Praise for

Voting in Fear

D1319262

"In developing the volume of essays for *Voting in Fear*, the United States Institute of Peace has assembled a comprehensive set of insights into the political, security, social, and economic factors that create vulnerabilities for electoral violence in Sub-Sahara Africa. As a result, this book represents an important contribution to understanding the conflict dynamics of such violence so that policymakers and practitioners can develop effective response measures to prevent, manage, and mediate electoral conflict."

—Jeff Fischer, Electoral Security Consultant

"This comprehensive volume introduces state-of-the-art-data that help focus debate and research on electoral violence in conflict. Featuring excellent case studies by prominent scholars, *Voting in Fear* is an accessible, well-researched book that offers thoughtful and realistic policy recommendations."

—Terrence Lyons, School for Conflict Analysis and Resolution, George Mason University

"This volume is an excellent addition to the growing body of work on electoral violence. It explores many of the key variables relating to the causes, actors, and impacts of electoral violence in Sub-Saharan Africa, providing much-needed depth and complexity to a phenomenon that many dismiss as inevitable and simplistic in its motivations."

— Lisa Kammerud, Electoral Conflict Specialist, F. Clifton White Applied Research Center, International Foundation for Electoral Systems (IFES)

Voting in Fear

Voting in Fear

Electoral Violence in Sub-Saharan Africa

Dorina A. Bekoe,

editor

UNITED STATES INSTITUTE OF PEACE PRESS
WASHINGTON, D.C.

The views expressed in this book are those of the authors alone. They do not necessarily reflect views of the United States Institute of Peace.

United States Institute of Peace
2301 Constitution Avenue, NW
Washington, DC 20037
www.usip.org

First published 2012

To request permission to photocopy or reprint materials for course use, contact the Copyright Clearance Center at www.copyright.com. For print, electronic media, and all other subsidiary rights e-mail permissions@usip.org

Printed in the United States of America

The paper used in this publication meets the minimum requirements of American National Standards for Information Science—Permanence of Paper for Printed Library Materials, ANSI Z39.48-1984.

Library of Congress Cataloging-in-Publication Data

Voting in fear : electoral violence in sub-Saharan Africa / Dorina A. Bekoe, editor.
   p. cm.
   ISBN 978-1-60127-136-5 (alk. paper)
   1. Elections—Africa, Sub-Saharan—History.   2. Political violence—Africa, Sub-Saharan—History.   I. Bekoe, Dorina Akosua Oduraa.
   JQ1879.A5V69 2012
   363.32—dc23
                                                            2012017405

Contents

Foreword by Ambassador Jendayi Frazer   vii

Acknowledgments   ix

1. Introduction: The Scope, Nature, and Pattern of Electoral
   Violence in Sub-Saharan Africa   1
        Dorina A. Bekoe

2. Democratization and Electoral Violence in Sub-Saharan
   Africa, 1990–2008   15
        Scott Straus and Charlie Taylor

3. Evaluating Election-Related Violence: Nigeria and Sudan
   in Comparative Perspective   39
        Timothy D. Sisk

4. Land Patronage and Elections: Winners and Losers
   in Zimbabwe and Côte d'Ivoire   75
        Catherine Boone and Norma Kriger

5. Postelection Political Agreements in Togo and Zanzibar:
   Temporary Measures for Stopping Electoral Violence?   117
        Dorina A. Bekoe

6. The Political Economy of Kenya's Crisis   145
        Susanne D. Mueller

7. Disturbance or Massacre? Consequences of Electoral
   Violence in Ethiopia   181
        Lahra Smith

8. Preventing Electoral Violence: Lessons from Ghana   209
        Franklin Oduro

9. Conclusion: Implications for Research and Policy 243
        Dorina A. Bekoe

About the Contributors 253
Index 257

Foreword

Voting in Fear: Electoral Violence in Sub-Saharan Africa is essential reading. Scholars, civic leaders, and government officials seeking to understand the conditions leading to electoral violence, and master the tools to prevent its occurrence, will find great value in this volume. Unlike other books on electoral violence in Africa, *Voting in Fear* draws on both quantitative and qualitative research to systematically investigate this important yet understudied phenomenon. When I served as the U.S. Assistant Secretary of State for African Affairs from 2005–09, I faced the challenge of responding to electoral violence especially in Kenya and Zimbabwe and would have benefitted tremendously from the information contained in this book.

Dorina Bekoe, sets out a comprehensive framework for analyzing the timing, triggers, perpetrators, and victims of violence that is relevant for sub-Saharan Africa and other regions. The book also features leading scholars of African politics that offer empirically rich studies of some of the most prominent cases of electoral violence in Africa, including Côte d'Ivoire, Ethiopia, Kenya, Nigeria, Sudan, and Zimbabwe. The reader will better understand why some countries are more susceptible to electoral violence and how to distinguish when common underlying and structural conditions are more or less likely to lead to violence, and what steps can be taken to counter its outbreak and mitigate its effects.

The book is especially welcome at a time when U.S. policymakers have elevated democratic progress in Africa as a key foreign policy goal. The lessons offered in *Voting in Fear* to end electoral violence will contribute to greater voter turnout, candidate participation, and the overall legitimacy of the electoral process in African countries. During this third wave of Africa's democratic advancement, the quality of governance and trust of society are keys to sustainable progress that are undergirded by peaceful or at least non-violent elections.

Africa has made significant strides over the past two decades especially its economic growth. Continued progress will require deepening good governance and consolidating democracy. It is especially important to open political space for inclusion of Africa's large youth population. The case studies in *Voting in Fear* offer concrete analysis both of what to avoid and to embrace to prevent electoral violence and build on Africa's more hopeful trends. The reader is exposed to the complexity of contemporary Africa, gaining insight into the political-economy and socio-economic and cultural diversity of several key countries across sub-Saharan Africa's four regions. This diversity when poorly managed, and accompanied by weak institutions, unable to accommodate difference, often is a recipe for electoral violence in Africa's relatively new democracies. Another key finding in the book, that postconflict states are more prone to electoral violence, should give pause to officials that elevate elections as the end state in peace agreements. Similarly, resorting to power-sharing arrangements to end electoral violence in the short-term is unlikely to end the cycle of violence without credible institutional reforms.

African practitioners and international institutions, diplomats, and nongovernmental organizations will find a treasure trove of useful policy recommendations to strengthen African institutions and guide policy interventions to avoid and mitigate electoral violence in Africa and beyond. Ultimately, by revealing the scope and variation of electoral violence in Africa, the book makes a major contribution to the literature on Africa's political development.

Ambassador Jendayi Frazer

Acknowledgments

A primary motivation for bringing together this edited volume was to provide an understanding of electoral violence's root and proximate causes, its perpetrators and their motivations, and its scope, thus enabling the policy and academic communities to organize more peaceful and credible elections. The idea grew out of several workshops held in Africa and the United States by the United States Institute of Peace (USIP) in collaboration with civil society organizations.

The first workshop took place in Abuja, Nigeria, two months before the 2007 elections. My colleagues and I were struck by civil society's resourcefulness and tireless determination to continue working for free and fair elections, this despite mounting evidence that Nigeria's 2007 elections would go down as among its worst organized, most disappointing, and least credible. The civil society workers felt helpless, however, in facing the seemingly inevitable violence that would accompany the polls. Subsequent workshops in Côte d'Ivoire and Sudan further confirmed that national and international programs were not geared to forestall the violence that ordinary people fear surrounding elections. A workshop organized at USIP in June 2009, bringing together scholars and practitioners to explore specific topics on electoral violence, served as the blueprint for this book.

I am especially grateful to my former colleagues at USIP for their collaboration in this work. Jacqueline Wilson, Linda Bishai, Kelly Campbell, and I worked together for several years in Nigeria, Côte d'Ivoire, and Sudan, organizing workshops aimed at better understanding the causes of electoral violence in Africa, and ways to prevent it. Debra Liang-Fenton joined us later in developing a course on preventing electoral violence in Africa for the USIP Academy for International Conflict Management and Peacebuilding.

Many people were indispensable in bringing this book to fruition. Above all, I thank the contributors. In addition to writing excellent chapters, they were quick and helpful in their responses. Also, heartfelt thanks to the staff at USIP Press and to the reviewers for their valuable insights on how to improve the manuscript. I am indebted to Michael Carr, in particular, for his careful editing.

And I thank my ever-patient husband, Kwaku Nuamah. He has been a sounding board for ideas, and a voice of encouragement throughout the project.

1

Introduction

The Scope, Nature, and Pattern of Electoral Violence in Sub-Saharan Africa

Dorina A. Bekoe

Seventeen African countries held presidential, legislative, or parliamentary elections in 2011.[1] In eleven countries (60 percent), the elections were violent in some manner. The type and degree of violence ranged from persistent harassment and intimidation experienced by Kizza Besigye, the presidential challenger in Uganda, to the intense violence that gripped Nigeria for three days following the presidential elections, killing 800 people and displacing 65,000. Indeed, the year started on a violent note, with news in the first quarter of 2011 dominated by the near civil war that broke out following the presidential elections in Côte d'Ivoire, taking some three thousand lives and displacing about one million over the course of four months.

Why does electoral violence happen in some places and not others? What are its triggers? What are its consequences? Who are the main perpetrators, and who are the victims? How can it be stopped?

This book provides some initial answers to these questions, through a theoretical and practical framework for thinking about and addressing them. It features pioneering work on the scope and nature of electoral violence in Africa, investigates the forms that such violence takes, and ana-

Heartfelt thanks to Scott Straus, Charlie Taylor, Tim Sisk, Catherine Boone, Norma Kriger, Lahra Smith, Franklin Oduro, and Susanne Mueller for their input at various stages of this project.

1. In this chapter, "Africa" refers to the forty-nine sub-Saharan countries on the African continent.

lyzes the stakeholders, structures, and strategies that can precipitate it, as well as those that can reduce or prevent it. While this phenomenon certainly happens in other regions, the book's focus on Africa is an opportunity to study electoral violence among a group of countries that have come of age and embarked on democratization at roughly the same time. This book is a first attempt to document the scope, quality, and circumstances of electoral violence in Africa using both quantitative methods and case studies.

What Is Electoral Violence?

The existing scholarly literature does not offer much guidance in thinking about elections and violence in Africa. Only a few books and articles aim to understand electoral violence as a specific phenomenon (Laakso 2007; Fischer 2002; UNDP 2009; USAID 2010; Bardall 2010). Therefore, what it is and when it occurs will likely remain a source of debate as more scholars begin to focus on it. But some researchers and institutions have begun to join around the notion that electoral violence is a subset of political violence distinguished by its timing, perpetrators and victims, objectives, and methods (UNGA 2010; Höglund 2009; Fischer 2002; Sisk 2008). These are important criteria because they help separate electoral violence from other types of violence that may happen to occur around election time; that is, that an act of violence occurs during the election period does not make it electoral violence.

When Does Electoral Violence Happen?

While electoral violence can take place at all stages of the electoral process—before the election, on election day, and after the election—defining precisely when it occurs is a point of contention. The danger in looking too far ahead of the polling date is that we may include incidents unrelated to the election. In contrast, looking too close to the polling date may result in underreporting electoral violence. This is especially true if politicians start to foment violence far ahead of the election date, as they did in Kenya in the early 1990s and in Zimbabwe in the past decade. Scott Straus and Charlie Taylor, in their chapter in this book, document electoral violence from six months before the election until three months after the election.

Election day, by several accounts (including the results of Straus and Taylor's analysis), is usually peaceful, which emphasizes the importance of focusing on the pre- and postelection periods (Höglund 2009, 416). The little quantitative research that has been done, including Straus and

Taylor's work in this volume, also shows that most elections in Africa—80 percent, in fact—are not as intensely violent as the ones in Nigeria, Kenya, Zimbabwe, and Côte d'Ivoire. In an early work on electoral violence, Jeff Fischer examined fifty-seven elections in 2001 to ascertain the level of violence, the perpetrators, and the opportunities for preventing violence. From a dataset spanning countries in Africa, Asia, Europe, and the Caribbean, he found that fourteen countries, or 24.5 percent, experienced conflict or violence (Fischer 2002, 4). Straus and Taylor find that 20 percent of all elections in Africa from 1990 to 2008 resulted in intense and destabilizing violence.

Who Are the Perpetrators, and Who Are the Victims?

In order to prevent future violence or properly understand its drivers, it is important to know who commits electoral violence and who suffers from it. Jeff Fischer, in his pioneering work documenting the extent of electoral violence, identifies victims as including voters who conflict with the state and disagree with the results of the election; perpetrators as including the state that disagrees with the protests lodged by the voters; and victims and perpetrators as including those in clashes between rival political supporters (Fischer 2002, 17). In the setting of a conflict-ridden society, Höglund, echoing other studies, explicitly identifies political parties (both government and opposition) as the "key organizers" of electoral violence. She expands Fischer's categories to include guerrilla and militia groups committing violent acts on behalf of politicians (Höglund 2009, 416; UNGA 2010, para. 20). Notably, in some cases, victims can also be perpetrators: in the aftermath of Kenya's 2007 elections, the Kikuyu were first persecuted by the Kalenjin before resorting to reprisal attacks. In the end, each case will determine the most relevant actors, but the critical factor in identifying the perpetrators and victims is to understand the objectives of electoral violence: which groups want to alter the outcome of the election, and which groups will be affected in their pursuit of this goal (Höglund 2009, 415–16; UNGA 2010, para. 24)?

While the most overt forms of violence—clashes between two opposing sides, state security services' violent suppression of demonstrators, political assassinations—are the easiest to document, less obvious forms of conflict are more difficult to recognize or quantify. In this volume, Straus and Taylor identify a broad set of actions characterizing electoral violence. These include not only overt acts that result in assassinations, deaths, and injuries, but also harassment and intimidation of political rivals, confiscation of newspapers, disqualification of candidates, and short-term arrests of political opponents. These last categories of violence may not directly cause deaths and injuries, but they can hinder the administration of, and participation in, elections.

Why Study Electoral Violence?

Some have dismissed the need to study electoral violence as a separate phenomenon, because, per capita, it is not a significant source of violence. Indeed, even in this volume, Straus and Taylor point out that electoral violence does not necessarily result in a significant spike in a country's overall level of violence; other sources of conflict are more significant. The paradox of electoral violence is that it is usually a brief, time- and event-bound period of violence, with generally low levels of tension but with enormous bearing on a country's democratization process and institutional reform priorities and on its leaders' legitimacy.

Electoral violence may affect the process or outcome of an election by determining voter turnout, candidates' participation in the electoral process, whether an election should be held, or a government's legitimacy (Höglund 2009, 417–19). In Zimbabwe, for example, the intense violence following the first round of the presidential election of 2008 resulted in the decision by the leader of the opposition Movement for Democratic Change, Morgan Tsvangirai, to withdraw from the second round. In contrast, many in Darfur called for postponement of Sudan's elections because of the region's instability and the fear of more violence. Violence can keep voters away. The threat—and, at times, reality—of violence by hired political thugs kept many away from the polls in Nigeria in 2007. Similarly, before Kenya's 1992 election, the violence that displaced hundreds of thousands of those opposing President Daniel arap Moi resulted in Moi's victory by rendering them unable to vote. Finally, violence can also weaken the internal and external legitimacy of an election and an elected official. In Nigeria, seven of thirty-six governors elected in 2007 were eventually removed from their positions after their election was deemed flawed by state election tribunals (Ilo 2011). Even the election of Nigerian president Umaru Yar'Adua was questioned: the Nigerian Supreme Court eventually ruled his election legitimate, but only twenty months after the polls. The cloud over the elections and the uncertainty of the electoral turnovers undermined officials' ability to govern.

Electoral violence can affect a country's regard for democratization. Citizens who experience repeated or intense electoral violence may view democratization in a less favorable light than do others who have not been so subjected. Some evidence for this is found in the survey results reported by Afrobarometer. Specifically, the 2006 surveys for Zimbabwe and Nigeria, both of which experienced violent elections, indicated a less favorable opinion of "elections as a means to represent the true voice of the people in government" than in Ghana, Namibia, and Botswana, where elections have been more peaceful (Afrobarometer 2006, 12). More general data from Afrobarometer indicate that 71 percent of those who viewed their country's last election as not free and fair or with major problems were not at all satisfied with democracy. In contrast, 50.7 percent of those who viewed their elections as free and fair or with minor problems were very satisfied with democracy. Moreover, when observers judged elections to be not free and fair, or free and fair but with major problems, only 40 percent of respondents thought of their country as a full democracy. In contrast, when observers judged the elections to be free and fair, or free and fair but with only minor problems, the number of respondents who classified their country as a full democracy rose (Alemika 2007, 7). Thus, from a policy perspective, if democratization is the goal, then reducing the prospect of electoral violence should also be one of the objectives. From a more academic perspective, the presence of electoral violence should be one of the variables included when seeking to explain the conditions under which democracy becomes consolidated.

New democracies face a particularly high risk of political violence in general, and electoral violence in particular. This is especially true for poorer, ethnically diverse, and postconflict countries. Thus, for institutions and governments promoting democratization to replace dictatorships, it is important to consider that the expected reduction in political violence has not materialized in new democracies. Rather, the opposite has occurred. Paul Collier argues that new democracies do not reduce political violence, because they do not usher in more accountability or more legitimacy (Collier 2009, 18–52). The lack of accountability means that governments do not fear repercussions for failing to live up to promises.

Collier's research demonstrates that electoral competition in poorer, newly democratizing countries does not entice governments to perform better, because the requisite checks and balances are missing. Rather, it provides incentives for politicians to employ the worst tools at their disposal (i.e., violence and repression) to win. Consequently, democracy in these settings does not make a government legitimate. The result is that democracy does not bring peace, and grievances continue to mount, making political violence in general, and electoral violence in particular, much more likely (Collier 2009, 18–52; Laakso 2007, 228–30; UNDP 2009, 8). Moreover, in an institutionally weak environment, without the attendant institutions to allow for tolerance of opposing views and the mitigation of

outbreaks of violence, nascent democracies cannot successfully accommodate and manage the diverse new political interests that emerge when the
political system opens up—especially if those new political views threaten
the status of existing elites (Mousseau 2001, 550–51; Laakso 2007, 227).
Furthermore, in new democracies with significant ethnic divisions, political
transitions can lead to ethnic violence as satisfying different ethnic groups
becomes ever more difficult (Laakso 2007, 226–27). Political coalitions,
which could hold together diverse interests in more mature democracies or
even in one-party systems, may be less binding in a competitive multiparty
environment with no history of political compromise or accommodation
(Mansfield and Snyder 2007, 163, 169–71).

Postconflict states, like some new democracies, may be more prone to
electoral violence. This is an important finding, given the tendency for
many peace agreements to proclaim the formal end of a conflict through
the organization of elections. Höglund highlights four features that make
postconflict states more vulnerable to such violence. First, postconflict
states are apt to have stronger patronage networks than other states, given
the divisiveness of conflict environments. In such an environment, where
the demands of loyalty supersede efficiency, inclusivity, and the rule of law,
electoral violence is likely because power is sought by any means necessary
(Höglund 2009, 420). Such extremism is particularly likely if elections are
held too early, before political parties have a chance to form properly or
before armed groups can fully make the transition into political parties
(Reilly 2002, 121–22, 133–34). Second, in some postconflict environments,
incomplete demobilization and disarmament results in the easy availability
of arms should the results of an election be unfavorable to one side. Politics
and institutions may not be demilitarized, allowing political actors to disregard opportunities for inclusiveness (Höglund 2009, 420; Lyons 2004,
44, 48). Clearly, such an environment enabled the postelection violence
in Angola (1992), the Republic of Congo (1993), the Democratic Republic of Congo (2006), and Côte d'Ivoire (2010) once the political leaders
rejected the results. Third, postconflict states may perpetuate a culture of
violence and intolerance if disputes are not resolved peacefully. And finally,
the suspension and weakening of many institutions in postconflict states
may result in a culture of impunity, allowing violence to pay (Höglund
2009, 421; Lyons 2004, 39–40).

Africa's ethnic diversity may, in some cases, also make the transition to
democracy and multiparty elections more difficult and violent. In many
African countries, political parties are based on ethnic, religious, or regional
divisions that operate in a highly centralized system (Mousseau 2001, 551;
Van de Walle 2003, 297–321). Indeed, some politicians explicitly build

their support through ethnic or religious appeals, exploiting existing cleavages and grievances for their own political gain. Constructing political battles that pit one ethnic or religious group against another reinforces the sense of marginalization that the losing group will feel (Diamond, Linz, and Lipset 1995). For elections in new democracies where contenders and supporters perceive zero-sum games, political and economic influence will accrue to the ethnic or political group whose candidate wins; losers will be marginalized—thus raising the stakes and the potential for violence (Diamond, Linz, and Lipset 1995; Collier 2009, 51–73).

Finally, electoral violence may serve as the impetus for a civil war. This was arguably the case in 1994 in the Republic of Congo (ROC) and nearly the case in Côte d'Ivoire's postelection violence of 2010. In ROC, after the October 1993 legislative election resulted in President Pascal Lissouba's victory, militias supporting him and those supporting the two other challengers clashed violently. Even after the election was rerun in November 1993, with Lissouba's party winning again, violence ensued. As many as 2,000 people were killed during November 1993 to January 1994 (U.S. State Dept. 1995; United Nations 1997). Four years later, in May 1997, these same political and ethnic cleavages resulted in more violence as the militias supporting Denis Sassou-Nguesso and Lissouba clashed again, this time over a dispute of the electoral rules, attempts by Lissouba supporters to stop the election, and Sassou-Nguesso's claims of assassination plots against him, along with other issues. During the six months of violence until Sassou-Nguesso seized the presidential palace, about 15,000 died (Bazenguissa-Ganga 1999, 39–42; De Beer and Cornwell 1999). Over the next two years, 20,000 more lives were lost (Polity IV 2010). Likewise, the four months of postelection violence in Côte d'Ivoire in 2010 and 2011 broke down along the same ethnic lines and issues that caused the civil war in 2002. Many feared that if a resolution was not reached in time, Côte d'Ivoire would return to full-blown war. Even so, with some three thousand dead and one million displaced—nearly the same numbers as in 2002—one may argue that civil war returned to Côte d'Ivoire in 2011.

Scope, Patterns, and Management of Electoral Violence in Africa

This book documents and analyzes the incidents of electoral violence in Africa through rich quantitative and qualitative approaches. The chapters reveal a number of significant interlocking and complementary insights as to the causes, warning signs, and prevention of electoral violence. Most prominently, the chapters demonstrate the high risks posed by close elections, a state's declining economic fortunes, and weak institutions. In seeking to prevent electoral violence, the chapters give policy recommendations that are designed to create inclusive forums for discussing divisive issues, developing programs that specifically focus on electoral violence, and starting violence prevention programs several months before the elections.

The book begins with the only known dataset of electoral violence in Africa, compiled by Straus and Taylor, spanning from 1990, the dawn of democracy's third wave, until 2008. The African Electoral Violence Dataset (AEVD) allows scholars and policymakers to determine the frequency, intensity, scope, and nature of electoral violence in Africa over eighteen years. Straus and Taylor's work shows that electoral violence has distinct patterns and that by recognizing them, policymakers, civil society activists, and scholars can devise strategies to mitigate—and even prevent—its occurrence. Notably, the data show the following:

- Most violence takes place *before* an election.
- For nearly half the countries in the database, electoral violence is a regular occurrence.
- The incumbent is usually the perpetrator of the violence that occurs.
- Presidential elections are slightly more violent than legislative elections.

Understanding these characteristics of electoral violence in Africa is an important first step in determining whether a country is at risk of violence, and in developing strategies to address it.

Straus and Taylor, in their chapter, also identify these six possible scenarios and motivators of electoral violence, suggested by the data:

- harassment and intimidation in protest or support of political candidates, not resulting in deaths
- elimination of the opposition through assassination, arrest, or torture
- violence in order to physically displace opposition supporters
- violence used to gain (or retain) access to resources in order to consolidate electoral support
- pockets of electoral violence, where violence is restricted to certain regions or districts
- protests over a result or process that lead to repression and violence

Many of the cases in the book illustrate these different scenarios of electoral violence. The first scenario, where electoral violence is least intense, appears in a number of chapters, embedded in analyses of more intense violence—illustrating the variation in electoral violence that can take place even concurrently in the same country. Incidents of harassment and intimidation that do not always lead to deaths are discussed in the cases of

Nigeria (Sisk), Zimbabwe (Boone and Kriger), Côte d'Ivoire (Boone and Kriger), Ethiopia (Smith), and Ghana (Oduro). The case studies presented by the chapter authors also feature the other specific scenarios of electoral violence described by Straus and Taylor:

- Eliminating the opposition: Some contenders in Nigeria's 2007 election lost their lives as political opponents tried to eliminate each other. The Ethiopian government imprisoned the leaders of the opposition following the 2005 elections.
- Redistricting: In 2005, Operation Murambatsvina in Zimbabwe displaced urban supporters of the opposition Movement for Democratic Change.
- Redistribution: Violence to redistribute resources was evident in the cases of Côte d'Ivoire, Kenya, and Nigeria.
- Pockets of violence: The violence in northern Ghana, which did not spread to the rest of the country, represents an "island of electoral violence," as did the violence in Zanzibar.
- Protests leading to violence: The protests before and after the 2005 elections in Togo were severely repressed by the government, leading to nearly 800 deaths.

The second chapter, thus, is both groundbreaking and foundational: it presents a critical first step in understanding both the scope and variation of electoral violence in Africa and the different scenarios in which it may occur.

The third and fourth chapters balance out the AEVD and reinforce each other by providing a broader context for electoral violence. Sisk frames electoral violence as a function of a country's progress on democratization, the political economy of state capture, the capacity of the electoral commission, and structural factors driving conflict. Sisk's chapter, which examines the factors that fuel violence in Nigeria (2007 and 2011) and Sudan (2010), may help explain why some countries are more prone to electoral violence than others even though they carry similar risk factors. Within this framework, for example, Nigeria's experience in 2007 demonstrates that the deep fissures in the ruling party, the centralization of political and economic resources, the culture of impunity, and the inability of the state police to investigate electoral offenses created an environment conducive to violence. More specifically, it made violence a likely tool in securing the vote, which explains why violence was prevalent before the election and on polling day.

Catherine Boone and Norma Kriger address the role that patronage resources play in fomenting violence during elections. In their analysis of the steadily deteriorating situations in Côte d'Ivoire and Zimbabwe, it is evident that as incumbents felt increasingly threatened by the opposition while also experiencing declining resources for sustaining patronage networks, the propensity to use violence increased. Complementing Sisk's discussion of institutions, the political economy of state capture, structural factors driving conflict, and the capacity of the electoral commission, Boone and Kriger illustrate the political and economic context that has led political leaders to use violence to win elections.

The fifth chapter (Bekoe), looking specifically at Togo and Zanzibar, examines the efficacy of postelection political agreements (PPAs) to break the cycle of intense electoral violence by creating power-sharing arrangements and examining the root and proximate causes of electoral violence. PPAs raise critical questions about the role of elections, the message they send regarding the use of violence in contesting electoral disputes, and their effects on democratization efforts. A key finding is that while PPAs may stop the violence in the very near term, if institutional reforms are not enacted or not credible, subsequent elections are likely to return to violence or, at least, high tension. In both Togo and Zanzibar, the persistent weakness of institutions was a key element in the opposition's distrust of the implementation of promised reforms.

The issue of institutional reform is critical in Mueller's chapter on Kenya's postelection violence. She documents the paradox of Kenya's seemingly strong institutions—benefiting from years of international donor support for reform—being unable to prevent the descent into violence. Mueller demonstrates that the persistence of informal, biased regulations enabled President Daniel arap Moi to distribute patronage and, in the process, arm supporters, in the effort to win elections. The resulting "diffusion of violence," Mueller argues, needed only the spark of the too-close-to-call 2007 election to precipitate a descent into ethnic killing. Beyond Kenya, Mueller's analysis sounds this cautionary note to the international community about its approach to, and assessment of, democratization efforts: beware the drawbacks of focusing too closely on formal institutions and ignoring the actual incentives that drive politicians to seek office. In Kenya, as in many transitional democracies, Mueller argues, politicians benefit from violence.

The payoff from electoral violence is at the center of Lahra Smith's chapter on Ethiopia's 2005 and 2010 elections. In 2005, nearly 200 people were killed and 30,000 opposition supporters were imprisoned, as the government cracked down on opposition supporters when the opposition's gains caught it by surprise. The effect was the "nonviolent" 2010 elections in Ethiopia—a result predicted by Höglund (2009). In 2010, voters chose the ruling party overwhelmingly—paradoxically, with a turnout of more than 93 percent—largely due to fears of repression. Moreover, civil society, which bore a heavy toll in the government's crackdown and was subjected to a harsher operating environment following the 2005 election, was noticeably absent from the electoral process. The Ethiopia case underscores the importance of understanding the broader context in which an election takes place, and illustrates the detrimental effects of violence.

The case studies end on a hopeful note, with Ghana demonstrating the real possibility of preventing electoral violence. Notably, the Ghanaian election was not entirely free of violence. As in Ethiopia and Kenya, it was a close election, but critical interventions at the national and local levels prevented violence from escalating and kept tensions from transforming into more violent confrontations. Oduro outlines state- and nonstate-led interventions that helped reduce tensions. For example, expatriate voting, which the opposition feared would invite fraud, was disallowed through an interparty advisory council. The ruling party's attempt to prevent the release of the results of the runoff election was overruled by the fast-track court, and the losing party's threat not to accept the results was resolved with the intervention of nationally recognized mediators. Coordinating across different sectors, the largest domestic election observation mission delivered early warnings of violence to the media, security agencies, the electoral commission, and other key stakeholders and public institutions. And on election day, the domestic observers used parallel vote tabulation to track the official results. As Oduro writes, these initiatives drove home the point that "the peaceful conduct and outcomes of elections are not the sole responsibility of the [electoral commission]."

To date, there are few multidimensional analyses of electoral violence. This book attempts to broaden academics' and policymakers' understanding of the conditions surrounding electoral violence—its scope, nature, patterns—the consequences it may generate, and what may be done to prevent or at least mitigate it. The dataset and the case studies suggest that electoral violence is not necessarily inevitable, may be prevented, and should be understood within its location-specific political context. Collectively, they reveal that a country's history of electoral violence, a close election, the presence of weak institutions, and declining state resources raise the risk of electoral violence. Thus, at a time when holding elections remains a key objective of many international institutions, nongovernmental organizations, and Western governments, it is important to distill the difficulties of doing so in the new and transitional democracies found in Africa and to develop strategies for avoiding the violence that often accompanies them.

References

Afrobarometer. 2006. "Citizens and the State in Africa: New Results from Afrobarometer, Round 3." Working Paper no. 61. May. www.afrobarometer.org/index.php?option=com_docman&Itemid=39.

Alemika, Etannibi Eo. 2007. "Quality of Elections, Satisfaction with Democracy and Political Trust in Africa." Afrobarometer Working Paper no. 84. Dec. www.afrobarometer.org/index.php?option=com_docman&Itemid=39.

Bardall, Gabrielle. 2010. "A Conflict Cycle Perspective on Electoral Violence." *Monday Developments* 28 (3): 15–16, 29. www.ifes.org/~/media/Files/Publications/Article/2010/1682/MD_March_10_small_2.pdf.

Bazenguissa-Ganga, Rémy. 1999. "The Spread of Political Violence in Congo-Brazzaville." *African Affairs* 98 (390): 39–42.

Collier, Paul. 2009. *Wars, Guns, and Votes: Democracy in Dangerous Places.* New York: Harper Perennial.

De Beer, Hanlie, and Richard Cornwell. 1999. "Congo-Brazzaville: The Deep End of the Pool." Institute for Security Studies, Occasional Paper no. 41, Sept. www.iss.org.za/Pubs/Papers/41/Paper41.html.

Diamond, Larry, Juan J. Linz, and Seymour Martin Lipset. 1995. "Introduction: What Makes for Democracy?" In *Politics in Developing Countries: Comparing Experiences with Democracy,* ed. Larry Diamond, Juan J. Linz, and Seymour Martin Lipset. Boulder, CO: Lynne Rienner.

Fischer, Jeff. 2002. "Electoral Conflict and Violence: A Strategy for Study and Prevention." IFES White Paper, Feb. 5. http://aceproject.org/ero-en/topics/elections-security/UNPAN019255.pdf/view.

Höglund, Kristine. 2009. "Electoral Violence in Conflict-Ridden Societies: Concepts, Causes, and Consequences." *Terrorism and Political Violence* 21 (3): 412–27.

Ilo, Udo Jude. 2011. "Restoring Electoral Accountability to Elections in Nigeria." *Vanguard,* Jan. 27. www.vanguardngr.com/2011/01/restoring-electoral-accountability-to-elections-in-nigeria/.

Laakso, Liisa. 2007. "Insights into Electoral Violence in Africa." In *Votes, Money, and Violence: Political Parties and Elections in Sub-Saharan Africa,* ed. Matthias Basedau, Gero Erdmann, and Andreas Mehler, 224–52. Uppsala: Nordic Africa Institute.

Lindberg, Staffan. 2006. *Democracy and Elections in Africa.* Baltimore: Johns Hopkins Univ. Press.

Lyons, Terrence. 2004. "Post-conflict Elections and the Process of Demilitarizing Politics: The Role of Electoral Administration." *Democratization* 11 (3): 36–62.

Mansfield, Edward D., and Jack Snyder. 2007. "Turbulent Transitions: Why Emerging Democracies Go to War." In *Leashing the Dogs of War: Conflict Management in a Divided World,* ed. Chester Crocker, Fen Osler Hampson, and Pamela Aall. Washington, DC: United States Institute of Peace Press.

Mousseau, Demet Yalcin. 2001. "Democratizing with Ethnic Divisions." *Journal of Peace Research* 38 (5): 550–51.

Polity IV Project: Political Regime Characteristics and Transitions, 1800–2010. 2010. "Polity IV Country Report 2010: Congo (Brazzaville)." Center for Systemic Peace. www.systemicpeace.org/polity/Congo2010.pdf.

Reilly, Benjamin. 2002. "Post-conflict Elections." In "Recovering from Civil Conflict." Special issue, *International Peacekeeping* 9 (2): 118–39.

Sisk, Timothy D. 2008. "Elections in Fragile States: Between Voice and Violence." Paper prepared for the International Studies Association Annual Meeting, San Francisco, Mar. 24–28. www.humansecuritygateway.com/documents/ISA_electionsinfragilestates.pdf.

United Nations. 1997. "Congo-Brazzaville: Background Brief on Congo-Brazzaville." Oct. 22. IRIN-WA Update 68-97 of Events in West Africa, Dept. of Humanitarian Affairs, Integrated Regional Information Network for the Great Lakes, 114–18. http://reliefweb.int/sites/reliefweb.int/files/reliefweb_pdf/briefingkit-27fe2a03f472c0ab94282cd752301eb5.pdf.

United Nations Development Programme (UNDP). 2009. *Elections and Conflict Prevention: A Guide to Planning and Programming.* Aug. http://web.undp.org/publications/Elections_and_Conflict_Prevention.pdf.

United Nations General Assembly (UNGA). 2010. "Report by the Special Rapporteur on Extrajudicial, Summary or Arbitrary Executions, Philip Alston: Election-Related Killings (Addendum)." A/HRC/14/24/Add.7. May 21.

U.S. Agency for International Development (USAID). 2010. *Electoral Security Framework: Technical Guidance Handbook for Democracy and Governance Officers.* Democratic Governance Group, Bureau for Development Policy. Jul. www.usaid.gov/our_work/democracy_and_governance/publications/pdfs/1-Electoral-Security-Framework.pdf.

U.S. State Dept. 1995. "Congo Human Rights Practices, 1994." Feb. http://dosfan.lib.uic.edu/ERC/democracy/1994_hrp_report/94hrp_report_africa/Congo.html.

Van de Walle, Nicolas. 2003. "Presidentialism and Clientelism in Africa's Emerging Party Systems." *Journal of Modern African Studies* 41 (2): 297–321.

2

Democratization and Electoral Violence in Sub-Saharan Africa, 1990–2008

Scott Straus and Charlie Taylor

I n Robert Dahl's classic text on democratization, he warned that political transitions are risky. To introduce competition and contestation into a previously closed political system invites the potential for
conflict between incumbents and opponents as each weighs the costs of
violence and toleration (Dahl 1971). Dahl's warning was not prominent
among international and domestic advocates who launched sub-Saharan
Africa's grand democratic experiment after the end of the Cold War.[1] In
very few years, the modal African political system switched from one-
party hegemony to multiparty competitive elections—a remarkably swift
and comprehensive set of regime changes across the continent.

In the first two decades of sub-Saharan Africa's grand experiment,
many democratic gains are evident. On average, African political systems

The authors wish to thank Dorina Bekoe, John Clark, Brett Lacy, Jacqueline Klopp, Melanie Manion,
Matt Scharf, Michael Schatzberg, Aili Tripp, and Crawford Young for detailed comments on earlier
drafts of the paper, and Staffan Lindberg for his data on multiparty elections from 1990 to 2003.
Earlier versions were also presented at the United States Institute of Peace, the 2009 annual meeting
of the American Political Association, and the Comparative Politics Colloquium at the University of
Wisconsin, Madison, where the authors received helpful comments and suggestions. The research was
supported with grants to Scott Straus from the Harry Frank Guggenheim Foundation and the Gradu-
ate School at the University of Wisconsin, Madison.

1. Throughout this chapter, "Africa" and "African" refer to the forty-eight states typically considered
sub-Saharan African states. (This excludes South Sudan which seceded from Sudan in 2011.)

are more competitive, repeat multiparty elections are more common, the media are more liberalized, civil society is stronger, public criticism of government is increasingly tolerated, and judiciaries are more independent. To take one common measure of the quality of democracies, the average Freedom House score for political rights and civil liberties for sub-Saharan states improved significantly from 1989 to 2008.[2] In short, there is much to applaud in Africa's democratic experiment.

The overall democratic gains mask an important empirical regularity, however—one that echoes Dahl's warning. The experience of many African democratic transitions, especially during electoral periods, has been violent. Especially in recent years, the risk that elections may produce political violence has been all too apparent. Three regionally important and moderately affluent states (in comparative Africa terms)—Kenya, Zimbabwe, and Côte d'Ivoire—experienced highly violent episodes directly tied to electoral contests. Yet these are not the only countries where serious election-related violence has occurred—from Equatorial Guinea to Togo, to Ethiopia, to South Africa's transition to multiracial democracy, violence has been a major feature of electoral periods.

Much of the early literature on Africa's democratic transition did not focus on the risk of violence. Rather, those foundational comparative works explained why the transitions occurred (Bratton and Van de Walle 1997), the critical ingredients of democratic transitions, such as civil society (Harbeson, Rothchild, and Chazan 1994), what "democracy" means to voters (Schaffer 1998), and what might lock in democratic gains (Lindberg 2006), among other themes. The early optimism has met with new skepticism, however, especially recently. In a new book, Robert Bates argues that political liberalization shortened the time horizons of African leaders during the past two decades, increasing the likelihood that state leaders would predate rather than develop institutions for the common good (Bates 2008).[3] In another recent influential book, Paul Collier argues that democratic elections increase the risk of political violence in poor countries (Collier 2009). These more Africa-oriented works dovetail with general arguments, made by Jack Snyder and others, that in countries with weak institutions, democratization increases the risk of nationalism and armed conflict (Snyder 2000). The terms of a critical theoretical debate,

---

2. Freedom House assigns individual countries a rating from 1 to 7 for political rights and another for civil liberties, with 1 denoting the most free and 7 the least free. In 1989–90, the average political rights and civil liberties scores for sub-Saharan African countries were 5.91 and 5.32 respectively; in 2008, the same scores changed to 4.19 and 3.94, down even from 2007, when the averages were 4.29 and 4.08.

3. In an earlier work, Bates (1983) argued that electoral competition could lead political actors to make ethnic claims to build winning coalitions.

one with clear policy implications, are now taking shape: does the onset of multiparty elections increase the risk of political violence, and if so, how, when, and why?

This chapter addresses these questions principally by providing a descriptive overview of the frequency and patterns of electoral violence in sub-Saharan Africa. Despite the vital importance of knowing how common electoral violence is, there is a surprising lack of published empirical work on how frequently it occurs. To address this question, we have created a new dataset on electoral violence in Africa from 1990 to 2008, called the African Electoral Violence Database (AEVD). In creating the dataset, we specify and disaggregate an outcome of interest, namely "electoral violence," in part because the existing literature provides little explicit specification of a dependent variable describing violence related to elections. As part of the conceptual discussion, we argue that electoral violence should be disaggregated into pre- and postelection violence, incumbent and challenger violence, and levels of violence. Although Dorina Bekoe, formerly at the United States Institute of Peace, and Leonardo Arriola at the University of California, Berkeley, have done similar research, we know of no other existing and published cross-national dataset that focuses specifically on electoral violence in Africa and that measures electoral violence across nearly two decades.[4]

This chapter describes the findings from the dataset. The first part specifies scope conditions, defines concepts, describes coding rules, and discusses source material. The next section describes the main findings, which include a table that sorts each election in the database into one of four levels of electoral violence. The chapter also describes a range of other findings on when electoral violence takes place, who the primary perpetrators are, and whether electoral violence rises or falls over time, among other things. One of the central findings from the study is that serious destabilizing electoral violence is not nearly as frequent as critics suggest, though frequent enough to warrant serious concern. Most elections in the dataset experience some violence, but mostly at low levels, in what is known as *violent harassment,* in which security forces sometimes break up rallies, or party supporters engage in violent confrontations. About 20 percent of the elections in the database result in violence above a specified substantive

---

4. Staffan Lindberg codes for violence in his dataset on African elections, which covers 1990–2003. Lindberg codes for whether an election was peaceful, had isolated incidents of violence, or experienced a campaign of violence. While his research remains critically important and we build from his dataset, violence was not the focus of his research, and we seek to improve on his conceptual categories and data collection. Since creating this dataset, we have learned of the work of Leonardo Arriola at the University of California, Berkeley, who also is in the process of creating a dataset on election-related violence in Africa (Arriola 2011).

threshold, involving high-level assassinations or generalized killing. There is considerable variation in whether elections trigger violence.

In addition to presenting data on the frequency and primary patterns of electoral violence, the chapter also describes the most common scenarios apparent in the database. More specifically, it identifies six primary scenarios that indicate significant variation in the ways that electoral violence takes shape and, by implication, in the logic of electoral violence. In some cases, for example, we find that incumbents seek to dismantle the opposition through assassination, long-term high-level arrests, and consistent disruption of political party activities. In other cases, we find that electoral contests create a window of opportunity to change access to vital resources, notably land but also, secondarily, marketplace rights and trade routes. Elections thereby politicize preexisting resource rivalries, and local actors in turn mobilize to gain or protect access to such resources, all of which creates the foundation for violent clashes. Local clashes take on a greater scale when they dovetail with national electoral incentives—when, to win national electoral contests, national political parties need the votes of rival local groups fighting for access to vital resources. Yet other cases involve protest against the real or announced results of a poll. Most commonly in this scenario, opposition candidates and supporters challenge rigged results, triggering repression and, potentially, generalized killing. But in some cases, incumbents decide to reject the results, leading to the annulment of a poll, followed by protest and repressive violence. To be sure, the different scenarios overlap in places. In the 2007 Kenyan elections, for example, the initial logic of violence was that of the latter scenario—protest followed by repression—but the violence quickly followed a logic of access to local resources, notably land, in the Rift Valley. Despite the occasional overlap of scenarios, it is helpful to map out the different ways in which electoral violence takes shape as part of the broader empirical overview that is the main focus of this chapter.[5]

Scope Conditions, Concepts, and Data Collection

There are three principal reasons for limiting the study of electoral violence to Africa. First, the research is a mid-range cross-national study, focused on one world region of nearly fifty countries during a nineteen-year period, rather than on a global sample across different historical periods. This regional and temporal focus affords a degree of control over the sample. Second, sub-Saharan African countries have experienced a historically

---

5. Many of the other chapters in this volume provide considerably greater detail on the main patterns and processes described here.

similar transition period. The end of the Cold War triggered a remarkable change from single-party rule to multiparty competition. Yet there is considerable variation within that experience, particularly in how many and which African states experienced electoral violence. Thus, sub-Saharan Africa is a region that underwent a historical shift in regime type but with significant variation in the dependent variable of interest: electoral violence. Third, in recent years, African elections have produced notable cases of electoral violence, particularly in Kenya, Zimbabwe, and Côte d'Ivoire. Therefore, the analysis has practical and policy implications—policymakers and others have an interest in anticipating and understanding how and when electoral violence is likely to occur.

Any study of such data should acknowledge that neither "violence" nor "electoral violence" is a concept with a consistent social-science definition, so we start by defining our terms. Indeed, one limitation of existing studies is a wide and inconsistent (across studies) definition of the dependent variable. In Collier's work, for example, "violence" includes civil war, riots, political strikes, and assassinations (Collier 2009). In Bates's work, the dependent variable for state failure (including violence) is a dummy variable for the formation of militias (Bates 2008, 147). Snyder's dependent variable is armed conflict (Snyder 2000). While these studies are impressive, we find the specifications not specific enough for evaluating whether and how multiparty electoral processes trigger violence, and not specific enough to capture the modal pattern of electoral violence (versus, say, wars or coups) in sub-Saharan Africa. Hence, we seek a more specific conception of violence related to elections, namely "electoral violence."

At the broadest level, by "political violence," we mean the deliberate use of physical harm or the threat of physical harm for a political purpose. Overt physical violence can take the form of beatings, torture, and murder, but violence is also evident by its threat—by coercive intimidation. "Electoral violence" refers to physical violence and coercive intimidation directly tied to an impending electoral contest or an announced electoral result.[6] One problem with this seemingly straightforward definition is that in some instances it can be difficult to know whether violence is directly related to an election. In coding, we sought to determine whether violence that occurred was directly related to an electoral contest.[7] For ambiguous cases, when coding we consider any politically related violence that

---

6. By "announced electoral result," we refer mostly to the announcement of electoral returns, rigged or not, that in turn trigger a chain of events that lead to violence. However, we also include the possibility that an election was annulled, leading to violence, as occurred in the 1993 Nigerian elections.

7. For example, ongoing violence that is clearly attributable to civil war fighting is not included in this definition of "electoral violence."

occurred from six months before an election until three months after an election to be electoral violence.[8]

Even if these conceptual parameters help clarify "electoral violence," the concept requires further disaggregation, which we propose to do in three dimensions. First, the concept of electoral violence encompasses at least two distinct logics of violence. Elections are generally formal contests between incumbents and challengers, and so incumbents and challengers may well use violence for different reasons and in different circumstances.[9] More often than not, incumbents who employ violence do so to maintain power, using the coercive means of the state or informal institutions that have state or ruling political party support, such as political party youth wing groups or militias. Challengers, by contrast, most often employ violence to challenge the power of the state or to contest results and typically do not have access to the coercive apparatus of the state. These two logics link up to distinct threads in the literature on violence: the former, to studies of state violence and repression; the latter, to studies of rebellion and protest. Therefore, a cross-national empirical study of electoral violence should at least record the origins of violence, which most existing studies of electoral violence do not do. The dataset has two categories: incumbent (referring to any state agent, militia, political party member, or hooligan who acts on behalf of the political party that controls the executive) and challenger (any party member, militia, or hooligan acting on behalf of a political party that does not control the executive). The categories are not mutually exclusive—in some cases, incumbents and challengers both commit violence in an election.

A second source of disaggregation concerns whether violence occurred before or after the election. Again we observe two distinct logics of violence—or at least the possibility for the presence of those two distinct logics. On the one hand, prevote violence occurs as political actors seek to shape voting behavior, preferences, and patterns. That is, prevote electoral violence occurs in periods with uncertainty about voting outcomes, when political actors seek to shape who votes, where they vote, and how they vote. By contrast, postvote violence generally expresses a logic of response to an outcome, either to an actual voting result or to an announced rigged

---

8. The longer time horizon before an election date reflects the fact that electoral campaigns usually take place for a substantial period before an election. The shorter period after an election reflects that responses to an electoral result will usually occur within a few months after an announced result.

9. Hypothetically, there could be a scenario where an incumbent or incumbent party stands down completely, leaving a formal contest between nonincumbent parties who use violence. Empirically, the dataset records only one such case: Nigeria in 1999, when the provisional military authorities did not contest the elections, yet electoral violence occurred. That case is an important one for Nigeria and the continent, but it represents an outlier—in most cases, the electoral contests in which violence occurs pit incumbents against challengers.

result. For the latter, violence is, at least typically, less an effort to shape uncertainty and more an effort to change a political direction. Both points highlight a general truism about elections: that they represent periods of fluid authority when *who* governs is in question, which in itself creates an opportunity for the use of violence.

The disaggregation between incumbent and challenger and between prevote and postvote violence suggests some initial hypotheses. In contrast to Collier and Vicente (2008), this study hypothesizes, for example, that because incumbents have access to the coercive apparatus of the state, they will be more likely than challengers to engage in electoral violence. Incumbents have greater capacity both to engage in violence and to respond to challenger violence. By contrast, even though challengers are less likely to engage in election violence overall, if they do resort to violence they are probably more likely to do so *after* an election. Before an election, given the coercive power asymmetries between incumbents and challengers, challengers would theoretically prefer persuasion (including patronage promises) because of the risk that violence would trigger a repressive response from the state, thereby removing the challengers from the contest. To be sure, challengers could seek to trigger incumbent violence to diminish the legitimacy of an election that they fear losing, but they would try to retain a high-ground position, thereby generating a legitimacy advantage. All other things equal, then, the study hypothesizes that challengers are less likely than incumbents to use violence before an election. By contrast, after an election, challengers have less to lose if an incumbent has declared victory; thus, if challengers use violence, they will be more likely to do so after an election result has been announced.

A third source of variation concerns the level of violence. Not all electoral violence should be lumped into the same category—that is, a case of incumbent security forces beating a few opposition supporters is categorically different from one in which incumbent security forces orchestrate the killing of a hundred opposition supporters, and the forced removal of many thousands more. In reflecting on this question and in consulting cases, the study has isolated four distinct levels of violence. The first level is simply that of no reported electoral violence before or after a vote (coded as 0). A second level of violence is violent harassment, indicated by police or security forces breaking up rallies, party supporters brawling in the streets, confiscation of opposition newspapers, candidate disqualifications, and limited short-term arrests of political opponents (coded as 1). A third level of violence is violent repression, indicated by high-level assassinations and targeted murder combined with long-term high-level arrests of party leaders, the consistent use of violent intimidation and harassment (as in category 1), or the use of torture (coded as 2). The fourth level is a highly violent campaign with generalized violence—that is, repeated, widespread physical attacks leading to a substantial number of deaths over time (interpreted as twenty or more deaths—coded as 3).

Available detailed data on electoral violence across Africa are not abundant and constitutes a limitation to any dataset on the topic. To be sure, some cases are well documented and well reported, but many are not. In choosing a data source to code cases cross-nationally, we sought a single source that was reliable and had comprehensive coverage for African states. One limitation of nongovernmental human rights organizations' reporting, for example, is that documentation is uneven across African countries. The same is largely true for international newspaper coverage as well as for available electoral observer reports. Therefore, in choosing a data source, we wanted to avoid any systematic reporting bias that stemmed from the data source's reporting patterns and to select a single source that would report on as many cases in the sample as possible.

The main source we rely on is therefore the U.S. State Department's annual Country Reports on Human Rights Practices. The State Department began issuing annual reports on all countries in 1993, and we consulted every report for a country with an election during 1993–2008. For the years 1990–92, we consulted three major sources, especially the Amnesty International and Human Rights Watch annual human rights reports, as well as journalism coverage in *Africa Report*. The data are not flawless, and in many cases the State Department reports are not highly detailed. However, the State Department reports in particular, as well as the combined reports for the years in which the State Department did not issue reports, provide a level of detail sufficient to code elections into the categories outlined above. Cingranelli and Richards (2010, 406) find a similar correlation.

Several other relevant criteria figured in constructing the AEVD. First, the dataset follows Staffan Lindberg's (2006), which records all multiparty elections from 1990 to 2003. The years not covered in his dataset are filled in by hand. The study follows Lindberg's decision to code only presidential and parliamentary elections and not local elections. Second, many countries hold parliamentary and presidential elections at different times, and one important question is whether violence is more or less frequent in one type of election or another—a matter addressed later in the chapter. But in practice, many elections are held in close temporal proximity, and distinguishing whether violence (if it exists) relates to the presidential and parliamentary elections can be difficult given the level of detail provided by the existing data sources. Thus, if parliamentary and presidential elections are held within three months of each other, even if in different years, we code them as a single electoral case. This leaves us with 221 election cases in the dataset.

In any cross-national coding exercise, there is always the risk of measurement error and arbitrary cutoff points. To address possible measurement error, where a case seemed ambiguous or where information was spotty, we consulted additional sources, primarily those cited above but also international election observer reports when available. The study also used intercoder reliability checks and consulted country experts on the coding of particular countries. To address concerns involving arbitrary cutoff points, we seek to be as transparent as possible in showing which countries and which elections fall into the various categories. While some observers may challenge the specific categorization of certain elections, the dataset is able to capture substantively important variation in levels of electoral violence. Also, with 221 observations, a few changes in the coding of specific countries will not affect the overall patterns of electoral violence that the chapter identifies.

General Patterns of Electoral Violence in Sub-Saharan Africa, 1990–2008

How common is electoral violence in African elections? Does serious electoral violence tend to happen before or after elections? And who most typically commits electoral violence: incumbents or challengers, or both?

Frequency of Electoral Violence at Different Levels

At the most general level, the most serious incidents of widespread electoral violence (those coded as 3 in the dataset) are somewhat rare: about 10 percent (N = 23) of all elections held in sub-Saharan African between 1990 and 2008 resulted in generalized killing and violence directly tied to the electoral contest. Nearly the same proportion of electoral periods resulted in repressive violence involving targeted assassinations and long-term high-level detentions combined with occasional cases of torture. The study finds 10 percent (N = 22) of all elections in that category. Putting the two categories together, the highest levels of electoral violence have occurred in about 20 percent of all electoral contests in Africa from 1990 to 2008. By contrast, cases in which limited violence exists but is not a central feature of an electoral period—what we label violent harassment (category 1)—occurred in about 38 percent (N = 84) of cases. About 42 percent (N = 92) of all cases show no reported electoral violence.

These results stand in contrast to the impression, given by Snyder, Bates, Collier, and some other critics, of democratization routinely instigating violence in poorer, weakly institutionalized countries. The results suggest instead that there is considerable variation among African electoral campaigns. If an election is held in Africa, according to the data, the most likely outcome by a significant margin is one of no or limited electoral violence. If electoral violence does occur, it will most likely be at the level of harassment, intimidation, and disruption, rather than at the level of eviscerating the opposition leadership or at the level of generalized killing.

For readers interested in how different cases are coded (and in the interests of transparency), table 2.1 lists how each election in the dataset is scored. If some ambiguity exists in the coding, a footnote is provided.

Clusters of Rare, Occasional, and Probable High Electoral Violence

Table 2.1 indicates some distinct clusters of countries. First, we see a number of African countries where no or low levels of electoral violence are the norm across multiple electoral periods. Some of these countries are the most stable democracies and the comparatively wealthier countries, such as Botswana and Mauritius. Some are also reliably democratic but comparatively poorer, such as Benin, Mali, and Zambia. However, some countries that have not experienced high levels of electoral violence are comparatively poor and have emerged from armed conflict, such as Mozambique. Other countries, such as Chad and Rwanda, have had recent periods of violent conflict and are largely authoritarian and yet, for different reasons, did not have highly violent electoral contests in the years coded in the dataset.[10] So there is no clearly apparent category of countries that consistently avoid high levels of electoral violence. In another cluster of cases, high levels of electoral violence are occasional—such violence occurs in some but not most electoral contests in the dataset. Here we find a mix of countries, from oil-rich Cameroun to conflict-ridden Central African Republic, from democratically stable Senegal in 1993 to fragile Madagascar and Guinea. For a third cluster of cases, if an election has occurred, it will most likely have resulted in high levels of electoral violence—that is, more than half the elections in the dataset produced high levels of violence. This category includes many of sub-Saharan Africa's largest and most economically and politically important states—Kenya, Zimbabwe, Sudan, Nigeria, Ethiopia, South Africa, and the Democratic Republic of Congo—as well as some smaller states, such as Togo and Equatorial Guinea.[11] To help visualize these patterns, table 2.2 divides the sample into cases where high levels of

---

10. Rwanda's August 2010 presidential election, which is not coded in the dataset, saw prevote targeted assassinations and would therefore be coded as 3.

11. We recognize that the criteria for characterizing high electoral violence (twenty deaths or more) may not fully capture the local significance of electoral violence—twenty deaths is a small number in a populous country, but a relatively large number in a less populous country.

Table 2.1   African Elections 1990–2008, by Level of Electoral Violence

No Violence (0)	Violent Harassment (1)	Violent Repression (2)	Large-Scale Violence (3)
Benin: 1995, 1996, 1999, 2001, 2003, 2006, 2007	Angola: 2008	Burundi: 2005	Angola: 1992
	Benin: 1991	Cameroun: 1997	CAR: 1992
	Burkina Faso: 1991, 2005	Comoros: 1992	DRC: 2006
Botswana: 1994, 1999, 2004	Burundi: 1993[1]	Eq. Guinea: 1993, 1996, 1999, 2004	Ethiopia: 2005
Burkina Faso: 1992, 1997, 1998, 2002, 2007	Cameroun: 1992, 1992, 1997, 2002, 2004, 2007		Guinea: 1993
		Ethiopia: 2000	Côte d'Ivoire: 2000
		Guinea: 1998	Kenya: 1992, 1997, 2007
Cape Verde: 1991, 1995, 1996, 2001, 2006	CAR: 1993, 1999, 2005	Côte d'Ivoire: 1995	Lesotho: 1998
	Chad: 1996, 2001, 2002	Mauritania: 1992	Madagascar: 2001
CAR: 1998		Niger: 1996	Nigeria: 1992, 1993, 2003, 2007
Chad: 1997, 2006	Comoros: 1990	Senegal: 1993[2]	
Comoros: 1993, 1996, 1996, 2002, 2004, 2006	Djibouti: 1993, 1997, 1999, 2005	Sudan: 1996, 2000	Rep. of Congo: 1993
		Tanzania: 2000	South Africa: 1994, 1999
Djibouti: 1992, 2003	Eq. Guinea: 2002, 2008	Togo: 1998, 1994, 2003	
Gabon: 1996, 1998, 2001, 2006	Ethiopia: 1995	Uganda: 2001, 2001	Togo: 1993, 2005
Gambia: 1997	Gabon: 1990, 1993, 2005	Zimbabwe: 2005	Zimbabwe: 2000, 2002, 2008
Ghana: 1996, 2000	Gambia: 1992, 1996, 2001, 2002, 2006, 2007		
Guinea: 2002			
Guinea-Bissau: 1999, 2004, 2008	Ghana: 1992, 2004, 2008		
Lesotho: 1993, 2002, 2007	Guinea: 1995, 2003		
Madagascar: 1997, 1998, 2002, 2007	Guinea-Bissau: 1994, 2005		
Malawi: 1994, 1999	Côte d'Ivoire: 1990		
Mali: 1992, 2002, 2007	Kenya: 2002		
Mauritania: 1996, 1997, 2006, 2007	Liberia: 1997, 2005		
Mauritius: 1991, 1995, 2000, 2005	Madagascar: 1993, 1993, 2006		
Namibia: 1994, 2004	Malawi: 2004		
Niger: 1993, 1995, 1996, 2004	Mali: 1997		
Rep. of Congo: 2002, 2002, 2007	Mauritania: 2001, 2003		
São Tomé & Prínc.: 1991, 1994, 1996, 1998, 2001, 2002, 2003, 2006, 2006	Mozambique: 1994, 1999, 2004		
	Namibia: 1999		
Senegal: 2001	Niger: 1999		
Seychelles: 1993, 1998, 2001, 2002, 2006	Nigeria: 1998, 1999		
Togo: 2007	Rep. of Congo: 1992		
Zambia: 1991, 2001, 2006, 2008	Rwanda: 2003, 2003		
	Senegal: 1998, 2000, 2007, 2007		

(table continued next page)

Table 2.1 African Elections 1990–2008, by Level of Electoral Violence
(continued)

No Violence (0)	Violent Harassment (1)	Violent Repression (2)	Large-Scale Violence (3)
	Sierra Leone: 1996, 2002, 2007		
	South Africa: 2004		
	Swaziland: 1993, 1998, 2003, 2008		
	Tanzania: 1995, 2005		
	Togo: 1999, 2002		
	Uganda: 1996, 2006		
	Zambia: 1996		
	Zimbabwe: 1990, 1995, 1996, 2008		

1. In October 1993, Melchior Ndadaye, Burundi's first democratically elected and Hutu president, was assassinated, triggering a wave of mass violence and civil war. We code the case as violent harassment for two reasons: (1) while ultimately the product of the electoral process, the assassination nevertheless was in response to policy reform proposals, particularly to the military, and not only in response to the electoral outcome; and (2) the assassination happened more than three months after the election and, thus, by our coding rules, is not categorized as "electoral" violence. Some observers might reasonably consider the case one of high electoral violence, and the logic indeed resembles one of the scenarios identified later in the chapter (where an incumbent or challenger protests the electoral results, leading to generalized violence).

2. A high-level electoral official was assassinated after the vote, triggering the arrest and torture of high-level political opponents of the ruling Parti Socialiste du Sénégal.

violence never happen, cases where such levels occur occasionally (in no more than half the elections), and cases where high electoral violence usually takes place (in more than half the elections). The countries in table 2.2 are divided into three columns according to how frequently their elections exhibit high levels of electoral violence (categories 2 and 3 in the dataset).

The patterns in table 2.2 have some theoretical implications. They suggest that variation in the incidence of electoral violence occurs not only across African states but also, over time, *within* African states. That variation raises two questions: Why do elections in some states tend to be highly (or rarely) violent? And why are elections in some states sometimes highly violent and sometimes not? The data suggest that the answers will lie in a combination of structural and historical factors: on the one hand, factors that recur across electoral periods and that consistently push some countries (but not others) toward mass violence; and, on the other hand, short-term dynamic factors that change every year or two. Although it is not the explicit focus of this chapter, an explanation of variation in electoral violence outcomes across and within states should seek to account for these structural and dynamic factors.

Table 2.2   Frequency of High Levels of Electoral Violence

Never High Electoral Violence	Occasional High Electoral Violence	Usual High Electoral Violence
Benin: 1991, 1995, 1996, 1999, 2001, 2003, 2006, 2007	Angola: 1992,* 2008	Côte d'Ivoire: 1990, 1995, 2000*
Botswana: 1994, 1999, 2004	Burundi: 1993, 2005	DRC: 2006*
Burkina Faso: 1991, 1992, 1997, 1998, 2002, 2005, 2007	Cameroun: 1992, 1992, 1997, 1997, 2002, 2004, 2007	Eq. Guinea: 1993, 1996, 1999, 2002, 2004, 2008
Cape Verde: 1991, 1995, 1996, 2001, 2006	CAR: 1992,* 1993, 1998, 1999, 2005	Ethiopia: 1995, 2000, 2005*
Chad: 1996, 1997, 2001, 2002, 2006	Comoros: 1990, 1992, 1993, 1996, 2002, 2004, 2006	Kenya: 1992,* 1997,* 2002, 2007*
Djibouti: 1992, 1993, 1997, 1999, 2003, 2005,	Guinea: 1993,* 1995, 1998, 2002, 2003	Nigeria: 1992,* 1993,* 1998, 1999, 2003,* 2004, 2007*
Gabon: 1990, 1993, 1996, 1998, 2001, 2005, 2006	Lesotho: 1993, 1998,* 2002, 2007	South Africa: 1994,* 1999,* 2004
Gambia: 1992, 1996, 1997, 2001, 2002, 2006, 2007	Madagascar: 1993, 1997, 1998, 2001,* 2002, 2007	Sudan: 1996, 2000
Ghana: 1992, 1996, 2000, 2004, 2008	Mauritania: 1992, 1996, 1997, 2001, 2003, 2006, 2007	Togo: 1993,* 1994, 1998, 1999, 2002, 2003, 2005,* 2007
Guinea-Bissau: 1994, 1999, 2004, 2005, 2008	Niger: 1993, 1995, 1996, 1996, 1999, 2004	Zimbabwe: 1990, 1995, 1996, 2000,* 2002,* 2005, 2008*
Liberia: 1997, 2005	Rep. of Congo: 1992, 1993,* 2002, 2002, 2007	
Malawi: 1994, 1999, 2004	Senegal: 1993, 1998, 2000, 2001, 2007	
Mali: 1992, 1997, 2002, 2007	Tanzania: 1995, 2000, 2005	
Mauritius: 1991, 1995, 2000, 2005	Uganda: 1996, 2001, 2001, 2006	
Mozambique: 1994, 1999, 2004		
Namibia: 1994, 1999, 2004		
Rwanda: 2003, 2003		
São Tomé & Prínc.: 1991, 1994, 1996, 1998, 2001, 2002, 2003, 2006, 2006		
Seychelles: 1993, 1998, 2001, 2002, 2006		
Sierra Leone: 1996, 2002, 2007		
Swaziland: 1993, 1998, 2003, 2008		
Zambia: 1991, 1996, 2001, 2006, 2008		

Italics: Substantial (high) violence (categories 2 and 3).
* Highest violence (category 3).

Trends over Time

The dataset on African electoral violence also indicates other important patterns. One question is whether there is a general trend, over time, across sub-Saharan Africa in the likelihood of high electoral violence. The short answer is no, at least according to the dataset. As figure 2.1 shows, the mean level of violence in the dataset is around .89, and twelve of the eighteen years in the dataset show an average violence level between .5 and

Figure 2.1   Average Level of Electoral Violence, by Year, 1990–2008

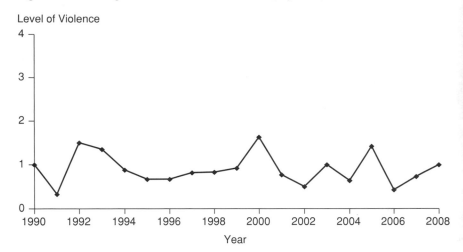

1. During two years in the early 1990s (1992 and 1993), when African states were holding their first elections after the transition from one-party regimes, we see a concentration of highly violent electoral periods. But on average, the years 2000 and 2005 were as violent as, or more violent than, 1992 and 1993. The result is counterintuitive: even though, on average, sub-Saharan African states are becoming more democratic—at least, as measured by Freedom House's scores on political and civil liberty—elections, on average, are not becoming less violent, at least through 2008.

Patterns of Pre- and Postvote Electoral Violence

When violence occurs in an electoral period, it is overwhelmingly in the prevote period. Of the 129 cases of some form of electoral violence, including harassment, either before or after the vote (or both), 122 cases (94.6 percent) took place during the electoral campaign before the polling date. By contrast, of the 129 cases with some form of violence, only 38 cases (29.5 percent) had violence after the voting. Of those cases, only seven had any form of postvote electoral violence *and* no prevote electoral violence.[12] There are forty-five cases of high electoral violence—that is, categories 2 and 3 in the AEVD. Of these, thirty-six (80 percent) occurred before the vote, and sixteen (36 percent) occurred after the vote. (Seven cases had high levels of violence both before and after the vote.) If electoral violence does occur before the vote, only 30 percent of cases in the sample reach a threshold of high electoral violence. By contrast, if violence happens after

---

12. Those countries were Burkina Faso (1991), Guinea-Bissau (2005), Lesotho (1998), Madagascar (2001), Mauritania (1992), Nigeria (1993), and Senegal (1993).

an election, 42 percent of cases in the sample reach a threshold of high electoral violence.

These results suggest three important findings that were not obvious before constructing the AEVD dataset. First, where electoral violence occurs in sub-Saharan Africa, it is most often part of an electoral campaign before voting takes place; violence is therefore most often an effort to shape voting behavior, patterns, and preferences. Second, if electoral violence occurs after an election, it is more likely to reach a high level than electoral violence occurring before an election. This finding suggests that after the election is held, the terms of the contest change—or, at least, the logic of violence is likely to be different. Third and finally, the findings suggest that postelection violence is very rare if preelection violence did not occur. In the sample, less than 3 percent of all elections experienced any form of postelection violence without any incident of preelection violence.

Regarding who commits the violence, the results strongly indicate that incumbents (or groups affiliated with incumbents) are the primary perpetrators. Of all the recorded election cases where pre- and postelection violence took place, incumbents were the unique primary perpetrators 75 percent of the time. By contrast, challengers were the unique primary perpetrators only 2 percent of the time.[13] And in 21 percent of cases, both incumbents and challengers were principal perpetrators of electoral violence. The percentages are similar if only high-violence cases are examined: in some 71 percent of high-violence cases (both pre- and postelection), incumbents were the primary perpetrators; by contrast, challengers were the sole perpetrators 2 percent of the time, and both incumbents and challengers engaged in high levels of violence 27 percent of the time. These patterns are apparent in table 2.3, which disaggregates the level of violence according to the type of perpetrator.

The data in table 2.3 reveal other important patterns. Some of the findings are consistent with a running theme so far: incumbents are the main perpetrators of electoral violence in general, but as table 2.3 shows, the finding also holds true if electoral violence cases are disaggregated by timing. Of the 122 cases of any preelection violence, incumbents were unique primary perpetrators 79 percent of the time, and challengers were the same only 2

---

13. The 2 percent represents two cases. The first is South Africa (1994), where the large-scale electoral violence was between the then-opposition parties, the African National Congress and the Inkatha Freedom Party. But the Inkatha Freedom Party is generally believed to have received the support of incumbent National Party supporters in the former apartheid security forces. The second case is Republic of Congo (1992), when former presidential incumbent Denis Sassou-Nguesso placed third in the first round of voting. In the subsequent runoff period, Sassou-Nguesso backed Pascal Lissouba, whose supporters clashed with those of Bernard Kolelas. Both cases strongly imply that incumbents were instrumental in fomenting the electoral violence. In short, according to the data, nonincumbent challengers are almost never the sole perpetrators of electoral violence.

Table 2.3   Cases of Electoral Violence by Level, Timing, and Perpetrators

	Incumbent Main Perp.	Opposition Main Perp.	Both Perpetrate
Preelection Violence			
Level 1	70	1	15
	(72%)	(50%)	(65%)
Level 2	19	0	2
	(20%)	(0%)	(9%)
Level 3	8	1	6
	(8%)	(50%)	(26%)
Postelection Violence			
Level 1	17	2	3
	(65%)	(67%)	(33%)
Level 2	4	1	0
	(15%)	(33%)	(0%)
Level 3	5	0	6
	(19%)	(0%)	(67%)

percent of the time. Both incumbents and challengers engaged in violence 19 percent of the time. Of the thirty-six prevote high-violence cases (categories 2 and 3 in the AEVD), incumbents were the primary perpetrators 75 percent of the time, while challengers were the primary perpetrators only 3 percent of the time, and both were involved 22 percent of the time.

The same pattern generally holds true for postelection violence. Of the thirty-eight cases of postelection violence, incumbents were the primary perpetrators 68 percent of the time. Challengers were the primary perpetrators 8 percent of the time—those three cases being Madagascar (1993), South Africa (1994), and the Central African Republic (1999)—and both sides perpetrated violence 24 percent of the time. Of the sixteen postvote high-violence cases, incumbents were the principal perpetrators 56 percent of the time. Challengers were the principal perpetrators 6 percent of time—the sole case being South Africa (1994)—and both sets of actors were involved in high levels of postvote violence 37.5 percent of the time. The main difference in these numbers is that if challengers are involved in electoral violence, whether as unique perpetrators or coperpetrators, they are, like incumbents, more likely to do so before the vote. (In 68 percent of cases where challengers engaged in electoral violence at any level, the violence took place before the election, as table 2.3 shows.) But in the election periods when challengers do engage in electoral violence, that violence is more likely to occur at a higher level after the election is held. Where electoral violence by challengers occurred before the vote, 36 percent of cases had high levels of violence, compared to 58 percent if the violence occurred after the vote.

The results are interesting on their face. First, no matter how we disaggregate electoral violence, incumbents are overwhelmingly the primary perpetrators. They use the coercive apparatus available to them to win contests

Table 2.4   Legislative versus Presidential Elections

	Presidential	Legislative	Both (within three months)
Violence level 0	19	50	23
	(32%)	(53%)	(34%)
Violence level 1	27	27	30
	(45%)	(29%)	(45%)
Violence level 2	6	10	6
	(10%)	(11%)	(9%)
Violence level 3	8	7	8
	(13%)	(7%)	(12%)

and to protect their power. That consistent finding runs squarely counter to some of Collier and Vicente's work, in which they claim that challengers are the primary wielders of violence (Collier and Vicente 2008). Second, if there is electoral violence, challengers are more likely to be involved in preelection than postelection violence, but if challengers engage in electoral violence, they likely will do so at higher levels after the polling takes place.

Legislative and Presidential Elections

Another important question to ask is whether presidential elections, legislative elections, or elections that are close to each other experience more or less violence than others. The theoretical expectation would be that any electoral period involving a presidential contest would be, on average, more violent than those that do not, given that African political systems tend to be presidential. However, while the data do not contradict this expectation, neither do they lend strong support for it, as table 2.4 shows.

Overall, there is a slightly higher incidence of the greatest level of violence in our dataset if a presidential context took place.[14] Of all such cases in the dataset (electoral period that is either presidential only or combined presidential and legislative), 13 percent had large-scale electoral violence, compared to 7 percent where a presidential seat was not being contested. Of the two highest levels of violence, the ratios change to 22 percent and 18 percent respectively. Similarly, 33 percent of contests involving a presidential election showed no electoral violence, whereas 53 percent of legislative-only races showed no electoral violence. On average, electoral campaigns in which a presidential seat is being contested are more violent, though not as dramatically as theory might suggest.

---

14. A chi-squared test of table 2.4 does not yield a significant result (p = 0.103). A chi-squared test of whether elections that include a presidential contest (meaning the "Presidential" and "Both" categories) differ from legislative elections does yield a significant result (p = 0.015). A chi-squared test of whether elections that include a legislative contest (meaning the "Legislative" and "Both" categories) differ from presidential elections does not yield a significant result (p = 0.296).

Electoral Violence and Other Political Violence

In the section on frequency and main patterns of electoral violence, one other important critical question remains: Are electoral periods in general more violent than nonelectoral periods in sub-Saharan Africa? Using data from the Political Instability Task Force (PITF) Worldwide Atrocities Event database, which records instances of political violence resulting in five or more noncombatant deaths, we calculate the log of the total number of deaths from recorded events for nonelection and election years for distinct African countries from 1995 to 2005. The time frame for the data is somewhat curtailed, and the coding scheme used by the PITF excludes a number of low-intensity violent events, but the analysis suggests that elections do not have a dramatic effect on the intensity of political violence in specific African countries. Indeed, the mean of the log of annual deaths for nonelection years is 4.93, while the mean for election years is 3.93.[15] Nonelection years seem to be somewhat *more* violent than election years. Thus, although countries such as Zimbabwe and Kenya have experienced a dramatic surge of political violence related to elections in recent years, the data show that when looking at the universe of recorded violence against civilians in Africa, elections are not the main source of violence. Violence is likely to be as prevalent, and of marginally greater magnitude, in nonelection years.

Findings

This section's main findings are six:

- First, electoral violence is not as frequent as critics suggest, though frequent enough to cause serious concern. That significant violence occurs in nearly one-fifth of all African electoral contests means that advocates and policymakers need to pay attention to the risks that democratic elections can trigger.
- Second, there is consistent cross-national variation—some countries rarely have significant electoral violence, other countries have occasional significant electoral violence, and still other countries almost always have significant electoral violence. Moreover, there is also important variation across time within countries. While not the focus of this paper, a major topic for future research is to explain the variation across and within countries.
- Third—perhaps unsurprising but still important and contrary to some scholarship—incumbent forces overall commit considerably

---

15. We log the annual numbers of people killed per country given the skewness in the PITF data, which includes some country-years with more than 10,000 deaths.

more violence than challenger forces. However—conforming to expectation—where challengers do engage in high levels of electoral violence, they are more likely to do so after an election than before.

- Fourth, electoral violence is generally much more likely to take place before the polling date than after, but if it occurs after the polling date, that violence is likely to be at a higher level. The logic of postelection violence may therefore be somewhat different from that of preelection violence.
- Fifth, elections in which a presidential seat is being contested are marginally more violent than those that involve only legislative contests, but the difference in violence attendant on the two types of elections is not as dramatic as anticipated.
- Finally, overall, elections per se are not the main drivers of violence in sub-Saharan Africa—on balance, nonelection years are marginally more violent than election years in the one existing dataset that annually measures political violence against civilians.

From a normative and policy point of view, the conclusions are somewhat middle-of-the-road. On the one hand, we find significant destabilizing elections to be infrequent enough to challenge a pessimistic view that multiparty elections per se are highly damaging. On the other hand, we do not find any trend over time to suggest that sub-Saharan Africa is shifting toward less violent elections, and the examples of highly violent electoral periods in the dataset indicate a real risk that such violence may take place. On the theoretical and policy side, as the study has indicated, there is a strong premium on determining which combinations of factors and conditions lead to high levels of electoral violence and which combinations do not.

Scenarios of Electoral Violence

In the course of creating the AEVD, we identified several pathways or scenarios of electoral violence, with an emphasis on high levels of electoral violence. This section identifies those scenarios and attaches some case examples to them, as part of the general descriptive overview of African electoral violence that the chapter presents. Six principal scenarios stand out. They overlap in some ways but are different enough to merit their own categories.

Scenario 1: Harassment and Street Brawls

One scenario of electoral violence can be characterized as low-level harassment. In these cases, two general types of violence take place. In one type, security forces are deployed against challengers to break up political party rallies, to raid opposition-identified newspapers, and, occasionally, to arrest opposition candidates. Typically, the violence does not reach the level of murder. In the other type of this scenario, party supporters (generally youth) clash—supporters of one party might attack the headquarters or an office of another political party; one party's rally might be heckled and taunted by supporters of another party. In general, these street brawls are not fatal or, if they are, are not part of systematic campaigns of killing. In this category of electoral violence, we find both targeted, directed, and planned instances of violent harassment, as well as more spontaneous instances. The main logic of violence is harassment and mild intimidation to contain and control opponents and to limit the scope of their power. The cases are somewhat frequent—38 percent of the electoral contests in the dataset—and they indicate that significant physical violence is not the primary strategy for securing victory for either incumbents or challengers, but that some form of intimidation is.

Scenario 2: Decapitating the Opposition

A second scenario, identified as violent repression, is to immobilize the high-level opposition. In general, the scenario is coded as level 2 in the dataset and is a strategy almost uniquely pursued by incumbents. The central aim of this form of electoral violence is to remove the main opponents from the electoral playing field. The violence is not generalized but, to the contrary, highly targeted. In contrast to a unique practice of violent harassment, the scenario of decapitation implies that incumbents calculate that arrest, disqualification, or expulsion of high-level opponents will not be sufficient; instead, they opt to remove their opponents physically from the electoral arena. Apt examples include the presidential elections in Togo in 1994, in Zimbabwe in 2005, and in Equatorial Guinea in 1993. In these cases, political opposition leaders were variously killed, arrested, and tortured. In general, this scenario of electoral violence takes place before an election, when an incumbent seeks to remove powerful contenders from the playing field; however, the move could also occur after an election, when incumbents seek to quell opposition to an announced electoral vote. The expectation would be that this type of electoral violence is primarily urban and targeted at specific individuals.

Scenario 3: Redistricting by Other Means

In this scenario, the focus of violence shifts from leaders, candidates, and their organs for disseminating ideas (such as newspapers) and toward supporters. As with the second scenario, this tends to occur when an incumbent victory is uncertain and the incumbent calculates that victory cannot be secured through intimidation, bribery, harassment, or disqualification. But unlike the second scenario, in these cases the violence is directed against voters as well as candidates. In general, we would expect the violence to be greatest in electoral districts where the opposing party has significant support but where the party that uses violence also has a chance of victory. Hence the term "redistricting by other means." In most cases, the perpetrators will be incumbents, the victims challengers. The Zimbabwe 2008 presidential elections are an apt example of this type of electoral violence.

Scenario 4: Redistributing by Other Means

A fourth scenario occurs when national and local electoral interests align to produce violence. For local actors, electoral periods are opportunities to redress access to vital local resources, in particular land and sometimes marketplace rights or other sources of wealth and power. For national actors, the interest lies in securing electoral victory. The study finds consistently that electoral contests trigger and intensify bitter claims over access to vital local resources, especially in areas with significant migration. The electoral claims thus generate within some groups indigenous, or "sons of the soil," arguments about their autochthonous rights to control a vital local resource. Those claims in turn generate fears in perceived outsider groups, who seek to protect themselves. Where these local resource grievances play out in constituencies or speak to ethnic audiences that are essential for a national party to put together a winning coalition, high electoral violence is most likely to occur. That is, high electoral violence happens when joint incentives align between a national party's electoral strategies and influential local actors who mobilize to change resource distributions in electoral periods. Kenya's 1992 and 1997 elections and Côte d'Ivoire's 1995 elections illustrate this scenario. In these cases, we would expect to see a combination of urban-based repressive electoral violence and regionally specific electoral violence, especially in those regions where national parties need to win and where access to local resources is contested during an electoral period.

Scenario 5: Islands of Intense Electoral Violence

A related but slightly different scenario occurs where electoral violence is confined to a single constituency or region. In these cases, as in the previous scenario, the electoral contest triggers highly localized claims to local resource access. However, the fight for control of local resources is distinct from national-level electoral strategies. In some cases where semiautonomous regions exist, or in a federal system where control of a regional or local administration is highly significant, we would expect to see greater violence. The consistent electoral violence in Zanzibar would be a good example—consistently high electoral violence in the islands, but rare violence on the mainland of Tanzania. Electoral violence in Nigeria's 2007 elections is another illustrative case. By contrast, where there is no federal or semi-autonomous structure and where the electoral contest triggers local-level resource conflicts without national implications, we would expect violence to be at a lower level. Northern Ghana illustrates this scenario of localized, generally low-level electoral violence over land claims, access to markets, and chieftancy disputes.

Scenario 6: Protest → Repression Electoral Violence

Another fairly distinct scenario occurs where an announced electoral result triggers protest, which in turn triggers repression and the potential for generalized violence. The most fitting example is the Kenya 2007 elections, where a widespread belief that the results were rigged in favor of President Mwai Kibaki triggered challenger protests, which led to repression from security forces. The announced results also unleashed a wave of violence related to the local resource grievances described in scenario 4, which led to revenge attacks. Another example is Nigeria's 1993 elections, which were annulled after the opposition candidate Moshood Abiola was widely expected to have won. The state security forces deployed massive repressive violence to quell opposition to the announced annulment. Côte d'Ivoire's 2000 elections and 2010 runoff elections are yet other examples. Typically in this scenario, the chain of violence is not directly related to shaping voting behavior, preferences, and opportunities but to repressing challengers who seek to overturn an announced outcome or to use violence to accomplish, in a period of uncertainty, what an election result was expected to accomplish, namely to redress local resource allocations.

Conclusions

This chapter has presented a descriptive overview of electoral violence in sub-Saharan Africa from 1990 to 2008. The empirical presentation is based on an analysis of the AEVD, an original dataset on electoral violence, created in part to fill an existing gap in the literature. Despite growing interest in the topic, we know of no other database focused specifically on the frequency and patterns of electoral violence in African elections.

　　What we lose in detail about the dynamics of specific cases, we hope to have offset in presenting an overview. The results are certainly not immediately obvious. The most important result is that significant electoral violence is relatively infrequent. Of the 221 national elections in the study's universe of African cases, 42 percent were nonviolent while 38 percent produced low levels of electoral violence—termed *violent harassment*. This means that about one-fifth of all elections yielded large-scale violence. The results are generally consistent over time: elections held in the early and mid-1990s were just as likely to result in the same levels of electoral violence as those in the early and mid-2000s, even though, on average, African states are becoming more democratic. Incumbents and their supporters commit most of the electoral violence, and most of it happens before a vote, with the apparent intention of shaping voting behavior, preferences, and opportunities (i.e., for whom one can vote). Where violence happens after an election, it is generally more severe. Electoral periods in which a presidential seat is at stake are generally more violent (though not dramatically so) than electoral periods where only legislative seats are contested. We also find that elections per se are not the main source of political violence on the continent: overall, election years in Africa are slightly less violent than nonelection years.

With some reservations, we can draw a number of conclusions about the relationship between elections and violence in Africa. The relative infrequency of serious electoral violence challenges the pessimistic view that multiparty elections are dangerous and should be avoided. However, that one-fifth of African elections *do* result in significant violence indicates the need for serious attention to the risk of violent destabilization that elections create.

The study's results demonstrate great variation across and within African states, and a critical next step in advancing a research agenda on electoral violence is to examine that variation. Why do some African states consistently produce electoral violence while others do not? Why are some elections but not others highly violent in the same African state? And what is the relationship more generally between electoral violence and other forms of political violence? These are critical questions with clear policy and theoretical implications. Other chapters of this volume address these questions with reference to specific cases, and we also hope to address them in future research.

References

Arriola, Leonardo. 2011. "Post-Election Violence and Power-Sharing in Africa." Paper delivered at the annual conference of the African Studies Association, Washington, DC, Nov. 18.

Bates, Robert. 1983. "Modernization, Ethnic Competition, and the Rationality of Politics of Contemporary Africa." In *State versus Ethnic Claims: African Policy*

Dilemmas, ed. Donald Rothchild and Victor Olorunsola, 152–71. Boulder, CO: Westview.

Bates, Robert. 2008. *When Things Fell Apart: State Failure in Late-Century Africa.* New York: Cambridge Univ. Press.

Bratton, Michael, and Nicolas van de Walle. 1997. *Democratic Experiments in Africa: Regime Transitions in Comparative Perspective.* New York: Cambridge Univ. Press.

Cingranelli, David, and David Richards. 2010. "The Cingranelli and Richards (CIRI) Human Rights Data Project." *Human Rights Quarterly* 32 (2): 401–24.

Collier, Paul. 2009. *Wars, Guns, and Votes: Democracy in Dangerous Places.* New York: Harper Collins.

Collier, Paul, and Pedro C. Vicente. 2008. "Votes and Violence: Evidence from a Field Experiment in Nigeria." CSAE WPS/2008-16. http://economics.ouls.ox.ac.uk/13198/1/2008-16text.pdf.

Dahl, Robert A. 1971. *Polyarchy: Participation and Opposition.* New Haven, CT: Yale University Press.

Harbeson, John, Donald Rothchild, and Naomi Chazan, eds. 1994. *Civil Society and the State in Africa.* Boulder, CO: Lynne Rienner.

Lindberg, Staffan I. 2006. *Democracy and Elections in Africa.* Baltimore, MD: Johns Hopkins University Press.

Schaffer, Frederic C. 1998. *Democracy in Translation: Understanding Politics in an Unfamiliar Culture.* Ithaca, NY: Cornell Univ. Press.

Snyder, Jack. 2000. *From Voting to Violence: Democratization and Nationalist Conflict.* New York: Norton.

3

Evaluating
Election-Related Violence

Nigeria and Sudan
in Comparative Perspective

Timothy D. Sisk

Electoral violence is common on the long transitional pathway from authoritarian rule or civil war to the consolidation of democracy. Recent African history provides a lesson: the democratization processes have frequently brought recurring violence in the heat of electoral struggles in transitions from one-party states and civil war contexts. The track record of elections in Africa is mixed. Indeed, Lindberg finds gradual improvement in participation, competition, and legitimacy in elections, particularly in those African countries that see third and subsequent rounds of ostensibly improving electoral processes over time (Lindberg 2003, 2006). In many countries, however, a period of initial transition has evolved into an apparently ongoing state of political instability and strife, or fragility, with the consolidation of democracy too often proving to be an elusive goal (Bratton and Mattes 2009).

This chapter explores the question, what are the underlying contexts, drivers, and manifestations of election-related violence in Africa? First, the chapter presents a framework for cross-case evaluation of election-related

The author would like to thank the following readers of earlier drafts of this chapter: Sead Alihodzic of International IDEA, volume editor Dorina Bekoe, and Anne Gloor of Peace Nexus, formerly of the Swiss Foreign Ministry.

violence, drawing on theoretical perspectives and comparative politics research. This framework builds on the literature on root causes of conflict to posit that structural and institutional drivers of conflict are found in historical path dependencies and demographic, social, economic, and environmental conditions that lead to competition over scarce resources and over control of the state. But the scramble for resources and largesse (or "rent") amid scarcity is only part of the picture. Often, mobilization occurs along ethnic or religious lines; thus, theories of root causes must look deeper than simple economic scarcity arguments, into the nexus between resource capture, state power, and identity politics.

Election-related violence in Africa is driven in some contexts by competition among elites for the state, and ill-managed, insecure electoral processes tend to exacerbate underlying root causes that are often grounded in perceptions of "horizontal inequalities," in which economic inequalities or opportunities overlap with ethnic or religious identity. Greed is often blamed for election-related conflict in Africa's fragile, resource-poor, prebendalist states.[1] But greed alone does not seem sufficient. Instead, accounts of elites' incentives for control of the resource-allocation authority of the state must be seen in parallel with their incentives for mobilizing on divisive ethnic themes. The analysis looks at the political economy of state capture in a particular social context that relates directly to the elites' incentives and stakes for perpetrating violence in order to prevail at the polls or to prevent opponents from gaining (or legitimizing their gain of) the state. These insights into causes and motives may help inform the conflict-prevention strategies and operational approaches that have become a critical concern of the United Nations, the African Union, and subregional organizations.[2]

Approach and Methods

As Straus and Taylor find in their chapter of this volume, around 20 percent of presidential and parliamentary electoral events in Africa have witnessed a high level of violence. Much of this violence has occurred in countries facing extended transitions, in which the onset of liberation or the advent of multiparty rule leaves democratization processes that are not

---

1. The term "prebendalism" was coined by Richard Joseph in his analysis of politics in Nigeria: "According to the theory of prebendalism, state offices are regarded as prebends that can be appropriated by officeholders, who use them to generate material benefits for themselves and their constituents and kin groups" (Joseph 1996, 3; 1987).

2. In late 2011, for example, the Economic Community of West African States, the African Union, and the United Nations adopted the Praia Declaration on Elections and Stability in West Africa, which states that "election-related violence continues to be one of the major challenges to political stability in the sub-region" and that "free and fair elections as a prerequisite to the peaceful transfer of power are the cornerstone of democracy" (UN Office for West Africa 2011).

yet consolidated, in which compliance with the rules of the electoral game becomes habituated.[3] Indeed, electoral violence is an ongoing problem for many African countries. (See, for example, France 24 2010.) In many "fragile" states in Africa, violence has accompanied electoral processes during transitions from an autocratic past or civil war (in some countries, both) toward a stable system of regular, credible elections in which social interests and differences are reconciled nonviolently through democratic institutions and concomitant electoral processes.[4]

To explore root causes of electoral violence, this chapter presents a structured, focused comparison of two case studies—Nigeria (2007) and Sudan (2010)—in which strife escalated because of national-level election processes.[5] These two cases loom large in informing the analysis of election-related conflict in Africa (both have seen high levels of violence overall) and, through comparison, can yield insights into electoral violence in similar contexts globally in which natural resource rent-seeking and state capture are pervasive traits of politics. While comparison of two case studies cannot yield truly robust contingent generalizations, it yields important insights about ways that election-related violence feeds into broader social conflict, the incentives for regime or opposition forces to engage in violence, and contemporary approaches to preventive action.

In Nigeria, electoral violence in 2007 escalated compared with the already violent 2003 elections, suggesting that the underlying drivers of conflict over religious and ethnic difference, over control of a petrostate, and over access to state authority have increased. An estimated 300 fatalities were attributed to the electoral process in early to mid-2007. Nigeria is very much a case of election violence in a protracted and unfinished transition to democracy in a country where political power is closely related to economic gain. While some have seen the 2011 elections in Nigeria as a step forward in that the election was relatively peaceful and transparent in some respects, actual fatalities throughout the entire process were actually higher (just over 1,000 fatalities) than in 2007, given the postelection riots and confrontations that occurred just after the 2011 results were announced. Thus, the Nigeria case reveals cyclical and sometimes worsening

---

3. For an overview of the recent scholarly literature on the issues and dimensions in democratization in Africa, see National Intelligence Council 2008.

4. This ongoing instability well after the initial turn to democratization is reflected in broader concerns over the prior prevailing view that democracy tends to be consolidated after the initial transitional period is overcome. See Carothers 2002.

5. These cases were selected based on their regional variation within Africa, their differing contexts in the dimensions and aspects of fragility (protracted transition, war-to-peace transition), and their importance on the international agenda. The case studies are linked by the fact that both are petrostates that have experienced high levels of political violence, have conflict along identity lines, and feature federal political institutions.

cycles of election-related violence despite improvements in the capacity of local electoral administration.

The 2010 elections in Sudan are the second case study. This analysis illustrates well that root causes must be seen within the broader transition framework reflected in the implementation of the 2005 Comprehensive Peace Agreement (CPA), which set up a war-to-democracy transition in this long-troubled state. In Sudan, election-related violence reflected the deep instability and fragility characterizing the war-to-peace transition in that country, and the use of national elections to legitimate a war-ending pact. Moreover, election-related violence was part of an overall strategy of specific, desperate incumbent elites to legitimate and retain their control of the state through the course of the uncertain transition from war to the country's partition in July 2011.

Exploring Causal Drivers

Causes-of-conflict analysis increasingly focuses on the underlying social and economic factors, or the intersection of "need, greed, and creed" (Arnson and Zartman 2005). But this chapter, in adapting this approach to the analysis of election-related violence, seeks to link this more generic causal analysis framework of underlying social, environmental, or economic factors to the election-violence research that emphasizes the stakes, incentives, and expectations of elites. Four points of analysis are critical: the context of democratization or political change in which violence occurs; the political economy of state power and the nature and patterns of political mobilization; the political economy of state capture; and the electoral system, integrity of electoral administration, and effects of violence-management efforts such as peace pacts and security-force performance. The contexts matter because the use of violence is strategic to a broader purpose. The political economy of state capture relates to the deep structural conditions that inform the stakes of controlling the commanding heights of governmental authority in high-natural-resource environments. The electoral system is important because it determines who wins, how, and by how much; it is often specifically manipulated for a specific aim. And finally, the question of electoral administration is critical because fraudulent or poorly administered elections are more likely than fair elections to produce challenges of illegitimate rule.

The Democratization and Mobilization Context

Violence escalates with a very specific political context that has both macro-level (national) and micro-level (local) levels of analysis. Thus, any analysis of root causes must also address the intersecting dimensions of statebuilding, democratization, and conflict at various levels and in consideration of key local factors—often spatial or territorial factors (Bratton and Chang 2006). Some African countries, such as Sudan, have yet to resolve basic questions of national identity and state formation. And clearly, in addition to the ethnic, demographic, or resource dimensions of conflict, the context of state formation is a critical factor (Deng 2005). Current assessment tools on the analysis and prevention of election-related conflict tend to focus on the immediate electoral threat and take preexisting conditions as a starting point. But it is essential also to evaluate critical issues such as regime type, since violence may be more likely in those countries in transition or facing considerable uncertainty. In the early stages of democratization, especially when there is high uncertainty, low information, and the perception of high stakes, the propensity for violence tends to rise. Yet for each of these generalizations, any integrated causal analysis must be based in a particular set of original conditions.

The democratization context also raises the need to focus on the patterns and nature of political mobilization. Analysis of the causes and manifestations of violence needs to address its usually organized and purposeful nature; while small-scale acts of violence may be perpetrated by lone individuals, endemic or chronic election violence is usually the consequence of extensive organization and mobilization. Africa has typically seen violence at various levels and in various forms (from relatively spontaneous to deliberate and organized). Examples drawn from Kenya and Nigeria, for example, suggest that both spontaneous and instrumentalized violence are common, whereas in postwar situations (e.g., Sudan and DRC), violence is more highly or regularly instrumental, perpetrated by organized political agents (Ong'ayo 2008).

Indeed, other research (such as Straus and Taylor's in this volume) shows distinct patterns of violence in Africa, for example between incumbents and challengers, or in preelection versus postelection violence. Studies of organized violence in internal conflicts have highlighted not only the role of political leaders who articulate grievances and organize and lead conflict organizations and of the masses who support them, but also the influence of midlevel mobilized elites (e.g., a local party functionary or provincial police or guerrilla commander) as critical players in the emergence and sustainability of violence at the local level (Höglund 2009). All this suggests that any account of root causes of election-related violence must take into account agency and elite behavior within a specific democratization and mobilization context.

The Political Economy of State Capture

Common accounts of the underlying root causes of vulnerability to violence in contemporary Africa pair deep-seated social grievances with the political economy of inequality or rent-seeking by sometimes predatory elites. Typical accounts of the structural grievances underlying conflict in Africa are found in land or chieftaincy disputes; political, cultural, or economic marginalization along identity lines; and state fragility and the politics of "neopatrimonialism." Disentangling the incentives for violence requires carefully thinking about the conditions under which electoral violence may be instrumentally useful to elites: when a deeply insecure party or faction expects to be systematically excluded from political power, it may well turn to violence either to prevent its own exclusion or to prevent the election's success (Höglund 2006).

Theories of election-related violence often highlight the perpetuation of highly personalistic or patronage politics or a system in which politicians are gangland-style "warlords" who control resources (such as access to jobs and income) and dispense public services such as housing, health care, and lucrative government contracts (Schwartz 2001). In Africa, these approaches relate directly to the stakes for state capture and the close association of presidentialism in Africa with clientelistic approaches to governance (Van de Walle 2003). As Boone and Kriger demonstrate in their chapter of this volume, electoral success may well translate into the direct capacity of elites to manipulate land rights, which in turn (as in Côte d'Ivoire or Zimbabwe) can directly affect identity-group relations. However, it is important to understand the incentives and stakes for state capture by predatory elites at both national and local levels, and how state power at these various levels affects the distribution of public goods and the exploitation or use of private resources (Van de Walle 2002).

Thus, the stakes of elections are often seen as opportunities to engage in corruption and economic rent-seeking. Importantly, these dynamics may be just as strong, or stronger, at the local level. At any level, the consequence is highly factionalized politics, often along religious, sectarian, or ethnic lines or party-political divisions, where control of the state leads to the reinforcement of class divisions or of economic opportunity along lines of social difference. Scholars have pointed to the existence and perpetuation of the overlap between control of the state, economic opportunity, and identity politics—known as "horizontal inequalities"—as strongly contributing to the likelihood of violent encounters (Stewart 2008). The stakes involved in electoral contests can be considered in several different ways and in various contexts. A common cause of election violence is that in many situations, especially in conditions of high scarcity and underdevelopment, the stakes of winning and losing valued political posts are incredibly high. When winning a state office is the key to livelihood not just for an individual but for the entire clan, faction, or even ethnic group, the stakes for prevailing in electoral competition are dangerously high. Bates's work on state failure in Africa and the challenges of political violence emphasizes the critical role of top state elites engaged in predation as a driver of conflict, whereas other researchers emphasize the challenges of "disruption from below" by aggrieved or marginalized groups (Bates 2008).

Structural and Institutional Drivers of Conflict

Most African countries have no shortage of underlying factors typically associated with vulnerability to conflict, and indeed, cross-national studies of fragility indicate that many African countries can be coded as either highly or moderately conflict-vulnerable. The deep drivers of conflict are often described in terms of social and demographic factors, environmental factors, and economic factors. Among the leading social factors are ethnic differences and a history of prior conflict along ethnic lines. Indeed, in some cases, such as Nigeria and Sudan, such differences may also be described along religious lines (principally, Muslim-Christian). Ethnic fragmentation is not a deep driver of conflict in its own right but is instead seen as a contingent factor that depends highly on the nature of social structure and of elites' mobilization along ethnic lines. Because of the multiethnic and multireligious character of most African states (and all those that have seen election-related violence), the linkages between ethnicity, electoral mobilization, and violence require close attention to the specific contexts in which they occur.

Also, to understand the control of the "commanding heights," analysis of root causes needs to happen at multiple levels, including local and subnational regional levels where power is dispersed in decentralized contexts. Indeed, as the case studies below show, much of Africa's electoral violence can be highly localized, at times occurring in marginalized or disparate areas. Because ethnicity is not universally salient in all cases of election-related violence, the conditions under which mobilization occurs on divisive ethnic or religious themes requires an approach that delves into the conditions under which ethnic differences become electorally salient. (See Posner 2006.) There is insufficient knowledge on the nature of mobilization and the collective-action aspects of election-related violence. Several recent case studies (Burundi, Kenya, Nigeria, South Sudan, and Zimbabwe) shed light on how mobilization and collective action works in the escalation of election-related violence in Africa.

It is increasingly clear that exclusion from natural resource allocations can lead to mobilization by those excluded and disaffected. Many internal conflicts—for example, in Aceh (Indonesia), Mindanao (Philippines), Nigeria, and Bolivia—are driven in part by the exclusion of local peoples from access to the extraction of, and profit from, local natural resources, whose revenues are controlled by either the central government or transnational corporations. Two other areas also come under scrutiny as background conditions that leave Africa's countries vulnerable to electoral violence. One set of variables is demographic, suggesting that high concentrations of youth (particularly young men), typically overlapping with few opportunities for formal-sector employment, provide a human resource base for recruitment into militias, armed gangs, or political movements and organizations. A second demographic aspect is rapid urbanization, which may account for both the intensity and the locality of election-related conflict in the periurban slums in and around Africa's major cities.

Finally, the search for root causes may go back up the causal chain, in some analysts' view, to bigger problems of environmental scarcity, particularly competition over land.[6] The environment-conflict nexus argument posits that deep-seated environmental change (e.g., desertification, water scarcity, land-quality deterioration) may create conditions of scarcity, and in turn, conflicts over access to resources. This driver is particularly salient in countries with either extreme scarcity (e.g., Somalia) or particularly lucrative commodity-resource endowments (e.g., Nigeria).

Election Management

Electoral processes themselves do not cause violence. Instead, they aid escalatory dynamics through mobilization and collective action of conflict groups and through the "precipitating event" aspects that fuel grievances when there are (as is often the case) charges of fraud, manipulation, or falsification of results (Rapoport and Weinberg 2001). That is, whether and how violence occurs also strongly depends on how state authorities conduct the entire cycle of election-related management. Countries can be initially vulnerable to violence—as in Kenya's 2010 Constitutional Referendum—but a well-managed process and a broader commitment to nonviolent contestation can prevent escalation. Thus, the electoral process itself, including the state's capacity to manage electoral processes, is a critical intervening variable between underlying driver and actual escalation of

---

6.   See Catherine Boone and Norma Kriger's chapter in this volume. For further analysis of the environment-conflict nexus, see UN Environmental Programme 2004.

conflict. Indeed, in Kenya in 2007–08, root-cause drivers did not escalate until there was a public perception of fraud and mismanagement by the election-management body.

Electoral systems matter in reflecting and shaping social divisions and in translating these social differences into political power, but, alas, there is no consensus on whether any single electoral system is always "best" for ameliorating conflict. Debates swirl around whether a majoritarian system (which most African countries feature) or proportional representation is more conducive to conflict management. The persistence of winner-take-all presidential electoral systems in Africa (especially those featuring two-round processes and first-past-the-post in single-member districts) may create special vulnerabilities to high-stakes elections and, thus, to violent conflict. Nonetheless, it is important to conduct context-specific analysis of the effects of electoral system choice on conflict dynamics both at the moment when the electoral system is chosen (often unilaterally by incumbent regimes, in constitution-making processes, or in peace talks) and over several electoral cycles. This is particularly true today in Sudan, for example, where the electoral system and dispersion of power may have some conflict-ameliorating effects. The ongoing and lively debate over whether Africa's diverse societies are best served by majoritarian or proportional electoral systems suggests that it is difficult to make blanket statements about the effects of electoral system choice on conflict or on democratic quality (Reilly and Reynolds 2000).

In addition to the electoral system, a final area for assessment is the quality of electoral administration and election-related security. State capacity, particularly in the area of electoral administration, election dispute resolution, and policing and security, is *the* pivotal variable in determining whether underlying vulnerabilities become violent encounters. Collier finds that the greatest constraint to democratization in Africa is the "three illicit electoral tactics" of bribing voters, intimidating voters, and committing deliberate, pervasive electoral fraud (Collier 2009). Massive cheating or fraud—such as vote buying, ballot tampering, fallacious counting, or other measures (e.g., releasing large numbers of prisoners to vote)—can be the stimulus for a violent reaction by those who react to such fraud. One of the common reasons for mass mobilization and violent resistance to state authority is allegations of stolen, cheating, or manipulated electoral processes and outcomes (Lehoucq 2003; CMI 2009).

From this comparative literature, a framework for evaluating election-related violence is presented, followed by application of the framework to the cases of Nigeria's troubled 2007 and 2011 elections and the 2010 elections in Sudan.

An Overview Framework for Evaluating Election-Related Violence

The Democratization Context

- How does the historical context of state formation and national integration set the stage for violent elections?
- How did the political process or sequencing affect vulnerabilities to violence?

Political Economy of State Capture

- What are common mobilization narratives about the nature of conflict that directly relate to the stakes, incentives, and outcomes of electoral competition?
- How did institutional incentives—particularly those created by the electoral system—affect perceptions of stakes and expectations?

Structural and Institutional Drivers of Conflict

- What social, political, and economic/resource conditions are argued to be root causes of vulnerability to conflict?
- What effect do underlying social and economic conditions have on the context in which electoral conflict turns violent?

Election Management Capacities

- How did the administration of state authority—particularly the role of the electoral management body and the security forces—affect the perception of a credible election?

Nigeria 2007

Nigeria's 2007 elections highlight a basic irony in the long-standing story of democratization there. The electoral process was highly compromised, both through deliberate rigging and professional incapability of the election management body and through the systematic and deliberate use of election-related violence through a widespread network of formal and informal actors and institutions. The elections produced the ill-fated regime of Umaru Yar'Adua of the People's Democratic Party (PDP), declared winner of the April 21 presidential election and sworn into office on May 29, 2007. The Independent National Electoral Commission (INEC) proclaimed that Yar'Adua had won the presidential poll with a handsome majority—24.7 million votes, or 72 percent of the votes recorded.

The 2007 election, following a long story of political intrigue, featured the handpicked successor of the outgoing president (Gen. Olusegun Obasanjo), Yar'Adua, against former military ruler Gen. Muhammadu Buhari of the All Nigeria People's Party. Obasanjo's former vice president, Atiku Abubakar, whom he fired and against whom corruption charges were filed, was eventually allowed to contest the poll for the Action Congress (AC), but only days before the vote, following his reinstatement by the Nigerian Supreme Court. Wole Soyinka wryly observed, "Long before the election itself took place, the election had failed. It had proceeded along unconstitutional lines, masterminded by one individual who had not yet given up his ambition of ruling that nation dictatorially, even after leaving office. . . . [That attempt] is linked to the manipulation of this election, the rigging into office of a number of cronies of the departing president . . ." (Soyinka 2007).

The violent and universally criticized election served the purpose of the PDP party apparatus: retaining power in Abuja and in twenty-eight of Nigeria's thirty-six federal states. The pathway of this violent election illustrates well the drive for capture and maintenance of state power as a common theme across a disparate theater of election-related conflict. Some 300 people died in the electoral process, adding to the nearly 12,000 deaths in political violence since Nigeria initially attempted the transition to democracy from military rule in 1999.

The regime was doomed in part due to ill health of the president, who died of an extended illness just two years after the polls and was succeeded by his deputy, the current president, Goodluck Jonathan. The Yar'Adua administration was also crippled by its having come to power in a grossly fraudulent election based on brutal intimidation and cunning manipulation of the electoral administration process, buoyed by a patronage system that the government and ruling party used, along with the instruments of state power—the police—to ensure electoral victory. President Yar'Adua's death and Jonathan's inheritance of power combined with economic strife and local-level dynamics to create a tipping point toward greater divisions and conflict in Nigeria. Indeed, by late 2011 and early 2012, the country saw increasing ethnic and communal conflict driven by deep-seated social and economic frustrations. International nongovernmental organizations (NGOs) sounded warnings about the fragility of the situation.

Nigeria's Democratization Context

Nigeria's history is replete with democratization's crises, setbacks, and sequences. Thus, there is concern that despite putatively democratic rule from 1999 onward, democracy is once again failing to yield a cohesive, consolidated state. Assessments of the 2007 election were initially promising, suggesting that it would be a turning point in consolidating a democratic order long fought for in the long years of military rule under a succession of corrupt dictatorships. The 2007 election was to be the first election since independence in 1960 in which one democratically elected regime would turn over the reins of power to a democratically elected successor (Rotberg 2007). As a third election—had it gone well—the 2007 poll in Nigeria would reaffirm Lindberg's hypothesis about "learning by doing" in gradual improvements in electoral processes (Lindberg 2003). But the 2007 election turned out even worse than 2003 in undermining the legitimacy of electoral politics as a way to reconcile a diverse society's myriad interests.

The immediate context for the election of 2007 is the period of democratization and return to civilian rule in 1999, following the failed first and second republics and twenty-nine years of military rule in the first thirty-nine years of independence. Military rule and venal democratic elites left a long historical shadow culture of corruption, patronage, and weak state institutions. The democratization story is also the story of the pervasively destructive politics of a petrostate: the ongoing struggles between federal government and state authorities to distribute revenue from oil—power struggles that are often violent and involve complicated and extensive networks among top-level government elites, bureaucratic elites in ministries, governors, and a diverse and often-changing network of local methods of co-optation and control (Lewis 2007). Resource conflict interacts with ethnoregional and religious identities. The reality is a deeply insecure Nigeria—especially in the north, south, and southeast—beset by episodic upsurges of ethnoregional violence and religiously inspired cycles of attack and revenge (Umar 2007).

Since independence, elections in Nigeria have been consistently fraught with severe election-management and logistical failings; public dissatisfaction over vote buying and secretly shifting coalitions and alliances; insecurity in a number of conflict-affected regions; and deep-seated regional, ethnic, religious, and party-political tensions. From the outset of the re-democratization period, the 1999 elections were marred by serious irregularities. Still, many Nigerians were willing to accept the overall outcome as legitimate and to acknowledge the progress the elections reflected in the long transitional process from military rule. The 2003 elections were mishandled, and in addition to being marred by election-administration ineptitude and incapacity, they left in their wake an estimated 100 deaths from election-related violence (HRW 2007, 14–17). Although better organized than in 1999, the elections had serious problems, including lack of transparency, lack of secrecy in voting, vandalized or stuffed ballot boxes, and results altered during tabulation. Violence was concentrated in Rivers, Kogi, and Enugu states especially. The 2003 elections generated widespread criticism of the INEC's lack of independence (and the procedures for its appointment by the president), voter registration irregularities, violence, partiality of the police, and the scandalous theft and stuffing of ballot boxes.

An immediate context of the run-up to the 2007 polls was the bitter public dispute within the PDP between the incumbent president, Olusegun Obasanjo, and Vice President Atiku Abubakar. The dispute stemmed from Obasanjo's apparent effort to amend the constitution to allow a third presidential term, and whether Abubakar, as leader of the opposition party, would be allowed to contest the polls.[7] In May 2006, Obasanjo lost an apparent bid to stay in power, when the National Assembly rejected the effort to amend the constitution to allow a third term for the president and state governors. The third-term debate and dispute between Obasanjo and Abubakar revealed deep rifts within the ruling PDP, which led to intraparty violence, especially during the volatile period of the primaries. It also bitterly divided PDP candidate-selection processes, heightening regional tensions and fueling debates over ethnoregional identities within the ruling party.

Capturing the State in Federal Nigeria

In Nigeria, the political economy of state capture occurs within the critical context of the federal institutions and the distribution of oil rents to capture and hold budgets of states and local government areas. Eighty percent of all government finances comes from centrally collected revenues, making every public official highly dependent on the ruling-party apparatus for access to resources. The overcentralization of resources has yielded a political system with intense partisan, ethnic and religious, and factional competition for control of the central government.[8] Access to the state is critical for highly valued—and extremely scarce—resources, including state revenues and spending, state positions, land and natural resources,

---

7. A last-minute Supreme Court decision—less than one week before the election—affirmed Abubakar's eligibility to run. Therefore, the INEC had to reprint ballots (in South Africa) and other documents and distribute these materials nationwide against a very tight time frame. This created significant logistical challenges.

8. The incentive for elite capture of state power was indeed codified in the provision of the Electoral Act of 2006 that allowed incumbents to remain in office in the event of a dispute over an election outcome. This increased the incentive to appeal, and to drag out appeals, in order to commandeer the largesse of the state for as long as possible. In Anambra State, for example, the winner of the 2003 elections was not installed until March 2006, when his opponent's erroneous declared victory in 2003 polls was finally nullified.

access to critical markets or sectors, and rents potentially gained from corruption. Nigeria, with the tenth-largest known oil reserves in the world, suffers from the resource curse: 36 percent of Nigerians live in severe poverty, with seriously compromised life expectancy due to deprivation of basic human needs (UNDP 2011).

Osaghae and Suberu argue that the federalism framework has served to exacerbate tensions at the local level because it has changed boundaries of representation away from ethnic representation and expanded access to politics—and all that this implies. They observe that "the creation of more states and local government areas has led to an expansion in the domain of salient identities, but at the same time, there has been a concentration of contestations and conflict around local issues. This has provided the impetus for the sharpening of communal identities and conflict, which have manifested in conflicts between 'indigenes' and 'non-indigenes,' 'sons of the soil,' and 'migrants and settlers' " (Osaghae and Suberu 2005, 13). These conflicts have been especially acute in the Niger Delta region, where core problems of poverty and environmental degradation fuel demands for control of natural resources. Opposition leaders seeking to advance these grievances have been the subject of violent threats and intimidation (Ibrahim 2007).

The basic factors of collective action—managerial control and control over patronage resources—are critical to the story of election-related violence. Many cite the case of the Bakassi Boys, in which provincial authorities in Anambra State reconstituted a violent gang as a government-sanctioned private army and ethnic militia of the governor Chinwoke Mbadinuju. The "Boys" began with considerable support as an informal institution that could represent the interests of a local trade association, and emerged as a state-sanctioned vigilante group. Meagher's research on the Bakassi Boys is compelling. She reports, "A key impetus beyond violent vigilantism is seen to lie in a reversion to traditional institutions for the maintenance of law and order, owing to the widespread disillusionment of the state to provide security" (Meagher 2006, 90).[9] Human Rights Watch (HRW) describes a "godfather" syndrome in Nigeria: "Many of Nigeria's ostensibly elected leaders obtained their positions by demonstrating an ability to use corruption and political violence to prevail in sham elections. In violent and brazenly rigged polls, government officials have denied any real voice in selecting their political leaders. In place of democratic competition, struggles for political office have often been waged violently in the

---

9. She notes, "References to charms and occult practices, while somewhat overstated, indicate a tendency to bolster the contemporary organizational structure of the Bakassi Boys with an older, informal repertoire of community security organization and secret societies" (Meagher 2006, 98).

streets by gangs of young men recruited by politicians to help them seize control of power" (HRW 2007).

Central to the elites' calculations for political control is the way in which a theoretically harmonizing electoral system has led to the evolution of a dominant-party, semiautocratic regime in Nigeria. At the level of president, the system provides a modified majority system with a provision for runoff rounds. To win the first round, a candidate must secure at least one-fourth of the votes cast in two-thirds of the states. If no such majority is attained, the two leading candidates have a runoff election. If, in the second round, no candidate meets the same requirement for a majority, a second run-off round is held, requiring a simple majority. Nigeria's choice of electoral system is closely linked to political party regulations that effectively bar overtly ethnic or regional parties. First, candidates must be registered by a political party, giving party elites exceptional control in internal nominating processes. Political party regulation is critical: provisions require that a name, symbol, or logo carry no ethnic or religious connotation or "give the appearance that the activities of the party are confined to a part only of the geographic area of Nigeria" (COG 2007, 20).[10] Thus, when the presidency is the prize (as it certainly is in Nigeria), there are powerful incentives for the ruling party to create a dense network of patronage relationships that have reach (and hegemony) in all thirty-six states.

Still, the actions of political parties and the disparate affiliations of officeholders, permanent staff, candidates, volunteers, supporters, and backers within the state and military seem critical in explaining the outbreak and perpetration of election-related violence. Scholars have identified that in countries with extreme poverty, vote buying is a ubiquitous strategy for perpetrating election fraud (Schaffer 2007). Nigeria corroborates this view. Afrobarometer survey results, reported in Bratton's research, show that the effects of campaign violence are widespread and significant and that the key factors affecting election outcomes are vote buying and violence. Elections are lost and won with the votes of the poor—the votes also most susceptible to financial incentive. And violence creates an overall "atmospheric condition" that affects all voters. Bratton reports, "Nigerians that encounter a threat against voting freely often withdraw from the electoral process entirely, that is, they abstain from voting, perhaps persistently. So political intimidation apparently has achieved an intended effect: it makes citizens so fearful that they abandon their right to vote" (Bratton 2008, 626–31).

---

10. Also, the Electoral Act of 2006 prohibits "campaigning on religious, tribal, or sectional basis" (COG 2007, 28).

Violence and the 2007 Elections

The 2007 polls opened on Saturday, April 14, with elections for state governors and state legislators, with polling the following week, on April 21, for the president and national legislature.[11] The election campaign revolved around two central issues: struggles for power in the national government and in the thirty-six states, and the long-simmering struggle in the oil-rich Niger Delta region. Inequality and environmental degradation in the Delta have begotten a violent insurgency, and the worsening security situation has seriously undermined the ability to administer the election and to deploy domestic and international election observers. The campaign, waged by some fifty political parties, was marked by very little dialogue on policy issues; instead, the campaign revolved around the personalities of the candidates, consolidation and mobilization of mass party support, and the reaffirmation of allegiance to political party identities.

The elections were seriously flawed and, in the views of close observers, deliberately rigged. Rawlence and Albin-Lackey of Human Rights Watch report:

> In states up and down the country very little voting took place as ballot papers were diverted to the offices and homes of government officials to be filled out with fabricated results. Elsewhere, ballot boxes were stolen and stuffed with pre-marked ballots. Where voting did proceed it was often marred by the intimidating presence of PDP officials who exploited the total lack of secrecy around the vote to watch closely as voters cast their ballots. In many areas, money was openly exchanged for votes as policemen stood by and watched. (Rawlence and Albin-Lackey 2007)

The central-power contestation, the Niger Delta insurgency, and the locally focused contests for parliamentary and state-level positions generated and catalyzed significant violence and intimidation in a long run-up to the elections (up to a year before the polls). Violence occurred not only during the election period itself (when the roughly 300 deaths were recorded) but well before the polling days and also afterward as the allegations of fraud, rigging, and abuse generated violent reactions from those who did not prevail in the balloting. Political violence at the state level was a recurring feature of Nigerian politics in recent years, evidenced by a spate of assassinations in mid-2006, including those of three high-profile candidates for governors in Lagos, Plateau, and Ondo states. In the long run-up to the 2007 polls, election-related violence was reported in Anambra, Adamawa,

---

11. The immediate context for the poll was the adoption of the Electoral Act of 2006, less than one year before the election. This started the process off well behind schedule and particularly affected registration for Nigeria's expected 65 million voters. The law established the sequencing and timing of elections and put into place a number of administrative procedures (that would eventually prove unworkable).

Delta, Edo, Enugu, Kogi, Nassarawa, Ogun, Ondo, and Rivers states. The violence involved a laundry list of dirty tricks and spontaneous clashes:

- violence related to primary contests within political parties, typically between supporters of opposing candidates
- cases of party switching (changing allegiance from one party to another)
- harassment of persons belonging to opposition parties or considered critical of government's mismanagement of the electoral processes
- arrest of opposition candidates, and their forcible transport to Abuja, hindering their ability to campaign but also having a chilling effect on their supporters
- attacks on rival parties, and clashes between supporters of rival parties during the general elections
- armed attacks on campaign meetings and rallies
- threats against potential voters
- attacks on polling stations, polling officials, and rival party agents

Additionally, reports of crimes, including election-related kidnappings, soared in the months preceding the poll, which suggests a close relationship between armed robbery, kidnapping, extortion, racketeering, and the organization and management of the political party base in a given locality (COG 2007; NDI 2007).

Violence worsened during the height of the election campaign, particularly following Obasanjo's ill-considered comment in February 2007 that the elections were a "do-or-die affair" for the PDP, and a "matter of life and death." Violence also escalated in Niger Delta, which saw a rise in kidnapping of international oil and humanitarian workers, and where threats by militant groups against the local population's participation reduced voter turnout (and prevented the deployment of international monitors). Violence occurred on polling day when frustrated voters turned up to vote and found polling places closed or opening late (e.g., in Katsina State, where four people were killed in violent protests). Violence continued into the proclamation period. In Benue State, ten people died and twenty houses were destroyed in clashes between PDP and AC supporters in post-election-day violence.

A recurrent theme in accounts of the 2007 election violence is the role played by armed vigilante groups under the direction of local midlevel political elites, and those elites' involvement in unleashing violence as a tactic for political gain. An often-cited case is that of Dr. Ayodeji Daramola, a PDP gubernatorial candidate in Ekiti State, who was assassinated in August 2006. His killing sparked a cycle of revenge and retaliatory attacks in the community.[12] Allegations of direct state involvement with violent vigilante groups were rife. Vigilante gang activity had escalated during the prior military regimes in the course of state-led anticrime initiatives and a dirty war that created a nationally led law enforcement apparatus able to act with impunity.

In the Niger Delta region, incidents in Bayelsa State reflected the upsurge in election-day violence, as machine-gun fire and explosions tore through the capital city, Yenagoa, when militants attacked a government house believed to be holding ballots and results sheets.[13] The Commonwealth Observers noted that at the heart of the violence was the problem of youth recruitment and the largesse that incumbency and political organization provide for mobilizing youth gangs into political violence:

> Stakeholders we met highlighted the link between political parties and "mal-adjusted" youths, or gangs. They indicated that some parties "buy" unemployed youths, and that such youths can easily be enticed to promote and perpetuate violence. On 13 April 2007, *Vanguard* reported that five persons were killed in Lagos following a clash between PDP and AC supporters. A representative of the Lagos State police described it as "a fight between local area boys," which is a term for gangs. (COG 2007, 31)

While not all election-related violence had direct ethnic or religious overtones, these patterns of collective recruitment of youths into politically mobilized militias are closely intertwined in Nigeria with ethnic identity: "A large part of youth identities is well entrenched in ethnicity and communalism, having emerged from redress-seeking struggles by aggrieved ethnic groups . . . this ethnicization of Nigeria youth culture has been promoted significantly by widespread socio-economic frustration and alienation (including relatively high levels of youth unemployment and underemployment" (Osaghae and Suberu 2005, 13).

Thus, the mobilization and manifestations of violence are at least partly rooted in a system of clientelism and corruption together with a large reservoir of recruitable young men mobilized along lines of community identity and the fight for resources.

Election Management Failures

As mentioned above, management of the 2007 elections was dismal, adding to frustrations and perceptions that the national, gubernatorial, and

---

12. The Web site devoted to Daramola's memory claims that he was killed by bandits. But his death had clear political implications—the Commonwealth Observer Group (COG) reports that his death resulted in revenge attacks on political opponents' homes. All those involved were active within the PDP (COG 2007).

13. The causes of the attack are uncertain, but one article speculated, "Either the militants are angry that last week's state elections were rigged, or they have been denied money they had requested to pay for security for Saturday's polls" (*BBC News* 2007).

state assembly elections were conducted under a shadow of irregularity and illegitimacy, especially in violence-prone areas. The ways in which the election was mishandled are well described by international and domestic observers:

- delay in distribution of balloting materials
- inadequate supply of materials, including ballots
- inaccurate materials, or materials lacking serial numbers (for the entire presidential elections, due to the final production of the ballots)
- intimidation of voters, election-station monitors, and INEC officials
- improper control of ballot papers and election materials
- theft of ballots and boxes
- improper activities by party representatives at polling stations
- lack of secrecy in voting
- voter registration irregularities and failure to display register
- underage voting
- allegations of partisan behavior by INEC and policy personnel

In particular, the INEC was criticized for serious and pervasive irregularities and for complicity in the disqualification of key candidates, including Vice President Abubakar, based on their indictment for corruption by a government administrative panel for corruption (a panel controlled by the ruling party). The INEC also delayed in accrediting domestic election-monitoring groups, and Nigeria security forces harassed NGOs and perceived opponents of the regime. The INEC failed to set a timetable for the election until August 2006, giving insufficient time for a wide range of preelection preparations, especially registration. These delays also generated problems of candidate registration, with allegations of bribes paid to register candidates. This also helped enable multiple and underage voting, disenfranchisement of voters, and widespread ballot-box stuffing.

The International Crisis Group (ICG) concluded that the elections were characterized by a "rigging epidemic" through which PDP ruling elites retained power through intricate and extensive manipulation of appointment procedures, and limits on the financial autonomy of the INEC.[14] ICG saw direct intervention by the security forces on behalf of the ruling party, including official harassment of opposition figures, failure to secure election materials, and failure to intervene to prevent violent incidents during the polls or in suppression of protests after proclamation (ICG 2007).

Civil society's capacity to monitor the elections was also severely constrained. A network of 170 organizations conducted action-oriented in-

---

14. Yar'Adua acknowledged the deficits in the electoral process and, just as in the 1999 and 2003 polls, promised an invigorated reform effort.

formation gathering and conflict tracking, as reported in the work of the South African NGO that facilitated the work, the Institute for Democracy in Southern Africa (Marco 2006). The Nigerian Federal Police came under criticism. A massive security campaign had the effect of militarizing the election and frightening voters while ultimately being unable to guarantee safety and security. Meanwhile, NGO efforts to prevent violence and encourage voter participation despite security concerns were apparently quite successful. In an empirical analysis of the effects of conflict-prevention public awareness campaigns during Nigeria's 2007 elections, Collier and Vicente found that antiviolence campaigns are effective "in providing an increased sense of security to the general population, and boosted empowerment to counteract electoral violence" (Collier and Vicente 2010).

U.S. observers from the National Democratic Institute (NDI) concluded, "In many places, and in a number of ways, the electoral process failed the Nigerian people" (NDI 2007, 3). An election racked by violence and conducted with serious and pervasive irregularities left in its wake a fragile state with questionable legitimacy. The 2007 elections and the associated violence have undermined norms on both conflict and democracy at a critical moment in Nigeria's political evolution: when the legitimacy of electoral outcomes is compromised, political elites become even more reliant on the political economy of patronage to govern, and avenues of accountability are foreclosed. Then frustration over a closed system of power and perceptions of group-based inequalities heighten future vulnerability to violence.

Several findings emerge from the 2007 elections in Nigeria. First, election-related violence in this case involved a very high level of intra-party rivalry and violence surrounding the primaries. This pattern reflects the high stakes of winning nomination in the ruling party as a surefire path to power and rents as an officeholder in a vertically integrated system of power that generates its resources externally. Second, the lack of prosecutions (which was also a problem following the 2003 elections) has created a perception that acts of violence can be carried out with impunity. In 2007, the Nigeria Police Force failed to investigate deliberate acts on behalf of the PDP cadres involving direct use of violence against citizens. According to the NDI monitoring group, "On election day ... NDI observers in Anambra, Enugu, Kaduna, and Ogun States witnessed security personnel standing by when polling stations were invaded by thugs who seized ballot boxes and scared away voters." Third, the effect of political violence was widespread and direct: violence suppressed voter turnout, especially between the voting on April 14, for state positions, and a week later, for national positions: "The invasion of police stations by thugs who destroyed voting materials stored there deterred many potential voters from turning out on election day" (NDI 2007, 27, 32).[15]

The 2007 elections were a low point for Nigeria. In subsequent polls, principally April 2011, there was a general perception of improved performance in election administration. Although there were still reports of significant and widespread irregularities, the polls were generally seen as an improvement over 2007. Among the continued challenges were the voter registration process (including the ill-considered use of expensive biometric technology), logistical failings, ballot snatching, intimidation, and slippage in the electoral timetable. With the results favoring the PDP and leading to the reelection of Goodluck Jonathan (a southerner) over former general Muhammadu Buhari (a northerner), violence escalated in the northern part of the country, where many victims were targeted based on religious identity, leading to more than 1,000 fatalities. Some northern politicians had asserted that according to the practice of rotating the presidency between the two regions (and, implicitly, religions), it was the north's turn to rule. In the resulting widespread rioting, according to the ICG, "Ethnicity and religion appear to have been intertwined with socioeconomic malaise and grievances about marginalisation" (ICG 2011). Thus, the 2011 electoral process reinforces the findings from 2007, especially concerning the role of electoral processes in exacerbating underlying social, economic, and ethnic tensions at a time when the ruling party's grip on power seems to be slowly weakening.

Sudan: 2010

Sudan's 2010 national elections—a benchmark in the implementation of the 2005 Comprehensive Peace Agreement (CPA), which formally ended twenty-two years of civil war in the South—were widely anticipated to be deeply violent.[16] The elections portended the possibility of sparking renewed civil war in the South, in a country that has proved exceptionally vulnerable to war recurrence. Absurdly, elections were to occur in Darfur, which has been ravaged by war since 2003 and has become the hallmark atrocity underscoring the persistence of gross violations of human rights into the twenty-first century. Moreover, the election was held in the context of a complicated power-sharing agreement through which the coun-

---

15. Turnout in the 2007 elections was estimated at 57.2 percent, compared with 64.8 percent in 2003. See also Alemika and Omotosho 2008.

16. Early warning was informed by reports of increased arms transfers, including the National Congress Party (NCP) regime's purchases of major offensive military hardware, and South Sudan's purchases of rocket launchers and antiaircraft artillery. See Almquist 2010; Gustafson 2010a.

try's elites had already effectively divided the country into distinct spheres of influence, in anticipation of South Sudan's secession. The split was the expected outcome of a plebiscite to be put to voters in a 2011 referendum.

Warnings of war recurrence in Sudan are well founded: the 2010 electoral process was deeply violent and fraudulent, although in a pattern different from that seen in Nigeria. In Sudan, violence and intimidation are part of a broader strategy by the dominant parties and their affiliated elites to govern fractious, geographically dispersed, militarized communities across the country. Innumerable local conflicts occur regularly and sometimes escalate into major episodes of intercommunal, interreligious, or interclan or subclan violence. In the North, the National Congress Party (NCP) reigns, led by Gen. Omar al-Bashir, the first sitting head of state under indictment by the International Criminal Court for war crimes and crimes against humanity. The South is led by Salva Kiir of the Sudan People's Liberation Movement, who served as first vice president in the power-sharing agreement that emerged as a transitional governance framework during implementation of the CPA. Kiir eventually emerged as president of South Sudan following independence in 2011.[17]

Indeed, those who predicted violence for the polls were essentially correct in their assessments. In each of the axes of the Sudan conflict imbroglio—North-South and Darfur—the electoral process was accompanied by violence and a wide range of intimidation, fraud, and abuse. However, the electoral process was more about *reflecting* power than contending for it, and thus the overt type of electoral violence seen in Nigeria (e.g., direct clashes and attacks within parties) was less frequent in Sudan. Where violence did occur during the 2010 polls, it was primarily "upstream," or well before the actual election. Indeed, many observers saw the low level of violence on and around polling day as indicative of how many Sudanese saw the election as, by then, not very meaningful—a charade of sorts.

Sudan's War-to-Partition Transition

The 2005 signing of the CPA to end Sudan's long-running war was a triumph of multilateral, multilevel diplomacy that, over time, leveraged the parties into an agreement for a war-to-democracy transition (Jarstad and Sisk 2008). It involved a period of interim power sharing, national elections midway through the six-year implementation process (the 2010 elections were to have occurred in 2008 but were delayed), and the 2011

---

17. Other key provisions of the CPA include a cease-fire, the withdrawal of all Sudan Armed Forces (SAF)—the withdrawal was generally accomplished by January 2009—and a formula for sharing the income derived from oil production. In the CPA, the Government of South Sudan (GOSS) was allowed to keep its military, the Sudanese People's Liberation Army (SPLA). Militias that had fought in the war were required to choose between joining the SAF and joining the SPLA.

referendum on an independent South. But the CPA emerged only after a long and costly war that was an extreme humanitarian and environmental catastrophe. The war was over resources—oil and water—but also over identity. The spark for the 1983 war (which was a recurrence of an earlier civil war, during 1956–72) was the imposition of Muslim sharia law in a largely non-Muslim South. Also, many see the discovery of oil in the southern regions in the early 1980s, with exclusion of key communities from the distribution of revenues, as the principal underlying cause of the 1972 pact's breakdown. The rifts in Sudan's "war of visions" are a mix of both inter- and intrareligious and interethnic struggles, and because of them, the project of national integration and social cohesion in Sudan never came to fruition. Francis Deng observed:

> The crisis of statehood and national unity in Sudan is rooted in the British attempt to bring together diverse peoples with a history of hostility into a framework of one state, while also keeping them apart and entrenching inequalities by giving certain regions more access to state power, resources, services, and developmental opportunities than other regions. . . . The inequities fostered by the system played out along regional, racial, ethnic, and cultural divisions, with the Muslim Arabs favored over the non-Arabs within the North, and with the South being by far the most neglected region. (Deng 2005, 41).

The transition in Sudan unfolds in the wake of the long civil war, from 1983 to 2005, along North-South lines, which cost an estimated two million lives and pushed four million people into internal or international displacement. The CPA, which ended the civil war in South Sudan, created a six-year transitional period of autonomy, followed by a referendum on southern independence, brokered by the regional organization the Intergovernmental Authority on Development, and with widespread international support. The North-South orientation of conflict and peacebuilding in Sudan is widened today by the Darfur conflict, which escalated in 2003 and which has added to the complexity of stabilizing the CPA and bringing peace to war-torn Sudan. (See De Waal 2005.) The CPA led to the creation of the GOSS, led by the former rebel forces, the Sudan People's Liberation Movement.

Human Rights Watch suggested that "the purpose of a six-and-half-year waiting period between the CPA and self-determination referendum is to allow time for the central government to make unity attractive to the southern voters through power-sharing, wealth-sharing, and other measures" (HRW 2006). The power-sharing system designed to do that over the five-year period seems to have failed. In the South, the power-sharing agreement gave the SPLM 70 percent representation in the autonomous southern government. The NCP got 15 percent representation, and other political forces made up the 15 percent balance. At the national level, the

NCP maintained a 52 percent majority in the legislature, and the SPLM got 28 percent representation in the legislature and 20 percent representation in the executive branch. This representation included the office of first vice president and several national and state ministerial positions.

Thus, the 2010 electoral process unfolded with the widespread expectation (which turned out to be true) that in 2011 the southerners would vote to secede. There was a high degree of uncertainty in the provisions for power sharing, the ultimate legal, sovereign status of the Government of South Sudan, and the ultimate disposition of disputed regions. This deep uncertainty over sovereignty and control framed the 2010 election contest, but ironically, this may also help explain why violence did not escalate further in the electoral process. Indeed, the actual days of voting in Sudan were surprisingly less violent than anticipated. This may have been due in part due to SPLM's decision in early April 2010 to boycott the elections in the North.

The results were as expected: al-Bashir was proclaimed winner of the GNU presidential vote with 68.24 percent, followed by the SPLM candidate for the GNU presidency, Yasir Arman, with 21.69 percent. The closest northern competitor, Hatim al-Sir of the DUP, garnered 1.93 percent of the votes. In the South, Kiir won the poll for southern president with 92.99 percent of the vote. In Northern Sudan, fourteen of the fifteen state governorships went to the NCP. (In contested Blue Nile State, the SPLM candidate, Malik Agar, retained the governership.) In the National Assembly, the NCP won 52 percent of the seats, the SPLM 28 percent, and other parties managed 4.4 percent (twenty seats, mostly from the proportional representation side of the mixed-system ballot, in which one vote is cast for candidates and another for political parties). In Darfur, the NCP won seventy-five seats, or 87 percent of the state assembly seats (Gustafson 2010a).[18]

State Capture(s) in the Post-CPA Era

A critical feature of Sudanese politics is a game in which the power contenders each work to consolidate and divide control rather than contend directly for it. Thus, there was little direct violence between the two major contending blocs during the electoral period. Much of this is explained by the political economy of state capture, in which political control is part of what Alex de Waal has described as "monetized, internationalized, and factionalized patronage systems." The relative balance of northern and southern elites defines the nature of the state and the ways in which electoral processes are designed, manipulated, and used to consolidate state power. De Waal argues that Sudan "is ruled by a hybrid of institutions and

---

18. For background on the NCP strategy of control in Darfur, see ICG 2010.

patronage systems, but the patronage systems have become dominant, as successive regimes have either dismantled or neglected social institutions and social norms." They have appropriated "all financial means—including state budgets and international borrowing—to fund gargantuan patrimonies" (De Waal 2010, 9, 16). Hemmer describes "an auction of loyalties" through which Khartoum governs provinces through loyalty inducements such as bribes, political positions, and threats and intimidation. He explains that in this political marketplace, "violence can become a powerful tool for those who seek to improve their ranking in the hierarchy of buyers and sellers" (Hemmer 2009).

The CPA establishes principles and mechanisms for sharing wealth and managing land-related disputes, so that control over the central state and the GOSS are critical for accessing the rents earned from extractive industries. For oil, the agreement calls for equally dividing oil revenue between North and South; thus, half of all net oil revenue from production in the South goes to the GOSS.[19] On other issues, the CPA called for creating a National Land Commission and a Southern Sudan Land Commission, with a provision for final arbitration of land matters by the Constitutional Court. The CPA envisioned that in 2011, the people of Abyei would vote whether to retain the special administrative structures set up for the transitional period or to became part of Bahr el Ghazal State in the South. (These votes did not take place according to the timeline.) Also, the CPA included special provisions for boundary demarcation for Southern Kordofan, Blue Nile, and Nuba Mountains states.

Underlying reliance on state patronage networks are the challenges of economic development and extreme poverty (90 percent of South Sudanese live on less than a dollar a day; the regional gross national income is ninety dollars per capita) and conflicts over oil, water, and grazing rights. And challenges stemming from decreasing oil revenues—the central source of revenue to governmental elites—have left the governments unable to pay civil service personnel and soldiers as well as demobilized veterans, which has led to munity by troops, and riots by veterans.

In the North, with external sanctions in place, the NCP experiences deep insecurities, especially around its lack of access to oil rents in the wake of southern independence. Although the regime's principal opponents in the North, the Democratic Unionist Party and the UMMA Party, are deeply divided, high marginalization and inequality suggest that many

---

19. The demarcated borders between Sudan and South Sudan are critical to the CPA's wealth-sharing provisions; however, the agreement excluded the disputed Abyei, an area ethnically and geographically defined as the nine chiefdoms of Dinka-Ngok. To resolve these matters, the CPA includes a provision for special administrative status, and a detailed special protocol that creates a complex administrative structure for this region.

northern Sudanese do not support the regime. Thus, the purchase of loyalty and the control of electoral processes that lead to capture of the state are absolutely essential to the party's core interests. In the South, there is little challenge to the SPLM's hegemony, despite the emergence of a small splinter faction from within its own ranks (the SPLM-Democratic Change), which challenged the dominant faction in the polls. Continued control of the state is critical to maintaining these patronage networks. The electoral process—in 2010 but especially concerning the referendum—has catalyzed the formation of networks to consolidate control over natural resources and rents.

The transition created a situation in which the two major parties, the NCP and the SPLM, divided the spoils and consolidated their power bases in the electoral process. This implicit bargain created a situation in which violence and intimidation needed to be used early to avoid any risk of an electoral outcome that would weaken either the NCP regime in Khartoum or the SPLM's hold on power through the GOSS in Juba and in the sub-provincial, or "state," governments of the South.[20]

The framework for the elections, codified in the 2008 National Elections Act, reflected this basic set of choices. The complicated formula provided for elections at six different levels, employing a complicated mixed majoritarian-proportional system. In Sudan's 2010 elections, many elections happened simultaneously:

- presidency of the Government of National Unity (first past the post)
- presidency of the Government of South Sudan (first past the post)
- state governorships (first past the post)
- National Legislature, on a mixed majoritarian (60 percent of seats) and proportional representation (40 percent) formula
- South Sudan Legislative Assembly and state legislative assemblies[21]

The implications of the electoral system choice at each level are quite easy to discern. In the North, control over the overall election management process and a "rally round the flag" effect from sanctions would assure the dominant NCP regime of a clear victory in presidential and national assembly levels; the proportional formula would allow just enough opposition representation to claim that Sudan is a multiparty democracy. (See O'Brien 2009.) Thus, the combination majoritarian-proportional formula would allow for some inclusivity without jeopardizing NCP control. In the

20. Gareth Curless observes that "the paralysis of the political opposition, a product of internal division and the authoritarian political climate, has encouraged the NCP and SPLM to unfairly protect the gains bestowed upon them by the CPA" (Curless 2010).

21. For details on the electoral system used for Sudan's 2010 elections, see Democracy Reporting International 2009; Gustafson 2010b.

South, SPLM's liberation-based lock on power was guaranteed to continue as long as the referendum loomed on the horizon, and the prospects for secession remained imminent. Now, with secession a fait accompli, SPLM, as the dominant independence party, seems set to govern for the foreseeable future.

Violence in the 2010 Sudanese Elections

Sudan's diverse and episodic violence is driven by a multitude of factors, including the ethnic and religious divides, especially the feeling of collective discrimination against South Sudanese. In addition to this deep and enduring enmity between North and South, ethnic tensions in the South have been a persistent driver of internal differences. South Sudan is highly diverse, and intergroup conflict over grazing rights, water, and access to resources has been a long-standing challenge.[22] Ongoing, pervasive threats to peace in Sudan escalated in the run-up to the election. In late April 2009, conflicts in the province of Jonglei led to an estimated 700 deaths, and in 2008, the United Nations estimated that some 187,000 people were internally displaced as a result of intergroup conflict in southern provinces such as the oil-rich Abyei region. Some argued that fighting in Abyei was escalating into full-scale war in advance of the electoral process, thereby affecting the outcome of the referendum on self-determination (Mozersky 2008). Indeed, tensions in the postindependence era remain high enough that in early 2012 there is recurring concern of full-scale civil war between the new nation of South Sudan and the rump state in the north.

The year 2009 saw many manifestations of intercommunal conflict in nearly every state of the South: between Murle and Lou Nuer communities in Jonglei, between Dinka groups in Warrap State, between Shilluk and Dinka in Upper Nile State, between rival factions of the SPLA along Dinka and Nuer lines, and between armed civilians and soldiers in Cueibet County in Lakes State (APG Sudan 2010). In May 2009, clashes in Southern Sudan over cattle and territory, which were believed related to the impending elections, led to the deaths of 900 people and displacement of 20,000. News reports linked these attacks to alleged interference by the NCP government and to the impending electoral process (Associated Press 2009). The entry of the Uganda insurgent group the Lord's Resistance Army into Southern Sudan further complicated the conflict context in the run-up to the 2010 elections. Indeed, GOSS is unable to manage internal interclan and ethnic struggles within Southern Sudan. In late 2009 and into early 2010, new violence pushed Sudan's overall in-

---

22. Indeed, some have linked intergroup conflicts in South Sudan to climate change conditions, in which there is increasing competition for arable land and water amid regional desertification.

ternally displaced persons figures to 4.9 million. This "upstream" violence in 2009 was in many instances directly related to the electoral process as the 2010 elections approached and, over the longer horizon, to the 2011 referendum on independence for the South and the disputed areas. Tensions rose within the power-sharing government and between the northern and southern elites in Khartoum as the April 2010 event loomed on the horizon. In December 2009, Pagan Amum, the most senior SPLM official in Khartoum, was arrested during a rally to protest President al-Bashir's attempt to preempt a referendum for the South, after accusing the NCP regime of a sinister plot to seize the South's oil wealth. The African Union Commission chairman remarked in January 2010 that Sudan is "sitting on a powder keg" (*BBC News* 2010). Indeed, much of the violence unfolded early in the process as the two major parties, particularly the incumbent party, consolidated power. (This finding reaffirms the large-N quantitative findings of Straus and Taylor in this volume.) In a detailed report covering much of the period in the lead-up to the election, Amnesty International found the pervasive use of Sudan's National Security Service to carry out a campaign of arbitrary arrests and detentions of opposition leaders, particularly in response to the International Criminal Court's warrant against al-Bashir and following an attack, near Khartoum, attributed to the Darfur rebel group Justice and Equality Movement (Amnesty International 2010).

Among the manifestations were voter registration fraud, harassment of opposition figures and political parties, ethnic and communal rivalries—especially in the zones where North and South meet, which also coincide with the oil-rich regions—intimidation of opposition, and contestation within SPLM for control of state positions in the South. Human Rights Watch found that during the critical voter registration, candidacy nomination, and constituency delimitation phases of the election, acts of violence prepared the way for an uncontested win by NCP and SPLM. The violence included arrests of observers and activists; harassment of opposition figures; violent breakup of opposition rallies; censorship of the press and manipulation of the state-owned media; and arrest, detention, and mistreatment of opposition candidates (HRW 2010). One of the concerns about the electoral framework was its effect on the ability of internally displaced persons to vote. Given that many displaced pople are from the South or Darfur, this would significantly limit their enfranchisement through the electoral process (McHugh 2008).

Observers from the Sudanese Group for Democracy and Elections (based in the South) and the Sudanese Network for Democratic Elections (based in the North) reported 194 incidents of intimidation, harassment, and violence, from every state in the South, during the seven-day voting period (HRW 2010, 19). Violence was less prevalent during the seven-day voting period than before the elections. Indeed, most observers found that the dirty work of intimidation, control of security forces, and undermining of opposition parties had begun well before the actual five (which grew to seven) days of voting. (With an outcome secured, violence was not needed for the power-consolidation aims of the two major power blocs, and the opposition forces were too weak to challenge either hegemonic bloc.)

The Carter Center observation mission reported, in addition to insecurity in Darfur and Eastern Sudan that limited its capacity to observe, isolated acts of violence during the seven-day voting period, particularly harassment of opposition by SPLM in Western Equatoria, Unity State, and Northern Bahr el Ghazel (Carter Center 2010, 11). The United Nations also documented a wave of postelection violence involving bitter losers, particularly in Jonglei and Upper Nile. Indeed, in the aftermath of the elections, the UN Mission in Sudan (UNMIS) received sixty-six reports of intercommunal violence in Southern Sudan, particularly in the very states where the Carter Center identified harassment and intimidation (UNMIS 2010 [S/2010/388], 9).

Electoral Management

Sudan has actually held many elections since independence: from 1953 to 2000, the country had seventeen national-level elections and referendums, although these were confined primarily to the North in areas of regime control (Willis, el-Battahani, and Woodward 2009). Indeed, a long litany of complaints of electoral manipulation and fraud perpetrated by the regime left expectations that there would be serious flaws in the electoral process and that malpractice and manipulation, as well as resource and organization failures, would undermine the prospects for a credible poll. Moreover, the United Nations repeatedly warned that electoral processes in areas of Sudan facing extreme insecurity were impossible, particularly in the areas of the South recently affected by conflict (UNMIS 2010). Among the specific disputes over electoral issues were the delimitation of electoral districts, the census that informed the distribution of seats (SPLM rejected the census outcomes), the drawing of candidate and party lists, election accounting, media control and access, and polling procedures.

Sudan's 2010 elections were riddled with misconduct and malfeasance from the outset. In particular, the Carter Center, which has maintained the most extensive international monitoring operation of the Sudanese elections in 2010, found violence and intimidation of observers by security officials, rebel forces, and other armed groups throughout the country. Unlike in Nigeria, the National Elections Commission was chosen by consensus of the various parties; however, it performed as poorly, with a range of operational and logistical problems such as the late arrival (or inadequate supplies) of voting material, incomplete and inaccurate voter lists, incorrect and insufficient ballots, and lack of consistency in procedures. The Carter Center concluded, "It is apparent that the elections will fall short of meeting international standards and Sudan's obligations for genuine elections" (Carter Center 2010). Although the Carter Center mission was willing to suggest that Sudan's 2010 elections were a benchmark in the implementation of the CPA, it ultimately declined to endorse their credibility.

Conclusion

The cases of Nigeria in 2007 and 2011 and Sudan in 2010 underscore that an underlying instigator of violence is the slipping of an incumbent regime's grip on power; when threatened by challengers, the government turns to election-related violence as a way to maintain power with the veneer of electoral legitimacy. In each of these cases, the common thread is state capture by elites, who represent themselves as agents of ethnic mobilization, to extract rent. However, for these rent-seeking elites in semiauthoritarian regimes, elections pose a dilemma: there is no alternative to legitimization by the ballot box, yet a credible election entails risk of losing power within a political party (as intraparty violence in both Nigeria and Sudan demonstrates), or risks of loss of control over the critical natural resources that produce rents (as both cases also attest). Electoral violence in these cases is thus driven in large part by the exigencies faced by elites in semiauthoritarian systems as they seek to legitimate their rule without losing control.

Several findings flow from this comparative analysis. First, in both these cases there was clear collaboration between the state and incumbent political parties to control the financial and legal levers through which a regime pays off potential adversaries, organizes militias and security forces, and gains control of the machinery to manipulate the electoral process through violence and intimidation. In both cases, violence was perpetrated well before the electoral event itself. In Africa, there are the traditional dangers of authoritarian control of elections, such as use of police forces to do the ruling party's bidding (as seen in both cases). Yet there are also new dangers in weak state environments, in which regimes and opposition elites—particularly local midlevel "godfathers"—who organize militias and gang leaders capture state power to seize rents and, thereafter, wield state authority to perpetuate their hold on political power. In both Nigeria and Sudan, there is ample evidence of the perpetration of violence by marginalized nonstate actors, or what Reno has termed "marginalized critics of corrupt rulers," who "try to gain as much utility from the existing political society as possible" (Reno 2002).

Second, there is very early manipulation of electoral rules, and the strategic use of electoral violence "upstream" in the process, to set the conditions for worry-free electoral fraud. Early election-related violence is highly strategic: used by strong incumbents to maintain a political grip through inducements (e.g., vote buying, co-optation) and fear (to suppress the opposition). But violence is also used by the weak to demonstrate their resolve against a corrupt and fixed system. And violence is equally opportunistic as a way for existing or aspiring political entrepreneurs to use preexisting criminal or ethnic organizations to solidify or achieve capture of the state. The implications of using election-related violence strategically show clearly in the Sudan case, where it was used early in the process so that risk to incumbent power in both North and South was minimized: all the pieces were in place for the dominant parties to win elections with very little uncertainty.

Third, it doesn't take much overt violence to deeply and widely influence the electoral process. In both cases, election-related violence is a relatively low proportion of overall political violence; many more die in clashes and conflicts that don't appear directly related to elections than where the linkage is more evident and direct. But elites have learned that election violence has both direct and indirect effects: directly, it affects victims and their compatriots; indirectly, in the absence of secrecy in balloting, it can sow widespread fear among voters. Overcoming this fear requires mass mobilization and the management of voter turnout. As the Nigeria case illustrates, ethnic appeals don't work there nearly as well as the financial incentives; the Nigerian electoral system instead has an equally perverse incentive structure that may contribute political organization through the financial patronage structures of the state.

While violence perpetrated to achieve or hinder state capture is clearly a leading factor in this analysis, greed is most politically salient when it interacts with identity construction: much electoral mobilization in Africa is along ethnic or religious lines, and other factors such as disputes over land and natural resources have affected the tenor of intergroup relations. Thus, it is at the intersection of greed-and-political-economy analysis with theories of mobilization and collective action along identity lines that we can glean particular insights into the nature of contemporary election-related violence in much of Africa. This means that the persistence of a "prebendal" or neopatrimonial state in Africa must be at the heart of causal accounts of the election violence phenomenon (Bratton and Van de Walle 1994). At the same time, such analysis does not account well for subnational election-related violence—highly prevalent in both cases—suggesting the urgent need to develop more sophisticated assessment frameworks that can better explain the ways in which national-level scrambles for control of the state are linked to local-level processes, where the worst violence often erupts.

References

Alemika, Etannibi E. O., and Shola B. Omotosho. 2008. *Nigeria's 2007 General Elections: Betrayal of Electorate Optimism and Participation.* Lagos and Abuja: Alliance for Credible Elections and CLEEN Foundation.

Almquist, Katherine. 2010. "Renewed Conflict in Sudan." Council on Foreign Relations, CPA Contingency Memorandum no. 7, Mar. www.cfr.org/sudan/renewed-conflict-sudan/p21678.

Amnesty International. 2010. "Agents of Fear: The National Security Service in Sudan." www.amnesty.org/en/library/asset/AFR54/010/2010/en/7b11e50c-3a0b-4699-8b6f-08a27f751c6c/afr540102010en.pdf.

APG Sudan. 2010. "On the Brink: Towards Lasting Peace in Sudan." APG Sudan report, Mar. 18. www.apg-sudan.org\\index.php\\parliamentary-hearings\\final-report.

Arnson, Cynthia J., and I. William Zartman. 2005. *Rethinking the Economics of War: The Intersection of Need, Creed, and Greed* (Washington, DC: Woodrow Wilson Center Press.

Associated Press. 2009. "Tribal Violence Threatens Sudan Election." May 21. www.msnbc.msn.com/id/30870512/.

Bates, Robert H. 2008. *When Things Fell Apart: State Failure in Late-Century Africa.* Cambridge, UK: Cambridge Univ. Press.

BBC News. 2007. "Nigerians Tense on Eve of Polls." Apr. 20. http://news.bbc.co.uk/2/hi/6576077.stm.

———. 2010. "Sudan Like a Powder Keg, Says AU Chief Jean Ping." Jan. 28. http://news.bbc.co.uk/2/hi/africa/8485890.stm.

Bratton, Michael. 2008. "Vote Buying and Violence in Nigerian Election Campaigns." *Electoral Studies* 27 (4): 621–32.

Bratton, Michael, and Eric Chang. 2006. "State Building and Democratization in Africa: Forwards, Backwards, or Together?" *Comparative Political Studies* 39 (9): 1059–83.

Bratton, Michael, and Robert Mattes. 2009. "Neither Consolidating nor Fully Democratic: The Evolution of African Political Regimes, 1999–2008." *Afrobarometer Briefing Paper* no. 67, May. www.afrobarometer.org/papers/AfrobriefNo67_19may09_final.pdf.

Bratton, Michael, and Nicolas van de Walle. 1994. "Neopatrimonial Regimes and Political Transitions in Africa." *World Politics* 46 (4): 453–89.

Carothers, Thomas. 2002. "The End of the Transition Paradigm." *Journal of Democracy* 13 (1): 521.

Carter Center. 2010. "Carter Center Election Observation Mission in Sudan Presidential, Gubernatorial, and Legislative Elections, April 2010: Preliminary Statement." Press release, Apr. 17. www.cartercenter.org/news/pr/sudan-041710.html.

CMI. 2009. "Electoral Mismanagement and Post-Election Violence in Kenya: Kriegler and Waki Commissions of Inquiry." CMI, Feb. www.cmi.no/research/project/?1353=electoral-mismanagement-and-post-election-violence.

Collier, Paul. 2009. *Wars, Guns, and Votes: Democracy in Dangerous Places*. New York: Harper Collins.

Collier, Paul, and Pedro C. Vicente. 2010. "Votes and Violence: Evidence from a Field Experiment in Nigeria." University of Oxford Department of Economics, Centre for the Study of African Economies. Aug. www.pedrovicente.org/violence.pdf.

Curless, Gareth. 2010. "Sudan's 2010 National Elections." Occasional paper, Exeter Center for Ethno-Political Studies, Univ. of Exeter. http://centres.exeter.ac.uk/exceps/downloads/Ethnopolitics%20Papers_No7_Curless.pdf.

Commonwealth Observer Group (COG). 2007. "Nigeria: State and Federal Elections, 14 and 21 April 2007." Report. www.thecommonwealth.org/shared_asp_files/GFSR.asp?NodeID=164967.

De Waal, Alex. 2005. *Famine That Kills.* Oxford, UK: Oxford Univ. Press.

———. 2010. "Sudan's Choices: Scenarios beyond the CPA." In *Sudan—No Easy Ways Ahead,* ed. Heinrich Böll, 930. Berlin: Heinrich Böll Foundation. www.boell.de/publications/publications-publication-sudan-democracy-8961.html.

Democracy Reporting International. 2009. "Assessment of the Electoral Framework: Final Report." Policy report, Center for Peace and Development Studies, University of Juba. www.democracy-reporting.org/files/sudan_091209_online.pdf.

Deng, Francis. 2005. "Sudan's Turbulent Road to Nationhood." In *Borders, Nationalism, and the African State,* ed. Ricardo René Larémont. Boulder, CO: Lynne Rienner.

France 24. 2010. "Pre-Election Violence Creates Climate of Fear in Kigali." *France 24,* July 30. http://observers.france24.com/en/content/20100727-pre-election-violence-creates-climate-fear-kigali-rwanda-kagame-fpr.

Gustafson, Marc. 2010a. "Elections and the Probability of Violence in Sudan." *Harvard International Law Journal Online* 51 (May 24): 47–62. www.harvard-ilj.org/wp-content/uploads/2010/09/HILJ-Online_51_Gustafson.pdf.

———. 2010b. "Electoral Designs: Proportionality, Representation, and Constituency Boundaries in Sudan's 2010 Elections." Rift Valley Institute. www.riftvalley.net/resources/file/Electoral%20Designs%20-%20Report%20on%20elections%20in%20Sudan.pdf.

Hemmer, Jort. 2009. "Ticking the Box: Elections in Sudan." Clingendael Institute policy report. www.clingendael.nl/publications/2009/20090900_paper_cru_hemmer_elections_sudan.pdf.

Höglund, Kristine. 2006. "Elections in War-Ravaged Societies: The Case of Sri Lanka." Paper presented at the Workshop on Power Sharing and Democratic Governance in Divided Societies, Center for the Study of Civil War, PRIO, Oslo, Aug. 21–22.

———. 2009. "Elections and Violence in Sri Lanka: Understanding Variation across Three Parliamentary Elections." In *The Democratization Project: Opportunities and Challenges*, ed. Ashok Swain, Rames Amer, and Joakim Öjendahl. London: Anthem Press.

Human Rights Watch (HRW). 2006. "The Impact of the Comprehensive Peace Agreement and the New Government of National Unity on Southern Sudan." Human Rights Watch policy report. www.hrw.org/legacy/backgrounder/africa/sudan0306/sudan0306.pdf.

———. 2007. "Criminal Politics: Violence, 'Godfathers' and Corruption in Nigeria." *Human Rights Watch* 19, no. 16A (Oct.). www.hrw.org/sites/default/files/reports/nigeria1007webwcover_0.pdf.

———. 2010. "Democracy on Hold: Rights Violations in the April 2010 Sudan Elections." HRW report, June 30. www.hrw.org/en/reports/2010/06/29/democracy-hold-0.

Ibrahim, Jibrin. 2007. "Nigeria's 2007 Elections: The Fitful Path to Democratic Citizenship." United States Institute of Peace Special Report 182. Washington, DC: USIP Press.

International Crisis Group (ICG). 2007. "Nigeria: Failed Election, Failing State?" Africa Report 126. www.crisisgroup.org/~/media/Files/africa/west-africa/nigeria/ Nigeria%20Failed%20Elections%20Failing%20State.ashx.

———. 2010. "Rigged Elections in Darfur and the Consequences of a Probable NCP Victory in Sudan." Africa Briefing 72, Mar. 20. www.crisisgroup.org/en/regions/africa/horn-of-africa/sudan/b072-rigged-elections-in-darfur-and-the-consequences-of-a-probable-ncp-victory-in-sudan.aspx.

———. 2011. "Lessons from Nigeria's 2011 Elections." Crisis Group Africa Briefing 81, Sept. 15. www.crisisgroup.org/~/media/Files/africa/west-africa/nigeria/B81%20-%20Lessons%20from%20Nigeras%202011%20Elections.pdf.

Jarstad, Anna, and Timothy D. Sisk, eds. 2008. *From War to Democracy: Dilemmas of Peacebuilding*. Cambridge, UK: Cambridge Univ. Press.

Joseph, Richard. 1987. *Democracy and Prebendal Politics in Nigeria: The Rise and Fall of the Second Republic*. Cambridge, UK: Cambridge Univ. Press.

———. 1996. "Nigeria: Inside the Dismal Tunnel." *Current History* 95 (601): 3.

Lehoucq, Fabrice. 2003. "Electoral Fraud: Causes, Types and Consequences." *Annual Review of Political Science* 6 (June): 233–56.

Lewis, Peter. 2007. *Growing Apart: Oil, Politics, and Economic Change in Indonesia and Nigeria*. Ann Arbor, MI: Univ. of Michigan Press.

Lindberg, Staffan I. 2003. "The Democratic Qualities of Competitive Elections: Participation, Competition and Legitimacy in Africa." *Commonwealth and Comparative Politics* 41 (3): 61–105.

———. 2006. *Democracy and Elections in Africa*. Baltimore, MD: Johns Hopkins Univ. Press.

Marco, Derrick. 2006. "The Context and Contents of the Strategic Assessment." In *Conflict Tracking Dossier: Toward the 2007 Elections in Nigeria*, ed. I. O. Albert, Derrick Marco, and Victor Adetula. Abuja: IDAS Nigeria, Madol Press.

McHugh, Gerard. 2008. "Electoral Reform in Sudan and Prospects for Peace in Darfur: Implications of the National Elections Act of 2008 for the Darfur Political Process." Conflict Dynamics International briefing paper, Oct. 13. www.cdint.org/CDI%20-%20Electoral%20Reform%20and%20Darfur%20Political%20Process%20FIN%2013%20Oct%202008.pdf.

Meagher, Kate. 2006. "Hijacking Civil Society: The Inside Story of the Bakassi Boys Vigilante Group of South-Eastern Nigeria." *Journal of Modern African Studies* 45 (1): 891–15.

Mozersky, David. 2008. "Abyei Conflict Threatens to Escalate to Full-Scale War." ICG, May 30. www.crisisgroup.org/en/regions/africa/horn-of-africa/sudan/op-eds/mozersky-abyei-conflict-threatens-to-escalate-into-full-scale-war.aspx.

National Democratic Institute (NDI). 2007. *Final NDI Report on Nigeria's 2007 Elections*. Washington, DC: NDI. www.ndi.org/files/2313_ng_report_election07_043008.pdf.

National Intelligence Council. 2008. *Democratization in Africa: What Progress toward Institutionalization?* Report, Feb. www.dni.gov/nic/PDF_GIF_confreports/african_democ_2008.pdf.

O'Brien, Adam. 2009. "Sudan's Election Paradox." Enough Project, June 10. www.enoughproject.org/publications/sudans-election-paradox.

Ong'ayo, Antony Otieno. 2008. "The Post-election Violence in Kenya: An Overview of the Underlying Factors." *Pambazuka News*, Feb. 14.

Osaghae, Eghosa E., and Rotimi T. Suberu. 2005. "A History of Identities, Violence, and Instability in Nigeria." CRISE Working Paper 6, Center for Research on Inequality, Human Security, and Ethnicity, Univ. of Oxford, 13.

Posner, Daniel N. 2006. "Regime Change and Ethnic Cleavages in Africa." *Comparative Political Studies* 40 (11): 1302–27.

Rapoport, David C., and Leonard Weinberg. 2001. "Elections and Violence." In *The Democratic Experience and Political Violence*, ed. David C. Rapoport and Leonard Weinberg. London: Frank Cass.

Rawlence, Ben, and Chris Albin-Lackey. 2007. "Nigeria's 2007 General Elections: Democracy in Retreat." *African Affairs* 106 (424): 497–506.

Reilly, Benjamin, and Andrew Reynolds. 2000. "Electoral Systems and Conflict in Divided Societies." In *International Conflict Resolution after the Cold War*, ed. Paul C. Stern and Daniel Druckman. Washington, DC: National Research Council.

Reno, William. 2002. "The Politics of Insurgency in Collapsing States." *Development and Change* 33 (5): 837–58.

Rotberg, Robert I. 2007. "Nigeria: Elections and Continuing Challenges." Council on Foreign Relations, CSR no. 27. www.cfr.org/nigeria/nigeria/p12926.

Rustad, Siri Aas. 2008. "Power-Sharing and Conflict in Nigeria: Power-Sharing Agreements, Negotiations, and Peace Processes." Occasional paper, Center for the Study of Civil War, Oslo (PRIO). www.prio.no/sptrans/-1415422889/Nigeria_full_report.pdf.

Schaffer, Frederick Charles. 2007. *Elections for Sale: The Causes and Consequences of Vote Buying.* Boulder, CO: Lynne Rienner.

Schwartz, Roland. 2001. "Political and Electoral Violence in East Africa." Working Paper on Conflict Management no. 2. Friedrich Ebert Stiftung and Centre for Conflict Research, Nairobi. http://library.fes.de/pdf-files/bueros/kenia/01398.

Soyinka, Wole. United States House of Representatives, Subcommittee on Africa and Global Health, hearing "Nigeria at the Crossroads: Elections, Legitimacy and a Way Forward," June 7, 2007, 26–27. Washington, DC: Committee on Foreign Affairs, Serial 11080.

Stewart, Frances, ed. 2008. *Horizontal Inequalities and Conflict: Understanding Group Violence in Multiethnic Societies.* London: Palgrave.

Umar, Muhammad Sani. 2007. "Weak States and Democratization: Ethnic and Religious Conflicts in Nigeria." In *Identity Conflicts: Can Violence Be Regulated?* ed. J. Craig Jenkins and Esther E. Gottlieb. New York: Transactions.

UN Development Programme (UNDP). 2011. "Human Development Report 2011: Nigeria." http://hdrstats.undp.org/images/explanations/NGA.pdf.

UN Environmental Programme. 2004. "Understanding Environment, Conflict and Cooperation." www.wilsoncenter.org/topics/pubs/unep.pdf.

UN Mission in the Sudan (UNMIS). 2010. "Report[s] of the Secretary-General on the Sudan." All reports: Jan. 19, Apr. 5, Apr. 27, July 19, Oct. 14, Dec. 31. www.un.org/en/peacekeeping/missions/unmis/reports.shtml.

UN Office for West Africa. 2011. "Praia Declaration on Elections and Stability in West Africa." Regional Conference on Elections and Stability, Praia, Cape Verde, May 20. http://unowa.unmissions.org/Portals/UNOWA/PRAIA%20DECL_ANG.pdf.

Van de Walle, Nicolas. 2002. "Africa's Range of Regimes." *Journal of Democracy* 13 (2): 66–80.

———. 2003. "Presidentialism and Clientelism in Africa's Emerging Party Systems." *Journal of Modern African Studies* 41 (2): 297–319.

Willis, Justin, Atta el-Battahani, and Peter Woodward. 2009. "Elections in Sudan: Learning from Experience." Report, Rift Valley Institute, Apr. www.riftvalley.net/resources/file/Elections%20in%20Sudan%20-%20Learning%20from%20Experience.pdf.

4

Land Patronage and Elections

Winners and Losers in Zimbabwe and Côte d'Ivoire

Catherine Boone and Norma Kriger

Q uestions of land rights and land access have played a prominent part in post-1990 electoral struggles in Kenya, North Kivu province of the Democratic Republic of the Congo, Côte d'Ivoire, and Zimbabwe. In each of these cases, political leaders have promised to transfer the land rights of "foreigners," in-migrants, immigrants, or minorities to their supporters. These political struggles over land have found expression in the introduction of new laws and the abrogation of old ones, constitutional changes and disputes, state-orchestrated displacements and disenfranchisements, regime violence against dissenters, violent actions of militias, and grassroots-level violence perpetrated by party militants and ordinary citizens attempting to gain or defend land rights.

The connection between land and elections calls for urgent attention. This chapter examines the phenomenon of rulers using (or promising to use) land rights as a patronage resource to mobilize electoral support. We first identify the phenomenon of using land as a patronage resource in

Thanks to Dorina Bekoe and the United States Institute of Peace for support and suggestions in preparing this chapter. An earlier version appeared in *Commonwealth and Comparative Politics*, and we thank that journal for permission to reuse some of that material here (Boone and Kriger 2010).

75

post-1990 electoral contests and then identify some aspects of the contemporary African political economy that help explain why this phenomenon has become so visible in that period.

The resort to land as a patronage resource in multiparty elections may be at least partly explained by the convergence of three specific constraints and incentives confronting politicians in many African countries. First, weak constitutional and legal restraints on rulers' ability to allocate and reallocate land rights—a constant in the modern history of most African states—create opportunities for politicians to use land as a patronage resource, and many have done so during the past five decades. Second, competitive elections, which became more common following the return to multiparty politics in many African countries since 1990, mean that politicians must now work harder to mobilize constituency support to win elections.[1] Third, the attractiveness of land compared to other patronage resources (e.g., investment in public goods such as schools in rural constituencies, or allocation of government jobs) is heightened when the state's fiscal capacity has dwindled, as it has in most African states since the late 1980s. Land rights can be offered as a patronage resource even when state coffers run low.

Although scholars of land tenure in sub-Saharan Africa have recognized the vulnerability of land rights to arbitrary state action—especially the unregistered, neocustomary land rights of African smallholders and peasants—most political scientists have not. In most of sub-Saharan Africa, there are few legal or constitutional restraints on government's ability to reassign rural property rights. Legally speaking, most small farmers are basically tenants at will of the state; central governments are legally empowered to give and take land almost as easily as they can give and take patronage resources such as jobs, funds for road-building, and food relief that are financed directly from state coffers (McAuslan 1998; Toulmin and Quan 2000; Alden Wily 2001; Juul and Lund 2002). The experience of Zimbabwe, where white farmers' privately owned land was unlawfully confiscated and became state land, suggests not only the insecurity of even this category of land rights (freehold title)—an estimated 2 to 10 percent of land in sub-Saharan Africa (Chimhowu and Woodhouse 2006, 346)—but also its vulnerability to becoming a source of political patronage. Political analysts need to pay more attention to how insecure land rights, not only where the state is the legal owner or "national guardian" of rural land but

---

1. In many places, the change over time constitutes a difference of degree rather than kind, since elections in Africa's one-party states sometimes both were competitive and created incentives for rulers to trade resources for votes.

also where private property rights exist, may become linked to insecure voting rights and to electoral politics.

Some scholarly work identifies connections between land politics and electoral politics in Africa. Studies of post-1990 Kenya and post-2000 Zimbabwe have tracked rulers' manipulation of land rights to reward or intimidate voters, contributing to literatures on elections and violence, elections and ethnic conflict, and elections and nationalism (e.g., Klopp 2002; Oucho 2002; Lynch 2008; Boone 2011; Scarnecchia 2006; Raftopoulos and Phimister 2004; Alexander and McGregor 2001). There is an excellent literature on what J. P. Chauveau has called the "political instrumentalisation of land conflicts" in post-1993 Côte d'Ivoire (Chauveau 2000; Marshall-Fratani 2006; Babo and Droz 2008). The work needed to integrate this into broader comparative frameworks, however, still needs to be done. Researchers have barely begun to conceive of land patronage as a general strategy for creating or mobilizing political constituencies, or of how this feeds a politics of displacement, dispossession, and disenfranchisement. This chapter begins to fill this gap in our understanding of political order and disorder in Africa.

We explore the relationship between electoral and land politics in Zimbabwe and Côte d'Ivoire, despite the two countries' often dramatic dissimilarities.[2] Because politicians have used land patronage as an electoral strategy in both countries, we can seek to understand the common factors driving this dynamic in these two cases. Politicians in the throes of electoral competition in the 1990s in Côte d'Ivoire, and during the 1990s and 2000s in Zimbabwe, resorted to land patronage to mobilize electoral support. Targeting those they labeled as "foreigners," "not true citizens," or "non-indigènes," politicians confiscated, denied or threatened to take away their acquired land rights, disenfranchised them, and used their land as a source of state patronage for regime supporters, who were portrayed as "loyal patriots." In Zimbabwe, the ruling party seized mainly white-owned private property to distribute to its constituencies; ZANU PF also identified black commercial farm workers on white-owned farms as "aliens" and often forcibly evicted them from their homes and livelihoods. In Côte d'Ivoire, southern politicians sought to mobilize electoral support among constituencies in the southwest by promising to recover the land rights that indigenous groups had lost to immigrants and migrants in earlier de-

---

2. For example, Côte d'Ivoire, a French colony, had a relatively smooth route to independence in 1960, whereas Zimbabwe, a British colony, won internationally recognized independence in 1980, after a war. The substantial private ownership of rural land by white settlers, and the colonial legacy of racial land inequities, that existed in Zimbabwe were not factors in Côte d'Ivoire at independence. Zimbabwe has had multiparty elections since independence in 1980 (and before); postcolonial Côte d'Ivoire reintroduced multiparty politics in 1990.

cades.[3] In both countries, legal and extralegal action to expropriate and re-distribute land and land rights involved violence by the architects of these initiatives, the would-be beneficiaries, and, in some cases in Côte d'Ivoire, those reacting to threats of displacement and dispossession.

Over the past few generations, African governments have taken land, given land, and awarded or assigned property rights as a core matter of political management and public policy. In many parts of Africa today, disputes over land ownership and allocation lie at the heart of contested relationships between the state and social groups, and of contested definitions of citizenship and entitlement. From this perspective, it is unsurprising that in contested multiparty elections, political leaders use land as a patronage resource; that is, they promise to give or revoke land rights in efforts to reward followers and punish opponents.

This case study of Zimbabwe and Côte d'Ivoire analyzes efforts instigated by national political leaders to reshape the electoral playing field through (a) using land as a patronage resource to mobilize and reward supporters; (b) displacing rival-party supporters so that they cannot vote, freeing up the properties left behind, so that these can be claimed by partisan supporters; and (c) stripping rival-party supporters of their citizenship rights and, thus, their voting rights and property rights (if only citizens can own land). Intimidation and violence are intertwined in all these maneuvers and are intended to have an electoral effect.

Elections and Land Patronage in Zimbabwe

Zimbabwe has had multiparty elections since 1980. Two factors made white farmers and their private property rights vulnerable to electoral populism, even when Robert Mugabe's Zimbabwe African National Union (ZANU PF) rule was secure (1980–99). First, European dispossession of African land left 4,500 white farmers in 1980 with a disproportionate share of land (15.3 million hectares, or 40 percent of the total land area). Second, both nationalist movements—Joshua Nkomo's Zimbabwe African People's Union (ZAPU) and Mugabe's ZANU—mobilized rural support during the liberation war by promising to return stolen lands, thus creating expectations of land redistribution.

ZANU PF's land redistribution policy was centered on the purchase of privately owned farms belonging to whites, for resettlement chiefly by Africans in the overcrowded communal lands covering 16.3 million hectares

---

3. Land conflicts in Zimbabwe's communal areas, as in Côte d'Ivoire, often revolve around newcomers and "first-comers" and have an electoral dimension.

(42 percent of total land area) (Moyo 1986, 168, 193). The party used the allocation of resettlement land as a patronage resource to build hegemony in the 1980s, but it was not a high-profile electoral strategy. After 1990, in the context of growing economic hardship and discontent with the government, ZANU PF weakened constitutional and legal constraints on compulsory land acquisition but escalated electoral threats to take white farmers' land. Faced with its stiffest-ever opposition in the 2000 parliamentary elections, combined with sharp economic decline, ZANU PF orchestrated often violent occupations, unlawful confiscations, and allocations of white farms to mobilize and reward loyalists and punish opponents. Although the Commercial Farmers' Union estimated that 800–900 farmers were fully or partially operating by February 2003 (ZHR NGO Forum 2007, 8), a government estimate said that in July 2003 there were still 1,332 farmers on just over 1 million hectares (Land Review Committee 2003, 27). Black farm workers on the white-owned commercial farms, who constituted about one-fourth of the total formal labor force (Amanor-Wilks 2000) and were perceived by ZANU PF to be supporters of Morgan Tsvangirai's Movement for Democratic Change (MDC), were disenfranchised on a massive scale through forcible displacement from their homes on the farms. Moreover, many farm workers and white farmers were deliberately disenfranchised by the Zimbabwe Citizenship Amendment Act, which came into force on July 6 2001, thus giving substance to ZANU PF's frequent depiction of both these groups as "aliens." In subsequent elections, ZANU PF continued its warnings that the opposition, the MDC, would return land and power to whites. And it continued transferring white-owned land to its clients and forcibly evicting farm workers and coercing those workers still on the farms to vote for ZANU PF.

The First Decade: Emerging Links between Land Patronage and Electoral Politics

In the 1980 election, ZANU PF promised to redistribute land to peasants and to build socialism by establishing cooperatives and collectives on resettlement land (Cliffe, Mpofu, and Munslow 1980, 48–49). The party recognized white farmers' economic significance: they accounted for most agricultural production and marketed farm output, significant foreign exchange earnings, linkages to industry, and one-third of formal employment (Mumbengegwi 1986, 210). ZANU PF also promised to respect unusually strong constitutional guarantees for private property rights, a product of the British-mediated peace settlement in 1979. For ten years, the government could acquire any land on a "willing seller, willing buyer" basis but could compulsorily acquire only underutilized land for resettlement. When the state compulsorily acquired property, compensation had to be "adequate" (understood to mean paid at market price) and paid "promptly" and in foreign currency if that was the owner's preference (Coldham 1993, 82, 86).

Under ZANU PF rule, whites became politically vulnerable. Government reassurances about the security of whites' land rights were intermingled with politicians' encouragement of land protests and defense of spontaneous land occupations, especially during 1980–85 (Selby 2006, 115, 131). Starting in 1983, farmers had to obtain court orders to evict squatters, and such orders became more difficult to secure or enforce. By 1986, several High Court orders of eviction were ignored by police, the squatters, and populist members of government and ZANU PF (Selby 2006, 168).

Before the 1985 parliamentary election, Mugabe reassured white farmers, who were nervous about politicians publicly advocating a radical land agenda (Selby 2006, 131). But after the election results revealed that many whites had voted for former prime minister Ian Smith's party, Mugabe castigated all whites for spurning reconciliation and threatened a government clean-up operation "so that we remain only with the whites who want to work with the Government." The rest "will have to find a new home" (Kriger 2005, 12).

Despite threats to whites and their land rights, the government purchased white-owned land on the market in the first decade of independence. By 1990, around 54,000 African families had been settled on 3 million hectares of land purchased from the whites at market rates (Selby 2006, 134). Model A resettlement schemes—individual arable plots of five hectares and communal grazing—rather than socialist cooperatives (model B) and state collectives (model C)—occupied most resettlement land and accounted for some 80 percent of new settlers.

Even in this first decade of independence, ZANU PF demonstrated that it was interested not only in land redistribution but in land as a patronage resource to build its party base. By 1989, about half the settlers on model A schemes were former squatters on commercial farms, many of whom were allocated land because of their support for ZANU PF politicians rather than their compliance with government criteria for settler selection. In Matabeleland, where ZANU PF was engaged not only in fighting antigovernment dissidents but also in an attempt to decimate its chief opponent, ZAPU, the violent conflict drove a number of white farmers to sell their farms. The state bought their land and, from 1985, leased it for a small fee to civil servants and politicians, all ZANU PF supporters (Kriger 2007). But land patronage politics were less prominent as an electoral mobilizing strategy in the 1980s than in subsequent decades, largely because opportunities for other forms of state patronage were available to the ruling party and because there was no risk of ZAPU, with a mainly Ndebele base, attracting support from the ruling party's predominantly Shona rural base.

The Second Decade: Deepening Links

ZANU PF agreed to unite with ZAPU in 1987, and Zimbabwe was a de facto one-party state in its second decade. Still, as the economy faltered and ZANU PF's legitimacy was increasingly challenged by mounting opposition, it fought hard to preserve its status as the hegemonic party. In this context, land redistribution became a higher-profile component of its electoral mobilizing strategies, even as the ruling party also threatened to withdraw other government resources, such as jobs and food relief, from opposition voters and to provide development benefits only for ruling-party voters (Kriger 2005, 16, 18–19, 23–24).

The March 1990 general and presidential elections took place amid the anticipated expiration, in April 1990, of constitutional guarantees for private property, as well as mounting economic problems and a new opposition party, the Zimbabwe Unity Movement (ZUM), led by the ruling party's former secretary-general. ZANU PF intensified land and race rhetoric leading up to the election.

ZANU PF called whites in Ian Smith's party, which had agreed to vote for ZUM, racist, antireconciliation, and the real force behind ZUM. Minister Shamuyarira warned that whites who voted for ZUM risked "putting their community in danger as soft targets" (Kriger 2005, 15). Mugabe and Joshua Nkomo, then a senior minister in the president's office, initiated a populist discourse on land (Selby 2006, 183). Nkomo and Mugabe called for a massive land transfer from commercial farmers to peasants and blamed white farmers for slowing the pace of resettlement by refusing to sell to the government (Arnold 1990, 60–61). In fact, from 1985 to 1990, the government chose not to exercise its legal right of first option to buy over 1 million hectares of white-owned land (Coldham 1993, 83 and fn 9).

In April 1990, the ZANU PF Parliament voted to weaken the restrictive constitutional clauses on compulsory land acquisition and compensation. Henceforth, the government could compulsorily acquire any land for resettlement, and compensation had to be merely "fair," paid within a reasonable time, and in local currency (Coldham 1993). These constitutional changes were reflected in the Land Acquisition Act of 1992, which also gave a statutory base to the National Land Policy. The policy's objective was to transfer 5 million hectares of white-owned farms to those who would use it productively (Selby 2006, 183, 186).

Land and race rhetoric intensified before and during the April 1995 parliamentary election and the March 1996 presidential election campaigns. Because the Forum Party—the chief opposition party—had some white support, ZANU PF called it a European party and its African leader a traitor to the armed struggle. Fueled by the black empowerment movement, which sought a larger share of the economy, the state and party media and party officials blamed white economic dominance for the country's economic problems (Kriger 2005, 20–21). Starting in September 1993, the party campaigned to discredit white farmers and their involvement in opposition politics (Selby 2006, 228). In April 1995, Mugabe condemned whites for refusing to sell their farms at concessionary rates (Kriger 2005, 23); in early 1996, he declared that land identification committees would target "racist" farmers first, and blamed them for the deadlock on the land issue (Selby 2006, 242, 244). During his presidential campaign, Mugabe said he did not want to send squatters to invade farms, but warned that he could consider it if the UK did not provide funding for the purchase of land for resettlement or if farmers remained intransigent (Selby 2006, 285–86, 246).

In November 1997, after designating almost 1,500 farms for compulsory acquisition, Mugabe said he would pay compensation only for land improvements and not for land itself (Selby 2006, 246). When white farmers successfully challenged the designations in court because the government failed to comply with its own criteria and the Land Acquisition Act, Mugabe again warned that the land issue would not be derailed by the courts (Selby 2006, 239). By mid-1998, thousands of blacks had occupied white-owned farms, encouraged by Mugabe's threats to "take" the land and by war veterans, so-called veterans, and ZANU PF party officials (ICG 2004a, xii). In January 1999, the attorney general reiterated the government's commitment to the designations and said it "would not let the law stand in its way" (Harold-Barry 2004, 268).

ZANU PF's bungled efforts at compulsory land acquisition meant that it acquired much less land in the 1990s than in the 1980s. The acquired land was used mainly to foster the ruling elites' land accumulation and retain their loyalty. By 1999, several hundred ruling-party elites—cabinet ministers, parliamentarians, judges, senior army officers, and civil servants—had obtained state leases to farm on resettlement land for nominal fees (Selby 2006, 222–23 and fn 490, 236–37).

The Third Decade: Full-Blown Links

By 1999, real income per capita was probably 15 percent lower than at independence, and 30 percent lower than its peak in 1974. The shrinking economy was dealt another blow when the IMF suspended balance-of-payments support in October 1999, principally because the government seemed uncommitted to the economic reform program but also because of uncertainties about the government's land policy and its reluctance to provide information on the true costs of its war involvement in the Democratic Republic of Congo since August 1998 (EIU 2000). From 1999 to 2000, the government budget deficit rose from 9.7 percent of GDP to 21.4 percent of GDP (Thaker 2008). Once the MDC appeared as a contender for power, ZANU PF made land and race issues the centerpiece of its electoral mobilizing strategy and initiated occupations of white-owned farms. However, land was not the only source of patronage used by the ruling party after 2000. ZANU PF purged the civil service and the security forces (police, Central Intelligence Organisation, and defense forces) of those believed to be supporters of the opposition and replaced them with party loyalists—something it had mainly threatened to do in the 1990s.

The constitutional referendum, 2000. ZANU PF appointed a commission to draft a new constitution, which was put to a referendum in February 2000 (Hatchard 2001). In January 2000, Mugabe unilaterally inserted a land clause, making it the British government's obligation to pay compensation for agricultural land compulsorily acquired for resettlement (Bowyer-Bower and Stoneman 2000, 11). Opinion polls before the referendum indicated majority support for the state's right to expropriate land for redistribution to the disadvantaged, but only about 15 percent favored expropriation without compensation (Shaw 2003, 88, fn 5). White farmers opposed the land clause and, along with most other voters, the increased presidential powers in the proposed constitution. They openly mobilized their black farm workers to vote no, as did the farm workers' organization, the General Agricultural and Plantation Workers Union of Zimbabwe (GAPWUZ) (Chambati and Magaramombe 2008, 236, fn 14).

In the referendum, 54 percent were not swayed by the populist appeal to land grievances, although only 26 percent of registered voters cast votes (Hatchard 2001, 215). Surprisingly, even in sixteen of forty-eight rural constituencies, a majority voted no. Adding these to the forty-six of fifty-six urban constituencies where a majority voted no, it became evident that the MDC could win a majority of the 120 elected parliamentary seats (the other 30 seats were not elected on a constituency basis and were effectively guaranteed to ZANU PF) and threaten ZANU PF's then twenty-year hold on parliamentary power (ZHR NGO Forum and JAG Trust 2007, 14). Mugabe seemed to accept his first electoral defeat since 1980.

Within days, land invasions of white-owned farms started. Whether these early land invasions were centrally organized by ZANU PF or, as some claim, were spontaneously initiated and organized by war veterans in an ad hoc way (Moyo and Yeros 2005, 2007; Sadomba 2008), soon after the 2000 land invasions began war veterans, aided by unemployed youth, received logistical support from party officials and the security forces. Using commercial farms as bases, veterans with their supporters used violence and intimidation to punish white farmers and their black workers for their no vote and used a liberation war discourse, liberation-style *pungwes* (nighttime meetings), and violence to prevent the MDC from gaining ground among farm workers on white-owned farms and in the communal areas. Both the MDC and ZANU PF wanted to capture the black farm workers' vote because of their numerical significance and vulnerability (Waeterloos and Rutherford 2004, 542). Before the land invasion, the estimated 300,000 to 350,000 farm workers, including their families, constituted an estimated 1 million to 2 million people (Rutherford 2001, 633; Waeterloos and Rutherford 2004, 540; Sachikonye 2003b, 17). A very high proportion of farm workers were in the three Mashonaland provinces, which had the bulk of large-scale commercial farms (Chambati and Magaramombe 2008, 219) and which were also ZANU PF strongholds. Most large agro-industrial estates (sugar, coffee, tea, and forest plantations) were located in the Eastern Highlands (Manicaland Province) and the Lowveld (Masvingo Province) and were not affected by the land acquisition program (Chambati and Magaramombe 2008, 219).

The 2000 parliamentary and 2002 presidential elections. ZANU PF's campaign slogan for the June 2000 parliamentary election was "land is the economy, and the economy is land" (COHRE 2001, 30). The party promised priority in land redistribution to peasants, war veterans and the youth who had supported them during the war, former political prisoners and detainees in the struggle for independence, young agricultural graduates and other professionals, and indigenous businesspeople who demonstrated capacity for farming (Xinhua News Agency 2000). The party highlighted its revolutionary nationalist credentials while portraying the MDC as a party of traitors and British puppets representing white interests and a return to white rule.

Mugabe instructed invaders and the police to ignore a March 2000 High Court order to remove invaders from the land, asserting that land was a political issue, which the courts should stay out of. In April 2000, the overwhelmingly ZANU PF Parliament passed a constitutional amendment to make compensation for compulsorily acquired resettlement land a responsibility of the UK government. Zimbabwe's government would pay compensation only for land improvements. Compensation no longer needed to be "fair," and compensation assessments had to take into account the availability of state resources and "any financial constraints that necessitate the payment of compensation in installments over a period of time" (Coldham 2001, 227). In May 2000, Mugabe used his presidential powers to temporarily amend the Land Acquisition Act to reflect the constitutional changes.[4]

By the June 2000 parliamentary election, 28 percent of all farms owned by Commercial Farmers' Union members (including black farmers) had been invaded (Harold-Barry 2004, 269). Of the 119 contested seats, ZANU PF won 62 and the MDC won 57—one by-election was held later. Thus, even with thirty guaranteed seats, ZANU PF lost the necessary two-thirds parliamentary majority to amend the constitution. The land occupiers—chiefly war veterans, peasants, and youth, all either loyal to ZANU PF or having to demonstrate party loyalty to get their plots, and the party elites, including army and police officers and party officials—almost certainly voted for ZANU PF (Sachikonye 2003a, 235; Chaumba, Scoones, and Wolmer 2003a, 541). To say that land redistribution won ZANU PF votes is not to diminish, as Sam Moyo does, the role of ZANU PF violence and electoral rule manipulation (Moyo 2000, 29).

The government announced a fast-track land reform program in July 2000 (Chaumba, Scoones, and Wolmer 2003a, 544). Its goal was to acquire 5 million hectares from commercial farmers by December 2001 (UNDP 2002, 7–8). There were two resettlement models. The A1 model provided small-scale holdings for the poor and landless in the communal areas and reserved 20 percent of plots for war veterans. The A2 model provided medium- and large-scale commercial farms for those with agricultural experience and capital to develop the land and repay the cost of the farm as determined by the government (Sachikonye 2003a, 240, fn 3). Land occupations became more formalized, and war veterans and ZANU PF officials made allocation decisions (Chaumba, Scoones, and Wolmer 2003b, 603; HRW 2002, 29–30). The Supreme Court ruled in November 2000 that the land invasions were illegal, but Mugabe told his party's congress in December 2000 to ignore the courts and portrayed whites as "foreign" and "a tiny racial minority," which owned and controlled the economy (Reuters 2000). Even as Mugabe and ZANU PF made the land issue also a race issue, black landowners who opposed the regime also had their farms occupied and confiscated, and black farm workers, generally perceived by the ruling party as MDC supporters, had their votes either captured by ZANU PF through violence, intimidation, and coercion or denied through violent

---

4. In November 2000, the Parliament passed the Land Acquisition Act amendment (HRW 2002, 10).

displacement from their homes and jobs on the farms. In 2001, land occupations were retroactively legalized, making it impossible for farmers to use the courts to remove the occupiers. Later that year, the Supreme Court, now packed with ruling-party loyalists, validated that legislation (HRW 2002, 13–14).

For the March 2002 presidential election, ZANU PF's slogan was again "land is the economy and the economy is land." The state newspapers ran advertisements calling on every patriotic Zimbabwean to reclaim a piece of land and advising MDC supporters to apply for land or lose out (Selby 2006, 294). ZANU PF depicted the land invasions as part of the Third Chimurenga, the revolution against neocolonialism, and linked it to the Second Chimurenga, the independence war. The MDC was again portrayed as stooges of British imperialists who sought to recolonize Zimbabwe. Mugabe repeatedly threatened to expel whites and take all their land, claimed that Tsvangirai planned to give the land back to the whites, and treated the UK and Prime Minister Blair as if they were contenders in the presidential race (ZHR NGO Forum 2002, ch. 7; HRW 2002, 14; Lamb 2007, 245).

Before the presidential election, the Citizenship of Zimbabwe Amendment Act stated that Zimbabweans with foreign citizenship must renounce their foreign citizenship, in accordance with the law of the foreign country of which they held citizenship, by January 6, 2002, or lose their Zimbabwe citizenship. The registrar general's office interpreted the law to mean that all Zimbabwean citizens with a potential right to a foreign citizenship had to renounce their foreign "entitlement" if they wanted to retain their Zimbabwean citizenship. Since many farm workers had a foreign-born father or paternal grandfather from Malawi, Zambia, or Mozambique, they needed to have the high commission of that country renounce their potential claim to citizenship, but these governments were unable to do so, and it was too expensive for most farm workers (Waeterloos and Rutherford 2004, 551, fn 14). One estimate is that 88,000 farm workers of "foreign origin" were disenfranchised by the amendment (Chambati and Magaramombe 2008, 228). ZANU PF's depiction of whites and black farm workers as "aliens" and "not belonging" (Rutherford 2007) thus became a legal reality for many. In 2004, another law was introduced to amend the act to exempt persons whose parents were from countries in the Southern African Development Community from having to renounce their potential non-Zimbabwean citizenship (Waeterloos and Rutherford 2004, 551, fn 14).

Mugabe was reelected president in March 2002, with 56 percent of the vote compared with MDC leader Tsvangirai's 42 percent. The justice minister called it a "runaway victory" that "was won on the issue of land"

(McGreal and MacAskill 2002). As in the 2000 election, land won ZANU PF votes, but victory also depended on violence and rigging. The fast-track land reform program, initiated in July 2000, was to end in August 2002, according to government ministers, but was officially announced to have ended on October 19, 2002 (Waeterloos and Rutherford 2004, 550, fn 5).

Land patronage: Beneficiaries and victims. The official land audit reported in August 2003 that 6.4 million hectares of the 9 million hectares acquired from commercial farmers by the fast-track land reform program between 2000 and 2002—nearly double the initial 2000 goal—had been allocated: 4.2 million hectares to 127,192 A1 households, and 2.2 million hectares to 7,260 A2 applicants (Land Review Committee 2003, 5). A more recent estimate is 140,775 A1 and 16,386 A2 settlers (Hammar, McGregor, and Landau 2010, 273).

The key beneficiaries of the A2 scheme were the ruling elite: party officials, cabinet ministers, governors, war veteran leaders, security sector members, civil servants, almost all the Supreme Court judges, and others in the judiciary, the church, and state media houses. Starting in 2002, when soldiers returned from fighting in the Democratic Republic of the Congo, they and other security sector members increasingly dominated land allocations (Selby 2006, 328–30).

Beneficiaries of A1 schemes are murkier. A study of a single ranch in Chiredzi District, Masvingo Province, found that a majority of settlers were young men (25–40 years old) who had left families in the communal areas, where they were landless or land poor. A significant minority were single mothers, usually divorcées or widows, who had no communal land. A high percentage of settlers were relatively rich, and a high percentage relatively poor, but all had political connections and ZANU PF loyalties (Chaumba, Scoones, and Wolmer 2003b).

The percentage of farm workers to benefit from land allocations was unsurprisingly small, given ZANU PF's depiction of them as pro-MDC, "alien," and "unpatriotic." According to some estimates, 2 to 10 percent of former farm workers received land allocations (Hammer, McGregor, and Landau 2010, 273, fn 47), though some national surveys reportedly indicate that up to 15 percent were beneficiaries (Chambati and Magaramombe 2008, 225).

The fast-track land reform program cost the vast majority of farm workers their jobs, and many were evicted from the farms, losing their homes and belongings. With nowhere else to live, many evicted farm workers returned to the farms (Rutherford 2001, 628). In 2008, the UNDP estimated that a million farm workers and their families had lost their homes and livelihoods as a result of the fast-track land reform program (NRC 2010, 44).[5] Violent displacement of farm workers was a deliberate electoral strategy from the start of the land invasions in 2000 (Kinsey 2010, 339). In many cases, workers were ordered to leave their houses instantly and were unable to collect their belongings. Ruling-party militants destroyed their homes to ensure that they would not return. The government refused to acknowledge that its fast-track land reform program had led to internal displacement, claiming that all former farm workers had a choice whether to leave the farms. The government therefore objected to the use of the term "internally displaced persons," and it restricted humanitarian agencies' access to displaced farm workers (NRC 2010, 44). In fact, many farm workers (and some others) suffered multiple successive displacements as they sought new livelihoods in urban or mining areas or even in neighboring countries (NRC 2009a, 49). Meanwhile, workers on the farms were subjected to violence and intimidation to ensure that they voted for ZANU PF.

After ZANU PF recaptured enough seats in the March 2005 parliamentary election to change the constitution, it continued to remove constitutional and legal constraints to the acquisition of agricultural land for resettlement. The party retroactively legalized the acquisition of land and removed the right to challenge those land acquisitions in the courts, made it a criminal offense for former owners or occupiers to stay on the land unless they had lawful authority (an offer letter from the lands minister, a state permit, or a lease), and authorized the courts to order the eviction of those on the land without lawful authority (Citizenship of Zimbabwe Amendment Act 2005, cl. 2; Gazetted Land [Consequential Provisions] Act 2006).

ZANU PF's hostility toward white farmers persisted. In September 2005, with senate elections pending, the state security and land reform minister said, "Operation *Murambatsvina* should also be applied to the land reform program to clean the commercial farms that are still in the hands of white farmers. White farmers are dirty and should be cleared out. They are similar to the filth that was in the streets before *Murambatsvina*" (ZHR NGO Forum and JAG Trust 2007, 15).

The state's title to resettlement land, along with the minister's power to issue and revoke offer letters, permits, and leases, was a reason why few farmers accepted ninety-nine-year leases on offer since November 2006

---

5. Estimates of displaced farm workers and of farm workers who remained on the farms vary considerably, reflecting not only different initial estimates of farm workers but also the changing situation on the ground.

(UNDP 2002, 30), because it gave ZANU PF a source of patronage that it could use again and again. For example, about a half million black settlers who occupied farms during the 2000 invasions were evicted during 2004 (Ploch 2009, 20). Early in 2008, with elections pending, the land reform and resettlement minister said the government had reclaimed at least 1,449 A2 farms allocated to black clients, because a land audit found the land vacant or unused (IRIN 2008). Similarly, in May 2008, before the presidential runoff election, the government instructed settlers on an old resettlement scheme who were believed to have voted for the MDC in the March 2008 election to vacate their homes immediately and return to the communal areas from where they had come twenty-six years earlier (Kinsey 2010, 360).

ZANU PF's slogan in the March 2008 presidential and parliamentary elections was "Defending the land and sovereignty." In the presidential election, Mugabe also campaigned with the slogan "100% Empowerment, Total Independence" and warned of the future takeover of foreign firms (Solidarity Peace Trust 2008b, 7). For the first time since 1980, ZANU PF lost its house majority, and Mugabe got fewer votes than an opposition presidential candidate. Because Tsvangirai did not win a majority, a runoff was necessary. In its violent runoff campaign, which eventually led Tsvangirai to withdraw from the contest, ZANU PF claimed that white farmers were returning to the country to reclaim their land in the event of an MDC victory (BBC 2008). Before the presidential runoff election, in April 2008 alone, an estimated 30,000 farm workers were again victims of forced displacement by ZANU PF supporters (Solidarity Peace Trust 2008a, 35). These evictees were only a fraction of those displaced in the election violence. ZANU PF's supporters in the runoff included elites with land to defend. Some of the newly landed elite used their farms, and co-erced farm workers, to organize electoral violence during the presidential runoff election (Solidarity Peace Trust 2008a, 49).

Following Mugabe's victory in the presidential runoff election, under conditions widely recognized as not free and fair, ZANU PF and the two MDC parties signed the Global Political Agreement (GPA) in September 2008, which established a power-sharing government in February 2009. Importantly, the GPA describes the land acquisitions and redistribution that have occurred since 2000 as irreversible (article 5.5), thus entrenching current occupations and ZANU PF patronage structures (RAU 2008, 4). White farms and farm workers continue to be evicted from the few remaining white-owned farms, and farm workers remain under constant threat of eviction from the new settlers.

Land Patronage and Elections in Côte d'Ivoire

Although Côte d'Ivoire was not subject to European settler colonialism on the scale known in East and southern Africa, the allocation of rural land since the early to mid twentieth century, as in many parts of sub-Saharan Africa, has been the legal prerogative of the central state.[6] With few exceptions, rights to rural land were established or claimed by kingdoms, communities, and families, and individuals had little or no constitutional or legal standing. In practice, the intensity of state intervention in the allocation of rural land in Côte d'Ivoire has varied across space: it has been most intensive in the center-west and southwest regions of the Ivorian forest zone. This is the part of the country where commercial agricultural development has been most rapid and extensive since the 1950s. To increase the land area under coffee and cocoa cultivation in what had been a sparsely populated region, the regime of Félix Houphouët-Boigny (1960–93) enabled massive inflows of settlers. The government protected the settlers and their acquired land rights against ever more resentful autochthonous populations.

With the opening of the electoral arena to multiparty politics after 1990, conflicts aroused by long-standing government land policies in center-west and southwestern Côte d'Ivoire spread from the local and regional level, where they had simmered under the repressive cover of the one-party state, to the national level. Land rights emerged as a highly charged issue and a potent mobilizing force in party competition for control over the central government itself.

Southern leaders used what can be called "land rights patronage" to construct electoral constituencies and, by the mid- to late 1990s, to forge a southern majority that could stand up to the challenge presented by northern politicians. The main mechanism for doing this is the land law reform that was pushed by southern politicians in the 1990s. Under the land law passed in 1998, land rights acquired by in-migrants in earlier decades were weakened or simply invalidated. The targets of this law—the most obvious land rights losers—were presumed supporters of northern politicians. The legal reform transferred these land rights to *autochtones* in the center-west and southwest who constituted the core of, or could be incorporated into, a winning southern electoral coalition.

Since the 1990s in both Côte d'Ivoire and Zimbabwe, politicians have attempted to win popular support and bolster their electoral chances by promising to undo the perceived injustices of past settlement histories and

---

6. On European plantation agriculture in Côte d'Ivoire, see Anyang' Nyong'o 1987. On land law, see Chauveau 2000, 2002a; Toulmin and Quan 2000; Lewis 2003; and Boone 2003, 218–20.

by using the powers of the central state to restore farmland to targeted beneficiaries who are cast as the rightful, authentic owners of the land. In Côte d'Ivoire as in Zimbabwe, this political strategy has involved the use of state power to dispossess and disenfranchise targeted communities via legal means, propaganda, mobilization of violent pro-government militias, and violence meted out directly by the state. Since the late 1990s, the Ivorian legislature has passed (and repeatedly confirmed) a new property law that restricts the right to own property to Ivorian citizens, identified as such under newly restrictive citizenship laws. It has simultaneously restricted voting rights and revised the constitution to "rededicate" the polity on the basis of a narrower, more exclusively defined citizenry. Exclusionary government policies have also involved state coercion against those targeted for dispossession, displacement, and disenfranchisement; tacit government association with militias that have propagated local-level violence and displacement; and the often willful failure of the state to protect residents and citizens from violence.

Land Policy, Political Patronage, and Elections under the Houphouët Regime

The regime of Houphouët-Boigny (1960–93) adopted a land strategy that combined a politically pragmatic commitment to upholding indigenous land claims (where this was convenient and helped reinforce local political control and elite accommodation at the center of the political system) with an economically ambitious program of land pioneering that encroached ever more invasively on customary claims in the center-west and southwest, the region of the country targeted for the rapid expansion of export-crop production.

By the Code Domanial of 1963, all land not registered under formal title was declared part of the "national domain," to be administered by the state. In practice, the government's often-repeated position on rural land rights was that "the land belongs to whoever is using it." This dictum had highest salience in the rural center-west and southwest, where the prefectoral corps—direct agents of the central state—played a key role in organizing, facilitating, and enforcing an open-door migration policy.

From the 1950s onward, migrants from central Côte d'Ivoire (especially the Baoulé V, the forest-savannah contact zone that was the heartland of Houphouët's Baoulé ethnic constituency) and northern Côte d'Ivoire, along with immigrants from Burkina Faso and Mali, settled in center-west and southwestern Côte d'Ivoire with the Houphouët government's encouragement and protection. By clearing land and establishing coffee and cocoa plantations, they drove the expansion of the export-crop economy. As Chauveau (2000, 2002a) explains, state agents encouraged or pressured

indigenous communities in the southwest to accept the migrants and immigrants and to provide them with access to land in exchange for nominal payments, symbolic exchanges, or cash or in-kind gifts. Government
agents worked to sustain at least the pretense of "landlord-stranger" relations in this region by *not attempting* to create or enforce a legal order in
which land transfers to "strangers" would be legally binding or permanent.
Immigrants and migrants in the forest zone were encouraged to defer to
their hosts and to make ongoing payments to their autochthonous "hosts,"
or tutors, for the rights to use the land.[7] Many migrant villages were located apart from those of the autochthones and were referred to as *campements*, or camps, signaling their legally and culturally ambiguous (liminal)
status. Muslim in-migrants from northern Côte d'Ivoire and immigrants
from Mali also played key roles in the development of the towns and commercial networks that knit together the economy of this region. Many of
the outsiders prospered as traders, transporters, moneylenders, and plantation owners (Lewis 1980; Chauveau 2000, 69; Bassett 2003b), adding a
classlike dimension to *indigène*-stranger relations.

The Ivorian government's aggressive land-pioneering policies in the
center-west and southwest fueled regional grievances against the Houphouët
regime. Resentment mounted during the late 1950s and 1960s as "the
state ... used a combination of intimidation and incentive to persuade
local populations to allow increasing numbers of migrants to break new
land" (Marshall-Fratani 2006, 20). One native of the Gagnoa region (who
was a well-placed ruling-party militant in 2010) recounted this history by
arguing that "the outsiders were imposed upon us *by force*."[8] In the years
of the Houphouët regime, a tight regional alliance between the president's
core constituencies in central Côte d'Ivoire and northern leaders effectively
silenced dissident voices from the center-west and southwest. Areas of
high in-migration around Gagnoa, Daloa, and Divo developed as the epicenter of popular rural resentment of the Houphouët regime, and the sites
of recurrent land conflicts between nonautochthones and autochthones.

The center-west has long been the political epicenter of the Ivorian forest zone west of the Bandama River. Land dynamics in the extreme southwest (Bas-Sassandra region, Departments of San Pedro and Tabou) are
similar within broad outlines to those in the Gagnoa-Daloa-Divo region,
with the caveat that in the extreme southwest, land-related pressures are
compounded by parastatal and private investment in large-scale plantation

---

7. On the political intervention of the state to "maintain the fiction of the *tutorat* system" (i.e., the
role of the Houphouët regime in resisting the formalization of conventions for land rights transfer or
delegation [e.g., sales, leasing]), see Chauveau 2000, 2002a, 2002b; Lewis 2003.

8. Author interview with Gagnoa resident, FPI facility, Abidjan, Oct. 20, 2010.

agriculture. Plantation agriculture, which occupied approximately two-thirds of the cultivated area in the Department of Tabou in 2001 (Babo and Droz 2008, 753), aggravated tensions in the smallholder sector in this area by acting as a magnet for in-migrants to the region and by enclosing land that otherwise would have been open to smallholder expansion. (See Schwartz 2000; Woods 2003; Babo and Droz 2008; and Babo 2010.) In some localities around Tabou, 80 percent of all cocoa farmers are in-migrants. In parts of the extreme southwest, two-thirds of all residents are in-migrants. (See Colin, Kouame, and Soro 2008.) In Gagnoa in 1970, an uprising against the ruling Parti Démocratique de Côte d'Ivoire (PDCI) government, driven in large part by the perceived illegitimacy of the government's land policy, was brutally suppressed by the Ivorian army, leaving at least several hundred (and possibly as many as 4,000) dead (Dozon 1985, 348; Marshall-Fratani 2006, 10, 21).[9]

By the late 1980s, an estimated 50–60 percent of the population of center-west and southwestern Côte d'Ivoire was not indigenous to this region.[10] For the indigenous population, there was little doubt that the Houphouët regime and the ruling PDCI had favored the non-indigènes or that outsiders—whether Burkinabè planters, Malians, Baoulé and Muslim settlers from other regions of Côte d'Ivoire, Lebanese, French neocolonialists, or international coffee and cocoa brokers—had reaped the lion's share of the benefits of economic development of the southwestern region.

In the one-party elections of the 1970s and 1980s, immigrants living in the southwest were given voting cards so that they could cast their ballots for the ruling party. Their votes for the PDCI were generally interpreted by outside analysts and PDCI politicians as a quid pro quo for Houphouët's gift of access to land and other economic opportunities in the Ivorian south.[11] Writing of the early 1990s, Bassett (2003b, 11) says that foreigners were both indebted to Houphouët's open-door policies "and fearful they would be forced home if he lost the election."

Return to Multipartyism: 1990–99

The return to multiparty elections in 1990 destroyed the geopolitical and electoral alliances of the Houphouët era and brought to the fore divisive questions about the role of the central government in allocating land rights

---

9. The officially reported death toll was 4,000. Strozeski (2006, 1) reports that between 4,000 and 6,000 were killed.

10. At the time, about one-fourth of the total population of about 15 million to 16 million was classified as non-Ivorian.

11. Crook (1997, 222–23) says that non-Ivorians had always been allowed to vote. In 1960–61, a wave of protest over foreigners' right to vote (and to government employment) swept Abidjan.

and voting rights. The land grievances of central-westerners and south-westerners emerged as a critical factor in national politics.

In 1990, long-time left-wing nationalist and Houphouët critic Professor Laurent Gbagbo rallied constituencies in the center-west, his home region, around a platform that blamed foreigners for Côte d'Ivoire's economic crisis and insisted that indigenous Ivorians reclaim the land.[12] As Barbara Lewis (2003) has explained, the Gbagbo candidacy was celebrated around the Divo region with the slogan "Gbagbo will chase out the strangers."

Gbagbo's Front Populaire Ivoirien (FPI) drew a direct link between the questions of party control over the national government and distribution of land rights in the Ivorian forest zone. The FPI denounced the Houphouët regime's distribution of voter cards to foreigners and individuals of "dubious citizenship," arguing that it was only the protection of the PDCI that had allowed noncitizens in the center-west and southwest to establish and retain control over so much land, and only the electoral support of these foreigners that kept the PDCI in power.

Citizenship: Who Can Benefit from Resources Allocated by the State?

Francis Akindès (2004, 33) called the question of citizenship in Côte d'Ivoire "a local expression of the political need to select those who have the right to ever more limited local resources." In the center-west and southwest, the issue of citizenship rights—and, by extension, voting rights—had strongly redistributive implications because of its connection to land.

In Côte d'Ivoire in the mid-1990s, the notion of "foreigner" was open to conflicting definitions that reflected, in part, the gap between the formal-legal definition of the Ivorian citizenry—which obviously included the country's Muslim citizens, who traced their ancestry to the northern part of the country—and an ethnonationalist vision of "a true Ivorian nation" made up of Christians and animists, whose ancestral roots in southern and central Côte d'Ivoire could be "traced back to the mists of time." For southerners who embraced the ethnonationalist ideal captured in the notion of "Ivoirité" that was promoted by the incumbent PDCI regime in the mid- to late 1990s, even their Ivorian-born northern compatriots were not true Ivorians.[13] In the villages, especially in the center-west and southwest, the gap between the formal-legal definition of citizenship and the prevailing popular (or folk) definition was even wider. In the villages, citizenship referred even more narrowly to members of autochthonous lin-

---

12. That indigenous Ivorians should reclaim the land has been the "consistent stance" of the FPI since the end of the 1980s (HRW 2003).

13. See Dozon 2000; Akindès 2004.

eages who claimed ancestral rights to land in their home localities. Under this most restrictive definition of citizenship, nonautochthones (foreigners, immigrants, and domestic in-migrants) were permanent guests in the localities—they could use land under provisional landlord-stranger contracts, but autochthony was a requirement for full political rights in the locality and for owning or controlling land. For indigenous populations of the center-west and southwest, this was the understanding of citizenship rights—and the entitlements associated with citizenship—that had been violated by Houphouët's land policies in the west.

Building a Southern Electoral Majority: Bédié, the 1994 Constitution, and the 1998 Land Law

Houphouët-Boigny and the PDCI won the presidential election in 1990 with an official vote share of 81 percent. The FPI, led by Gbagbo, gathered almost all the opposition vote.[14] The ruling party also won legislative elections in 1993. The demise of the PDCI, the political behemoth that had dominated Ivorian politics since the late 1950s, began in December 1993, when Houphouët died in office. In a fraught and disputed transition, power passed to his dauphin, Henri Konan Bédié.

Under Houphouët, the core of the PDCI power bloc was an alliance between populations and elites in Houphouët's home region, the Baoulé region of central Côte d'Ivoire, and the ruling elite of Korhogo, who were the political linchpins of the mostly Muslim northern region. Under this arrangement, the center-west and southwest had been marginalized, politically repressed, and, in the eyes of native southwestern populations, systematically exploited. This constellation of political forces did not survive the death of Houphouët. In early 1994, a reformist group from within the ruling PDCI, centered in the northern wing of the old PDCI, and some key southern leaders and members of Parliament defected to form their own political party, the Rassemblement des Républicains (RDR). The RDR gathered its forces to make a bid for political power in presidential and legislative elections scheduled for 1995 and 1996 (Crook 1997, 224–27). Bédié was left with the central and southeastern strongholds of the once-hegemonic PDCI, but even in these regions his party faced electoral challenge from both the RDR and the FPI.

Bédié's strategy was to expand his political base by forging a new coalition with long-marginalized and long-aggrieved southwestern constituencies, including FPI supporters and other disaffected (anti-Houphouët)

---

14. Turnout rate in 1990 was 69 percent, with Houphouët's official share of the vote at 81.7 percent. The FPI, led by Gbagbo, got 18 percent of the vote (Fauré 1993, 318–19).

constituencies in the south.[15] He envisioned a new electoral coalition made up of the non-Muslim, nonnorthern Ivorians, who could be pulled together as the peoples of the "Greater South" (Le Grand Sud). Together, the non-Muslim populations of the southeast, center, center-west, and southwest would make up some 55–60 percent of the Ivorian population—an electoral majority (Bassett 2003a, 19).

The political challenge facing the Bédié government was twofold. The first was to weaken the RDR as an electoral force. The second was to win over the center-west and the southwest, stronghold of the anti-Houphouëtist, anti-PDCI movement. To these ends, the Bédié regime promulgated the virulent nativist ideology of Ivoirité, sponsored a revision of the constitution, revision of the electoral code, and a new land law. "Ivoirité" defined indigenous southerners as the "pure-blood Ivorians" (*ivoiriens de souche*) who possessed a moral right to preferential access to national political office and to jobs, land, and other resources allocated by the state.

As many analysts have emphasized, Ivoirité was a political gambit—a risky *fuite en avant*—that must be understood in the larger macroeconomic context (Campbell 2003). The recession of the mid-1990s, deep structural unemployment, privatization of state enterprises, and vigorous attempts by external creditors to impose austerity on government spending all conspired to severely constrain Bédié's options for mobilizing electoral support and for building the base of popular support that his government so obviously lacked. For the external creditors, this was one of the *goals* of the austerity programs—in the name of economic liberalization and to curb rent-seeking, they sought to limit government's ability to use public funds to fuel patronage machines and buy political support. Under structural adjustment programs, the government budget deficit was reduced from US$280 million in 1993 to US$57 million in 1995. In 1996, there was a budget surplus of $23 million (IMF 2005, 241). Meanwhile, from 1985 to 1998, poverty rates soared, income gaps widened, and the quality of public services—including secondary and tertiary education—declined precipitously (IMF and IDA 2002, 4–5).[16]

The new, narrow vision of national identity and national citizenship was written into the 1994 Ivorian constitution and the December 1994 electoral code. The new constitution stipulated that any candidate for the presidency must have two Ivorian-born parents. This clause was aimed directly at Alassane Ouattara, the RDR candidate, whose father's citizenship

---

15. In the 1990 presidential election, the FPI got 50 percent of the vote in the Agni region (Fauré 1993, 231).

16. On the political effects of the economic recession, see Gyimah-Boadi and Daddieh 1999; Sindzingre 2000; Campbell 2000, 2003; Boone 2007. On structural blockages in the export economy, see Chauveau 2000; Woods 2003.

status was in dispute. The new electoral code stipulated that no foreigner could vote in an Ivorian election. Police, the military, and gangs across the south took it upon themselves to enforce this provision by confiscating and destroying the national identity cards of Muslims and individuals with northern-sounding surnames, on the grounds that the identity documents may have been acquired fraudulently or under the patronage of the now-defunct Houphouët regime. Observers inside and outside Côte d'Ivoire decried the violent "new racism" that was sweeping the country (HRW 2001; Scheuer 2002). The opposition press accused the Bédié government of Hitlerism and tribalism (*La Voie* 1995a; Djébi 1995).

In the March 1995 election run-up, the FPI and RDR "announced a formal alliance based on a call for the withdrawal of the new Code Electoral" (Crook 1997, 229). The government refused, unsurprisingly, and the two opposition parties then boycotted the 1995 presidential elections. In the rural areas of the center-west and southwest, the land-related implications of national-level electoral struggles were clear to all. Around Gagnoa, the FPI stronghold, some members of autochthonous communities responded to FPI calls for an "active boycott" to disrupt the upcoming elections. Long-simmering disputes over land access and ownership fused with the immediate struggle against the PDCI's attempt to use a noncompetitive election to ratify its hold on power. In the three Gagnoa electoral constituencies and around Saïoua and Soubré (Buyo), youth groups and opposition party militants harassed and intimidated Baoulé farmers, driving them off their farms, burning *campements,* purging localities of PDCI supporters, and, in some cases, allowing autochthones to seize their land (Crook 1997, 235, 138; Chauveau 2000, 115). An estimated 10,000 Baoulé were displaced in the *"tensions electorales"* of 1995. According to one estimate, about half of these fled the center-west permanently and returned to their home regions (Babo and Droz 2008; Etou and Mamadou 1995).[17] Barbara Lewis wrote that around Divo, most Baoulé thought that in spite of the election-time violence, their land rights were ultimately secure "because they were convinced that the PDCI would prevail" in the elections Lewis (2003, 24). The ruling party itself, in its efforts to mobilize the votes of immigrants in this region, emphasized the tight link between the electoral outcomes and land rights: "In the export crop producing regions of the West, instructions to vote in favor of the PDCI were accompanied by the threat [for those of Burkinabè, Malian, and Guinean origin] of expulsion from their land in the case of an FPI victory" (Chauveau 2000, 111). The PDCI appears to have employed the same tactic on members of its presumed "natural constituency" as well. The opposition press rou-

---

17. Violence against in-migrants started in 1994. See Babo and Droz 2008, 752, 754–60.

tinely accused the PDCI of holding Baoulé farmers in the center-west and southwest "hostage" with threats that an FPI victory would lead to their immediate expulsion from the region, while a PDCI victory would guarantee that in-migrants and their farms would be protected by the Ivorian army (Etou and Mamadou 1995; *La Voie* 1995c).

Because of the opposition boycott of the 1995 presidential race, Bédié won with 95 percent of the vote (with an official turnout rate of 57 percent of the registered electorate). Outside observers and the FPI again accused the PDCI of allowing fraudulently registered foreigners and other non-citizens to vote.

The opposition front of 1995 turned out to be short-lived, and the RDR and FPI competed against each other in the November 1996 legislative contest and the municipal elections shortly thereafter.[18] As the three-way battle for political dominance continued, many political leaders and cadres from both the FPI and the PDCI rallied their constituencies at the local level by stoking antiforeigner, antimigrant, and anti-Muslim sentiments (Dembele 2003, 37). As this happened, the RDR was forced onto the political defensive as the representative and political voice of "Le Grand Nord," which included not only the 14 percent of the Ivorian population that actually lived in the north, but also the 33 percent of the southern population made up of Ivorians who traced their family ties and ancestry to the north. Bassett points out that by the 1998 census, 39 percent of Ivorians were Muslim. In the worldview of the propagandists of Ivoirité, northerners and Muslims were outsiders, usurpers, and not "truly Ivorian" (Bassett 2003a, 19).

The PDCI embraced a nativist agenda designed to unite the non-Muslim, autochthonous populations of "Le Grand Sud." Anna Bednik referred to Ivoirité as Bédié's attempt "to federate the populations of the South, in lieu and in place of the material pay-offs and upward social mobility that the regime could no longer provide" (Bednik 2006). Ivoirité did have material appeal in the land rights domain, however. It tapped straight into the land-related grievances of indigenous communities in the center-west and southwest.

This connection became explicit in the Bédié government's major legislative initiative of 1998, which was a new *Code Foncier*, or Land Code. The new land law confirmed the primacy of *customary* land rights—understood both in the law and in popular consciousness as autochthony-based land rights—in the more than 95 percent of the national territory where informal tenure arrangements prevailed. It provided for the granting of

---

18. Baldé (2006) reports a 45 percent turnout rate in the 1996 legislative elections. The PDCI ended up with 146 deputies, the FPI with 14, and the RDR with 14.

formal ownership rights to land hitherto held under a myriad of neocustomary or informal arrangements—but only to those able to prove that they were true Ivorian citizens. Lewis argues that the FPI popularized the most restrictive interpretation of the law, in which land ownership was reserved for autochthones only, thus excluding not only those of foreign origin (i.e., Burkinabès, Malians, and Guineans) but also all *allochtones* (i.e., those not native to the locality) (Lewis 2003, 35–36, 39). The FPI version captured its constituents' land-related demands precisely, for it would prevent Baoulé farmers, as well as foreigners and their descendants, from obtaining landownership rights in the center-west and southwest, and force these outsiders to renegotiate the terms of land access with autochthones now armed with the force of a law that vested legal ownership of the land in autochthonous landholders.

In the months before the National Assembly vote on the Code Foncier, members of Parliament visited localities throughout the Ivorian south, especially localities in the center-west and southwest, in official *tournées de sensibilisation*. Babo and Droz (2008) note that in the center-west and southwest, PDCI politicians used these sessions—usually held in the seats of prefectoral administration and in the presence of mayors, prefects, and local cadres—to focus autochthones' land frustrations on farmers of Burkinabè, Malian, and Guinean origins rather than on their "Baoulé brothers" (Babo and Droz 2008).[19] Yet by this time, many Baoulé had already sized up the political situation and had left or were leaving the region to return to their home districts in the central part of the country (Babo and Droz 2008).

On December 23, 1998, the National Assembly, with 146 PDCI members and 14 members from each of the other two parties, voted almost unanimously for a new Code Foncier (Loi 98-750), which recognized customary land rights, arguably for the first time in Ivorian law, and excluded foreigners from land ownership.[20] The law stipulated that decentralized committees of elders at the local level could be called on to settle questions and disputes over "customary rights" at the village level. In the center-west and southwest, where land rights were most contentious, this handed the prerogative to local actors who were committed to defining citizenship in

---

19. The International Crisis Group (ICG) reported that in the far west, land-related tensions between "authentically Ivorian" Baoulé settlers and indigenous Guéré was higher than between Guéré and Burkinabè immigrants (ICG 2005, 11, fn 50).

20. The practical meanings of the terms "noncitizen" and "citizen" that appeared in the 1998 land law were open to interpretation by whoever controlled the government that would eventually implement and enforce the legislation. RDR legislators would surely invoke this justification for having voted for the law, as could PDCI legislators with Baoulé constituents who had acquired land rights as nonautochthones in the southwest. The RDR seemed trapped by the language of the law: to protest would have suggested that RDR legislators had doubts about the citizenship status of their supporters.

the narrowest possible terms (as *autochtonie*). Chauveau argues that the redistributive implications of the new Code Foncier were clear (Chauveau 2000; 2002a; 2002b, 65; Koné 2002, 184). The law undercut the acquired land rights of migrants and immigrants to the forest zone and created legal provisions and procedures for transferring these rights to the autochthones.

In the political context of Côte d'Ivoire in 1998, the 1998 land code can be read as a PDCI-led initiative that delivered on the party's nationalist, antiforeigner agenda while simultaneously delivering selective benefits to key constituencies in a swing region—the center-west and southwest— and thus playing for their electoral support. The land code was built around the central plank of the FPI's political platform (and, some say, in response to urging and pressure from FPI cadres), and it delivered what autochthonous communities in the center-west and southwest had been demanding since the late 1960s, if not before: state recognition of autochthones' ancestral land rights (Chauveau 2002a, 2002b, 66; Toulmin and Quan 2000; HRW 2003, 8 fn 11, 43–44). Autochthones in the center-west and southwest stood to be the leading beneficiaries of the new code: the land ownership issue was most politicized in the center-west and southwest, and the largest numbers of nonindigenous farmers were found in this region.[21] In the mid- to late 1990s, the Bédié regime had little else to offer by way of patronage resources in its efforts to win their support.[22]

In 1997 and 1998, Bédié was hamstrung by privatizations, austerity measures, and severe financial constraints on public spending. His government was rocked by strikes by state employees, teachers, cocoa producers, and students who protested job losses, pay cuts, low producer prices, rising costs, tuition hikes, unemployment, inflation, and declining living standards. Structural adjustment programs (SAPs) and liberalization had delegitimized and de-funded redistributive measures that had helped sustain national cohesion in the more prosperous decades of Houphouët's rule (through 1985), pushing the country, in the late 1990s, into what Gyimah-Boadi and Daddieh (1999, 143) called a SAP-induced recession. Under these circumstances, land patronage could look like a low-cost, high-yield political strategy.

Lewis wrote, "The picture of enormous amounts of Ivoirian property, already '*mis en valeur*' [in production] but vacant by the stroke of a legal

---

21. Calls for expropriation of foreigners, and restitution of native land rights also resonated in the southeastern coastal strip, and especially in Sud-Comoé (Bonoua), where migration from Burkina Faso in the 1960s and 1970s had helped drive the development of commercial agriculture.

22. The FPI press did not fail to point out that in 1995, the PDCI had not protected the property of thousands of Baoulé farmers who were victims of election-time house-burnings and displacements. See *La Voie* 1995b.

pen, excited many Ivoirian villagers, both the presumed winners of the vacated lands and the losers" (Lewis 2003, 29). Local leaders, members of Parliament, and youth groups encouraged autochthonous people to assert their newly sanctioned landownership rights. As Chauveau put it, "Conflict broke out" after villagers were informed of the provisions of the new law (Chauveau 2000, 115). In many localities, gangs of villagers led by youth seized farms and destroyed the *campements* of those effectively dispossessed by the new Code Foncier. The year following the passage of the new Code Foncier was marked by the expulsion of tens of thousands of nonautochthones from villages and *campements* in the southwest and center-west. In October 1999, approximately 12,000 Burkinabè farmers were driven out of Tabou in the southwest in the most notorious incidents. Locals invoked the terms of the 1998 land law in justifying the expulsions (Babo and Droz 2008, 755). After Tabou, local-level land clashes then spread to Saïoua, Oumé, Gagnoa, and Daloa, bringing the total number of Burkinabè farmers and farm workers expelled from the rural areas of the center-west and southwest in 1999 to approximately 20,000. Authorities in Abidjan and the local *forces d'ordre* mounted tepid, restrained attempts to contain and mitigate the spread of violence. By several accounts, prefects and gendarmes protected Baoulé communities while leaving northerners and foreigners exposed to violence in local *affrontements* (Chauveau 2000, 96, 116; Babo and Droz 2008).

During the 1990s, the land ownership question had emerged "at the forefront of electoral preoccupations and arguments" (Chauveau 2000, 113) and as "the main rallying point for those seeking to promote anti-foreigner ideology" (ICG 2003, 37). This decade of decay of the old polit-ical-economic order, and of attempts to forge a new majority, came to an end with the December 24, 1999, coup d'état of General Robert Guéi, a westerner and a non-Muslim. Guéi led a corps of mutineers drawn from northern military and security units that had been disbanded by Bédié.

Elections: Land Rights and Citizenship Disputes, 2000–2005

Guéi organized national elections for October 22, 2000, and ran for presi-dent. As part of his political platform, he embraced the southern ultra-nationalism known as Ivoirité, despite his having renounced this nativist ideology when he seized power (Akindès 2004). Thus, the year 2000 found Bédié, Guéi, and Gbagbo all promoting some version of Ivoirité, all com-peting for the electoral majority required to win the presidency.

Guéi sponsored a July 2000 referendum on the constitution, which affirmed that candidates for the presidency must have two Ivorian-born parents. Gbagbo endorsed this constitutional change. The initiative was aimed at the RDR's presidential candidate, Ouattara, whose citizenship status was still in dispute. The new version of the constitution also affirmed the principle that only "pure-blooded Ivorians" would have full citizenship rights, including land ownership rights (under the 1998 land law). The run-up to the vote revealed much about the stakes in this referendum: it was marked by widespread violence and destruction of the "fraudulent" or "suspicious" national identity cards of Muslims and individuals with northern-sounding surnames, and harassment and persecution of those suspected of being "immigrants born in Côte d'Ivoire."

Meanwhile, court rulings disqualified not only Ouattara (for dubious citizenship credentials) but also Bédié (for corruption) from running in the 2000 election. Guéi's two most formidable rivals were thus out of the competition. The presidential election itself was violent, with a low official turnout rate (37 percent). Protests over Guéi's early closing of the polls (when he appeared to be losing) engulfed Abidjan in three days of street fighting.[23] The ruling junta split, and Ivorian security forces (gendarmes) and FPI militants took to the streets to impose an outcome. The FPI candidate, Laurent Gbagbo, was ultimately proclaimed winner of the election, with 59 percent of the vote (to Guéi's 32.7 percent). In the ten days following the elections, government security forces hunted down, harassed, and beat RDR militants and supporters, executing at least fifty young men in the process and burying the bodies in mass graves in the Abidjan suburb of Yopougon.

For the next decade, Gbagbo clung tenaciously to his unlikely, compromised victory. In 2000–2002, persecutions of northerners and Muslims intensified, centered largely on the confiscation of voting cards and other identity papers.[24] In the first two years of the Gbagbo presidency, expropriations of the farms and crops of nonautochthones spread throughout the southwest, becoming commonplace and often violent. At the village level, locals acted on the knowledge that previous rules regarding the land rights of migrants "had been overturned" (Koné 2002, 28). The regions of contested land rights saw many confrontations at the local level. Koné reported, "In May 2001, in an attempt to ease tensions between rural communities and 'clarify' the situation, the Minister of Defense and Civil Protection in the new FPI government stated that the land belongs to its owner and not the person using it" (Koné 2002, 32). The FPI government was clearly giving the green light to village-level displacements, land ap-

---

23. On Guéi's background and intrajunta politics leading up to the election, see N'Diaye 2005, 30, 41–44.

24. The RDR won the largest number of votes nationwide in the 2001 municipal elections (Bassett 2003a, 25).

propriations, and renegotiations of land access agreements on terms far more favorable to autochthones. Through this process, Gbagbo's constituencies received precisely the benefit that their leader had promised. Youth militias aligned with the party were often at the vanguard of intimidation and thuggery against "foreigners" in the center-west and southwest, with the authorities turning a blind eye to much of the local violence. An indicator of the scale of this process is the estimated 100,000 Burkinabè who were estimated to have left the country by mid-2002, with many additional thousands forced off the land and into refugee camps within Côte d'Ivoire. One source estimated that 300,000 Burkinabè were driven into Abidjan (NRC 2010, 31).

In September 2002, northern and western soldiers attempted a military coup against Gbagbo. The northerners said that they had taken up arms "to demand their Ivorian national identity cards" (ICG 2005, 17; Banégas and Losch 2002).[25] Gbagbo and his government survived with the assistance of France. The mutineers were pushed back to Bouaké, in the center of the country, where rebel forces gathered and proclaimed themselves the Forces Nouvelles. From late 2002 until the Ouagadougou Accords of March 2007, Côte d'Ivoire was formally divided in two, in a geopolitical stalemate brokered with the support of France. The government remained in control of the south, and the Forces Nouvelles occupied the north and far west.

With Côte d'Ivoire now in a de facto state of war, many more tens of thousands of nonautochthones were driven from villages and farms in the center-south and southwest. The Norwegian Refugee Council (NRC) reported that 158,000 Burkinabè were forced to leave Côte d'Ivoire in the first six months after the military coup (NRC 2009b, 10). This brought the total number of Burkinabè people expelled from Côte d'Ivoire by the end of 2003 to about 250,000 (ICG 2003).[26] The NRC (2010, 35) also estimated that the number of internally displaced persons in Côte d'Ivoire peaked at 1.1 million in 2003, during the hottest period of military confrontation.

With a cease-fire in 2004, military operations gave way to a period of "no peace, no war." Localities in the center-west and southwest saw continuing ethnic cleansing (via displacement, mostly) and farm expropriations that were orchestrated by local militias, village defense committees (which were often encouraged by municipal politicians and linked to the national-level FPI wheels), and the FPI youth militia, the Jeunes Patriotes. They took control of plantations, villages, and roads, using threats and vio-

---

25. On France's assistance to Gbagbo's government, see Smith 2003.

26. ICG reports the government of Burkina Faso's estimates. See also Banégas and Otayek 2003; HRW 2007.

lence to drive out nonautochthones and "reclaim the land" (ICG 2004b, 2, 18–19; 2005).[27] Citing a UN Office for the Coordination of Humanitarian Affairs (OCHA) estimate, Human Rights Watch reported that as of 2007, there were 700,000 displaced persons in the southern, government-held areas of the country. By that time, an estimated 350,000 people of Malian origin had left the country, along with 450,000 Burkinabè, many of them second- or third-generation migrants to Côte d'Ivoire (HRW 2007, 20).[28]

Although no elections were held in Côte d'Ivoire from the end of 2000 to October 2010, the country remained in an almost continual state of preelection mobilization. The Marcoussis Accords, brokered by France and signed by Ivorians in January 2003, called for, among other things, revision of the 1998 land law to protect "acquired rights" that predated its enactment, and amendment of the Code de la Nationalité to broaden naturalization provisions. The National Assembly, controlled by the FPI, did not budge. In late 2003, the International Crisis Group (ICG) reported, "The FPI promises its southwestern constituency that they will recover land in the wake of a campaign to identify true citizens and apply the 1998 law" (ICG 2003, 38).

The attempt to mount a campaign to identify "true citizens" remained the stumbling block to progress on both land rights and elections. In 2003–05, the ruling party maintained that enfranchising foreigners and individuals of dubious or contested nationality, as called for in the Marcoussis Accords, was a clear ploy to modify the *corps electoral* in favor of the opposition, in anticipation of elections. Marc Yevou of *Fraternité Matin*, the official government newspaper, explained: "Land rights are also an issue upon which the FPI bases its objection to [the nationality code reforms contained in Marcoussis]. Those newly nationalized would become land owners by their new status as citizens" (Yevou 2004).[29]

The 2005 Pretoria Agreement proposed a reconciliation plan that would lead from disarmament to *audiences foraines* (itinerant tribunals with local public hearings) to issue identity cards to bona fide citizens, to elections in October 2006, but conflict derailed both disarmament and the national registration process. The 2007 Ouagadougou Accords allowed for administrative reunification of Côte d'Ivoire and restored Ouattara's Ivo-

---

27. Human Rights Watch documents extensive violence against civilians, especially in the rebel-controlled region of Dix-huit Montagnes in 2002–03 (HRW 2007, 19). ICG reported systematic, widespread violence against Burkinabès and Malians from Sassandra up to Duékoué: "Local militias and village self-defense committees are involved, as well as gendarmes, and police. Humanitarian workers claim that even village elders have been used to draw Burkinabè back to their plantations, where they are killed by local youths" (ICG 2003, 26).

28. The 700,000 figure includes people who fled the north to take refuge in the south.

29. The government calculated that the changes proposed in the Marcoussis Accords would enfranchise 500,000 people, or about 8 percent of the electorate.

rian citizenship, but conflicts over the issuing of national identity cards and the constitution of voter rolls repeatedly derailed plans for elections. Scheduled elections were deferred five times during 2005–10. The 2009 postponement came at a time when the government was attempting to accelerate implementation of the 1998 land law "in a context of population displacement" in which it was almost impossible for the displaced to defend their land claims and rights (NRC 2009b, 1–3, 11).

On October 31, 2010, the FPI competed against the RDR and PDCI in a long-awaited presidential election. This led to the November 28 runoff between Gbagbo and Ouattara for the presidency.[30] Ouattara's majority vote in these elections (54 percent, according to the Independent Electoral Commission) was declared invalid by the Constitutional Council that Gbagbo had appointed, and Gbagbo refused to relinquish power. The Forces Nouvelles mobilized to displace him by force. Violence, including widespread violence against civilians in Abidjan and the western part of the country, came close to devolving into civil war before French and UN troops captured Gbagbo in Abidjan in April 2011. This brought an ignominious end to the Gbagbo regime and cleared the way for formal installation of Ouattara as president. In November 2011, Gbagbo was transferred to The Hague, where, as of January 2012, he was facing charges in the International Criminal Court for his role as an "indirect perpertrator" of violence that killed an estimated 3,000 people in the four months following the November 2010 runoff election.

With peace, reunification, and more political stability, the land question will resurface as a sensitive and potentially divisive issue on the national agenda. Koné wrote in 2006 that "the land question is one of the issues that will determine the future of the country in the short and medium term," which is surely correct (Koné 2006, 22). The balance of power at the national level now shifted back to Ouattara's supporters and the core of the Houphouëtist bloc in the PDCI. This means that at a minimum, in the words of journalist Daniel Balint-Kurti, "It will be harder for locals to throw the [ethnic outsiders] off of the land" (IRIN 2009).

Conclusion

Multiparty elections can be held in democratic, democratizing, or "competitive authoritarian" states. The phenomenon of using land as a patronage resource to mobilize electoral support became dramatically visible in

---

30. The official provisional result of the first-round election, as of November 4, 2010, was Gbagbo 38.3 percent, Ouattara 32.8 percent, and Bédié 25.2 percent. Turnout was over 80 percent in an electorate of 4.7 million voters, a third of whom were in Abidjan.

the context of competitive multiparty elections in Zimbabwe and Côte d'Ivoire, and it revealed profound weaknesses in basic constitutional order in both states. Both countries were characterized by weak legal restraints on the arbitrary use of state power, including on rulers' ability to allocate and reallocate land rights. In both countries, the line between citizens and noncitizens was highly vulnerable to manipulation by opportunistic politicians who proposed denying political and economic rights to targeted subgroups. As history shows (and as has been argued extensively in the comparative politics literature), elections alone do not guarantee or produce democracy in Africa or elsewhere.

Our study shows how national leaders in Zimbabwe and Côte d'Ivoire, faced with the need to win constituencies in multiparty elections and with existing land grievances, used land rights and land access as a patronage resource for mobilizing electoral support. Weak constitutional and legal guarantees on privately owned agricultural land in Zimbabwe, and on rural land cultivated by peasant farmers in Côte d'Ivoire, enabled politicians to pursue this strategy. The selective apportionment of land, like the selective allocation of government jobs, allowed politicians to offer an excludable and reversible benefit to voters in exchange for their political support.

In Zimbabwe, beginning in 2000, the regime organized the violent occupation, unlawful confiscation, and allocation of private land (owned chiefly by whites but also by black opponents of the regime) to stimulate electoral support against the newly formed popular MDC opposition. In Côte d'Ivoire, politicians with southern, center-west, and southwestern constituencies undertook legal reform to transfer the acquired land rights of nonautochthonous communities to the politicians' electoral constituents or potential supporters. Low-ranking officials, militia members, and others then used or endorsed violence in many places to make these transfers a reality. In both countries, attacks on acquired land rights were accompanied by portrayals of minorities (white farmers in Zimbabwe) or migrants and immigrants (in Côte d'Ivoire) as foreigners who had stolen land from "authentic" indigenous owners, the true patriots of the country. In Zimbabwe, black commercial farm workers were also portrayed as foreigners by the ruling party, though only one-fourth of them were foreign when land invasions began in 2000. In both countries, too, electorally inspired land rights redistribution also was accompanied by violent displacement and loss of voting rights by targeted populations.

The variables identified as critical constraints and incentives in generating electoral politics in which politicians seek to redistribute land rights are found in many parts of Africa today: competitive multiparty elections, state fiscal crisis, and weak constitutional and legal restraints on the power of central rulers to reallocate land rights. This mix of factors proved condu-cive to politicians' exploiting land grievances for electoral gain.

One of Straus and Taylor's electoral violence scenarios (in chapter 2 of this volume) concerns resource-related conflict, and we see this in the cases of Zimbabwe and Côte d'Ivoire. Yet this chapter goes beyond Straus and Taylor's descriptive typology by providing analytic leverage on why elections politicize some resource conflicts, and why elections have this effect in some places but not in others. The analysis shows that in the case of Côte d'Ivoire, it is wrong to suppose that elections politicized conflicts that were nonpolitical in the era preceding multipartism. In the case of Zimbabwe, the analysis shows how the highly political issue of land, in-herited from the colonial period, was a politicized issue in every election since independence, though it was only in 2000, with the emergence of a popular opposition party that seemed poised for electoral victory, that a new style of land politics was introduced and became entangled with elec-toral violence. The cases underscore the deep and long-standing political involvement of national-level leaders in the land conflicts that emerged as a locus and focus of election-time violence in these two countries. Highly politicized allocation of land was a *structural feature* of land control in the regions that were engulfed in land-related electoral violence in Zimbabwe and Côte d'Ivoire. The same holds true for Kenya.

This chapter has focused on the land-related violence in these two countries that fits Straus and Taylor's stipulation of violence that is *directly related to an electoral contest*. It is important to note that these cases also saw election violence that was not related to land, including the violent perse-cution of opposition supporters. Meanwhile, over many decades, there has also been land violence unrelated to elections per se, although land-related conflict has often been closely connected to contestation over political power and state authority.

References

Akindès, Francis. 2004. "The Roots of the Military-Political Crises in Côte d'Ivoire." Nordic Africa Institute Research Report no. 128, NAI, Uppsala.

Alden Wily, Liz. 2001. "Reconstructing the African Commons." *Africa Today* 48 (1): 77–99.

Alexander, Jocelyn, and JoAnn McGregor. 2001. "Elections, Land and the Politics of Opposition in Matabeleland." *Journal of Agrarian Change* 1 (4): 510–33.

Amanor-Wilks, Dede. 2000. "Zimbabwe's Farm Workers and the New Constitu-tion." SADC Center of Communication for Development, Harare. http://apic.igc.org/rtable/ded0002.htm.

Anyang' Nyong'o, Peter. 1987. "The Development of Agrarian Capitalist Classes in the Ivory Coast, 1945–75." In *The African Bourgeoisie*, ed. Paul Lubeck, 185–248. Boulder, CO: Lynne Rienner.

Arnold, Guy. 1990. "The Land Dilemma." *Africa Report* 35 (1): 59–61.

Babo, Alfred. 2010. *Les jeunes, la terre, et les changements sociaux en pays baoulé (Côte d'Ivoire)*. Paris: Karthala.

Babo, Alfred, and Yvan Droz. 2008. "Conflits fonciers, de l'éthnie à la nation: Rapports interéthnique et 'ivoirité' dans le sud-ouest de la Côte d'Ivoire." *Cahiers d'Etudes Africaines* 48 (4): 741–63.

Baldé, M. Sory. 2006. "Côte d'Ivoire: Situation Institutionelle." CEAN. www.etat. sciencespobordeaux.fr/institutionnel/cotivoir.html.

Banégas, Richard, and Bruno Losch. 2002. "La Côte d'Ivoire au bord de l'implosion." *Politique Africaine* 87 (Oct.): 139–61.

Banégas, Richard, and René Otayek. 2003. "La Burkina Faso dans la crise ivoirienne: Effets d'aubaine et incertitudes politiques." *Politique Africaine* 89 (Mar.): 71–87.

Bassett, Thomas. 2003a. " 'Nord Musulman et Sud Crétien': Les moules médiatiques de la crise ivoirienne." *Afrique Contemporaine* 206 (2): 13–27.

———. 2003b. "Dangerous Pursuits: Hunter Associations (Donzo Ton) and National Politics in Côte d'Ivoire." *Africa* 73 (1): 1–29.

BBC. 2008. "Zimbabwean Activists 'Beaten Up.' " *BBC World News UK*, Apr. 8.

Bednik, Anna. 2006. "L'Afrique et ses matières premières: Tempête sur le cacao de Côte d'Ivoire." *Le monde diplomatique*, July. www.monde-diplomatique. fr/2006/07/BEDNIK/13656.

Boone, Catherine. 2003. *Political Topographies of the African State*. Cambridge, UK: Cambridge Univ. Press.

———. 2007. "Africa's New Territorial Politics: Regionalism and the Open Economy in Côte d'Ivoire." *African Studies Review* 50 (1): 59–81.

———. 2011. "Politically Allocated Land Rights and the Geography of Electoral Violence: The Case of Kenya in the 1990s." *Comparative Political Studies* 44 (10): 1311–42.

Boone, Catherine, and Norma Kriger. 2010. "Multiparty Elections and Land Patronage: Zimbabwe and Côte d'Ivoire." *Commonwealth and Comparative Politics* 48 (Apr.): 173–202.

Bowyer-Bower, T. A. S., and Colin Stoneman. 2000. "Land Reform's Constraints and Prospects: Policies, Perspectives and Ideologies in Zimbabwe Today." In *Land Reform in Zimbabwe: Constraints and Prospects*, ed. T. A. S. Bowyer-Bower and Colin Stoneman, 1–23. Aldershot, UK: Ashgate.

Campbell, Bonnie. 2000. "Reinvention du politique en Côte d'Ivoire." *Politique Africaine* 78 (June): 142–56.

———. 2003. "Defining Development Options and the New Social Compromises in the Context of Reduced Political Space: Reflections on the Crisis in Côte d'Ivoire." *African Sociological Review* 7 (2): 29–44.

Centre on Housing Rights and Evictions (COHRE). 2001. *Land, Housing and Property Rights in Zimbabwe.* COHRE Africa Programme Mission Report, Sept. www.internal-displacement.org/8025708F004CE90B/(httpDocuments)/ 30109DB1609F1659C12576E100581F0B/$file/COHRE2001.pdf.

Chambati, Walter, and Godfrey Magaramombe. 2008. "The Abandoned Question: Farm Workers." In *Contested Terrain: Land Reform and Civil Society in Contemporary Zimbabwe,* ed. Sam Moyo, Kirk Helliker, and Tendai Murisa, 207–38. Pietermaritzburg, South Africa: S&S.

Chaumba, Joseph, Ian Scoones, and William Wolmer. 2003a. "From *Jambanja* to *Planning*: The Reassertion of Technocracy in Land Reform in South-eastern Zimbabwe." *Journal of Modern African Studies* 41 (4): 533–54.

———. 2003b. "New Politics, New Livelihoods: Agrarian Change in Zimbabwe." *Review of African Political Economy* 30:585–608.

Chauveau, Jean-Pierre. 2000. "Question foncière et construction nationale en Côte d'Ivoire: Les enjeux silencieux d'un coup d'état." *Politique Africaine* 78 (June): 94–145.

———. 2002a. "Une lecture sociologique de la loi ivoirienne de 1998 sur le domaine foncier." L'Institut de Recherche pour le Développement (IRD), Réfo. Doc. de Travail n. 6, Unité de Recherche 095, sept. IRD working paper, Montpellier, France.

———. 2002b. "La loi ivoirienne de 1998 sur le domaine foncier rural et l'agriculture de plantation villageoise: Une mise en perspective historique et sociologique." *Land Reform/Réforme Agraire/Reforma Agraria* 2002 (1): 62–79.

Chimhowu, Admos, and Philip Woodhouse. 2006. "Vernacular Land Markets in Sub-Saharan Africa." *Journal of Agrarian Change* 6 (3): 346–71.

Citizenship of Zimbabwe Amendment Act. 2001. No. 12 of 2001, Jan.

———. 2005. (No. 17) Act, 2005 (gazetted Sept. 14).

Cliffe, Lionel, Joshua Mpofu, and Barry Munslow. 1980. "Nationalist Politics in Zimbabwe: The 1980 Elections and Beyond." *Review of African Political Economy* 7 (18): 44–67.

Coldham, Simon. 1993. "The Land Acquisition Act, 1992 of Zimbabwe." *Journal of African Law* 37 (1): 82–88.

———. 2001. "Land Acquisition Amendment Act, 2000 (Zimbabwe)." *Journal of African Law* 45 (2): 227–29.

Colin, Jean-Philippe, Georges Kouame, and Debegnoun Soro. 2008. "Outside the Autochthon-Migrant Configuration: Access to Land, Land Conflicts, and Inter-ethnic Relations in a Former Pioneer Area of Lower Côte d'Ivoire." *Journal of Modern African Studies* 45 (1): 33–59.

Crook, Richard. 1997. "Winning Coalitions and Ethno-Regional Politics: The Failure of the Opposition in the 1990 and 1995 Elections in Côte d'Ivoire." *African Affairs* 96 (383): 215–42.

Dembele, Ousmane. 2003. "Côte d'Ivoire: La Fracture Communautaire." *Politique Africaine* 89 (Mar.): 34–48.

Djébi, Valence. 1995. "Les causes du génocide rwandais sont en gestion en Côte d'Ivoire." *La Voie*, n. 1102, May 29, 2.

Dozon, J. P. 1985. *La société Bété*. Paris: Karthala.

———. 2000. "La Côte d'Ivoire entre démocratie, nationalisme, et ethnonationalisme." *Politique Africaine* 78 (June): 45–62.

Economist Intelligence Unit (EIU). 2000. *Country Profile 2000. Zimbabwe*. London: EIU.

Etou, César, and Bamba F. Mamadou. 1995. "Incidents survenus lors de l'élection presidentielle à Gagnoa, Guibéroua et Bayota: 10 morts, 10.000 déplacés dans un conflit stupide." *La Voie*, n. 1232, Nov. 2, 6–7, 10.

Fauré, Yves. 1993. "Democracy and Realism: Reflections on the Case of Côte d'Ivoire." *Africa* 63 (3): 313–29.

Gazetted Land (Consequential Provisions) Act. 2006. Chapter 20:28 Act 8/2006.

Gyimah-Boadi, Emmanuel, and Cyril Daddieh. 1999. "Economic Reform and Political Liberalization in Ghana and Côte d'Ivoire: A Preliminary Assessment and Implications for Nation-Building." In *State Building and Democratization in Africa*, ed. Kidane Mengisteab and Cyril Daddieh. Westport, CT: Praeger.

Hammar, Amanda, JoAnn McGregor, and Lauren Landau. 2010. "Introduction. Displacing Zimbabwe: Crisis and Construction in Southern Africa." *Journal of Southern African Studies* 36 (2): 263–83.

Harold-Barry, David. 2004. "Chronology." In *The Past Is the Future*, ed. David Harold-Barry, 261–73. Harare: Weaver Press.

Hatchard, John. 2001. "Some Lessons on Constitution-Making from Zimbabwe." *Journal of African Law* 45 (2): 210–16.

Human Rights Watch (HRW). 2001. "The New Racism: The Political Manipulation of Ethnicity in Côte d'Ivoire." Human Rights Country Report 13, no. 6 (A), Aug.

———. 2002. "Zimbabwe: Fast Track Land Reform in Zimbabwe." Report, vol. 14, no. 1 (A). Mar. www.hrw.org/legacy/reports/2002/zimbabwe/.

———. 2003. "Côte d'Ivoire: Trapped between Two Wars: Violence against Civilians in Western Côte d'Ivoire." Vol. 15, no. 14 (A), Aug. 6. www.hrw.org/reports/2003/08/05/trapped-between-two-wars.

———. 2007. "Côte d'Ivoire: 'My Heart Is Cut.' Sexual Violence by Rebels and Pro-Government Forces in Côte d'Ivoire." Report, vol. 19, no. 11 (A), Aug. www.hrw.org/reports/2007/08/02/my-heart-cut.

International Crisis Group (ICG). 2003. "Côte d'Ivoire: 'The War Is Not Yet Over.'" Africa Report no. 72, Nov. 28. www.crisisgroup.org/en/regions/africa/west-africa/cote-divoire/072-cote-divoire-the-war-is-not-yet-over.aspx.

———. 2004a. "Blood and Soil: Land, Politics and Conflict Prevention in Zimbabwe and South Africa." Africa Report no. 85, ICG. www.crisisgroup.org/en/

regions/africa/southern-africa/~/media/Files/africa/southern-africa/Blood %20and%20Soil/contents_foreword_and_executive_summary.ashx.

———. 2004b. "Côte d'Ivoire: Pas de paix en vue." Africa Report no. 82, July 12. www.crisisgroup.org/fr/regions/afrique/afrique-de-louest/cote-divoire/082-cote-divoire-no-peace-in-sight.aspx.

———. 2005. "Côte d'Ivoire: Les demi-mesures ne suffiront pas." Briefing Afrique n. 33, Oct. 12. www.crisisgroup.org/fr/regions/afrique/afrique-de-louest/cote-divoire/B033-cote-divoire-halfway-measures-will-not-suffice.aspx.

International Monetary Fund (IMF). 2005. *International Financial Statistics Yearbook*. Washington, DC: IMF.

International Monetary Fund (IMF) and International Development Association (IDA). 2002. "Côte d'Ivoire: Enhanced Initiative for Heavily Indebted Poor Countries (HIPC)." Mar. 12.

IRIN. 2008. "Zimbabwe: New Land Owners Face Eviction." Feb. 11. www.irinnews.org/Report.aspx?ReportId=76682.

———. 2009. "Côte d'Ivoire: Clearing the Highest Hurdle—National Identity." Jan. 22. www.irinnews.org/Report/82523/COTE-D-IVOIRE-Clearing-the-highest-hurdle-national-identity.

Juul, Kristine, and Christian Lund, eds. 2002. *Negotiating Property in Africa*. Portsmouth, NH: Heinemann.

Kinsey, Bill. 2010. "Who Went Where . . . and Why: Patterns and Consequences of Displacement in Rural Zimbabwe after February 2000." *Journal of Southern African Studies* 36 (2): 339–60.

Klopp, Jacqueline. 2002. "Can Moral Ethnicity Trump Political Tribalism? The Struggle for Land and Nation in Kenya." *African Studies* 61 (2): 269–94.

Koné, Mariatou. 2002. "Gaining Rights of Access to Land in West-Central Côte d'Ivoire." Working paper, International Institute for Environment and Development (IIED) and Groupe de recherche et d'échanges technologiques (GRET), Mar.

———. 2006. "Quelles lois pour résoudre les problèmes liés au foncier en Côte d'Ivoire?" *Grain de Sel: Inter-réseaux développement rural* 36 (Sept.–Nov.). www.inter-reseaux.org.

Kriger, Norma. 2005. "ZANU(PF) Strategies in General Elections, 1980–2000: Discourse and Coercion." *African Affairs* 104 (414): 1–34.

———. 2007. "Liberation from Constitutional Constraints: Land Reform in Zimbabwe." *SAIS Review of International Affairs* 27 (2): 63–76.

La Voie. 1995a. "Comme les principes de la race aryenne d'Hitler: L'Ivoirité fait des victimes." N. 1040, Mar. 13, 2.

———. 1995b. "Le mensonge rattrapé." N. 1239, Nov. 10, 2.

———. 1995c. "M. Henri Dassé, Député FPI (A propos du conflit Bété-Baoulé): Il faut éviter que les Baoulé partent de Gagnoa." N. 1233, Nov. 3, 5.

Lamb, Christine. 2007. *House of Stone: The True Story of a Family Divided in War-Torn Zimbabwe.* Chicago: Lawrence Hill.

Land Review Committee. 2003. *Report of Presidential Land Review Committee on the Implementation of the Fast Track Land Reform Programme, 2000–2002 ("The Utete Report").* Zimbabwe: Government of Zimbabwe. www.kubatana.net/docs/landr/plrc_utete_report_0310.pdf.

Lewis, Barbara. 1980. "Ethnicity and Occupational Specialization in the Ivory Coast: The Transporters' Association." In *Values, Identities, and National Integration,* ed. John N. Paden, 75–87. Evanston, IL: Northwestern Univ. Press.

————. 2003. "Citizens or Strangers: Ivoirian Land Law and the Succession Crisis." Paper presented at the annual meeting of the African Studies Association, Boston.

Lynch, Gabrielle. 2008. "Courting the Kalenjin: The Failure of Dynasticism and the Strength of the ODM Value in Kenya's Rift Valley Province." *African Affairs* 107 (429): 541–68.

Marshall-Fratani, Ruth. 2006. "The War of 'Who Is Who?': Autochthony, Nationalism, and Citizenship in the Ivoirian Crisis." *African Studies Review* 49 (2): 9–43.

McAuslan, Patrick. 1998. "Making Law Work: Restructuring Land Relations in Africa." *Development and Change* 29 (3): 525–52.

McGreal, Chris, and Ewen MacAskill. 2002. "Mugabe Victory Leaves West's Policy in Tatters." *Guardian* (UK), Mar. 13. www.guardian.co.uk/world/2002/mar/14/zimbabwe.chrismcgreal.

Moyo, Sam. 1986. "The Land Question." In *Zimbabwe: The Political Economy of Transition 1980–1986,* ed. Ibbo Mandaza, 165–202. Dakar, Senegal: Codesria.

————. 2000. "The Interaction of Market and Compulsory Land Acquisition Processes with Social Action in Zimbabwe's Land Reform." Paper presented at the Sapes Trust Annual Colloquium on Regional Integration: Past, Present and Future, Harare.

Moyo, Sam, and Paris Yeros. 2005. "Land Occupations and Land Reform in Zimbabwe: Towards the National Democratic Revolution." In *Reclaiming the Land: The Resurgence of Rural Movements in Africa, Asia and Latin America,* ed. Sam Moyo and Paris Yeros, 165–208. London: Zed.

————. 2007. "The Radicalized State: Zimbabwe's Interrupted Revolution." *Review of Political Economy* 34 (111): 103–21.

Mumbengegwi, Clever. 1986. "Continuity and Change in Agricultural Policy." In *Zimbabwe: The Political Economy of Transition, 1980–1986,* ed. Sam Moyo and Paris Yeros, 203–22. Dakar, Senegal: Codesria.

N'Diaye, Boubacar. 2005. "Côte d'Ivoire: The Miracle That Wasn't, Flawed Civil-Military Relations, and Missed Opportunity." In *Not Yet Democracy: West Africa's Slow Farewell to Authoritarianism,* ed. Boubacar N'Diaye, Abdoulave S. Saine, and Mathurin C. Houngnikpo, 19-50. Durham, NC: Carolina Academic Press.

Norwegian Refugee Council (NRC). 2009a. *Internal Displacement. Global Overview of Trends and Developments in 2008.* Geneva: NRC Internal Displacement Monitoring Center. www.internal-displacement.org/8025708F004BE3B1/ (httpInfoFiles)/82DA6A2DE4C7BA41C12575A90041E6A8/$file/IDMC_Internal_Displacement_Global_Overview_2008.pdf.

————. 2009b. "Whose Land Is This? Land Disputes and Forced Displacement in the Western Forest Area of Côte d'Ivoire." Oct. www.internal-displacement. org.

————. 2010. *Internal Displacement: Global Overview of Trends and Developments in 2009.* Geveva: NRC.

Oucho, J. O. 2002. *Undercurrents of Ethnic Conflict in Kenya.* Leiden, Netherlands: Brill.

Ploch, Lauren. 2009. *Zimbabwe.* Congressional Research Service Report for Congress. 1 April, 7-5700, RL32723. Washington, DC: Congressional Research Service. http://assets.opencrs.com/rpts/RL32723.20090401.pdf.

Raftopoulos, Brian, and Ian Phimister. 2004. "Zimbabwe Now: The Political Economy of Crisis and Coercion." *Historical Materialism* 12 (4): 355–82.

Research and Advocacy Unit (RAU). 2008. "Reckless Tragedy: Irreversible?" Justice for Agriculture (JAG) and General Agricultural and Plantation Workers Union of Zimbabwe (GAPWUZ). www.kubatana.net/docs/landr/jag_gapwuz_reckless_tragedy_hr_viol_081212.pdf.

Reuters. 2000. "Zimbabwe's Mugabe Urges Blacks to 'Strike Fear in Heart of White Man.'" *CNN.com,* Dec. 14. http://archives.cnn.com/2000/WORLD/africa/12/14/mugabe.zimbabwe/.

Rutherford, Blair. 2001. "Commercial Farm Workers and the Politics of (Dis) placement in Zimbabwe: Colonialism, Liberation and Democracy." *Journal of Agrarian Change* 1 (4): 626–51.

————. 2007. "Shifting Grounds in Zimbabwe: Citizenship and Farm Workers in the New Politics of Land." In *Making Nations, Creating Strangers: States and Citizenship in Africa,* ed. Sara Dorman, Daniel Patrick Hammett, and Paul Nugent, 105–22. Leiden, Netherlands: Brill.

Sachikonye, Lloyd M. 2003a. "From 'Growth with Equity' to 'Fast-Track' Reform: Zimbabwe's Land Question." *Review of African Political Economy* 96 (30): 227–40.

————. 2003b. "The Situation of Commercial Farm Workers after Land Reform in Zimbabwe." Report for the Farm Community Trust of Zimbabwe. www.kubatana.net/docs/landr/fctz_farm_workers_0305.pdf.

Sadomba, Wilbert Z. 2008. War Veterans in Zimbabwe's Land Occupations: Complexities of a Liberation Movement in an African Post-Colonial Settler Society. PhD diss., Wageningen Univ., Netherlands.

Scarnecchia, Tim. 2006. "The 'Fascist Cycle' in Zimbabwe, 2000–2005." *Journal of Southern African Studies* 32 (2): 221–37.

Scheuer, Benoît. 2002. "La xénophobie submerge la Côte d'Ivoire." Document posted on the Web site of Prevention Genocides, Jan. 2001. (www.prevention-genocides.org/fr/campagne/textes/rapnov2000.pdf.

Schwartz, Alfred. 2000. "Le conflit foncier entre Krou et Burkinabè: à la lumière de l'institution krouman." *Afrique Contemporaine* 193 (1): 56–66.

Selby, Angus. 2006. Commercial Farmers and the State: Interest Group Politics and Land Reform in Zimbabwe. PhD diss., Univ. of Oxford.

Shaw, William H. 2003. " 'They Stole Our Land': Debating the Expropriation of White Farms in Zimbabwe." *Journal of Modern African Studies* 41 (1): 75–89.

Sindzingre, Alice. 2000. "Le contexte économique et sociale du changement politique en Côte d'Ivoire." *Afrique Contemporaine* 193 (1): 27–37.

Smith, Stephen. 2003. "La politique d'engagement de la France à l'épreuve de la Côte d'Ivoire." *Politique Africaine* 89 (Mar.): 112–26.

Solidarity Peace Trust. 2008a. *Punishing Dissent, Silencing Citizens: The Zimbabwe Elections 2008*. Johannesburg, May 21. www.solidaritypeacetrust.org/download/report-files/punish_and_silence.pdf.

———. 2008b. *Desperately Seeking Sanity: What Prospects for a New Beginning in Zimbabwe?* July 29. www.solidaritypeacetrust.org/download/report-files/desperately_seeking_sanity.pdf.

Strozeski, Joshua. 2006. The Role of Land Ownership in Localized Conflicts between Bété and Burkinabé Households in the Central Western Forest Regions of Côte d'Ivoire. PhD diss., Howard Univ.

Thaker, Prathiba. 2008. EIU economist, e-mail exchange with author, Dec. 8.

Toulmin, Camilla, and Julian Quan. 2000. "Registering Customary Rights." In *Evolving Land Rights, Policy and Tenure in Africa*, ed. Camilla Toulmin and Julian Quan, 209–12. London: DFID/IIED/NRI.

United Nations Development Programme (UNDP). 2002. "Zimbabwe. Land Reform and Resettlement: Assessment and Suggested Framework for the Future." UNDP Interim Mission Report, Jan. www.eisa.org.za/PDF/zimland reform.pdf.

Van de Walle, Nicolas. 2001. *African Economies and the Politics of Permanent Crisis, 1979–1999*. Cambridge, UK: Cambridge Univ. Press.

Waeterloos, Evert, and Blair Rutherford. 2004. "Land Reform in Zimbabwe: Challenges and Opportunities for Poverty Reduction among Commercial Farm Workers." *World Development* 32 (3): 537–53.

Woods, Dwayne. 2003. "The Tragedy of the Cocoa-Pod: Rent-Seeking, Land, and Ethnic Conflict in Ivory Coast." *Journal of Modern African Studies* 41 (4): 641–56.

Xinhua News Agency. 2000. "Zimbabwean Ruling Party Unveils Election Manifesto." Mar. 23. www.zimbabwesituation.com/march23.html.

Yevou, Marc. 2004. "Débats sur la nationalité: Les partis se radicalisent." *Fraternité Matin*, July 15. www.allafrica.com/stories, 200407150294.html.

Zimbabwe Human Rights (ZHR) NGO Forum. 2002. "Human Rights and Zimbabwe's Presidential Election: March 2002." Special Report, Harare: ZHR NGO Forum. wwwhrforumzim.com/frames/inside_frame_special.htm.

Zimbabwe Human Rights (ZHR) NGO Forum and the Justice for Agriculture (JAG) Trust. 2007. *Adding Insult to Injury.* "A Preliminary Report on Human Rights Violations on Commercial Farms, 2000 to 2005." ZHR NGO Forum and JAG Trust, June. www.kubatana.net/docs/hr/hrf_hr_violations_farms_070616.pdf.

5

Postelection Political Agreements in Togo and Zanzibar

Temporary Measures for Stopping Electoral Violence?

Dorina A. Bekoe

In chapter 2, Straus and Taylor's pioneering work shows that just 10 percent of all cases of electoral violence in sub-Saharan Africa are of the violent kind experienced by Kenya after its 2007 elections. The month of violence killed 1,500 people and displaced 300,000. These few cases tend to steal all the attention on elections in Africa and attract the involvement of the international and regional communities in breaking the cycle of electoral violence. In some cases of intense electoral violence, little was done to punish the perpetrators, compensate the victims, or try to understand the root and proximate causes. In a handful of cases, however—Kenya included—the opposing political parties entered into a power-sharing arrangement after the violence. These postelection political agreements (PPAs) are a bid to resolve the underlying drivers of conflict and prevent future violence. Indeed, given that electoral violence has been cyclical in several cases in Straus and Taylor's study—suggesting that unresolved grievances resurface during elections and fuel violence— it seems appropriate to treat these extreme cases by tackling their root causes. Moreover, with the growing recognition of the *responsibility to protect*, which calls for intervention in cases where the national government

117

is committing or allowing humanitarian atrocities, there is an increasing call to put a stop to electoral violence (which was arguably a factor in the international response to Kenya).

PPAs aim to identify the factors that drove the violence and the accompanying institutional and structural factors that need reforming. But it is not clear what impact these agreements have on future episodes of electoral violence, or whether they actually result in reducing it. Moreover, the intervention with a power-sharing agreement raises an important threat of moral hazard: does a power-sharing agreement "reward" the perpetrators of violence, sending a message that violence pays, increasing the chance that election results will be violently disputed? The early offer by the former president of Côte d'Ivoire, Laurent Gbagbo, to enter into a power-sharing arrangement with internationally recognized presidential election winner Alassane Ouattara suggests that this may have been the case in Côte d'Ivoire. Regional and international mediators adamantly refused to allow a discussion of power sharing. Tragically, the violence in Côte d'Ivoire continued for four months, taking three thousand lives and displacing a million people, before the pro-Ouattara forces, with considerable help from French and UN forces, put an end to it by taking control of Abidjan and arresting Gbagbo. Thus, an important question for policymakers who must decide quickly on how to address cases speedily degenerating into violence is how to stop the violence without rewarding those who fomented it. In other words, if power sharing must be arranged to stop electoral violence, what will be the cost to a country's democratization process, which has as its most basic tenet to award the office to the winner? This chapter evaluates the conditions under which PPAs can succeed in breaking the cycle of violence.

Although Kenya and Zimbabwe have received much attention, they are only the latest among a handful of countries that have tried to address electoral violence through PPAs. PPAs have also been signed in Lesotho (1999), Togo (2006), and Zanzibar (1999 and 2001). A power-sharing agreement was also proposed after the first round of presidential elections in Angola in 1992 and after the electoral standoff in Madagascar in 2002. As table 5.1 shows, PPAs range from being very limited, specific arrangements to containing broad provisions of reform.

All the agreements in table 5.1 involve a degree of joint governance, and each focuses on different issues of reforms. They begin to differentiate themselves, however, when addressing justice for victims and breaking the cycle of violence. In this regard, of the five agreements noted above, Lesotho's is among the least comprehensive, focusing narrowly on the electoral system's need for reform, while Kenya's and Zimbabwe's feature a more comprehensive approach that targets historical, institutional, and struc-

Table 5.1 Variation in PPAs, from Least Comprehensive (Lesotho) to Most Comprehensive (Zimbabwe)

Key Tasks/Reforms in PPAs	Lesotho	Zanzibar	Togo	Kenya	Zimbabwe
Joint Governance Structures					
Interparty process/government of national unity	x	x	x	x	x
Broad Institutional Reforms					
Revision of the constitution	x	x	x	x	x
Depoliticization of institutions	x	x			x
Security sector reform			x		x
Judicial reform		x	x		
Media reform		x	x		
Devolution of power				x	
Addressing Election-Related Offenses					
Reform of electoral commission and processes	x	x	x	x	
Ending of political harassment	x	x	x		x
Repatriation of refugees/assistance to victims		x	x	x	x
Inquiry into the electoral violence		x	x	x	x
Level political playing field	x				x
Justice					
Punish electoral offenses			x	x	x
Addressing Deeper Causes of Conflict					
Correction of long-standing grievances				x	x
Creation of ethnic/social reconciliation processes				x	x
Promotion of economic growth and youth employment				x	x

tural sources of violence. While it is still too early to assess whether the more comprehensive agreements signed in Kenya and Zimbabwe have affected electoral violence, lessons may be gleaned from the early agreements in Togo and Zanzibar, which are also relatively comprehensive, reflecting the moderate trend in similar agreements.

This chapter examines the impact that the agreements in Togo and Zanzibar have had on the overall electoral environment in those countries. An improved electoral environment includes not just a reduction in electoral violence but also an explicit choice by politicians to eschew violence as a means of securing a win, and to resolve electoral conflicts using existing institutions rather than calls to arms, which increase the chances of violence.

Improving the Electoral Environment

Three distinctive attributes characterize PPAs: power-sharing arrangements, international involvement, and a program of key reforms. Of these, the hallmark is the creation of some type of power-sharing arrangement, as seen in table 5.1.

PPAs can have varying degrees of power sharing. Arrangements between contentious political parties could include a combination of joint membership in committees, joint monitoring activities, and the administration of a national unity government. Much of the rationale for creating power-sharing arrangements in the wake of a problematic election finds its roots in the conflict resolution literature. In postconflict settings, power-sharing arrangements are attractive because they are seen to redress grievances of political, economic, or social marginalization (Lijphart 1990; Horowitz 1985). Indeed, power sharing is typically advised in cases of ethnic conflicts or divisions (Zartman 1998). In some cases, such as Lebanon, power sharing is an enduring institutional arrangement; in others, such as Liberia and the Democratic Republic of Congo, it is a transitional arrangement. Inviting warring parties to share power is also thought to reduce the chance of spoilers in the peace process, since all members of the power-sharing arrangement have a stake in belonging to the new political dispensation (Stedman 1997).

Beyond the rationale of addressing the roots of a conflict or satisfying insurgents' demands, creating institutions of joint governance or administration also draws on the literature showing that cooperation (for peace, in this case) may increase with increased interactions between the parties (Axelrod 1984; Schelling 1980). Repeated interactions may provide opportunities to resolve tension before it escalates into a violent clash, may dispel rumors, and, finally, may demonstrate the political commitment to work on resolving the conflict.

What type of power is shared matters greatly. If power is not shared meaningfully or equally—meaning that one side is left with relatively less political power—then the power-sharing arrangement may dissolve. Research conducted by Hartzell (1999) shows that peace agreements with institutional arrangements to guarantee security and the redistribution of political and economic power are likely to result in a more durable peace than are those without such arrangements. A more sinister consequence is the possibility that power sharing may result in more conflict: as groups view participation in government as their reward for threatening violence, the power-sharing arrangement may encourage splinter groups vying for their own seats in government; or the majority group may begin to lament that too much power is being shared (Tull and Mehler 2005; Atlas and Licklider 1999). In both Togo and Zanzibar, dissatisfaction with the power being shared led to the main opposition groups' withdrawal from the PPA process.

Inducements from the international community and the enactment of credible reforms can provide incentives to adhere to the terms of the PPA

Figure 5.1 Key Variables Affecting the Electoral Environment

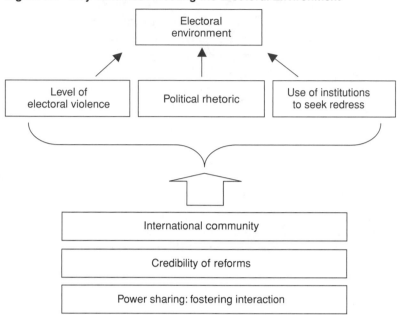

and refrain from violence. International organizations routinely condition aid on specific political outcomes—a strategy that has been applied to elections as well. For example, several international donors withheld development assistance to Ethiopia in protest of the regime's violent response to protestors against the 2005 parliamentary elections.

Undertaking credible institutional reforms can also lead to more peaceful elections. Often, opposition groups opt to seek redress through street protests because existing institutions are considered politically biased against them. For example, Raila Odinga, who was declared the loser of the 2007 Kenyan presidential election, justified his call for street protests by pointing to the perceived bias in Kenya's judicial system. Thus, for reform to be credible, the main opposition groups must regard the ruling party's actions as a sign of the political will to increase the transparency and objectivity of state institutions.

This chapter will evaluate the effects that the international community, the credibility of reforms, and the power-sharing arrangements have on the electoral environment. As figure 5.1 shows, those effects are evidenced by the level of electoral violence, the political leaders' willingness to seek redress through institutions, and the political parties' commitment to holding peaceful elections.

Overview of Togo and Zanzibar

Although both Togo and Zanzibar have instituted multiple PPAs to address electoral and political violence, this chapter will focus on the Togo 2006 and Zanzibar 2001 agreements. In Togo's case, the Comprehensive Political Accord (known by its French acronym, APG), signed in August 2006, is the twelfth attempt since 1990 at political dialogue between Togolese political opposition forces and the ruling party. Togo had experienced political instability since its transition to multiparty politics, and violence had occurred during nearly every electoral period. But the APG distinguishes itself in being a direct outgrowth of the intense violence of the 2005 presidential election period, and it is thus the focus of this chapter. Similarly, Zanzibar's first Muafaka Accord was signed in 1999, after the flawed 1995 elections. This accord remained largely unimplemented until the violence after the 2000 general elections precipitated a second agreement, Muafaka II, which is the focus of this chapter. Thus, in each case, the agreements studied are those reached after elections turned violent.

While the elections following both Togo's and Zanzibar's PPAs were less violent, there were qualitative differences between the two countries. A review of the experiences of both reveals that incentives from the international community and the interaction between the political parties were key determinants in whether the political actors toned down incendiary rhetoric, chose to protest results through institutions rather than in the streets, and urged their supporters to eschew violence.

In Togo, the European Union (EU) conditioned its reengagement of developmental assistance—which would have triggered reengagement of other international development assistance—on the organization of free, fair, and transparent legislative elections. In contrast with the 2010 presidential elections in Togo and the 2005 general elections in Zanzibar, where the international donor community placed no such conditions, the 2007 legislative elections in Togo were peaceful and adhered to international standards. Arguably, the promise of international aid influenced the political rhetoric and choices. In Togo's legislative elections, the political parties emphasized the need for a peaceful campaign, respect for the electoral process, and use of the existing institutions to redress electoral conflicts. In Zanzibar, on the other hand, the electoral period was characterized by insecurity, harassment and violence, a four-year boycott of the parliament by the losing (opposition) party, and a threat of postelection street violence by the opposition party.

Meaningful power-sharing structures also made a difference. In Togo in 2006, the structure designed to foster sustained interaction, namely the Comité de Suivi, met regularly to monitor implementation of the agreement, serving as a platform for the long-standing opposition group's active participation in the transitional government and thereby defusing tension. In Zanzibar's 2005 general elections and Togo's 2010 presidential election, this was not the case. Zanzibar's Joint Presidential Supervisory Committee barely met, and the Togolese main opposition group withdrew from the electoral commission, the intraparty dialogue process, and the national assembly. The resulting electoral environment in both countries was markedly more tense and violent than in Togo in 2007.

Finally, the credibility of the reform process is important. Opposition groups in particular must be convinced that the ruling party is committed to political reform. Thus, failure to make substantial and irreversible progress on reform during the periods between elections will eventually erode the gains made by the international community or intraparty structures to foster cooperation for peaceful elections, increasing the chance for continued violence during elections. In both Togo and Zanzibar, the opposition groups concluded that the government was not committed to reform, and this contributed to continued violence and protest during subsequent elections.

Togo

Background to Electoral Violence

Until recently, nearly all of Togo's elections since the adoption of multiparty democracy in 1991 have been accompanied by violence and boycotts by the political opposition. Indeed, Togo's elections have resulted in some of the deadliest incidents of violence in sub-Saharan Africa.[1] In January 1994, nearly 600 people died, some 500 of them civilians caught in the crossfire during clashes between Togolese security forces and dissidents who attacked from Ghana with the aim of overthrowing President Gnassingbé Eyadéma (U.S. State Dept. 1995). Most recently, before and after the 2005 presidential elections, between 400 and 800 Togolese and foreigners were killed when security forces and militants of the ruling party retaliated against opposition members demonstrating against elections that they claimed were fraudulent and unconstitutionally organized.[2] Smaller numbers of people were killed in 1993 and 2003.

---

1. The tally of electoral violence is the number of fatalities measured from three months before until three months after an election. Forms of electoral violence that do not result in fatalities are left out of this calculation.

2. The United Nations Office of the High Commissioner for Human Rights (OHCHR) estimates that 400 to 500 were killed, while the Ligue Togolaise des Droits de l'Homme (LTDH) estimates that 800 were killed (UN OHCHR 2005a, 18–22; 2005b).

After the 1993 legislative contest, the EU withdrew financial support to Togo, citing electoral irregularities and a "democratic deficit" (Gilmore 2006). In 2004, after more than ten years of sanctions, President Gnassingbé Eyadéma began talks with the EU for renewed diplomatic and development relations. Renewed relations would be conditioned on the fulfillment of twenty-two commitments that included holding credible legislative elections, promises of institutional reform, broadening political participation, ending impunity for crimes against humanity, and critical electoral reforms (European Parliament 2007b).

2005 Electoral Violence: Precursor to the APG

Talks between Togo and the EU over the renewal of development assistance were under way when Eyadéma, in power since 1965, died in 2005 (Roberts 2008). The ensuing electoral violence was Togo's worst yet. The origins of the 2005 postelection violence lay in the unconstitutional manner in which President Eyadéma's son, Faure Gnassingbé, was installed as president. According to the constitution, in the event of a presidential vacancy, the speaker of the house, Fambaré Natchaba Ouattara, was to serve as interim president, and elections were to take place within sixty days. Instead, the speaker, who was traveling at the time, was prevented from reentering the country, and Gnassingbé was sworn in as president after the constitution was hastily changed for this purpose. There was an immediate outcry from the regional and international communities. The Economic Community of West African States (ECOWAS) suspended Togo's membership. Protests from the political opposition led to clashes with security forces, resulting in several deaths, injuries, and arrests (LTDH 2005, 13–33; UN OHCHR 2005a, 14–15).

Under pressure, the Togolese government decided to hold presidential elections in April 2005. After Gnassingbé was declared the winner, the main opposition party, the Union des Forces de Changement (UFC), exhorted its supporters to take to the streets to protest the results, which it viewed as fraudulent and manipulated by the government. In the ensuing clashes with security agents and in attacks by state security agents and groups affiliated with the ruling Rassemblement du Peuple Togolais (RPT), many more lost their lives. In the end, the tally of Togolese and foreigners killed before and after the presidential election totaled about 500, according to the United Nations. The Ligue Togolaise des Droits de l'Homme (LTDH) estimated the death toll at just under 800 (UN OHCHR 2005b).

Given that past violence has been tied to disputes over the validity of results and to the belief that the government manipulated the process, preventing future electoral violence lay in improving the reliability of election results and reducing the chances of fraud. For Togo, this meant not only reforming the Constitutional Court, which validates the elections, but also investing it with credibility such that aggrieved political parties would seek redress through the courts rather than in the streets. To reduce fraud, the Electoral Commission, or Commission Electorale Nationale Indépendant (CENI), had to be made stronger, independent, and transparent. Finally, the security forces had to be retrained in how to protect rather than attack the population.

Comprehensive Political Accord

In light of the violence following the 2005 presidential elections, the EU decided to continue withholding development assistance and pressured the government to negotiate with the political opposition (Roberts 2008, 559). In August 2006, the Togolese government, five opposition parties, and two civil society representatives signed the APG, following a mediation process facilitated in Ouagadougou by Burkinabè president Blaise Compaoré. Conforming to the twenty-two commitments agreed to during the rapprochement talks in 2004, a key factor in restoring development assistance was the organization of free and fair legislative elections. To that end, the APG promised electoral reform, a revised voters' list, revised rules on managing challenges or grievances with the electoral process, a census-based redistricting of voting constituencies, regulation of political party financing, and equitable access to the media (APG 2007, sect. 1). In addition, the government, political opposition, and civil society agreed to enact reforms to the constitution, the judicial sector, the security sector, the media, and the electoral commission in a bid to prevent the recurrence of violence in future elections.

Since mistrust lay at the root of the grievances cited by political parties, perhaps the most important aspects of the APG were the number of interactions (degree of power sharing) that it promised between the government, the political opposition, and civil society. The APG promised to usher in a new spirit of collaboration through the formation of a government of national unity (GNU), a committee (Comité de Suivi) that would supervise implementation of the APG, and a framework for dialogue between the opposition and the ruling party (Cadre Permanent du Dialogue, or CPD). Key reforms included an expanded CENI, which would include opposition groups. Equally important was the stipulation that in the event of differing interpretations of the APG, Compaoré would act as the arbiter (APG 2007, sect. 5.8).

These structures and procedures facilitated collaboration in administering the elections and managing some of the necessary reforms and invested the signatories in staying in the peace process, thus helping reduce the incentives for violence during the electoral period. Consequently, politicians emphasized nonviolence and chose to seek redress through the courts, the security forces were restrained, and electoral violence was not a factor, all of which improved the electoral environment.

Fostering Interaction

The APG provided two main avenues through which the opposition, civil society, and the ruling party could interact to monitor implementation of the agreement and work toward fulfilling the transition process: the government of national unity and the Comité de Suivi.

Government of National Unity. The GNU was tasked with, among other things, implementing the APG, speeding the reintegration of the refugees who fled the 2005 violence, seeing that the security forces acted within the constraints of the law, and working toward the reengagement of development partners and the implementation of the twenty-two commitments with the EU (APG 2007, annex II).

All the signatories of the APG, except the UFC, chose to become members of the GNU. The UFC was not opposed to the concept of a unity government but felt that the government did not adequately consult the political parties on the choice of prime minister, the government's capacity to correct past injustices, and an equitable distribution of ministries. Instead, the UFC noted, the RPT controlled the majority of the ministries (twenty out of thirty-five). Some members of the UFC, notably Gnassingbé Amah, the UFC's second vice-president and one of the party's founders, joined the GNU in their individual capacities. The UFC promptly dissociated itself from him (UFC 2006, 2007a; Dzikodo 2006).

Comité de Suivi. The Comité de Suivi (CS) served as the most important institution to emerge from the APG, and one of the main reasons for the UFC's signing of the agreement (UFC 2007a). All signatories were members of the CS, which met monthly from November 2006 to August 2007 in Ouagadougou, Burkina Faso, under the leadership of Burkinabè president Compaoré, to assess the APG's progress. The CS provided guidance for the decision-making process at the CENI and called for weekly meetings between the government, the CENI, the EU, UN Development Programme (UNDP), and other development partners; sought to improve the communication between the CENI and the Togolese voting public by holding more press conferences; and made recommendations about using digital photos on voters' identity cards (CDPA 2006, 2007b, 2007c; Aziadouvo 2007).

Despite the importance attached to the CS, the UFC voiced much criticism about its decisions and role. One of the most controversial decisions was the CS's outline for how the CENI should make decisions in order to avoid a blockage. Specifically, the CS decided that if the CENI should

Table 5.2 Composition of the CENI in 2005 and 2007

CENI 2005	CENI 2007
1 magistrate*	5 RPT*
5 RPT*	2 UFC
2 moderate opposition*	2 Parti pour la Démocracie et le Renouveau (PDR)*
3 traditional opposition	2 Comite d'Action pour le Renouveau (CAR)
1 civil society representative*	2 Convergence Patriotique Panafricaine (CPP)*
1 civil society representative	2 Convention Démocratique des Peuples Africains (CDPA)
	1 Group de Réflexion et d'Action Femmes, Démocratie et Développement (indep. civil society org.)
	1 Réseau des Femmes Africaines Ministres et Parlementaires/Togo (REFAMP/T)*
	2 government representatives*
Total: 13	Total: 19 (17 voting members)
Government bias: 9/13	Government bias: 12/19 (10/17 voting members)

Source: IRI, IFES, and NDI 2005, 10 (2005 data); European Parliament 2007a, 3 (2007 data).
*Supporters of government's view.

fail to reach consensus (the preferred strategy), the CS would undertake two rounds of voting to arrive at a decision (CDPA 2007a). The UFC denounced this decision by the CS a few days later, saying that it violated the APG's requirement that the facilitator, President Compaoré, should decide all cases where decisions could not be reached by consensus. The UFC noted that because RPT members were in the majority in the CENI, decisions reached by two rounds of voting would likely represent the RPT views; thus, there would be little to encourage consensus. Also, the UFC viewed the two-round voting rule as a strategy for the RPT to control the CENI or to incorporate fraudulent practices (Aziadouvo 2007).

Despite these concerns, the UFC remained a member of the CS. It used its membership to pronounce views on various issues such as the electoral code of conduct, the persistence of impunity, delays in the delivery of identity cards, and the composition of the Constitutional Court (UFC 2007b). This indicated the UFC's commitment to remaining a member of the CS and to implementing the APG.

Key Reforms

CENI. The APG specified reforms intended to increase the representation of opposition groups in the CENI. In 2005, the CENI comprised thirteen members, nine of whom supported the government. In 2007, membership was increased to nineteen. The nineteen-member CENI included five members from the ruling party, ten from the other political parties of the APG (two each from five parties), two from civil society, and two from the government. The two from the government did not have voting rights (European Parliament 2007a, 3). Table 5.2 compares the CENI's composition in 2005 and 2007.

Still, the CENI's 2007 composition did not differ substantially from that of 2005, given that ten of the seventeen voting members ostensibly supported the government: besides the five members of the ruling party, two of the "opposition parties"—the PDR and the CPP—are considered moderate and, thus, supportive of the government's view; and one of the civil society organizations (REFAMP/T) consists of parliamentarians, who did not include the UFC, since the UFC had boycotted the legislature.

Reform of the Constitutional Court. The APG called for the recomposition of the Constitutional Court, the sole body charged with validating the results of elections and ruling on contentious issues linked to the electoral process. (The opposition and civil society had frequently criticized the Court for its bias toward the ruling party.) Although the recomposition of the Constitutional Court did take place, the political opposition and civil society were not at all pleased with the results. In particular, they criticized the selection of three of the six new members for their past membership on the Court. The opposition and civil society members charged that the presence of three previous members continued to bias the Court in favor of the government, and preferred to see six new members instead (Hetcheli, Ahianyo Kponzo, and Gnacadja 2007).

Thus, the UFC did not view the institutional reforms and new political arrangements as an unqualified success. Still, by all accounts and judging by its continued participation in the CS, the UFC seems to have been vested in the reforms in the run-up to the 2007 legislative elections.

Role of the International Community

The EU played a critical role in sparking and sustaining the momentum for signing a political agreement, because a key factor in restoring EU relations with Togo was political reform, including the dialogue between the ruling party and the opposition, and the organization of free and fair elections that met international standards. Indeed, the EU signaled its support of the new political framework early on, when development assistance resumed at the first meeting of the Comité de Suivi in November 2006, sending a strong signal to the Togolese parties (CDPA 2006).

In the first year after the EU's reengagement, a total of €57 million was projected to assist with eight projects encompassing a range of institutional reforms, infrastructure repairs, and debt relief. In comparison, before the meetings of the Comité de Suivi, the EU had but two projects—in the microenterprise and health sectors—totaling approximately €22 million (European Commission 2008, 23–26).

In 1990, net official development assistance (ODA) stood at US$57.3 per capita; the disengagement by the international community plunged net per capita ODA to $11.4 in 2001 (European Commission 2008, 34). The intervening years also saw a steep deterioration of other developmental indicators. By 2006, Togo was in dire need of international development assistance, and a resumption of EU engagement would pave the way for reengagement with the World Bank, the IMF, and the African Development Bank. Thus, Togo had great incentive to undertake the agreed-upon institutional reforms, and it paid off. The administration of legislative elections that were judged free and fair resulted in a 2008 conference, in Brussels, of development partners focused on Togo (European Commission 2008, 4).

The 2007 Legislative Elections

The 2007 elections handed a victory to the RPT: of the eighty-one seats in the legislature, the RPT won fifty, the UFC twenty-seven, and the CAR four (Roberts 2008, 580). The CENI noted a number of irregularities, which bolstered the UFC's claim that the results were unreliable, especially in the UFC's stronghold of Lomé. But most observer groups did not feel that the irregularities pointed out by the UFC affected the outcome of the vote (Roberts 2008, 580; UFC 2007c).

The UFC felt differently and challenged the irregularities—in the Constitutional Court rather than by staging street protests, as it had done in the past. It called for a recount, but the Court rejected this. The UFC also announced that it would boycott parliament, though it did not carry through with the threat (Roberts 2008, 580). The recourse to the Constitutional Court is significant because, in the past, the UFC had charged that the Court was too biased, and had instead taken its grievances to the streets. According to Isabelle Ameganvi, third vice president of the UFC and a member of parliament, the UFC decided to go through the Court because it felt that given the lower stakes of legislative elections, the Court would hear its case fairly. In other words, fraud and political bias in favor of the RPT would be more expected in the presidential election, where the stakes were much higher. Ameganvi pointed out that the UFC felt a measure of confidence in the Court (Ameganvi 2010). Indeed, the UFC's recourse to the Constitutional Court is not surprising, given that the UFC had signaled its intention to participate in governance by remaining in the CS despite the CS's perceived shortcomings.

The APG resulted in an improved electoral environment. Electoral violence decreased, the UFC used existing institutions to seek redress, and political parties emphasized the need for peaceful elections. The EU's em-

phasis on free and fair elections, along with the regular meetings and interactions fostered by the CS, provided incentives to organize internationally
acceptable elections and remain committed to the peace process. But the
APG did not change the underlying complaints about the system—that it
was opaque, prone to fraud, and politically biased—as seen in the UFC's
criticism of the changes in the all-important Constitutional Court. Indeed,
the APG engendered very little institutional reform. In 2010, following
Faure Gnassingbé's disputed win, the opposition coalition, Front Répub-
licain pour l'Alternance et le Changement (FRAC), called its supporters
out into the streets almost every weekend.

The 2010 Elections

In many ways, the presidential elections of 2010 would be a stronger test of
whether the APG had positively affected the Togolese electoral process. In
2010, the aspects that made cooperation possible during the APG had been
compromised: the UFC withdrew from the Cadre Permanent de Dialogue
et de Concertation (CPDC), the CENI, and the National Assembly.

The CPDC, which was a more permanent replacement for the Comité
de Suivi, had been set up in February 2009 to create a forum for the APG
signatories to meet and discuss the rights and responsibilities of the political parties and the pertinent reforms outlined in the agreement: constitutional reform, electoral reform, and equal media access by political parties
(APA News 2009). But just six weeks later, the UFC withdrew after accusing the government of trying to dilute the UFC's influence by increasing
the number of representatives in the CPDC (Ameganvi 2010).

In February 2010, weeks before the presidential polls, the UFC withdrew its representatives from the CENI, citing the government's "unilat-
eral management," the short time for the revision of the voters registry, the
choice of the company contracted to conduct the census, the involvement
of minors in the CENI's work, and failure to properly authenticate the
ballots by requiring officials to sign the ballots (*Panapress* 2010). The UFC
also complained that the RPT had not honored the agreement to make
decisions consensually but had instead used its majority status to enact
decisions according to its preferences (Ameganvi 2010).

The UFC and the CAR also withdrew from the National Assembly,
because the government pushed an amendment to retain the CENI's 2007
makeup. The UFC was opposed to retaining the 2007 CENI makeup,
claiming that the constitution did not allow it, that the commissioners'
terms had expired, and that the conditions of 2007 did not apply to 2010.
But with the RPT dominating, the amendment passed.

The withdrawal of the UFC and CAR, beyond acknowledging the RPT's inevitable power in the National Assembly (especially in the CPDC), indicated the two opposition groups' lack of support and political investment in the governing institutions. This they blamed on the absence of any spirit of cooperation by the government (Ameganvi 2010). Notably, the international community did not play the pivotal role it had in 2007, for it had already begun the resumption of development assistance after the legislative elections took place.

Comparing the 2007 and 2010 Elections

The FRAC did not wait for the official results to announce that it had won the presidency. When the CENI declared Faure Gnassingbè the winner, the FRAC proclaimed that there had been massive fraud. Unlike in 2007, the FRAC took to the streets with its protests, explicitly eschewing any recourse to the Constitutional Court (Xinhua 2010). Protests occurred weekly, once with allegedly 200,000 demonstrators (UFC Togo 2010). Fortunately, unlike in other years, the security forces did not open fire on the demonstrators, and large-scale loss of life was avoided.

What the 2010 elections tell us is that the APG could effect a change in how parties interacted and addressed their grievances in the very short term, through a temporary environment of cooperation and inclusion. But because the required institutional reforms were not enacted—the CENI and the Constitutional Court remained largely unchanged—the next election reverted to the status quo. There was insufficient impetus to enact the institutional change needed to avoid tension and violence in the medium to long term. Thus, we can see that although a PPA, by enabling parties to influence policies directly, may provide for a peaceful election in the immediate wake of its signing, it may not necessarily provide for a sustainable peace unless long-term credible institutional changes are made.

One could argue that the UFC gave the RPT the benefit of the doubt and, upon concluding that nothing had really changed, refused to continue cooperating. For the reform and peace processes to move forward, all the stakeholders must be seen as taking positive steps to ameliorate the conditions that led to violence. In Togo's case, that means a Constitutional Court with a more balanced set of magistrates, a CENI with more independence and transparency, and an accepted forum—such as the Comité de Suivi—for political parties to discuss differences. Also, the international community should consider playing a more robust role in providing incentives for a peaceful poll.

Zanzibar

Background to Electoral Violence

Although Zanzibar, comprising the islands of Pemba and Unguja, is part of Tanzania, the 1964 union government agreement that joined it to Tanganyika recognizes Zanzibar as a semiautonomous entity and entitles it to a separate parliament and president, in addition to representation by the union president and parliament.

Although elections on the mainland have happened relatively smoothly since the first multiparty election in 1995, all of Zanzibar's elections have been problematic. In each (1995, 2000, and 2005), the process has been marred by violence, inequities, and accusations of fraud. While the charges of irregularities have been leveled by both the opposition Civic United Front (CUF) and the ruling Chama Cha Mapinduzi (CCM), the CUF has been the more vocal and more aggrieved.

The violence in Zanzibar's elections was due to clashes between CCM and CUF and clashes between CUF and state security services. The rivalry is rooted in Zanzibar's history and reflects the ethnic, geographic, and economic differences between the parties' supporters. Pemba is a CUF stronghold, whereas Unguja has historically supported CCM. CUF is also tied to Zanzibar's Arabic heritage, while CCM supporters trace their lineage to the Tanzanian mainland and Zanzibar's African community. These divisions greatly polarized the island, with Pembans feeling politically and economically marginalized by the dominant CCM (Kaiser 2003, 107).

The most violent elections in Zanzibar were those of October 2000. Not only was the run-up to the polls marred by politically motivated harassment, intimidation, and assault, but in January 2001, as CUF protested that CCM had won through a flawed electoral process, security forces killed from thirty-five to sixty-seven CUF supporters.[3] Afterward, some 2,000 Zanzibaris fled to Kenya, fearing for their lives. In the wake of the violence, the Muafaka-II was signed in October 2001.[4]

Muafaka-II

The second Muafaka (which means "accord" in Swahili) reiterated the provisions of the first accord but attempted to be more binding, in a bid to avoid the fate of Muafaka-I. Broadly, Muafaka-II promised compensation to the victims of the January 2001 shooting; by-elections in sixteen CUF

---

3. Human Rights Watch (2002) verified thirty-five deaths, while CUF estimated sixty-seven. The government reported that twenty-three people were killed.

4. Muafaka-I was signed in 1999, following the protests over the 1995 polls, but was never implemented.

constituencies where logistical and material delays had prevented polling in October 2000; a timeline for implementation; and a Joint Presidential Supervisory Commission (JPSC) to oversee implementation. To confer a measure of legality, Muafaka-II was enshrined as a bill in the House of Representatives (Cameron 2002, 329).

Further, Muafaka-II committed CUF and CCM to a number of key reforms, initiatives, and principles to ensure that subsequent elections would be credible, free, and fair. Foremost among the reforms were amending Zanzibar's constitution and electoral laws to reflect the tenets of a multiparty system, and working to create an independent and professional judicial system. Reforms to the Zanzibar Electoral Commission (ZEC) included provisions to transform it into an independent and impartial entity and create a permanent voters registry. The Muafaka-II also called for reforms in the media to ensure equitable political coverage, and measures to guarantee that political activities could be conducted without fear of harassment and intimidation. Finally, Muafaka-II compelled the parties to provide redress to students, civil servants, and other citizens who had suffered violence (CCM and CUF 2001).

Although the Muafaka leaves the door open for joint government, CCM repeatedly opposed a government of national unity (CCM and CUF 2001, art. 5). Nonetheless, provisions in the accord allowed for CUF's involvement in governance. The JPSC, which would oversee implementation of the accord, would be cochaired by one representative from CUF and one from CCM. CUF and CCM would also jointly review appointments to the parliament and House of Representatives, boards of parastatals and other public institutions, diplomatic posts, and participation in official trips abroad (CCM and CUF 2001, arts. 5–12). The accord also calls for establishing a "permanent mechanism of dialogue and confidence building," and forming an "Inter-Party Consultative Committee, which shall bring together leaders of all political parties in the country" (CCM and CUF 2001, arts. 14–17).

Regarding elections specifically, the accord requires retraining of security forces to understand their duties and responsibilities in a democratic system; impartiality of state institutions; an investigation into the violence of January 26–27, 2001; release of all people detained in connection with the January events; and the return of the 2,000 Zanzibaris who fled to Kenya in the wake of the January violence (CCM and CUF 2001).

Fostering Interaction

The two most important institutions in the Muafaka-II are the JPSC and the ZEC. Together, they were meant not only to guide the country in holding more transparent, peaceful, and free elections but also to remove the imprint of political bias from governance in Zanzibar. Both institutions failed. The JPSC was unable to fulfill its very basic task of serving as a forum for CUF and CCM to discuss problems with the electoral process. ZEC could not shake its partisan nature, and CUF charged it with depriving nearly 47,000 Zanzibaris of their right to vote (IRIN 2005). Considering that the final register listed 507,000 voters, CUF's allegation amounted to a potentially decisive number of disenfranchised voters (Commonwealth Secretariat 2005, 23).

Joint Presidential Supervisory Commission

The JPSC comprised ten members (five each from CUF and CCM) and was cochaired by one representative each from CUF and CCM (CCM and CUF 2001, apps. 1, 2). The JPSC would oversee implementation of Muafaka-II; reform of ZEC, the media, and the judicial sector to institute impartiality; creation of a credible permanent voters registry; and the constitutional reform process (JPSC 2001, art. 5[1]). The decisions of the JPSC were to be reached by consensus (JPSC 2001, arts. 4[1]–5). The JPSC was voted into law by the Zanzibar House of Representatives on December 5, 2001. Ostensibly, it was felt that enshrining it into law gave it weight and importance that Muafaka-I did not have. It was also entrenched in the Zanzibar constitution through new amendments approved by the parliament (Oloka-Onyango and Nassali 2003, 20).

The first eighteen months of the JPSC were notable for the cooperation exhibited by both CUF and CCM (Ladhu 2010). The immediate task was to organize the Pemba by-elections in sixteen CUF constituencies that could not hold elections in 2000, due to logistical and material difficulties. By all accounts, the elections went well, and they were praised by observer missions. CUF viewed the success of the by-elections as evidence that it was possible to hold free and fair elections if the political will to do so existed (Ladhu 2010).

But after the Pemba by-elections, the JPSC effectively ceased to function, according to Ismail Jusa Ladhu, CUF's director for foreign relations and adviser to Seif Sharif Hamad, CUF's secretary general and presidential candidate. Indeed, in 2003, both CUF and CCM lamented the absence of cooperation on implementing the Muafaka. In fact, CUF had written to President Benjamin Mkapa four times during 2003–05, asking for a meeting to restart the Muafaka process. After CUF and CCM agreed in July 2004 to meet monthly, their first meeting was not scheduled until June 2005. But before this meeting could take place, CCM pulled out, citing an attack by CUF on the home of Jakaya Kikwete (Rawlence 2005, 518–19).

The JPSC finally met on July 3, 2005, after urging by President Mkapa. The commission discussed the current political atmosphere, the Muafaka implementation process, and the creation of an all-inclusive party committee (which would include other political parties) and explored the possibility of a power-sharing arrangement. The creation of an all-inclusive party committee took place shortly after the meeting. A follow-up meeting took place on July 16. While both CUF and CCM thought the meeting had gone well, it failed to resolve the problems and violence experienced during voter registration. It also failed to settle the lack of impartiality in ZEC, or the issue of CCM-sponsored youth camps, whose members CUF accused of committing violent acts against CUF supporters (FEWER 2005, 7). Despite the two meetings in quick succession, these efforts seem to have come too late because, before those meetings, the JPSC had not met in the past year (FEWER 2005, 10). Not surprisingly, by the time of the July 3 meeting, the JPSC was not being taken seriously, either by those following the implementation of Muafaka-II or by the JPSC members themselves. In fact, it was reported at the time that the JPSC members did not trust each other (FEWER 2005, 7). The JPSC formally ended its work in September, and elections took place in October.

The Reforms

The Muafaka-II made a number of recommendations for the reform of ZEC, with a view primarily to increasing ZEC's independence, creating a permanent voters registry (PVR), and reducing the role of the shehas, community leaders who worked with the voter registration process. The new seven-member commission was to include two commissioners recommended by the leader of government business and two recommended by CUF. Since ZEC had to make decisions by consensus, the inclusion of CUF was meant to provide an opportunity for diverse views (NDI 2005, 12). However, the operation and results of the 2005 elections show that ZEC continued to be partial to CCM. It did not respond to concerns of fraud raised by CUF or take suitable steps to make the process transparent and equitable (TEMCO 2006, 6–8).

The PVR did not unfold as planned. While it went well in the CUF stronghold of Pemba, it didn't in Unguja, which had supporters of both CCM and CUF (Rawlence 2005, 519). More problematically, ZEC did not show CUF a copy of the PVR until the day before the vote. Moreover, CUF claims that ZEC never gave it a clean copy of the PVR; the document it did provide was so disorganized, it was too difficult to analyze. This made it more difficult for CUF to determine whether the PVR was credible (CUF 2008b, 12). Furthermore, CUF claimed that 47,000 voters were "blocked from voting" (IRIN 2005). Other problems with the registration process included CUF allegations that mainlanders were being brought in to register to vote for CCM candidates. These allegations then resulted in a backlash against legitimate Zanzibari residents who had originated from the mainland (TEMCO 2006, 18).

ZEC reforms also included a reduced (though not eliminated) role for the shehas, who help identify residents of a community. In the past, shehas were seen to discriminate against CUF supporters, thus denying them the opportunity to register (TEMCO 2006, 6; Mjatvedt 2006, 10–11). The shehas were just as biased in the 2005 elections: assigned to assist the registration officers in the voter registration exercise, many shehas acted as the registration officials themselves, denying or approving voter registration applications based on whether they felt that the applicant would support CUF or CCM, and allowed the registration or multiple registration of thousands of minors and nonresidents of Zanzibar (East Africa Law Society 2005, 8–10). According to CUF, 12,000 people claimed that shehas had prevented them from registering. No action was taken to investigate these allegations (Mjatvedt 2006, 10–11; NDI 2005, 19; Commonwealth Secretariat 2005, 23).

While the international community did respond by creating a donor basket fund for implementation of the Muafaka, by and large, the international community did not offer a clear signal on the need for reform (European Commission Delegation 2004, 23). Unlike in 1995, when the donors suspended development aid to Zanzibar in protest over the flawed elections, the problematic polls in 2000 did not result in a suspension of assistance. The international community's lukewarm response to the 2000 elections may have been tied to its strong relationship with Tanzania, which many consider an oasis of peace and a model of economic reforms in a troubled region (Rawlence 2005, 522). Still others viewed CUF as an Islamic "fundamentalist" party (Cameron 2002, 328; Kaiser 2003, 116). Moreover, from CUF's point of view, the international community did not seem committed to ensuring that elections would be held in a free and fair environment (Ladhu 2010).

The 2005 and 2010 Elections

In 2005, CCM won most of the House of Representatives, with thirty seats against CUF's nineteen. Although CUF conceded that the 2005 elections were administered well in Pemba—its stronghold—it pointed to many irregularities in Unguja. Indeed, CUF's acknowledgment of ZEC's ability to manage the elections well in Pemba only strengthens the allegation that ZEC was deliberately complicit in rigging the elections in CCM's behalf:

in areas where CCM had no chance of winning, such as Pemba, ZEC organized well-managed elections with few irregularities. But in areas where CCM was more competitive, the elections were administered less transparently, with a number of irregularities (CUF 2008a). Other problems with the elections included lack of transparency surrounding transportation of ballots, counting, and collation of votes; the botched PVR process; allegations of multiple voting; disenfranchisement of CUF voters; the presence of nonresidents; and the aggressive behavior of the security forces (NDI 2005; CUF 2008a).

There were many incidents of violence. In Unguja, security forces chased voters and beat CUF supporters, while the CUF targeted CCM supporters (CUF 2008b, 520). Both parties used youth groups to threaten and harass each other: CUF employed the "Blue Guards," whereas CCM employed the "Janjaweed" (TEMCO 2006, 14). CUF supporters were threatened, intimidated, harassed, physically assaulted, or killed. In one incident, forty-eight CUF and CCM supporters were injured when they clashed following campaign rallies. CUF threatened to unleash "people power" should the process continue to be so biased (TEMCO 2006, 42). Possibly, a stronger JPSC could have tamped down the violence. Instead, the tension had ample space to grow.

Despite the irregularities, violence, and belief that the election was stolen, CUF opted not to demonstrate or boycott. By its own admission, "Previous boycotts have yielded little and simply handed the government to CCM on a plate" (CUF 2008b). Instead of unleashing the "people power" that it had threatened on the campaign trail, CUF refused to recognize the CCM government, boycotting the Zanzibar House of Representatives until November 2009 (Commonwealth Secretariat 2010, 9).

CUF felt that unleashing "people power" would surely result in violent clashes with the security forces, given the large number of security personnel who had been transported to Zanzibar. Moreover, in light of the international community's support for CCM's initiatives, CUF felt that the international community would not support its protests. The risks were thus too high: possible loss of lives for very little progress (Ladhu 2010). Others have noted that the Muafaka-II process may also have given CUF the impression that dialogue could reduce the probability of violence or that there also seemed to be some union government support for Muafaka-II, since, on a number of occasions, former President Mkapa urged the parties to use the JPSC to resolve their differences (FEWER 2005, 5). But others argue that the dialogue and Mkapa's role were inconsequential at best and deliberately deceptive at worst, citing Mkapa's intention to play "good cop" to CCM's "bad cop" (Burgess 2005, 2).

In conclusion, while the 2005 elections did not result in the high number of fatalities seen in 2001, the electoral process was still violent. Government security officers clashed repeatedly with CUF supporters, and no dialogue occurred between CCM and CUF about these issues, beyond the accusatory charges in the press. The mechanisms envisioned to facilitate these discussions—namely the JPSC meetings—did not materialize. CUF was also marginalized in ZEC, with many decisions openly favoring CCM.

In July 2010, a referendum in Zanzibar approved the creation of a permanent government of national unity (GNU) as a constitutional amendment. Under the GNU, the second-place winner of the October 2010 presidential elections would be first vice president. Both CUF and CCM, the two major parties, were thus guaranteed a place in government, regardless of the outcome. By all accounts, the 2010 election was free of violence and incendiary political rhetoric. CCM won the presidency, while CUF got the first vice presidency. But this surely deals a harsh blow to the meaning and role of multiparty elections.

Concluding Observations

The cases of Togo and Zanzibar show that the combination of structures that foster interaction, incentives by the international community to organize free and fair elections, and the strength and credibility of reforms all affect the electoral environment. They affect the level of violence in an election, the political rhetoric used, and politicians' choices whether to protest through existing institutions or in the streets.

The electoral environment in Togo's 2007 legislative election and Zanzibar's 2010 election stand in sharp contrast with the electoral environment in Togo's 2010 presidential election and the Zanzibari 2005 election. This suggests that the dominant factor affecting the political parties' decisions and actions is their ability to meet in forums (a) to defuse tension, (b) to affect the implementation of the agreement and the planning of the election, and (c) to challenge the dominance of the ruling party. Thus, reforms or institutions that create opportunities to foster interaction between opposing political parties have the potential to elicit politicians' cooperation to hold peaceful elections, seek redress through institutions rather than in the streets, and stop exhorting their supporters to use violence. The extreme case of Zanzibar's constitutional amendment instituting a permanent government of national unity resulted in the first peaceful election there since 1995. Although the new permanent GNU gets rid of the competition—and, by extension, the violence—of an electoral campaign, it also erodes the democratization process.

The international community can play an important role in setting the expectations and boundaries for political behavior. Again, the Togolese elections of 2007 are instructive: when compared with Togo's 2010 presidential elections and the 2005 general elections in Zanzibar, Togo's 2007 legislative elections were notable for their adherence to international standards. The conditioning of renewed development assistance on holding transparent and acceptable legislative elections was an important factor in holding all stakeholders accountable. In contrast, donor assistance did not put pressure on presidential elections. Equally telling, the CUF in Zanzibar felt that the international community would not punish the CCM for holding flawed elections. The U.S. ambassador refused to attend the CCM inauguration, but few other members of the international community made such overt protests. Paradoxically, the sense of abandonment by the international community also weighed on the CUF's decision to protest the results. CUF felt that violence would not yield any positive results, because the world would not pay attention. This raises different but important questions about how the international community reacts to crises, and the perverse incentives that may develop when the world forgoes conflict prevention measures in favor of addressing conflict only after violence erupts. Instead of remaining silent, the international community could have more actively promoted peaceful elections under Muafaka-II.

Finally, the strength and credibility of reforms matter. While the international community and structures encouraging interaction can provide sufficient incentives to political actors to work toward peaceful elections in the first election following a PPA, subsequent elections may depend more on the substance and credibility of reform measures. In the run-up to the 2010 presidential elections in Togo, the UFC pulled out of the National Assembly, the CENI, and the CPD because it concluded that the ruling party was not committed to political reform. Isabelle Ameganvi indicated that the UFC had given the RPT the benefit of the doubt. But when the RPT revealed that it had no intention of reforming the institutions, the UFC also disengaged. The result was a tense electoral period. Indeed, Togo's two elections provide an important insight: any gains from a PPA will be short-lived if the interim period is not used to enact political reforms that reduce the dominance of the ruling party, provide an even playing field for electoral campaigns, and ensure free and fair elections.

Yet, as stated at the beginning of the chapter, PPAs may also have the perverse potential to engender violence. By holding peace hostage, some political players may reason that they could expect an offer of joint governance. In fact, this was the discussion in the wake of Ivorian president Laurent Gbagbo's offer to consider a power-sharing agreement with Alassane Ouattara, the internationally recognized new president. All major stakeholders explicitly rejected power sharing as a solution. However, as a power-sharing deal continued to elude President Gbagbo, violence persisted: at the end of nearly four months of clashes between pro-Gbagbo and pro-Ouattara forces, about three thousand people were killed and nearly one million displaced. Could these deaths have been avoided with a power-sharing arrangement in place? Are these deaths the cost of standing on principle? And is the cost too high? Under what conditions should a power-sharing agreement be considered? These important questions must be actively debated, because the creation of a power-sharing agreement holds the potential for becoming a norm.

International and regional institutions that intervene to resolve electoral violence must approach proposals for power-sharing agreements with care; it is a deliberate choice of less democracy for more peace. The long-term implications of a power-sharing agreement that ignores the basic tenets of democracy—namely, that the winner of a presidential election should occupy the seat of government—may undermine any short-lived peace achieved through a PPA. Indeed, the Togo and Zanzibar cases show that without substantial and credible reforms, governments of national unity and other forms of joint governance can bring only temporary relief to violent electoral conflicts. Unless the period of joint governance is used for credible reform, the parties will revert to the tactics used before, increasing the likelihood of an ongoing cycle of electoral violence.

References

Accord Politique Global (APG). 2007. "Accord Politique Global: Un véritable pacte pour le renouveau." Feb. 11. www.consultations-nationales-togo.org/files/fichiers/documents/12ACCORD_POLITIQUE_GLOBAL.pdf.

Ameganvi, Isabelle. 2010. Telephone interview with author, Sept.

APA News. 2009. "Togo: Création d'un cadre permanent de dialogue et de concertation au Togo." *Jeune Afrique*, Feb. 5. www.jeuneafrique.com/Article/DEPXXIJ20090205T072317/.

Atlas, Pierre M., and Roy Licklider. 1999. "Conflict among Former Allies after Civil War Settlement: Sudan, Zimbabwe, Chad, and Lebanon." *Journal of Peace Research* 36 (1): 35–54.

Axelrod, Robert. 1984. *The Evolution of Cooperation*. New York: Basic Books.

Aziadouvo, Zeus. 2007. "Patrick Lawson: 'Que l'ordre ancienne survive ... cela n'est plus possible.'" Interview, Jan. 25. www.ufctogo.com/Patrick-Lawson-Que-l-ordre-ancien-1652.html.

Burgess, G. Thomas. 2005. "Analysis of the 2005 Elections in Zanzibar." National Intelligence Council Associates Report, Dec.

Cameron, Greg. 2002. "Zanzibar's Turbulent Transition." *Review of African Political Economy* 29 (92): 311–30.

CCM and CUF. 2001. "Political Accord between Chama Cha Mapinduzi (CCM) and the Civic United Front (CUF) on Resolving the Political Crisis in Zanzibar." Oct. 21. www.kituochakatiba.org/.

Commonwealth Secretariat. 2005. "The Elections in Zanzibar, United Republic of Tanzania, 30 October 2005." Report of the Commonwealth Observer Group, London. www.thecommonwealth.org/shared_asp_files/uploadedfiles/903C0A27-DA0B-4AF1-8361-0F512980FB0A_COGElectionsZanzibar 2005.pdf.

———. 2010. "Tanzania General Elections." Report of the Commonwealth Observer Group, Oct. 31. www.thecommonwealth.org/files/232431/FileName/FinalReport-TanzaniaCOG.pdf).

Convention Démocratique des Peuples Africains (CDPA). 2006. "Communiqué du Comite de suivi de l'accord politique global du dialogue inter-togolais à l'issue de sa deuxième session." C.S/APG/002/12/06 (second session), Dec. 16. www.cdpa_togo.com/suivi_APG/com_2.htm.

———. 2007a. "Communiqué du Comité de suivi de l'accord politique global du dialogue inter-togolaise à l'issue de sa troisième session." C.S/APG/003/01/07 (third session), Jan. 16. www.cdpa-togo.com/suivi_APG/com_3.htm.

———. 2007b. "Communiqué de Comite de suivi de l'accord politique global du dialogue inter-togolaise à l'issue de sa quatrième session." C.S./APG/004/03/07 (fourth session), Mar. 10. www.cdpa_togo.com/suivi_APG/com_4.htm.

———. 2007c. "Communiqué de Comite de suivi de l'accord politique global du dialogue inter-togolaise à l'issue de sa cinquième session." C.S./ APG/005/04/07 (fifth session), Apr. 12. www.cdpa-togo.com/suivi_APG/com_5.htm.

CUF. 2008a. "Betrayal of Popular Hopes: Report on the General Election in Zanzibar of October 2005." Executive Summary. http://hakinaumma.wordpress.com/2008/09/18/betrayal-executive-summary/.

———. 2008b. "Betrayal of Popular Hopes: Report on the General Election in Zanzibar of October 2005." ZEC and PVR. http://hakinaumma.wordpress.com/2008/09/18/betrayal-zec-and-pvr/.

Dzikodo, Dimas. 2006. "La base désavoue son leader." *Forum de la Semaine* no. 191, Sept. www.icilome.com/nouvelles/news.asp?id=39&idnews=7399.

East Africa Law Society. 2005. "The Report of the East Africa Law Society's Mission to Zanzibar of 16th to 20th May 2005." Jul. 15. www.afrimap.org//english//images//documents// file43873dc89881b.doc.

European Commission. 2008. "Coopération Togo/Union européenne Rapport Annuel Conjoint 2007." http://ec.europa.eu/development/icenter/repository/jar08_tg_fr.pdf.

European Commission Delegation. 2004. "Cooperation between the European Union and the United Republic of Tanzania: Annual Report 2004." http://ec.europa.eu/development/icenter/repository/jar04_tz_en.pdf.

European Parliament. 2007a. "Delegation for the Observation of the Parliamentary Election in Togo (11 to 16 October 2007)." www.europarl.europa.eu/intcoop/election_observation/missions/2004-2009/20071014_togo_en.pdf.

————. 2007b. "The Situation in Togo on the Eve of the 2007 Parliamentary Elections." Director-general for external policies of the union, Directorate B (Policy Department). Note, Sept. Annex 2. http://eu-information-service.rsconsulting.com/Policy%20Department%20for%20External%20Relations/Countries%20and%20Regions/ACP%20Countires%20%28African,%20Caribbean,%20Pacific%29/2.%20Country%20Notes/Togo/The%20situation%20in%20Togo%20on%20the%20eve%20of%20the%202007%20parliamentary%20elections.pdf.

FEWER. 2005. "Electoral Violence and Reconciliation in Zanzibar." Report, Aug. 19. www.fewer-international.org/pages/africa/english_publications_37.html.

Gilmore, Inigo. 2006. "Ethiopia Condemns Aid Pull-out." *Observer,* Jan. 1. www.guardian.co.uk/society/2006/jan/01/internationalaidanddevelopment.hearafrica05.

Hartzell, Caroline A. 1999. "Explaining the Stability of Negotiated Settlements to Intrastate War." *Journal of Conflict Resolution* 43 (1): 3–22.

Hetcheli, K. Folly Aimé, Claudine Ahianyo Kponzo, and Constant C. Gnacadja. 2007. "Les réels défis des élections législatives au Togo: Le début de confiance des acteurs." West Africa Network for Peacebuilding, *WARN Policy Brief,* Aug. 31. www.wanep.org/wanep/attachments/article/90/pb_togo_aug07.pdf.

Horowitz, Donald. 1985. *Ethnic Groups in Conflict.* Berkeley, CA: Univ. of California Press.

Human Rights Watch. 2002. " 'The Bullets Were Raining': The January 2001 Attack on Peaceful Demonstrators in Zanzibar." Report, Apr. www.hrw.org/node/78557.

International Republican Institute (IRI), International Foundation of Electoral Systems (IFES), and National Democratic Institute (NDI). 2005. "Report of the Joint IRI, IFES, NDI Togo Assessment Mission, March 15–April 4, 2005." www.ifes.org/publication/14598f6b4e1b52ad184faffa2cb7649b/CEPPS_Togo_Final_Report.pdf.

IRIN. 2005. "Tanzania: Zanzibar Opposition Says It Will Sit in Parliament, despite Presidential Poll 'Fraud.' " Nov. 7 http://news.irinnews.org/Report/57026/TANZANIA-Zanzibar-opposition-says-it-will-sit-in-parliament-despite-presidential-poll-fraud.

Joint Presidential Supervisory Commission (JPSC). 2001. Act MP/10 of 2001. www.kituochakatiba.org/index2.php?option=com_docman&task=doc_view&gid=115&Itemid=27.

Kaiser, Paul. 2003. "Zanzibar: A Multilevel Analysis of Conflict." In *From Promise to Practice: Strengthening UN Strategies for the Prevention of Violent Conflict,* ed. Chandra Lekha Sriram and Karin Wermester. Boulder, CO: Lynne Rienner.

Ladhu, Ismail Jusa. 2010. Phone interview with author, Oct.

LTDH. 2005. "Stratégie de la terreur au Togo (II): 'Un règne aussi court que sanglant'—Violations des Droits de l'Homme commises au Togo depuis le coup d'état du 5 février 2005." Rapport Préliminaire d'Investigation, Mar., 13–33. www.fidh.org/IMG//pdf/TogoRappPreliminaireFinal.pdf.

Lijphart, Arend. 1990. "The Power-Sharing Approach." In *Conflict and Peacemaking in Multiethnic Societies*, ed. Joseph Montville, 491–510. Lexington, MA: Lexington Books.

Mjatvedt, Annie-Lise. 2006. "Zanzibar: Presidential and House of Representatives Elections, October 2005." Norwegian Center for Human Rights (NORDEM), Report 5/2006. www.jus.uio.no/smr/english/about/programmes/nordem/publications/nordem-report/2006/0506.pdf.

National Democratic Institute (NDI). 2005. "2005 Zanzibar Elections, October 30, 2005. Final Report." Dec. 11. www.ndi.org/node/13521.

Oloka-Onyango, Joseph, and Maria Nassali. 2003. "Constitutionalism and Political Stability in Zanzibar: The Search for a New Vision. Report of the Fact Finding Mission Organized under the auspices of Kituo Cha Katiba, Oct. http://library.fes.de/pdf-files/bueros/tanzania/02112.pdf.

Panapress. 2010. "Togo: Party Suspension Does Not Affect CENI, Says Togo's Electoral Body." Feb. 14. www.panapress.com/pana-lang2-index.html.

Rawlence, Ben. 2005. "Briefing: The Zanzibar Election." *African Affairs* 104 (416): 515–23.

Roberts, Tyson. 2008. "The Legislative Election in Togo, October 2007." *Electoral Studies* 27 (3): 558.

Schelling, Thomas. 1980. *The Strategy of Conflict*. Cambridge, MA: Harvard Univ. Press.

Stedman, Stephen John. 1997. "Spoiler Problems in Peace Processes." *International Security* 22 (2): 5–53.

Tanzania Election Monitoring Committee (TEMCO). 2006. "The 2005 General Elections in Zanzibar." Feb. www.tz.undp.org/ESP/docs/Observer_Reports/2005/TEMCO_Report_Zanzibar_2005.pdf.

Tull, Denis, and Andreas Mehler. 2005. "The Hidden Costs of Power-Sharing: Reproducing Insurgent Voices in Africa." *African Affairs* 104 (416): 375–98.

UFC. 2006. "Déclaration de l'UFC relative à la Nomination de Premier Ministre et à la Formation du Gouvernement." Communiqué, Sept. 20. www.ufctogo.com/Declaration-de-l-UFC-relative-a-la-1533.html.

———. 2007a. "Conférence de presse de l'UFC: Il est temps de tirer la sonnette d'alarme." APG, Jan. 8. www.ufctogo.com/Conference-de-presse-de-l-UFC-Il-1632.html.

———. 2007b. "Evaluation du processus électorale par l'UFC." *Legislatives* 2007, June 7. www.ufctogo.com/Evaluation-du-processus-electoral-1752.html.

———. 2007c. "La Ceni Saisit la Cour Constitutionnelle pour la proclamation des résultants des législative de Lomé." *Dépêches,* Oct. 22, 2007 www.ufctogo. com/+La-CENI-saisit-la-Cour+.html.

UFC Togo. 2010. "Togo: Près de 200 000 personnes dans les rues de Lomé pour dénoncer la fraude électorale de Faure Gnassingbé." Mar. 13. www.ufctogo.com/togo-pres-de-200-000-personnes-dans-les-rues-de-lome-pourdenoncer-la-fraude,2320.html.

UN OHCHR. 2005a. "La mission d'établissement des faits chargée de faire la lumière sur les violences et les allégations de violations des droits de l'homme survenues au Togo avant, pendant et après l'élection présidentielle du 24 avril 2005." Aug. 29. www2.reliefweb.int/rw/RWB.NSF/db900SID/EVOD-6H3JDK?OpenDocument.

———. 2005b. "Togo: Human Rights Group Says 790 Killed in Election Violence." IRINNEWS, May 13. www.irinnews.org/report.aspx?reportid=54415.

U.S. State Dept. 1995. "Togo Human Rights Practices, 1994." Feb. http://dosfan. lib.uic.edu/erc/democracy/1994_hrp_report/94hrp_report_africa/Togo.html.

Xinhua. 2010. "Présidentielle: Jean-Pierre Fabre rejette le recours à la Cour constitutionnelle." *IciLome,* Mar. 10. www.icilome.com/nouvelles/news.asp?id= 2010&idnews=14716&f=.

Zartman, I. William. 1998. "Putting Humpty-Dumpty Together Again." In *The International Spread of Ethnic Conflict: Fear, Diffusion, and Escalation,* ed. David A. Lake and Donald Rothchild. Princeton, NJ: Princeton Univ. Press.

6

The Political Economy
of Kenya's Crisis[*]

Susanne D. Mueller

'So this is how it begins' (Kenyan political scientist, Nairobi, January 2008).

To the outside world, Kenya in 2007 was a model of stability and future possibilities. The draconian repression experienced under former President Moi in the 1980s and 1990s had finally ended. It was replaced with hard fought for freedoms of speech, press, and association. They emerged towards the end of Moi's rule and expanded after President Kibaki's election in 2002. The days of imprisonment, detention without trial, and torture of opposition party supporters were gone. A once vibrant economy had been decimated and brought to its knees by Moi. By 2007, just five years after installing a new government, Kenya had an annual growth rate of over 6 per cent and was poised to do even better. The mood was optimistic and most thought Kenya was back on an economic roll. Some in government spoke of Kenya following East Asia's tigers and becoming another Newly Industrialized Country (NIC). This was one side of the story.

The other was Kenya's low scores on the World Bank's Governance Indicators, which placed it below the mean for sub-Saharan Africa in three out of the following four areas: government effectiveness (28/28 per cent), political stability (15/35.6 per cent), control of corruption (16/30 per cent,

---

*Chapter was previously published as "The Political Economy of Kenya's Crisis" by Susanne D. Mueller, *Journal of Eastern African Studies* (2008) Vol. 2:2, 185–210. Reprinted by permission of the publisher (Taylor & Francis Ltd., www.tandfonline.com).

and the rule of law (15.7/28.8 per cent).[1] Kenya was rocked by financial scandals at the top of government, infrastructure continued to crumble, and foreign companies were still skittish about investing.[2] Crime, from gunfights in the central business district of Nairobi to carjacking, hold-ups in houses, and gangland-style murders, peppered the lives of ordinary Kenyans as well as others. This duality of both positive transformation and imminent decay aptly characterized Kenya in the post-Moi era.

The thesis of what follows goes somewhat beyond the above description of duality. It argues that Kenya was precariously perched and poised to implode even prior to the election because of three underlying precipitating factors.[3] These factors put Kenya on a dangerous precipice notwithstanding the many impressive changes experienced under its new government. The argument here is that the 2007 election, which was too close to call beforehand and contested afterwards, was the spark that ignited them. Hence, Kenya's descent into a spiral of killing and destruction along ethnic lines and the consequent fracturing of the fragile idea of nation was not altogether surprising.

This article identifies these underlying precipitating factors as follows: a gradual decline in the state's monopoly of legitimate force and a consequent generalized level of violence not always within its control; deliberately weak institutions, mostly overridden by a highly personalized and centralized presidency, that could and did not exercise the autonomy or checks and balances normally associated with democracies; and political parties that were not programmatic, were driven by ethnic clientism, and had a winner-take-all view of political power and its associated economic byproducts. The argument here is that: violence was diffused, could be ignited easily but not controlled, and was not; institutions outside the presidency normally associated with vetting a contested election were not viewed as being sufficiently neutral to do so and did not; and the nature of Kenya party politics predisposed both leaders and followers to see politics as a do or die zero sum game, which is what this election became. Had the election not been so close, these same factors may have been held in check for a while. Nevertheless, they were dangerous and looming problems. The aim of this article is to discuss these factors and show why the contested 2007 election triggered them. It argues that two of the three factors (e.g.

---

1. World Bank, *Governance Indicators*. Available from http://info.worldbank.org/governance/wgi 2007/sc_country.asp.

2. Between 1999 and 2002 140 foreign companies left Kenya. Katumanga, 'A City Under Siege', 517.

3. This author mentioned this during visits to Kenya in 2005 and 2006 in discussions with individuals in government and with donors.

weak institutions and ethnically driven clientist political parties) are common in Africa and therefore cannot alone be viewed as causal. It maintains that diffused violence, however, upped the ante, with a too close to call election raising the stakes in causal terms.

The intent of what follows is both to identify and outline these factors in the context of Kenya's political history. It is also to place the discussion within the framework of contemporary political economy analysis as well as to raise questions concerning the transition to democracy. It argues by implication that false optimism about Kenya and other transition economies has two causes. First, scholars and policy-makers often have focused on the formal aspects of institutions such as parties, parliament, administrative structures, and elections rather than on the incentive systems guiding the behaviour of political actors in them. This has led to overly positive views about how institutions both in and outside government actually function and false enthusiasm about the future. Second, concentrating on the formal nature of institutions as sui generis entities has also meant neglecting how these institutions really operate. In this case there was a deliberate hollowing out of formal institutions by those in power in the face of a diffusion of violence over more than a generation.

The conclusions reached here from the study of Kenya are of interest for three reasons. Firstly, in many democracies, from Bangladesh to the Philippines and Kenya, politicians depend on violence to build electoral influence. The role of violence in democratic electoral competition is largely unexplored in the literature. This study does not examine the still open question of when violence becomes important and when it does not, but it does document the long-run consequences for democratic sustainability. Secondly, policy-makers and academics have advocated formal institutional reform (e.g. decentralization, proportional representation and strengthened parliaments) as a solution to political violence. The analysis here suggests that violence is not purely a social phenomenon in need of being re-channelled through different types of formal institutional vehicles of political competition and decision-making. Instead, it is in part a product of political competition itself and for that reason may threaten the sustainability of any institutional reform that is devised to control violence. Furthermore, as the discussion below makes clear, institutional innovation that attempts to graft formal technical changes onto old systems will be undermined by prevailing norms and will not work. Thirdly, the civil conflict literature has focused on conflict triggers ranging from greed to grievance and on both the macro causes of violence (poverty) and the micro causes (the ability of rebels to finance insurgency). Elections are usually taken at face value in the literature and democracies are not distinguished according to the quality or specific dynamics of electoral competition. The violence in Kenya suggests that this is a mistake. Although all the major drivers of conflict are present (e.g. historic and significant inter-ethnic conflict over land), a key driver here has been the deliberate use of violence for electoral advantage and to maintain power indefinitely if possible. This is important because of its potential to destroy the integrity of the state itself as is clear from what follows.

Diffused Violence

'Government Has Lost Control of Some of This Country' (*Nation*, 28 January 2008).

'Gangs Are Driving the Political Agenda' (*Nation*, 6 February 2008).

For Max Weber, the defining characteristic of a state is its ability 'to control the monopoly of legitimate force over a given territory'.[4] Without this monopoly a state cannot maintain order, ensure peace and security, or govern effectively and it becomes vulnerable to descending into a Hobbesian state of nature. Hence, for Weber this characteristic of the state is essential. For a variety of reasons to be discussed below, the state under President Moi, while exercising a draconian level of violence against those opposed to it, also manufactured institutionalized violence outside of the state, both by design and neglect. Over time, these sources of violence, some of which were generated by the state to support it, began to take on a life of their own and, often, the state could no longer control them. It is in this sense that the state slowly began to cede its monopoly. Even when there was no crisis, the violence which the Moi state had generated was there to explode, with or without its blessing. When Kibaki took over government in 2002, extrastate violence had not been checked, had trickled down into the general population, and was out of control and ready to be tapped on call in a variety of ways, as it was after the 2007 election.

The discussion which follows discusses four types of extra-state violence that emerged under the Moi regime: that of politicians having their own bodyguards and goon squads; the emergence of groups of young thugs who were used by the state and its politicians to kill and displace opposition supporters in the Rift Valley, the Coast, and other provinces prior to two multi-party elections in the 1990s; the resulting Mafioso violent shakedown gangs that began to emerge and operate as shadow states in

---

4. Weber, *Basic Concepts in Sociology*, 119–23.

Nairobi's slums, in other cities, and in the countryside, as well as in support of certain politicians; and the generalized level of crime and violence that thereby confronted ordinary citizens from the 1980s onward and has continued to do so ever since.

The Kenyatta period was not without violence. However most of it, including the assassination of three politicians, the use of the provincial administration and preventive detention laws to repress opposition politics, and the harnessing of regular and paramilitary security forces to disrupt student and political rallies, was controlled by the state.[5] Although some writings on this period mention the role of the Kenya African National Union (KANU) party youth wingers, their role was relatively minor, did not threaten the state's authority, and did not come up in discussions with the Kenya People's Union (KPU) party and other opposition supporters concerning repression.[6] Their negative experiences came mainly from the state itself and those who discriminated against them out of fear of being associated with the opposition.[7]

The Moi era was infinitely more repressive than that of Kenyatta's rule, with some authors describing this period as an 'imperial presidency'. Throup and others argue that after independence Kenyatta had a good deal of patronage he could use to consolidate support, in contrast to Moi.[8] Kenyatta's supporters received jobs in the civil service and land, both of which had opened up with the exit of settlers. In addition, the coffee boom generated revenue for the state and prosperity for Kenya's many farmers. In contrast, by the time Moi took over, none of the above handouts were available. In addition, coffee prices had plummeted while the cost of oil had gone up. Moi also faced a recalcitrant Kikuyu elite, who had tried to overthrow him before he took office, Kalenjin supporters who wanted to 'eat', and a growing population waiting for perks.

Unlike Kenyatta, who could give without taking away, Moi had to take away before he could give. Hence, the means Moi used both to consolidate support and control those opposed to him were cruder and more repressive.[9] This entailed 'destroy[ing] Kikuyu hegemony and dismantl[ing] the economic foundations of the Kenyatta state' to 'build Kalenjin privileges

---

5. Mueller, 'Government and Opposition in Kenya'; Mueller, 'Political Parties in Kenya'. Also see Branch and Cheeseman, 'Politics of Control', 11–28.

6. Mwangola, 'Leaders of Tomorrow', 147–48.

7. Mueller, 'Government and Opposition in Kenya', 407–26; and Mueller, 'Political Parties in Kenya'.

8. Throup, 'Construction and Destruction', 34–36, 57–73; Throup and Hornsby, Multi-Party Politics, 26–27; Asingo, 'Political Economy of Transition', 23; Odhiambo-Mbai, 'The Rise and Fall of the Autocratic State', 65.

9. Ibid.

into the structure of the state'.[10] This was important because controlling the state was the means to entrench an ethnically defined class and to ensure its enrichment. Moi's methods were to tax and destroy Kikuyu agricultural associations, to fill the civil service, parastatals, and the university with unqualified individuals from his own ethnic group, and to replace the elected Nairobi City Council with an appointed commission to undermine Kikuyu control of the city.[11] He also plundered the treasury, in part to support a constantly changing inner circle, in contrast to that of Kenyatta's, which was more stable.[12] All of this gave rise to outrage in some quarters. Moi, in turn, responded by having his critics and even their friends followed, detained, tortured, and killed. He used indiscriminate violence against ordinary citizens, particularly against the poor and defenceless.[13] He and his politicians also began to use extra-state violence early on, possibly initially as a prophylactic antidote to the formal security forces, whose loyalties may have been in question, a tendency that increased during his 24-year rule. Ironically, the more extra-state violence was used to consolidate Moi's rule, the greater was its potential to erode the state's monopoly of legitimate force.

The Privatization of Public Violence and Bodyguards

Even in the early and mid-1980s, politicians such as Nicholas Biwott, William Ntimama, and others had personal bodyguards and gangs of supporters, something mostly not experienced during the Kenyatta period. The meting out of private justice through personal gangs was something opposition politicians and their supporters experienced as the Moi regime became more entrenched and more violent. This was the beginning of what Katamunga aptly has called 'the privatization of public violence' when the state both invoked extra-legal forces to retain power and became criminalized itself. This period, particularly after Kenya became a 'de jure' one-party state in 1982, also coincided with a 'revival of the KANU Youth Wing', a tool used 'to monitor, silence, and even punish dissidents, usually the lumpens in urban and rural Kenya'.[14]

---

10. Barkan 'Divergence and Convergence', 24–29; Chege, 'Return of Multi-Party Politics', 59; and Cowen and Kanyinga, 'The 1997 Elections', 135.

11. Stren, Halfani and Malombe, 'Coping with Urganization', 185–86.

12. Barkan, 'Divergence and Convergence', 27.

13. Katumanga, 'City Under Siege'; KHRC, *Where Terror Rules*, 1–26; Carver and Kirschke, *Deadly*, 15–25.

14. Katumanga, 'City Under Siege', 505, 508; Kagwanja, 'Youth, Identity, Violence', 90.

Multi-Party Democracy and Privatized Extra-State Violence

The great leap forward in the privatization of violence came in 1991 when the legislation which had turned Kenya from a de facto one-party state in 1969 into a de jure one in 1982 was finally repealed following pressure from internal critics and financial sanctions from donors. After this the Moi regime was faced with the prospect of multi-party elections for the first time in twenty-two years. Moi's thoughts on multi-partyism were well known: he detested the idea and wanted to stay in power.[15] His means were to use hired gangs to displace and kill those opposed to him in key electoral areas. Dead and displaced people don't vote. These groups and gangs were made up of young unemployed males and were recruited and hired by key KANU politicians, who wanted to win at any cost.[16]

The new rules on elections, designed to appeal to the marginalized areas, necessitated three conditions for winning the presidency: being elected as an MP, obtaining a majority of votes, and receiving more than 25 per cent of the votes in five out of Kenya's eight provinces. The adhesive which kept Moi in power for 24 years was a mixture of repression and anti-Kikuyu epoxy. He used the latter to consolidate support among his own and other marginal ethnic groups in the Rift Valley and other parts of the country. As Anderson has noted, '[u]nder Moi, KANU bec[a]me KADU reborn'.[17] This revived coalition, known by the acronym KAMATUSA, also appealed to other marginal ethnic groups at the Coast and elsewhere.[18] At independence they had opted for the opposition party, the Kenya African Democratic Union (KADU), for a federal system known as *majimboism*, and for a regional constitutional arrangement.[19] They were worried about being dominated by Kikuyus and other 'upcountry' groups, as well as the latter's monopoly of jobs and their acquisition of land outside their 'home' areas. KADU nevertheless folded and joined the governing party KANU in 1964, just one year after independence. In part, this was because majimboism had been so diluted in various constitutional conferences that it had become unviable both economically and politically. Hence, KADU MPs slowly gave up and crossed the floor.[20] Kenyatta also soothed the pain

15. Moi, *Nationalism*, 174–83.

16. Asingo, 'Political Economy of Transition', 37–38; Anderson, 'Vigilantes, Violence, and the Politics of Public Order', 547–53.

17. Anderson, 'Yours in the Struggle for Majimbo', 563. For a further elaboration of this point also see Anderson, 'Decline et Chute de la KANU'; Ngunyi, 'Resuscitating the "Majimbo" Project', 183–213; Kanyinga, 'Contestation over Political Space', 18.

18. The acronym KAMATUSA is a shorthand for Kalenjin, Masai, Samburu, and Turkana.

19. Anderson, 'Yours in the Struggle for Majimbo', 552–53, 555.

20. Ibid., 561–63.

and enticed the top echelon of the party with ministerial appointments, parastatal and other jobs, and access to choice land in the Rift Valley.[21] When asked later why he and his cohorts had never tried to bring back majimboism with a constitutional amendment from 1978 to 1990 when one of their own was president, William Ntimama, the MP for Narok and a minister in Moi's cabinet, answered, 'Power is sweet'.[22]

However, even afterwards, these same past issues continued to be salient for ex-KADU ethnic groups who thus found Moi's anti-Kikuyuism appealing. Population pressures in the Rift, the comparative poverty of ordinary pastoralists as opposed to agriculturalists, and land scarcities continued to increase.[23] Pressures on the land were rising, jobs were in scarce supply, and many individuals in these areas were illiterate. All of this combined to feed already existing feelings of resentment of outsiders and marginalization. Many 'outsiders' in fact were long-term residents who had lived in parts of the Rift and elsewhere for over 30 to 40 years with some going back longer. In addition, a number of contentious land issues arose from local elites grabbing land illegally from their own poor co-ethnics through their control of local land committees and their influence over the provincial administration.[24] Hence, mobilizing resentment against outsiders over land dovetailed with the self-interest of local elites and with efforts to ensure Moi's political survival after 1991.

Faced with a new multi-party situation and new rules for elections, Moi and his entourage were determined to win at any price. He was particularly worried about the demographics of the Rift, with its increasing influx of Kikuyu, as well as Luhya and Luo. Moi feared that their vote for upcountry opposition politicians running for president might keep him from obtaining 25 percent of the ballots cast, which he needed to win the Rift Valley Province. He also worried about losing seats to opposition politicians elsewhere, something which potentially could eat away at his parliamentary majority.

Politicians in multi-party democracies always face the possibility of losing. They have two options: to appeal to potential constituents and try to wean them away from the opposition or to get rid of the opposition itself. One way of eliminating a defined group of opposition opponents is to gerrymander them out of a district. Another method, used by James Curley, the corrupt Irish Catholic mayor of Boston, was to get his Protestant Brahmin opponents, whom he referred to as 'an inferior race', to move out

---

21. Bates, *Beyond the Miracle of the Market*, 61–63; Widner, *The Rise of a Party State in Kenya*, 55.

22. Quoted in 'Is Majimbo Federalism', *Nation*, 20 May 2001.

23. Wilcove, *No Way Home*, 91–93.

24. Mwangi, 'Subdividing the Commons', 825–26, 829.

of Boston entirely and into the suburbs, thereby eliminating their votes in the city. His means were to let their part of the city fall apart, and direct all public works, infrastructure, and new jobs to his Irish Catholic base. His strategy worked and he managed to stay in power for over 40 years even though his redistributive methods led to both Boston and his own constituents being worse off. Economists Glaeser and Schleifer have named this syndrome 'the Curley Effect': doing whatever is necessary to increase the size of one's base to retain power through 'distortionary wealth reducing policies', even if it leaves your supporters worse off than before.[25] This argues against more conventional theories, which assume politicians need to curry favour with constituents to get re-elected or they will be thrown out of office and against those who argue that multi-partyism thereby induces sounder economic policies.[26]

Moi's use of violence outside the state, in a parody of Clausewitz's statement on war, might be called gerrymandering or Curleyism by more drastic means. The means employed by Moi in both the 1991 and 1997 multiparty elections were violent attacks on his political opponents in the Rift and elsewhere, literally designed to eliminate them. He used privatized violence or gangs. In most cases these gangs were formed, aided, or abetted by the state's security apparatus and the provincial administration. Gangs of youth were organized by key KANU politicians who were identified by name in both human rights reports and those produced by a government commission. In the 1992 election, these tactics in the Rift and elsewhere led to the killing of over 1,500 individuals and the displacement of over 300,000 others, most of whom were Kikuyu. Consequently, they were not able to vote.[27] This included 15,000 voters who were pushed out of Narok, when the Masai MP William Ntimama used the right of eminent domain to reclaim the land and evict inhabitants who might vote against him. Before the election, he had told Kikuyus to 'lie low like envelopes' and other politicians were equally virulent in their warnings.[28]

Later, in 1997, government again used similar tactics. In both cases, coded hate messages were used at rallies, including discussions of majimboism. As Judge Akiwumi, who later conducted an inquiry into the 'tribal clashes' of the 1990s in the Rift Valley, Western, Coast, and Northeastern Provinces, noted with respect to the Rift, 'majimbo according to the evi-

---

25. Glaeser and Schleifer, 'The Curley Effect', 1–2, 9–12.

26. See also Bates, 'Institutions and Development', 28, 31. Bates argues multi-party elections may distort economic policies if politicians feel at risk and there is no accountability.

27. Africa Watch, *Divide and Rule*, 70–72,79–80; KHRC, *Kayas of Deprivation*, 48–49; KHRC, *Kayas Revisited*, 38–47; Republic of Kenya, *Akiwumi Report*.

28. Africa Watch, *Divide and Rule*, 30.

dence presented to us was not federalism in the real sense of the word, but an arrangement in which each community would be required to return to its ancestral district or province and if for any reason they would be reluctant or unwilling to do so, they would by all means be forced to do so'.[29] According to Boone, they were. The total combined fallout from the two elections in the 1990s was 2,000 killed, 500,000 displaced, and others intimidated into not voting.[30] Even after the 1992 election, Africa Watch argued that the political landscape of the Rift had been permanently altered. Boone confirms this, noting that 70 per cent of those who had been pushed off their land in the 1990s had not returned by 2002.[31] For Moi, this was mission accomplished.

Those who participated in the violence in many cases were dressed as warriors, and paid according to whether they destroyed huts, permanent structures, or killed people.[32] Some were promised land but, according to the testimony of one witness to the Akiwumi Commission, most did not get it.[33] Another report by the Jesuit Refugee Service of East Africa argues that 'land was allocated to the corrupt', while Africa Watch notes some was bought at 'sums below market prices' or was 'illegally occupied by squatters'.[34] Boone notes that land was given as patronage to reward 'supporters . . . party militants, local officials, and unemployed youth'. However, the extent to which this happened is not clear.[35]

There appears to be no systematic information about whether those who killed and destroyed the property of Kikuyus and other upcountry inhabitants in the Rift and other marginal areas were forcibly impressed into service, or motivated by long-standing grievances, pay, prospects of land, or other perks. This is an unfortunate gap in our understanding of what happened and why. Nevertheless, Kamungi argues that one important side effect of the clashes, particularly in northern Kenya, was an 'arms race' and a general 'militarization of society' as individuals increasingly felt a need to defend themselves when government did not.[36]

A good deal of statistical work in the political economy literature on conflict argues persuasively that conflict, particularly civil war, is driven

---

29. Republic of Kenya, *Akiwumi Report*, 78.

30. Boone, 'Winning and Losing', 9.

31. Ibid., 20.

32. Africa Watch, *Divide and Rule*, 52.

33. Republic of Kenya, *Akiwumi Report*, 88.

34. Kamungi, 'The Current Situation', 11–12, 23; Africa Watch, *Divide and Rule*, 70, 77, 2.

35. Boone, 'Winning and Losing', 19.

36. Kamungi, 'The Current Situation', 13, 15.

mainly by greed rather than grievance, while others disagree.[37] From the standpoint of the elite, many of whom already owned large tracts of land in the Rift and elsewhere, greed for political power, both by MPs from the area and by President Moi, appears to have been the motivating factor in the face of multi-party elections. Grievance over the dominance of land and jobs by upcountry individuals in the marginal areas was long standing. However, one needs to explain why, after living side by side for many decades, extra-state violence was employed systematically only with the reintroduction of multi-party elections as well as why it became an attack on upcountry voters rather than on the indigenous landed elite by the indigenous poor. In the case of the actual perpetrators, the motives are less clear. At the Coast, Digo youth who invaded the Likoni Police Station to obtain arms to be used to attack inhabitants from upcountry were organized by local politicians, but were also reacting against long-standing harassment of them by non-coastal government officers occupying the police and administrative apparatus.[38]

The result of the above is that while the state had aided and abetted the ability of groups who were formed from groups outside the state to perpetrate violence, these nonstate actors continued to exist even after the elections as they were never punished. Hence, 'privatized violence' was there to be used again for similar or different purposes or to act on its own some other day for some other end. The main point here is that the very violence used by the state for its own ends at one time frittered away its future monopoly of legitimate force.

Urban Gangs and Mungiki

During the 1980s and 1990s, urban crime also became a serious problem. The urban poor were increasingly harassed by the state, evicted from certain areas, and had some of their jua kali markets destroyed.[39] At the same time, due to the criminalization of the state itself, Nairobi's City Council and later the City Commission began to ignore many of its own city ordinances, simultaneously taking over land illegally, constructing buildings while bypassing its own regulations concerning safety, and allowing the poor to set up shacks and kiosks in areas where they were prohibited. What began as an initial lapse in ethics in the 1980s when the new head of

---

37. Collier, *The Bottom Billion*, 23–32; Collier and Hoeffler, 'Greed and Grievance in Civil Wars', 563–95; Ballentine and Sherman, *Political Economy of Armed Conflict*.

38. KHRC, *Kayas of Deprivation*; KHRC, *Kayas Revisited*.

39. Katumanga, 'City Under Siege', 513.

Nairobi's City Commission, Brigadier Shigolla, bought overpriced drapes for his office in City Hall, soon turned into more flagrant errors of judgement, including an unexplained decision to let garbage rot in public areas rather than collecting it. As a result, Nairobi, 'city in the sun', began to be transformed into an increasingly unattractive city of thieves and underworld activities, where ordinary citizens felt threatened and began to see their once thriving middle-class city decay. Gone were the days when pink and purple bougainvilleas adorned *Uhuru* highway's centre divide.

It was into this milieu of decay that urban gangs began to appear as significant actors. The largest and most prominent of these was 'Mungiki', a gang that began as a Kikuyu cult cum religious revival group in Laikipia District in the mid-1980s. Its origin, nature, and activities have been discussed and disputed in numerous articles.[40] However, its main raison d'être from the mid-1990s onward was as a violent, Mafioso-style shakedown gang. It operated almost as a shadow state in some Nairobi slums and in parts of the countryside and began to control certain businesses, such as *matatus*, by demanding 'protection money'. The gang had a known leader, was hierarchically organized like an army or an urban inner-city gang in the US, and by the mid-1990s was said to have somewhere between 3.5 and 4 million members.[41] The 1990s were a significant point of departure for Mungiki as a number of its members were Kikuyu who had been displaced from the Rift Valley by Moi's ethnic cleansing operations during the multi-party elections of the 1990s.

Initially, Mungiki claimed some moral authority where it operated by offering security, protection, and services in Nairobi's slums and the working-class housing estates that had been largely abandoned by the state. However, its main import soon became that of a well-armed violent gang. It intimidated and demanded payment from citizens, murdered those who refused to cough up, settled disputes, and meted out justice in the slums. In some areas, it became a shadow state, even charging for the use of pit latrine toilets. Mungiki began to expand into the matatu urban transport arena, vying violently for control over certain routes. It also engaged in other business activities, including demanding payments from *jua kali* car repair men working on Kirinyaga road, claimed effective hegemony to govern certain areas, and routinely got into wars with gangs, such as the Luo Taliban and others. Their wars were usually over turf rather than ethnicity, although the two often coincided, something not so surprising given

---

40. Anderson, 'Vigilantes, Violence, and the Politics of Public Order', 531–55; Kagwanja, 'Facing Mount Kenya or Facing Mecca?' 25–49; Kagwanja, 'Power to Uhuru', 51–75; Gecaga, 'Religious Movements and Democratization', 58–89.

41. Katumanga, 'City Under Siege', 513.

the earlier organization of self-help groups along ethnic lines. For instance, in one case the Luo Taliban attacked Kikuyu slumlords for raising rents in Kibera, which invited counterattacks by Mungiki, which was Kikuyu.[42] However, the Mungiki did not discriminate and was equally virulent in its attacks against other Kikuyu in Nairobi, Central Province, and elsewhere.

Various authors have suggested that Mungiki both received guns from and was aided by state security forces. The main point as made by Gecaga is that notwithstanding its origins, Mungiki evolved into a classic capitalist operation. It was a gang for hire. It operated on a willing-buyer willing-seller basis, anxious to sell its services 'to the highest bidder'.[43] That explains its interaction with security forces which it initially claimed it detested, as well as its alleged willingness to support a myriad of politicians, ranging from some in Kenneth Matiba's FORD ASILI to Moi's KANU and his candidate for president in 2002, Uhuru Kenyatta. The latter seems odd given that some Mungiki members were originally displaced by Moi from the Rift Valley in the 1990s. This decision seems less odd, however, when one considers that in exchange for supporting Moi, Mungiki was then 'allowed to take over certain transport routes'.[44]

In extorting from the poor as well as the rich Mungiki members, at least those at the top, were doing very well financially from their criminal activities. As Katumanga estimates, the annual value of the 'bandit economy' in 2004, including resale of highjacked cars, was about $3.8 million a year, while the subscriptions Mungiki raised from its members were around $58,000 per month as early as the mid-1990s.[45] This information also tends to support both Collier's argument about greed rather than grievance being the motivating factor in conflict as well as the upwardly mobile material motivations of hierarchically organized gangs.[46]

When Kibaki took over power in 2002, he banned Mungiki. As recently as 2007, after Mungiki beheaded certain matatu drivers who refused to be shaken down, the former Minister of Security, John Michuki, went after Mungiki with a shoot-to-kill policy. However, Mungiki still continued to operate, available for business and for hire. The main point from the standpoint of this article is that long before the 2007 election, Mungiki had become a virtual shadow state in certain areas. While reputedly sometimes used by the state and its politicians from Moi onwards, it nevertheless also operated outside state control. As such, it reduced the state's monopoly of

---

42. Ibid., 512

43. Gecaga, 'Religious Movements and Democratisation', 78, 80, 83–85.

44. Katumanga, 'City Under Siege', 513.

45. Ibid., 513–17.

46. Collier, *The Bottom Billion*, 22–25; Levitt and Dubner, *Freakonomics*, 89–116.

legitimate force, which had been severely compromised by the time of the 2007 election.

Gangs and Politicians

While Mungiki may be the largest and the most written-about gang for hire in Kenya, there were others that also frittered away at the state's monopoly of legitimate force. Their names alone were provocative: Kamjeshi, Baghdad Boys, Jeshi la Mzee (the elder's battalion), Jeshi la Embakasi, Kaya Bombo Youth, Chionkororo, Amachuma, The Rwenjes Football Club, the Jeshi ya King'ole, Jeshi la Mbela, etc. They operated in various parts of the country: Nairobi, Kisumu, Mombasa, Kwale, Taita Taveta, rural Kisii, Ukambani, Murang'a, and elsewhere.[47]

These gangs had various functions: shakedown gangs engaged in survival, gangs defending themselves from violence by the state security forces, gangs used to disrupt opposition rallies, gangs organized to support state politicians afraid of the opposition, and vice versa.[48] Politics by other means had taken root all over the country while various gangs both appeared and disappeared. All of this was a further indicator that the state's monopoly of legitimate force was being challenged and diminished. This diffusion of violence fits into Bates' observation that 'the shift to competitive politics appears to heighten the level of political disorder'. Elites fear losing power and lose incentives to 'refrain from predation', while citizens 'anticipate' this and 'prepare to defend themselves'.[49]

Trickle-Down Violence

Aside from the above, there also were trickle-down effects from the diffused violence that emanated from formal gangs. Freelancers operated as well and there was a demonstration effect arising from the general diffused violence that had plagued Kenya for so long. Ordinary citizens were constantly plagued by violence in their daily lives. Their vehicles were carjacked, their houses were invaded, and they were often robbed, duct-taped, or raped in their apartments. Their friends were murdered in their homes, on their way to church, or while waiting for a guard to open their gates.

---

47. Anderson, 'Vigilantes and Violence', 547–53; KHRC, *Kayas of Deprivation*; Katumanga, 'City Under Siege,' 512; Kagwanja, 'Politics of Marionettes', 72–100.

48. Anderson, 'Vigilantes and Violence', 547–53; KHRC, *Kayas of Deprivation*; Katumanga, 'City Under Siege', 512; Kagwanja, 'Politics of Marionettes', 72–100; Asingo, 'The Political Economy of Transition in Kenya', 37–38.

49. Bates, 'Institutions and Development', 57.

Certain parts of Nairobi and even certain routes into the countryside became no-go areas. Everyone from every class was touched by violence, although those in poor housing estates and in certain rural areas experienced the worst of it.

By the time of the 2007 election, this was the situation facing the majority of Kenyans. In contrast to the Moi period when they mostly feared the heavy hand of the state, they now had to worry about gang violence, freelance violence, and everything connected with both. A recent survey indicated that only 16 per cent of all respondents did not fear violence and that 30 per cent had been threatened by politicians.[50] What began as an attempt by Moi and his entourage to ensure their hegemony and win elections had escalated so severely that the state was in jeopardy of losing its monopoly of legitimate force. Violence was biding its time in the corridors of Nairobi and the countryside, waiting to explode when and if it was tapped. It was and it did after the 2007 election results were announced amidst cries of rigging. Given the way in which the state had ironically abandoned its monopoly while trying to strengthen it, the explosion was not so surprising.

Deliberately Weak Institutions

'A nation state is failed when its institutions no longer work' (*Nation*, 26 January 2008).

'[There is] a failure of our institutions to come up with results that are auditable and verifiable' (*East African Standard*, 28 January 2008).

One of the hallmarks of democracy is its system of checks and balances among the executive, legislative, and judicial branches of government. Douglas North argues that government, as well as other organizations, operates according to 'rules of the game' that determine how it actually works. Formal rules of the game are laid down in written constitutions, laws, and organizational directives. Informal rules of the game consist of unwritten norms that are enforced through often unspoken sanctions and rewards. Both, but particularly informal rules of the game, tend to support the status quo and the interests of the actors which they serve. This is why attempting to transpose systems from one part of the world to another mostly does not work; old norms undermine new systems.[51]

---

50. 'Ethnicity, Violence, and the 2007 Election in Kenya', 3.

51. North, 'Economic Performance through Time', 360–62, 366.

Since independence, the formal rules of the game in Kenya have been changed over time to buttress a strong executive at the expense of other parts of government. The informal norms increasingly have undermined even these changed formal rules by trumping the autonomy of independent branches of government in favour of a highly personalized presidency. Hence, the independence of institutions outside the presidency has been weakened deliberately by those whose interests it supports.

This phenomenon of deliberately weak autonomous institutions outside the presidency was a precipitating factor in explaining why Kenya imploded after the 2007 election. When both internal and external election observers challenged the legitimacy of the election on numerous counts, the question arose as how these challenges could be dealt with and resolved. Parties to the election as well as citizens did not believe that the Electoral Commission of Kenya (ECK) was independent from the executive and felt that the results it announced had been doctored either there or in the field.[52] Less than two months before the election, President Kibaki replaced all of the ECK's commissioners, simultaneously appointing his former lawyer as the ECK's Vice-Chairman. This violated an informal agreement from 1997 that all parties would have a say in appointing commissioners to the ECK.[53] Also, in contrast to past practices, commissioners were now responsible for overseeing election results in their own provinces as well as hiring returning officers, who in turn owed them loyalty. Overall, this dissipated confidence in the ECK.[54]

Furthermore, when the Attorney General said that disputes over the results should be resolved in the courts, there was a huge outcry. The reason was that on important issues, Kenya's judiciary is viewed as partisan rather than impartial and as tied to the executive rather than independent from it. This has been a long-standing problem, but was exacerbated in the run-up to the election when a new bill created 57 judicial vacancies in the high court and 17 others in the court of appeals.[55] Hence, the argument over who won the presidency took to the streets after the ECK announced the election results. The crisis sparked by contested results ignited this second underlying precipitating factor: that of deliberately weak institutions. Again, had the election not been so close, and had there not been allega-

52. Kibara, 'The Challenges and Efficiency of Election Monitoring', 284–302. Nyamu, 'Managing Elections in Kenya', 265–89; Aywa and Grignon, 'As Biased As Ever?', 102–05.

53. *Africa Confidential* 48, nos. 23 and 25, 16 November and 14 December 2007. For a further elaboration of this point see the testimony of the U.S. Deputy Assistant Secretary of State for Africa. Swan, 'The Political Crisis of Kenya'.

54. International Crisis Group, 'Kenya in Crisis', 13.

55. *Africa Confidential* 48, no. 25, 14 December 2007.

tions of riggings, it might not have come to this. But it did, in the face of
elections that were too close to call beforehand and contested afterwards.

The Executive Presidency

From the standpoint of formal rules, the history of the presidency has
been one of increasing personalized power at the centre. Odiambo-Mbai
notes that after passing a constitutional amendment in 1964 that made
Kenyatta both head of state and head of government, KANU put through
nine other amendments by 1968 that increased the power of the executive
at the expense of other organs of government. During this period, federalism was abolished, the opposition parties at independence folded, KANU
became an arm of the state, and the influence of local authorities was
denuded.[56] These amendments included the notorious preventive detention act. As early as 1970, the powers of government revolved exclusively
around Kenyatta and Leys referred to his home as a 'court'.[57] At the same
time, parliament became little more than a rubber stamp for the executive.

In terms of the formal rules of the game, opposition parties were legally
allowed until an amendment to the constitution in 1982 prohibited them.
However, those who joined the opposition KPU in 1966 were punished
when they crossed the floor, losing jobs, parastatal appointments, and being harassed.[58] Those who came back to the fold were in turn rewarded.
These were the well known informal rules of the game which everyone
understood. As Kenyatta himself said at the time when he went to Gem
constituency in Nyanza in an attempt to wean back the opposition, 'Kenyatta has the sugar, . . . go lick his hands'.[59] Most did.

Under President Moi, numerous other amendments to the constitution
were passed, including Section 2A of the constitution, which turned Kenya
into a de jure one-party state in 1982. By 1991, the constitution had been
amended about 32 times. Although Section 2A was removed in 1991, the
other clauses pertaining to 'personal rule' were 'left intact'.[60] In addition,
Moi erased distinctions between party and state, took away the lifetime
security of tenure of the Attorney General, Solicitor General, and judges,
and introduced queue voting for elections in 1988.[61]

---

56. Odhiambo-Mbai, 'The Rise and Fall of the Autocratic State', 60–63.

57. Ibid., 64.

58. Mueller, 'Government and Opposition in Kenya', 406–26.

59. Quotation from field notes of Malcolm Valentine, cited in Mueller, ibid., 423

60. Odhiambo-Mbai, 'The Rise and Fall of the Autocratic State', 69.

61. Kanyinga, 'Limitations of Political Liberalization', 103–04.

The Continued Weakness of Autonomous Institutions Post-2002

Even after the creation of multi-partyism in 1991, Asingo argues correctly that those in favor of democracy did not 'creat[e] strong political institutions, structures, and processes supportive of democratic values'.[69] Furthermore, rules were often non-existent or ignored, particularly when it came to party nominations and election financing.[70] Acemoglu and Robinson argue that institutional innovation tends to take place normally under two conditions: first when a ruling group is entrenched and there is no fear of losing from innovation, and second, when they face a high degree of competition and not making innovations might lead to their replacement.[71] When neither of these conditions applies, politicians tend to fear institutional innovation because innovating might lead to losses of political power and rents. The conditions favoring institutional change do not apply in Kenya. Hence, while the political atmosphere and the economy in Kenya greatly improved after the election of the NARC government, it is not surprising that institutions outside the presidency still continued to be weak and deliberately so.

A few examples will suffice. They show how large parts of government ignored the formal rules of the system, which were mostly paper rules that did not govern actual behavior. It also demonstrates that while ignoring the formal rules meant the checks and balances on the presidency did not work at one level, at another level the informal rules of the game worked very well for those in power. Under Moi and Kibaki, there were two big financial scandals: Goldenberg under Moi and Anglo-Leasing under both presidents. One involved the fictitious export of non-existent gold to take advantage of an export compensation scheme while the other consisted of air contracts to non-existent foreign companies abroad. Under the former, about US$1 billion left the Central Bank illegally, while the latter also involved several hundred million dollars in transactions, each in part having to do with campaign financing. In both cases, the formal rules of the Central Bank and the Ministry of Finance were suspended and ignored. In the Goldenberg case there was a long commission hearing. In the Anglo-Leasing case some ministers were dismissed temporarily and then reinstated. No higher-ups were ever punished. Both cases involved gross corruption and bypassing all the formal financial controls in the system, something that had profoundly detrimental effects on the economy and the integrity of the political system. The Anglo-Leasing case occurred under the new

---

69. Asingo, 'The Political Economy of Transition in Kenya', 26.

70. Ibid., 42–47; Oloo, 'The Contemporary Opposition in Kenya', 100–08.

71. Acemoglu and Robinson, 'Economic Backwardness in Political Perspective', 117.

National Rainbow Coalition (NARC) government, which had come in on an anti-corruption platform. Even before the public became aware of the Anglo-Leasing scandal, which involved a number of high-level ministers, Kibaki had hired John Githongo to be his anti-corruption tsar in the office of the president. Githongo brought the corruption emanating from the scandal to the attention of the president and his inner circle. His reward was being threatened for having betrayed his boss and fleeing the country in fear for his life.

Later in 2007, there was the mysterious case of the so-called 'Armenian brothers', two individuals who apparently were not Armenian but were closely involved with the alleged daughter of the President and his 'second wife', Mary Wambui. The 'Armenians' appeared to be implicated in contraband activities, including drugs, and possibly in undercover security operations, although none of this was ever made clear. For reasons not entirely obvious, they had a scam which involved suspending airport security and allowing them to pretend to be coming back into the country while carrying guns and clearing some imports thought to be contraband. All formal rules governing airport security were violated to allow this fictitious re-entry to take place after officials at the airport received a call from the president's daughter. Before that she had been working in a ministry where she never appeared. Shortly afterwards, *The East African Standard* newspaper was invaded and pulverized by a masked gang, allegedly attempting to prevent the publication of a damaging story about the 'Armenian' brothers, what they were doing in Kenya, their links to the president's family, and possibly other matters.

As mentioned earlier, in the last year before the election, the president appointed new commissioners to the Electoral Commission of Kenya (ECK) and three new judges to Kenya's High Court, where contested election appeals would be adjudicated. In all of the above cases formal rules or laws were ignored, bent, or misused in contrast to their original intent. The informal rules rewarded the perpetrators and punished those who did not play ball. Aside from further destroying the integrity of the state, the malleability of formal rules to accommodate executive and inner circle whims opened up the door to massive corruption, this time under President Kibaki. Given Kenya's long history of changing formal rules to increase presidential power and of undermining the autonomy of other institutions designed to provide for checks and balances in favour of informal norms designed to weaken them, Kenya's contested election presented a serious systemic challenge. Institutions such as the ECK and the courts, which in theory could have dealt with these challenges, were not viewed as independent or credible. They were seen as part of the presidency, not as separate from it. The apparent pressure to announce results at the ECK, allegations of rigging in the field both at the polling and constituency levels, changed numbers on forms and missing forms, ECK officials in the field who could not be reached, delays in tallying results and votes reaching Nairobi, as well as implausibly high turnouts and significant differences between the presidential and parliamentary vote in some areas, fuelled suspicions of rigging. Suspicions were further heightened when the head of the ECK, under pressure from both domestic and foreign observers, said he himself did not know who had won the election (a point he has since reiterated), and President Kibaki was sworn in secretly amidst allegations of rigging and then quickly appointed half of his cabinet. Hence, the historic and contemporary problem of deliberately weak and non-autonomous institutions outside the presidency was sparked by a too close to call contested election. It pushed the resolution of Kenya's elections off the table and into the streets.

Non-Programmatic Clientist Political Parties

'We failed to develop democratic struggles where opponents do not become enemies' (*Sunday Nation*, 27 January 2008).

'The only time government and opposition agree is when they want to fatten their pay checks' (*Nation*, 22 January 2008).

The third underlying precipitating factor ignited by the contested 2007 election was non-programmatic clientist parties based on ethnicity. Although Kenya has many ethnic groups who have lived side by side for years, politicians polarized and politicized ethnicity negatively in the run-up to the election. This ignited fears on both sides about what would happen if their parties did not win. When irregularities concerning results raised questions that were not resolved, some local opposition politicians and elders apparently organized ethnically driven violence in Eldoret and other parts of the Rift Valley among their supporters to protest the results and attack the Kikuyu, who supported Kibaki. Spontaneous violence also erupted in Nairobi, Kisumu, and elsewhere. Government responded with a shoot-to-kill policy in both Kisumu and Nairobi. Violence continued to escalate and then counter-violence, organized as ethnic retribution by supporters of government in Nakuru and Naivasha, also matured until Kenya was engulfed in death and destruction in many parts of the country. Human rights organizations and Western governments maintain that some of this violence, on both sides, was organized and orchestrated by politicians and businessmen. To understand why they chose to tap ethnicity, one must understand more about Kenyan politics and its political parties.

Political Parties

Kenya's political parties are not programmatic. Their ideologies, policies, and programs are largely indistinguishable and are not seen as particularly salient.[72] Politics is viewed primarily as a winner-takes-all zero-sum ethnic game. The national economic cake is the prize. Various ethnic groups argue openly that it is their turn to 'eat'.[73] The means to this end is controlling the state and having a fellow co-ethnic become president. As parties are not programmatic and institutions are weak, politicians are seen primarily as personal distributors of private rather than public goods.[74] Even though alliances and cross-ethnic coalitions are necessary to win the presidency, the winner is seen by others as the chief ethnic in charge. Hence, the importance of winning and not losing, particularly as political losses have meant being excluded from 'access to state resources'. This historical reality has encouraged what Cowen and Kanyinga call a 'communal logic' of 'tribalism' from above and 'below' to 'access state resources through one of our own because this is the only way to eat'.[75]

Kenyan politicians obtain power mostly by using ethnic arithmetic and clientage as mobilizing factors, whether articulated openly or not. As such, Kenya's leaders and politicians have shifted from party to party and in the process made strange bedfellow alliances with each other.[76] Even those who are in opposition now have been in each other's governments and cabinets at one time or another. For instance, Kibaki was Moi's Vice-President in KANU from 1978 to 1988. Odinga as head of the Liberal Democratic Party (LDP) joined Kibaki's NARC government until he broke with him over a watered-down constitutional referendum in 2005 designed to create the post of Prime Minister and decentralize government. Before that, Odinga was a minister under Moi until 2002 when Moi anointed Uhuru Kenyatta as his would-be KANU candidate in the upcoming election to succeed him as president. Piqued at being sidelined Odinga then went

---

72. Oloo, 'The Contemporary Opposition in Kenya', 95, 100–03.

73. See Jonyo, 'The Centrality of Ethnicity in Kenya's Political Transition', 155–79.

74. For discussions of why politicians in 'young democracies' find it cheaper and more efficient to deliver targeted private, as opposed to public goods, see Keefer, 'Clientism, Credibility and Policy Choices', 804–21, and Keefer and Vlaicu, 'Democracy, Credibility, and Clientism'.

75. Cowen and Kanyinga, 'The 1997 Elections', 170.

76. Wanyande, 'The Politics of Alliance Building in Kenya', 128–84; Ajulu, 'Kenya's 1992 Election'; Ajulu, 'Kenya: Reflection on the 2002 Elections'.

into a rainbow coalition of parties known as NARC with Kibaki. More recently, before the 2007 election, Kibaki made a seemingly unholy alliance with Moi and Biwott of KANU and with Uhuru Kenyatta, who by that time had shifted to the PNU, Kibaki's new party. Odinga then in another alliance of convenience to gain votes in the Rift Valley and other marginal areas joined hands with questionable KANU majimboist stalwarts, who either faced gross corruption charges or had been named as perpetrators in the ethnic cleansing operations of the 1990s. All of the above was possible given the parties' lack of ideology and their meagre differences in party programs. Many other parties (aptly called 'briefcase parties') have no offices, no national network, and no apparent ideology. They spring up at election time to allow individuals to stand as MPs. This phenomenon has increased, particularly now that MPs, mostly untaxed salaries have risen to about $190,000 annually. For instance, in the 2007 election, Limuru District in Kiambu Province had 25 individuals running on as many different parties to be the MP while 2,248 candidates ran for 210 parliamentary seats.[77]

Given the non-programmatic nature of Kenyan political parties, the lack of institutional checks on the president, his consequent personal power, and the expectations of benefits from clients, ethnicity is seen as critical in determining the distribution of national resources. In part, this explains the length to which leaders and followers are willing to go to get their leader in power and the means they are willing to use to achieve their ends. Hence, politically inspired violence has accompanied successive multi-party elections from 1992 until 2007. Under these circumstances it is not so surprising that some of Odinga's supporters threatened to burn up his farm and other property in Nyanza if he did not return home from negotiations with the presidency.

During Kenyatta's rule, other ethnic groups argued that the Kikuyu benefited, obtaining land and civil service jobs at their expense. Moi in turn used his power to destroy the Kikuyu's economic base while rewarding his own ethnic Kalenjin and other marginal groups with jobs and appointments to government. Since assuming power, Kibaki also has been criticized for favoring the Kikuyu from his area, known as the 'Mount Kenya Mafia', and ignoring high-level corruption in his inner circle. Even when such views do not always tell the whole story, they take on a heightened significance, in part explaining why politics is seen as a zero-sum ethnic game.

Literature in political science has termed the above syndrome as 'prebendalist', 'patrimonial', and 'neo-patrimonial'. Nevertheless, recent dis-

---

77. *Africa Confidential* 48, no. 25, 14 December 2007.

cussions of ethnicity suggest that 'co-ethnics' often do not benefit from having one of their own in power and may even be taxed more than non-co-ethnics. This happens for two reasons: either it is assumed they will vote for a co-ethnic anyway and hence do not need to be bought off or because well-to-do intermediaries who mobilize the general co-ethnic population benefit at the latter's expense.[78] Furthermore, co-ethnics also may vote for one of their own as a defensive strategy, effectively against another ethnic group assuming power. As Kasara notes, 'co-ethnics supporters are reluctant to oust rulers for fear that rival ethnic groups will take power and make them worse off '.[79] Under these circumstances, it also may not be necessary to shower supporters with rewards to obtain their votes.

This in part explains the pattern of voting in the 2007 Kenyan election and the hate and violence that was able to be mobilized in case of a loss. The voting was as much against large coalitions of ethnic groups as it was in favour of any one. The old Gikuyu Embu and Meru Association (GEMA), a defensive ethnic alliance initially created during Kenyatta's time to keep Moi from becoming president, and its allies feared Kikuyus would be displaced from their land and jobs if ODM came to power with Odinga's ex-KADU majimboist allies. The '41 against one campaign' (all 41 ethnic groups against the Kikuyu) and all that implied frightened them. Moi, Biwott, and the Kenyatta family all joined interethnic hands to support Kibaki as president, principally to protect their fortunes in spite of ethnic and other past squabbles. This protection was perceived as necessary as ODM had promised to go after corruption and return what had been looted from the Treasury. Odinga's run satisfied the Luo's belief that it was 'their turn' for the presidency, something majimboists from marginal areas were prepared to stomach to put KADU back in power and rid themselves of the Mount Kenya Kikuyus. Hence, the 2007 election was as much about what one might call exclusionary ethnicity and who would not get power and control the state's resources as it was about who would. Understood this way and given the saliency of ethnicity due to the personalization of power, the weakness of institutions, the lack of programmatic parties, and the perceived importance of clientism, it is easy to see how politicians could use political loss to politically ignite ethnic violence.

Political economists examining the question of the circumstances under which ethnicity can be polarized and mobilized for political ends, including using violence, argue that the size of ethnic groups is a factor.[80] Hence,

---

78. Kasara, 'Tax Me If You Can', 159–72.

79. Ibid., 161.

80. Collier, *The Bottom Billion*, 25–26; Posner, 'The Political Salience of Cultural Differences', 529–45.

this sort of mobilization is not characteristic of Tanzania or Zambia, where there are large numbers of small groups rather than a few large groups. Furthermore, Posner argues the size of ethnic groups tends be redefined as larger in multi-party as opposed to single-party elections, something that has happened in Kenya.[81] In the 2007 presidential election, for instance, Odinga took on the old KADU anti-Kikuyu alliance and hence ODM was perceived in those terms by some PNU Kibaki supporters. Conversely, ODM increasingly viewed the PNU as another GEMA Kikuyu power grab, given its own MPs' exclusion from Kibaki's cabinet over the 2005 referendum and Kibaki's refusal to honor a Memorandum of Understanding before the 2002 election that would have created the post of Prime Minister for Odinga. As former MP Koigi wa Wamwere has noted, 'Today, many express surprise that we are fighting. They say we buried negative ethnicity in 2002. We did not. As all united against the Kikuyu during the [2005 constitutional] referendum and last elections, in 2002, all united against KANU, Moi and the Kalenjin.'[82]

None of this alone explains the post-election violence, but demonstrates how the nature of non-programmatic winner-take-all clientist political parties fed into the polarization of ethnicity for political ends, which could be ignited violently after a contested election and was. Nevertheless, as Fearon and Laitin argue, just because individuals are 'mobilize[d] along ethnic lines does not mean ethnic diversity is the root cause'.[83] In the case of Kenya, the violent mobilization of ethnicity had been a political project to win elections (as well as to control the state, and gain access to its resources) since the 1990s, which was never checked and hence thrived because of certain underlying conditions.

Post-Election Violence and Its Escalation

'Those who came to kill me are the same people I had come to regard as relatives' (*Nation*, 23 January 2008).

'Both ODM and PNU painted each other as ethnic demons' (*Sunday Nation*, 27 January 2008).

The above argument is that Kenya was already on a precipice because of the three factors just discussed. The 2007 disputed election was the cata-

---

81. Posner, 'Regime Change and Ethnic Cleavages', 1302, 1304–05.

82. Daily Nation, 15 February 2008.

83. Fearon and Laitin, 'Ethnicity, Insurgency, and Civil War', 88.

lyst that ignited them and led to Kenya imploding with violence that was already sitting in wait in large parts of the country ready to be tapped.[84] Violence infused the run-up to the 2007 elections and escalated afterwards along ethnic lines, engulfing large parts of the country. By February 2008, an estimated 1,000 people were dead and over 350,000 had been displaced in camps. Individuals who had lived their whole lives in different parts of the country fled for safety, fearing former friends, and neighbors as well as organized gangs. Some went east and some west, often to places they had never lived, now designated their ancestral homelands. Essentially, the idea of nation had been fractured, and Kenya appeared to be turning rapidly into a set of politically and economically unviable, ethnically homogeneous Bantustans.

The diffused violence after the election and the frittering away of the state's monopoly on legitimate force also took their toll in ways that can only be described as chilling. Gangs not only began to patrol slums and various parts of the countryside, but also moved into middle-class urban and rural areas, with reports of new militias arming along ethnic lines to exact retribution, as well as to rob, kill, maim, and take over the control of various areas. This raised the question of who was in charge: government or gangs.

Gang wars in Nairobi's slums continued unabated as before. During the election campaign, the Kenya National Commission of Human Rights (KNCHR) and the local press documented the following problems: intimidation, threats or attacks on parliamentary candidates, hate speech, the distribution of hate leaflets, violence between groups of rival supporters, shootings, plus ethnic clashes and the displacement of 2,000 families in Mount Elgon and Kuresui, with police doing nothing even when they had been informed in advance.[85] They also noted that an assistant minister and another MP were transporting weapons in their vehicles, while journalists mentioned a run on pangas (machetes) in Nairobi's upscale supermarket chain, Nakumatt. Some Kikuyu in parts of the Rift Valley that had experienced election violence reported being intimidated by gangs of youth and having their voting cards ripped up in front of them. In the Dandora housing scheme in Nairobi, Kikuyu small businessmen said their shops were marked for takeover in anticipation of an opposition win. Without more information, it is impossible to assess the extent of these activities.

---

84. The examples discussed below come from discussions and news reports from the Nation, the East African Standard, and the international media.

85. KNCHR, *Still Behaving Badly.*

Although the election itself was peaceful, violence escalated when Raila Odinga's early lead for the presidency began to dissipate and the results were delayed amidst allegations of rigging. Violence consisted initially of spontaneous violence, destruction of property and killings along ethnic lines, first by ODM supporters in Kisumu and then in the ethnically mixed slums of Nairobi, where youths armed with machetes and Mungiki gang members went on a killing spree. It then quickly spread to other parts of the country with ethnically mixed populations, particularly after 30 December when the ECK declared Kibaki president and he was swiftly and secretly sworn in. Often, victims spoke of having been attacked by neighbours and fellow workers whom they viewed as friends.

Organized violence of Kalenjin gangs against Kikuyus in Eldoret area quickly took over. Whole families of Kikuyu were burnt alive in a church in Kiambaa, property was torched, and many others were killed with machetes in other parts of the Rift and elsewhere in the country. In Uasin Gishu, properties of departed residents were stripped of their old signs and renamed. In response, individuals of different ethnic groups then began to set up road-blocks out of Nairobi towards Limuru and then on the main roads in and out of various parts of the Rift, including in and out of Naivasha, Nakuru, Kisumu and parts of Kisii. Citizens of various ethnic groups in different areas who happened to be in the 'wrong' place were dragged from their cars, homes, and shops, and hacked to death or had their property destroyed. If they were from a minority ethnic group, they were asked for their identity cards, names, or to speak the language of their attackers and then brutally killed if they had the 'wrong' name or spoke the 'wrong' language. Property also was destroyed and towns such as Kisumu were decimated.

The police finally stepped in, but with a shoot-to-kill policy, particularly in Kisumu, which was criticized both by the opposition and human rights groups. Retaliatory violence then began in Nakuru and Naivasha with Kikuyu gangs, alleged to be Mungiki, going after both Luos and Kalenjins. Accusations mounted that ex-majimboist politicians in the opposition were responsible for the organized killings in Eldoret just as they had been in the 1990s, while the ODM accused government and pro-Kibaki businessmen of hiring Mungiki to carry out retaliatory raids. In addition, freelance violence escalated with resulting robberies, looting of shops, rapes, and other crimes. Meanwhile, text messaging was full of hate and cries to get rid of the *madoadoa* (spots).

Schools and universities, which always had attracted students and faculty from different parts of Kenya, were unable to protect them and everyone who could decamped to their so-called 'ancestral homes'. Local

officials at Baraton University, a religious college in the Rift Valley, had
to plead with gangs to allow a bus of ethnically mixed evacuees out of the
compound. Individuals from western Kenya working in the Kikuyu tea and
coffee estates and the Bata shoe company around Limuru took refuge in
camps for internally displaced people (IDP) in Tigoni. Kikuyus who had
lived and had businesses in Kisumu escaped to Uganda, while horticultural
enterprises in Naivasha provided shelter for their workers from western
Kenya, as they worried about their wilting roses and not being able to fly
out their flowers to meet their Valentine's Day quota in Europe. Kikuyu,
Luo, and Luhya who had made their homes in Eldoret and other parts of
the Rift for decades decamped, vowing never to return. Even in Nairobi,
some middle-class workers in the upscale Kabete and Lower Kabete areas,
who were concerned for their safety, decided to move to more ethnically
homogeneous parts of the city. Businesses, such as polling firms, could not
send staff out to do surveys because of the potential for violence against
workers whose ethnicity was different from those in the areas where they
were going work. The atmosphere in certain ethnically mixed offices was
chilly and some workers worried about being poisoned.

Recently diffused violence and the state's diminished monopoly on legitimate force also took their toll in ways that were frightening. Gangs
patrolled the slums and moved into more middle-class urban and rural
areas. Here, they intimidated their hapless victims, meting out justice and
robbing them. In Nakuru, young men demanded 'youth levies' from residents. Mungiki, in turn, threatened journalists with text messages. Sometimes the motive appeared to be political, sometimes not, indicative of the
state's impotence or its abnegation of responsibility for maintaining law
and order.

In mid-February, a gang of thirty masked men invaded the house of
ODM James Orengo, in upper-class Runda, while other MPs asked the
state for protection and body guards. In Nairobi, Kisumu, Nakuru, and
elsewhere in both urban and rural areas, ordinary citizens found gangs
rather than the state's security forces in charge. They 'issued threats', 'maintained segregation' between groups, used the pretext of hunting for 'particular communities' to enter people's houses and rob them, threatening those
in mixed marriages, and forced them to move. In defence, some citizens
organized their own security, arming themselves with guns and machetes.
Hence, as discussed earlier, the diffusion of violence away from the state
increasingly began to jeopardize the very integrity of the state itself.

At the same time non-state violence was escalating and becoming more
diffuse, the two political parties took two months to agree to a power-
sharing agreement on a new government, with future discussions concern-

ing legal, constitutional, and other arrangements still pending. However, even if mutually agreeable changes come to pass, new formal rules of the game may not solve Kenya's problems. The reason is, as earlier sections of this article have indicated, informal rules and enforcement mechanisms in the past have tended to support the status quo and the interests of their actors while undermining formal rules, especially new ones that might disrupt it. There is no reason this could not happen again, particularly as political parties are clientist, nonprogrammatic, and revolve around the chief ethnic group in charge winning and capturing the state. The additional assumption that decentralization would be a panacea also is suspect. The same informal rules of the game that have governed politics nationally could just be transferred downwards. Furthermore, as Treisman notes, in countries that are economically underdeveloped, federalism or decentralization actually increases rather than decreases corruption, contrary to current popular mythology.[86] When legal systems are not effective, increasing the number of actors heightens corruption, something that also could be a problem for Kenya given its long history of having created deliberately weak institutions with little autonomy from the president. Also, with its new power-sharing arrangement, Kenya now may have backtracked into a one-party state, at least for the life of this parliament, raising further questions concerning its transition to democracy; beyond this, diffused violence could easily be ignited once again.

Conclusions

'In history, the stories of failure are more frequent than the stories of success' (Mantzavinos, North and Shariq, 'Learning, Institutions and Economic Performance', 2004)

In the 1990s, policymakers and academics greeted Africa's embrace of multi-party democracy and its ensuing elections with euphoria. They assumed incorrectly that most countries were heading down a one-way path to democracy and development. Later some scholars critiqued this overreliance on elections, renaming the transition entities in both Africa and the former Soviet Union 'virtual democracies'.[87]

The point of this article has been to dissect what happened in Kenya and why. It suggests a need to look more closely at political economy fac-

---

86. Treisman, 'The Causes of Corruption: A Cross-National Study', 399–457.

87. See Carothers, 'Democracy Without Illusions" 22–43; Joseph, 'Democratization in Africa', 363–82; Joseph, 'Africa, 1990–1997', 5–19.

tors outside the electoral process itself. These include the incentive systems driving the state, violence, institutions, and the nature of political parties, among others. The 2007 election ignited deep-seated historical trajectories underlying each of these factors. In many cases they suggest what Douglas North has aptly described as 'path dependence', the tendency of systems to revert to stasis and rely on established rules of the game, rather than easy prospects for fundamental change.[88] For this reason and others discussed in the introduction to this paper, both the incentive system and these trajectories need to be explored further in Kenya and elsewhere.

Acknowledgments

I dedicate this article to the memory of Appollo Njonjo, my life-long friend and colleague, who spent his life fighting for democracy and against the twin evils of tribalism and violence. I would like to thank Phil Keefer for his astute comments on an earlier draft of this article as well as many unnamed colleagues in Kenya, the UK and Europe whose ideas, writings, and friendship have enhanced my understanding of Kenya over the years most of whose names are listed in my bibliography. I would also like to thank the editors of the journal for many interesting exchanges and for their collegiality.

References

Acemoglu, D., and J. A. Robinson. "Economic Backwardness in Political Perspective." *American Political Science Review* 100, no. 1 (2000): 115–31.

Africa Confidential. 2002–2007.

Africa Watch. *Divide and Rule: State-Sponsored Ethnic Violence in Kenya.* New York: Human Rights Watch, 1992.

Ajulu, R. "Kenya: A Reflection on the 2002 Elections: Third Time Lucky or More of the Same?" IGD Occasional Paper No. 39. Braamfontein, South Africa: Institute for Global Dialogue, November 2003.

———. "Kenya's 1992 Election and Its Implication for Democratisation in Sub-Saharan Africa." FDG Occasional Paper No. 9. Braamfontein, South Africa, March 1997.

Anderson, David M. "De cline et Chute de la KANU: Politique Partisane et Succession de Moi (Kenya)." *Politique Africaine*, no. 90 (June 2003): 37–55.

———. "Vigilantes, Violence, and the Politics of Public Order in Kenya." *African Affairs* 101, no. 405 (2002): 531–55.

---

88. North, 'Economic Performance through Time', 365–67.

————. "'Yours in the Struggle for Majimbo': Nationalism and the Party Politics of Decolonization in Kenya." *Journal of Contemporary History* 40, no. 3 (2005): 547–64.

Asingo, P. O. "The Political Economy of Transition in Kenya." In *Politics of Transition in Kenya: From Kenya to NARC*, edited by W.O. Oyugi, P. Wanyande, and C. Odhiambo-Mbai. Nairobi: Heinrich Böll Foundation, 2003, 15–50.

Aywa, F. A., and F. Grignon. "As Biased as Ever? The Electoral Commission Prior to Polling Day." In *Out for the Count: The 1997 General Elections and Prospects for Democracy in Kenya*, edited by M. Rutten, A. Mazrui, and F. Grignon. Kampala: Foundation Publishers, 2001.

Ballentine, Karen, and Jake Sherman, eds. *The Political Economy of Armed Conflict: Beyond Greed and Grievance*. Boulder, CO: Lynne Rienner, 2003.

Barkan, Joel, ed. *Beyond Capitalism vs. Socialism in Kenya and Tanzania*. Boulder, CO: Lynne Rienner, 1994.

————. "Divergence and Convergence in Kenya and Tanzania." In *Beyond Capitalism vs. Socialism in Kenya and Tanzania*, edited by Joel Barkan. Boulder, CO: Lynne Rienner, 1994, 1–45.

Bates, R. H. *Beyond the Miracle of the Market: The Political Economy of Agrarian Development in Kenya*. Cambridge: Cambridge University Press, 1989.

————. "Institutions and Development." *Journal of African Economics* 15, Supplement 1 (2006): 10–61.

Boone, C. "Winning and Losing Politically Allocated Land Rights." Unpublished paper for the African Studies Association Meetings, New York, 2007.

Branch, D., and N. Cheeseman. "Briefing: Using Opinion Polls to Evaluate Kenya Politics, March 2004–January 2005." *African Affairs* 104, no. 415 (2005): 325–36.

Branch, D., and N. Cheeseman. "The Politics of Control in Kenya: Understanding the Bureaucratic Executive State, 1952–78." *Review of African Political Economy* 107 (2006): 11–31.

Carothers, T. "Democracy Without Illusions." *Foreign Affairs* 76 (November–December 1997): 22–43.

Carver, R., and L. Kirschke. *Deadly Marionettes: State Sponsored Violence in Africa*. London: Article 19, International Centre Against Censorship, 2007.

Chege, M. "The Return of Multi-Party Politics." In *Beyond Capitalism vs. Socialism in Kenya and Tanzania*, edited by Joel Barkan. Boulder, CO: Lynne Rienner, 1994, 46–74.

Collier, P. *The Bottom Billion: Why the Poorest Countries Are Failing and What Can be Done About It*. Oxford: Oxford University Press, 2007.

Collier, P., and A. Hoeffler. "Greed and Grievance in Civil War." *Oxford Economic Papers* 56, no. 4 (2004): 563–95.

Cowen, M., and K. Kanyinga. "The 1997 Elections in Kenya: The Politics of Communality and Locality." In *Multi-Party Elections in Africa*, edited by Michael Cowen and Liisa Laakso. Oxford: James Currey, 2002, 128–71.

"Ethnicity, Violence and the 2007 Elections in Kenya." Unpublished paper discussing survey research, 8 February 2008.

Fearon, J. D., and D. D. Laitin. "Ethnicity, Insurgency, and Civil War." *American Political Science Review* 19, no. 1 (2003): 75–90.

Frederiksten, B. F. "Politics, Popular Culture, and Livelihood Strategies Among Young Men in a Nairobi Slum." In *African Alternative*, edited by U. Engel and L. Haan. Leiden and Boston: Brill, 2007.

Gecaga, M. "Religious Movements and Democratisation: Between the Sacred and the Profane." In *Kenya: The Struggle for Democracy*, edited by Godwin Murunga and Shadrack W. Nasong'o. London and New York: Zed Books, 2007, 58–89.

Gimonde, E. A. "The Role of the Police in Kenya's Democratisation Process." In *Kenya: The Struggle for Democracy*, edited by G. Murunga and S.W. Nasong'o. London and New York: Zed Books, 227–60.

Glaeser, E. L., and A. Schleifer. "The Curley Effect: The Economics of Shaping the Electorate." *Journal of Law, Economics and Organization* 21, no. 1 (April 2005): 1–19.

Hornsby, C. "The 2007 Kenya General Election: What Can We Tell From the Data." Unpublished paper, 22 January 2008.

Hulterstrom, K. "The Logic of Ethnic Politics: Elite Perceptions About the Role of Ethnicity in Kenyan and Zambian Party Politics." In *Political Opposition in African Countries*, Discussion Paper No. 37, edited by Henning Melbert. Uppsala: Nordiska Afrikomstituet, 2007, 7–38.

International Crisis Group. "Kenya in Crisis." Brussels: International Crisis Group, 21 February 2008.

Jonyo, F. "The Centrality of Ethnicity in Kenya's Political Transition." In *The Politics of Transition in Kenya: From KANU to NARC*, edited by W.O. Oyugi, P. Wanyande and C. Odhiambo-Mbai. Nairobi, Kenya: Henrich Böll Foundation, 2003, 155–79.

Joseph, R. "Africa, 1990–1997. From Abertura to Closure." *Journal of Democracy* 9, no. 2 (1998): 1–17.

———. "Democratization in Africa After 1989: Comparative Theoretical Perspectives." *Comparative Politics* 29, no. 3 (April 1997): 363–82.

Kagwanja, P.M. "Politics of Marionettes: Extra-Legal Violence and the 1997 Elections in Kenya." In *Out for the Count: The 1997 General Elections and Prospects for Democracy in Kenya*, edited by M. Rutten, A. Mazrui, and F. Grignon, Kampala, Uganda: Fountain Publishers, 2001, 72–100.

———. "Clash of Generations? Youth, Identity, and the Politics of Transition in Kenya, 1997–2002." In *Vanguard or Vandals: Youth, Politics, and Conflict in Africa*, edited by J. Abbink and I. van Kessel. Leiden and Boston: Brill, 81–109.

———. "Facing Mount Kenya or Facing Mecca? The Mungiki Ethnic Violence and the Politics of the Moi Succession." *African Affairs* 102, no. 406 (January 2003): 25–49.

―――. " 'Power to Uhuru': Youth, Identity, and Generational Violence in Kenya's 2002 Elections." *African Affairs* 105, no. 418 (January 2006): 51–75.

Kamungi, P. M. "The Current Situation of Internally Displaced Persons in Kenya." Unpublished report, Jesuit Refugee Service (EA), March 2001.

Kanyinga, K. "Contestation over Political Space: The State and Demobilization of Party Politics in Kenya." CDR Working Paper 98/12. Copenhagen: Center for Development Research (CDR), November 1998.

―――. "Limitations of Political Liberalization: Parties and Electoral Politics in Kenya, 1992–2002." In *The Politics of Transition in Kenya: From KANU to NARC*, edited by W. Oyugi, P. Wanyande, and C. Odhiambo-Mbai. Nairobi, Kenya: Heinrich Böll Foundation, 2003, 96–127.

―――. *Redistributing From Above: The Politics of Land Rights and Squatting in Coastal Kenya*, Research Report No. 115. Uppsala: Nordiska Afrikainstitutet, 2000.

Kasara, K. "Tax Me If You Can: Geography, Democracy, and the Taxation of Agriculture in Agriculture in Africa." *American Political Science Review* 101, no. 1 (February 2007): 159–72.

Katumanga, M. "A City Under Siege: Banditry and Modes of Accumulation in Nairobi, 1991–2004." *Review of African Political Economy*, no. 106 (2005): 505–20.

Keefer, P. "Clientism, Credibility, and Policy Choices of Young Democracies." *American Journal of Political Science* 51, no. 4 (October 2007): 804–21.

Keefer, P., and R. Vlaicu. "Democracy, Credibility and Clientism." *Journal of Law, Economics and Organization*, 2 December 2007. DOI:10.1093/jleo/ewm054.

Kenya Human Rights Commission (KHRC). *Kayas of Deprivation, Kayas of Blood: Violence, Ethnicity and the State in Coastal Kenya*. Nairobi: Kenya Human Rights Commission, 1997.

―――. *Kayas Revisited: A Post Election Balance Sheet*. Nairobi: Kenya Human Rights Commission, 1998.

―――. *Where Terror Rules: Torture By Kenyan Police in North Eastern Province*. Nairobi: Kenya Human Rights Commission, 1998.

Kenya National Commission on Human Rights (KNCHR). *Living Large: Counting the Cost of Official Extravagances*. Nairobi: Kenya National Commission on Human Rights and Transparency Kenya, January 2006.

―――. *Still Behaving Badly: Second Periodic Report of the Election Monitoring Project*. Nairobi: Kenya National Commission on Human Rights and Transparency, December 2007.

Kibara, G. "The Challenges and Efficiency of Election Monitoring." In *The Politics of Transition in Kenya: from KANU TO NARC*, edited by W. Oyugi, P. Wanyande, and C. Odhiambo-Mbai, Nairobi, Kenya: Heinrich Böll Foundation, 2003, 96–127.

Kimenyi, M. "Ethnicity, Governance and the Provision of Public Goods." *Journal of African Economics* 15, Supplement 1 (2006): 62–69.

Levitt, S. D., and S. J. Dubner. *Freakonomics: A Rogue Economist Explores the Hidden Side of Everything.* New York: HarperCollins, 2005.

Mantzavinos, C., D. North, and S. Shariq. "Learning, Institutions, and Economic Performance." *Perspectives on Politics* 2, no. 1 (March 2004): 75–84.

Moi, D.T. arap. *Kenya African Nationalism.* London: Macmillan, 1986, 174–83.

Mueller, S. D. "Government and Opposition in Kenya, 1966–1969." *Journal of Modern African Studies* 22, no. 3 (1984): 399–427.

———. "Political Parties in Kenya: Patterns of Opposition and Dissent: 1919–1969." Ph.D. diss., Princeton University, Princeton, NJ, 1972.

Mwangi, E. "Subdividing the Commons: Distributional Conflict in the Transition from Collective to Individual Property Rights in Kenya's Masailand." *World Development* 5, no. 5 (2007): 815–34.

Mwangola, M. "Leaders of Tomorrow: The Youth and Democratisation in Kenya." In *Kenya: Struggle for Democracy*, edited by G.R. Murunga and S.W. Nasong'o. London: Zed Books, 2007.

Ngunyi, M. "Resuscitating the 'Majimbo Projects': The Politics of Deconstructing the Unity State in Kenya." *In Challenges to the Nation State in Africa*, edited by A. O. Olukoshi and L. Laaska. Uppsala: Nordiska Afrikainstitutet, 1996.

North, D. C. "Economic Performance through Time." *American Economic Review* 84, no. 3 (1994): 359–68.

Nyamu, H. J. "Managing Elections in Kenya." In *The Politics of Transition in Kenya: From KANU to NARC*, edited by W. Oyugi, P. Wanyande, and C. Odhiambo-Mbai. Nairobi, Kenya: Heinrich Böll Foundation, 2003, 51–95.

Odhiambo-Mbai, C. "The Rise and Fall of the Autocratic State in Kenya." In *The Politics of Transition in Kenya: From KANU to NARC*, edited by W. Oyugi, P. Wanyande, and C. Odhiambo-Mbai. Nairobi, Kenya: Heinrich Böll Foundation, 2003.

Oloo, A. G. R. "The Contemporary Opposition in Kenya: Between Internal Traits and State Manipulation." In *Kenya: The Struggle for Democracy*, edited by G. Murunga and S.W. Nasong'o. London and New York: Zed Books, 2004, 90–125.

Oyugi, W. "The Politics of Transition in Kenya, 1992–2003: Democratic Consolidation or Deconsolidation." In *The Politics of Transition in Kenya: From KANU to NARC*, edited by W. Oyugi, P. Wanyande, and C. Odhiambo-Mbai. Nairobi, Kenya: Heinrich Böll Foundation, 2003.

Posner, D. N. "The Political Salience of Cultural Differences: Why Chewas and Tumbukas Are Allies in Zambia and Adversaries in Malawi." *American Political Science Review* 98, no. 4, (November 2004): 529–45.

———. "Regime Change and Ethnic Cleavages in Africa." *Comparative Political Studies* 40, no. 11 (November 2007) 1302–27.

Republic of Kenya and The Commission of Inquiry Act (Cap. 102). *Report of the Judicial Commission Appointed to Inquire Into Tribal Clashes in Kenya (Akiwumi Report).* Nairobi: Government Printer, 31 July 1999.

Rutten, M., A. Mazrui, and F. Grignon, eds. *Out for the Count: 1997 General Elections and Prospects for Democracy in Kenya*. Kampala, Uganda: Fountain Publishers, 2001.

Stren, R., M. Halfani, and J. Malombe. "Coping with Urbanization and Urban Policy." In *Beyond Capitalism vs. Socialism in Kenya and Tanzania*, edited by J. Barkan. Boulder, CO: Lynne Rienner, 1994, 175–200.

Swan, J., and U.S. State Department. "The Political Crisis in Kenya: A Call for Justice and Peaceful Resolution," Statement before the House Africa and Global Health Sub-Committee Hearing, Washington, DC, February 6, 2008.

Throup, D. "The Construction and Destruction of the Kenyatta State." In *The Political Economy of Kenya*, edited by Michael Schatzberg. New York: Praeger, 33–74.

Throup, D. W., and C. Hornsby. Multi-Party Politics in *Kenya: The Kenyatta and Moi States and the Triumph of the System*. Oxford: James Currey, 1998.

Treisman, D. "The Causes of Corruption: A Cross-National Study." *Journal of Political Economy* 76, no. 3 (June 2000): 399–457.

wa Wamwere, K. *The People's Representative and the Tyrants: Kenya Independence Without Freedom*. Nairobi: New Concept Typesetters, 1993.

Wanyande, P. "The Politics of Alliance Building in Kenya." In *The Politics of Transition in Kenya: From KANU to NARC*, edited by W. Oyugi, P. Wanyande, and C. Odhiambo-Mbai. Nairobi, Kenya: Heinrich Böll Foundation, 2003, 128–54.

Weber, M. *Basic Concepts in Sociology*. New York: Kensington Publication Corporation, 2002, 119–23.

Widner, J. A. *The Rise of a Party State in Kenya: From 'Harambee!' to 'Nyayo!'* Berkeley: University of California Press, 1992.

Wilcove, D. S. *No Way Home: The Decline of the World's Great Animal Migrations*. Washington, DC: Shearwater Books, Center for Resource Economics, 2008.

World Bank, Governance Indicators. Available from http://info.worldbank.org/governance/wgi2007/sc_country.asp.

7

Disturbance or Massacre?

Consequences of Electoral Violence in Ethiopia

Lahra Smith

While elections in developing countries have been the trigger for violence for some time, the evolving nature of electoral politics in sub-Saharan Africa has also shifted the nature, timing, and extent of this violence. In a few countries, violence has been a perennial feature of elections, regardless of whether those elections were genuinely competitive. In other places, as dominant political regimes have faced increasing public dissatisfaction, a more coherent and organized opposition, and international pressure to hold more transparent elections, incumbent elites have used violence to manipulate outcomes and intimidate voters, typically in the preelection phase. Other instances involve contestation over election results, typically initiated or led by opposition politicians and their supporters. This violence has had certain similar features, such as a significant level of citizen protest and, far too often, the use of excessive force by state security forces. In many cases, the narratives about the causes, consequences, and solutions to this election-related violence are widely divergent, providing critical insights into the triggers and sustaining factors in conflict and violence around elections.

Comparative study of electoral violence can give state actors, civil society, domestic peace activists, and international donors the opportunity to prevent, prepare for, and respond to incidents or sustained periods of

Extremely helpful comments on this chapter were provided by Dorina Bekoe and fellow participants in two United States Institute of Peace conferences held in June 2009 and February 2010, and by several colleagues who prefer to remain anonymous. Any errors or omissions are my own.

conflict around electoral processes. Because of the "increased importance of elections in post-war societies," both as a tool of peace promotion and democratization and because some kind of electoral process is likely to remain central in the political systems of most African states, consideration of the forms and motivations behind electoral violence calls for urgency and attentiveness by crucial actors at all phases of the process (Höglund 2009, 413). This should necessarily involve cross-national empirical study as well as case study knowledge. In chapter 2 of this volume, Straus and Taylor point to certain patterns of timing, forms of violence, and distinct constellations of violent actors through a cross-national analysis of all incidents of electoral violence in Africa from 1990 to 2008. This work finds that significant electoral violence is somewhat less frequent than has been assumed, and also that "if electoral violence occurs after an election, it is more likely to reach a high level than electoral violence occurring before an election" (Straus and Taylor, chapter 2 of this volume).

To complement this comparative study, this chapter considers Ethiopia, a country that provides a mid-range case of electoral violence. In Straus and Taylor's analysis, Ethiopia has seen a steady escalation of violence, from level 1 (violent harassment) in 1995 to level 2 (violent repression) in 2000, to level 3 (large-scale violence) in 2005. However, one of the important sets of questions obscured by this kind of large-N analysis involves the forms of violence and the sets of national-level discourses about that violence. First, the authors include only that violence occurring from six months before until three months after an election. This is reasonable in a quantitative coding process and important in analytically distinguishing electoral violence from other forms of political violence in multicountry, longitudinal studies of this type. But in Ethiopia, the most significant protests of the post-2005 election occurred five to six months after the election. Even more interestingly, although the more recent May 2010 violence would be coded as level 2 because of high-level assassinations and targeted murder in the preelection period, combined with long-term high-level arrests of party leaders, most people viewing the elections inside and outside Ethiopia would classify the 2010 elections as "peaceful" when compared to the sustained and substantial loss of life and property, as well as national confidence, after the 2005 elections. The popular understanding of these two elections stands in stark contrast to their coding here, and this "common narrative" of the elections is critical both in voter choices in future elections and in shaping the actions of the state between election cycles. The Ethiopian experience suggests that electoral violence has patterned and multielectoral-cycle implications, and that it conditions not only voters' and potential voters' choice sets in subsequent elections but the state or ruling party's actions as well.

Another set of factors that the Straus and Taylor dataset does not account for involves the locations and forms of violence, particularly when they do not directly involve the incumbents and challengers. Ethiopia provides the opportunity to make critical distinctions between those areas of the country where violence did occur and those where it did not. Most of the country saw little or no postelection violence in 2005. Of significant note, there were no reports of widespread or even localized intercommunal violence after the elections. Not only was election-related violence mostly an urban phenomenon, but also, it did not activate local grievances in Ethiopia in the way that it did in Kenya, for instance. This is somewhat unexpected since, in Ethiopia as in other places across the continent (e.g., Kenya, Côte d'Ivoire, and Zimbabwe), the relationship between the types of crucial political issues that were the focus of the electoral competition and the grievances of members of ethnic and communal groups are complex and intertwined. Also, despite a history of intercommunal tension and a significant focus on some of these controversial topics (e.g., land reform, ethnicity and the 1995 Constitution, and port access issues and relations with Eritrea) during the campaign, most of the violence in Ethiopia was localized and noncommunal in nature, and most of the lethal violence was perpetrated by the security forces, not by members of ethnolinguistic, regional, or religious communities against each other. Therefore, this chapter adds to the existing literature on electoral violence in Ethiopia by elaborating on the specific locations and forms of protest and violence by both the state and the wider society in Ethiopia in the post-2005 period.

Finally, the role of nonstate peace actors in preventing, stalling, and mediating electoral conflict deserves attention. In Ethiopia, a nascent but active set of civil society actors attempted to play a role in the 2005 elections, but its influence was sharply curtailed by the incumbent regime. This contrasts with Ghana, for example, where civil society has been instrumental in creating the conditions for electoral peace, or Kenya, where civil society has played a substantial role in postviolence peace promotion. This chapter assesses the critical nature of nonstate involvement in preventing and mediating electoral violence, in an attempt to shed light on possible policy interventions for future election cycles.

Sources of data are a challenge, and this chapter uses published human rights reports of the U.S. State Department and international advocacy groups, as well as the Ethiopian parliamentary report on the 2005 postelection violence (both the official parliamentary report and the "unofficial," disputed report). Also, I analyzed news accounts of the violence, and reports from various international nongovernmental organizations. It should be noted that, unlike in Kenya, no high-level delegations, either international or domestic in composition, were sent out to investigate incidents of electoral violence in the postelection period. Ethiopia does not have a trail of reports analogous to Kenya's postelection commissions. Similarly, because Ethiopia's civil society and media are beleaguered by the regime, high-quality, informative, and trustworthy reports from local organizations and media outlets are extremely rare.

The Electoral Context

Ethiopia does not have a long history of competitive multiparty elections. Perhaps because of this, neither does it have a long history of election-related violence. Ethiopia's most recent political transition began in the early 1990s, with the fall of the socialist military dictatorship of the Derg, and the flight of its leader, Mengistu Hailemariam. Under both the imperial government of Haile Selassie and the Derg, the ruling elite controlled all aspects of electoral politics despite efforts by students and grassroots movements to bring about meaningful social and economic reforms. After 1991, the newly formed Ethiopian People's Revolutionary Democratic Front (EPRDF) leadership, of which the Tigray People's Liberation Front was the founding member, made radical changes to the institutional structures of the Ethiopian state. Snap elections for local government were held in 1992. The EPRDF used intimidation and force to consolidate its political hold, particularly over the most substantial competitor, the Oromo Liberation Front (OLF). The OLF leadership had been admitted to participate in the elections and the newly established government, though it eventually withdrew and later fled into exile after facing significant political violence in its strongholds in western Oromiya (Pausewang, Tronvoll, and Aalen 2002). The EPRDF has controlled the political process ever since. Early attempts at a constituent assembly, while symbolically significant, were marred by withdrawals of key elites representing mostly distinct ethnolinguistic and regional communities. These groups have continued to contest the arrangements made during the transitional period. Despite the establishment of a multiparty system, the EPRDF has remained the dominant party throughout the past two decades (Rahmato and Ayenew 2004; Pausewang, Tronvoll, and Aalen 2002). Most notable among the political changes represented by this period were the establishment of a federal arrangement centered on ethnolinguistic identities, the 1993 Eritrean referendum on independence, and the scheduling of multiparty elections.[1]

---

1. Ethiopia has a parliamentary system, and unless otherwise noted, the elections referred to in this chapter were for the national and regional state parliaments. Under the current federal system, the country has been divided into nine regional states based primarily on the inhabitants' ethnicity, as well as two special administrative regions: the multiethnic cities of Addis Ababa and Dire Dawa. See Smith 2007.

In the 1995 elections, the major opposition political parties refused to participate, citing the ruling party's domination of the media, and the party registration process. Some of the major opposition parties did participate in the 2000 and 2001 elections, but they were fragmented and unable to challenge the ruling party effectively. In the 2000 national elections, the opposition won only 30 seats in the 547-member House of People's Representatives (Arriola 2008; Pausewang, Tronvoll, and Aalen 2002). Many of these political parties represented distinct local constituencies, and few had national constituencies. In each of these elections, observers cited the use of government structures to "subdue the rural population and any expression of opposition" (Tronvoll 2000).

By any measure, the election cycle in May 2005 represented a substantial change. By late 2004, opposition political parties had formed coalitions based on differing policy perspectives and nationalist visions. The main political parties—including the EPRDF, the United Ethiopian Democratic Forces, and the Coalition for Unity and Democracy (CUD), as well as smaller parties such as the Oromo Federalist Democratic Movement—campaigned on specific policy positions. The ruling party and the opposition reached an agreement on a formula to allocate access to important state-controlled media sources, including television and print media. International aid supported civic education. In the days before the election, large political rallies were well attended and peaceful. However, the ruling party blocked the changes to the electoral law suggested by major opposition political parties, including a change from plurality voting to proportional representation. The presence of the African Union, European Union, and Carter Center observer missions added some international legitimacy to the exercise, although the exclusion of local observer missions (discussed below) minimized that legitimacy. There was some preelection violence, including the killing of opposition party leaders and members in certain regions (U.S. State Dept. 2006).

Despite some problems, there were many promising signs in the preelection period. Televised debates, also broadcast on the radio and reported in the state-owned and private press, offered refreshing new sources of information for voters. For the first time, public debates between high-profile candidates of the main political party coalitions provided a forum for discussing some of the most controversial and important political issues, including policies on land ownership, economic development, language and education policy, and ethnic self-determination (Arriola 2008).

With all these controversial and substantive issues at play, voter turnout was high, and observer missions reported only minor irregularities on election day.[2] Rumors of unofficial results that put the opposition in the lead started to spread almost immediately after the election. Official results from the National Electoral Board of Ethiopia (NEBE) trickled out through June 2005, and the final official results were not announced until September, in part because an ad hoc complaints investigation process was initiated in June and July for some disputed constituencies.[3] Based on complaints reviewed, reelections were ordered in thirty-one constituencies and were held on August 21, 2005, together with the delayed polls in Somali regional state. The ruling party eventually won all these seats (Carter Center 2009). Official full results were then announced on September 5, 2005, with the combined opposition winning a total of 174 seats (32 percent of the total vote) out of 547 in the federal parliament.[4] The CUD did particularly well, winning 109 seats, including all the seats in Addis Ababa, where high-profile EPRDF members and cabinet ministers lost in stinging defeats. However, the EPRDF held on to its parliamentary majority, allowing it to appoint the prime minister and control the agenda and committees of the parliament.

The main opposition parties disputed the final results and the NEBE investigation process and outcomes. But the panic and brinkmanship of the main contenders quickly undermined the gains of the preelection period described above. With the ruling party and the main opposition party, the CUD, both claiming victory before counting was complete, and with a newly announced ban on demonstrations in Addis Ababa beginning on election night, a violent confrontation could have been avoided probably only if the government had shown restraint, which it did not. Demonstrations in early June and again in early November led to violent crackdowns by security forces, and the deaths of 193 civilians and six security officers, as well as the arrests of tens of thousands of others, as discussed in detail below.

Patterns of Violence in the 2005 Elections

The location, timing, and types of postelection violence in Ethiopia are instructive to an analysis of electoral violence in general. As in earlier elec-

---

2. Turnout was about 82 percent of the 22 million Ethiopians registered to vote—strikingly higher than in recent elections. See Harbeson 2005; Carter Center 2005 and 2009; European Commission 2005b.

3. The NEBE, together with representatives of the main political parties, implemented an ad hoc investigation process in the summer of 2005 to consider charges of fraud and abuse. But most of these investigation panels found in favor of the ruling party and rarely in favor of the opposition parties. Despite the potential of this process to address vote fraud, these panels mainly failed. See Arriola 2008; Harbeson 2005; Lyons 2006; European Commission 2005a, 2005b; Carter Center 2005, 2009.

4. The 2005 elections were also for regional state parliaments. The opposition also made significant progress in particular regional state parliaments. See assessments of the elections in Arriola 2008; Harbeson 2005; Lyons 2006.

tion cycles, there were some incidents of state-sponsored violence in the preelection period. The State Department Human Rights report of 2006 noted the killing of several members of the All Ethiopian Unity Party in Amhara region, and of several supporters and members of the Oromo National Congress (ONC) in Oromia region, and others in Southern Nations, Nationalities and Peoples region (SNNPR). These killings occurred at the hands of local *kebele* officials or militia members affiliated with the ruling party (U.S. State Dept. 2006). Unfortunately, this was not all that uncommon in Ethiopia. What was new was the postelection violence, which we consider in greater depth here.

There were two main periods of election-related violence following the May 2005 elections. The first occurred in early June, shortly after the elections. These incidents followed competing claims of electoral victory by the ruling party and the CUD, delays in the NEBE's announcement of official results, and the immediate clampdown by state security forces. On election night, the prime minister issued a ban on all public demonstrations, heightening tensions. The widely used text messaging system was shut down soon afterward.[5] Heavily armed troops moved into the capital city. On June 6, university students demonstrated in support of the opposition's claim of having won a greater share of the seats in Parliament. On June 8, a transportation strike was attempted. In those few days, security forces clashed with demonstrators, and official reports put the death toll at from thirty-seven to forty-two, with many more wounded. Observer missions such as the Carter Center condemned the "excessive use of force by security personnel" in this period.[6] State Department reports note that the protesters were unarmed (U.S. State Dept. 2005). Most of the violence was limited to the capital, though retaliatory arrests began to occur across the country. The violence was accompanied by arrests and surveillance of some political opposition party members and leaders as well as vocal civil society and media representatives.

Even as the violence occurred in early June, heads of various diplomatic missions, civil society leaders, and prominent Ethiopians were making behind-the-scenes attempts to broker peace. These continued through June and July, and the public quietly waited for some type of elite agreement to be reached. But hard-line factions blocked any compromise offered by the so-called plan for peace, and no agreement was reached. Similarly, civil society efforts at a postelection code of conduct were mostly

---

5. For a succinct discussion of these tense days with claims of electoral wins by both the EPRDF and the CUD, and the NEBE's trickle of reporting on electoral results, see Carter Center 2009.

6. See Carter Center 2009, which gives a figure of "more than 40 dead." See also U.S. State Dept. 2006, which cites an Ethiopian Human Rights Council figure of forty-two dead. The Carter Center also specifically identifies the murder of the newly elected Oromo National Congress leader.

ignored by the political elites and, therefore, failed to influence peaceful outcomes, as elaborated below. Most of the opposition party members assumed their parliamentary seats in September 2005. But after an internal split in the CUD, some of its more prominent members chose not to take their seats, thereby dividing the party and their voting constituencies. The ruling party quickly moved to strip these parliamentarians-elect of their immunity because they did not assume their seats, and in late October and early November, most were arrested and charged with a range of serious offenses against the Ethiopian Constitution.

Throughout October, there were periodic rumors of planned demonstrations, then denials of the calls, or postponements by leaders of the opposition who had not taken their seats in Parliament. A tense public waited. Almost inevitably, a further episode of violence occurred in early and mid-November 2005, again mainly in urban areas, especially the capital, and some larger towns in Oromiya regional state, Amhara regional state, and SNNPR. As in June, this involved calls for peaceful protests and work stoppages, though some protesters committed limited incidents of violence.[7] There was also a protest that involved various public transport drivers honking their horns in the capital city during a meeting of the African Union. For the most part, though, these were spontaneous and poorly organized demonstrations against the regime's actions concerning the elections and were not targeted at particular communities or categories of citizens. Again, as in June, the security forces acted with extreme force.

A parliamentary commission of inquiry into postelection disturbances was established in December 2005, after the federal police commissioner's report to the Parliament. The report, in October 2005, denied any excessive force by security personnel. Parliament established the inquiry commission to "investigate the disorder and report to the House so as to take the necessary measures and to further promote the peace and democratic process of the country" (Samuel 2006). After eight months of work, the 11-member commission concluded that 199 individuals had died, including 6 members of the security forces. But reports of political pressure on the commission led to a leaked report that blamed Ethiopian security forces for using excessive force. The chairman and deputy chairman and at least one other commission member fled the country, citing political intimidation and harassment by the ruling party (Samuel 2006; Amnesty International 2006).

The official report included the same figure of 193 civilian deaths and 6 police deaths—far above previous government estimates—but, notably, concluded that the actions of the security forces did not constitute excessive

---

7. U.S. State Dept. (2005) cites protesters with machetes and hand grenades.

force (Amnesty International 2006; U.S. State Dept. 2007). The inquiry commission found that violence at the hands of demonstrators involved the use of stones and fire, while the police used firearms, truncheons, and tear gas. Property damage was "mostly caused to public transport buses" rather than to private businesses, for instance (Samuel 2006). Even the October 2005 statement of the federal police commissioner demonstrates that where protesters were violent, in nearly every case the violence was directed at agents of the state, such as police officers, not at fellow citizens (Gebeyehu 2005). At least 30,000 individuals were arrested in the six-month period of June–November 2005, though many were never charged (Amnesty International 2006; U.S. State Dept. 2007). The vast majority of these were young people detained on charges such as "dangerous vagrancy," and many were released after some time, with no charge or without a trial. The message was clear: no public demonstrations of any kind, peaceful or otherwise, were to be tolerated, and all political activity was to come to a halt.[8]

The highest-level arrests of October and November included members of the main opposition political parties who refused to take their parliamentary seats when the House of People's Representatives opened in September 2005. In addition, several journalists and civil society representatives were arrested and later charged with a range of crimes. Others were charged in absentia. Delays and postponements marked the court proceedings. In June 2007, the Federal High Court found thirty-eight senior opposition members guilty of serious offences. Although the prosecutor's office sought the death penalty, the sentences given ranged from life in prison for CUD leaders, to lesser sentences for journalists and others. However, through the intervention of an informal group of Ethiopian elders, the political opposition leaders eventually submitted a letter requesting pardon to the Board of Amnesty, which approved their requests. The president of Ethiopia, Girma Wolde Giorgis, granted pardons to thirty-eight CUD leaders in July 2007.[9] Just weeks before, the Parliament had passed a motion declaring unoccupied seats to be vacant and calling for by-elections for those seats in early 2008. While the pardon restored the political rights of the CUD leaders to vote and stand for election, the conditions of the pardon meant that they would have to stand again for elec-

---

8. There is evidence that some protests, smaller in scale, did continue in the following months, particularly in Oromiya region, but these have not been analyzed.

9. Netsanet Demissie and Daniel Bekele, the two members of civil society who had been arrested along with the political opposition and were being tried together, refused to request a pardon at the time. The civil society leaders had requested to have their case heard separately from the political party leaders (a request that was denied), and they were the only defendants to recognize the Court and mount a defense. They were found guilty of lesser charges and eventually signed a separate pardon in April 2008.

tion to their seats in Parliament. The party was thoroughly fragmented, however, and several released leaders went abroad almost immediately and have not returned to Ethiopia.[10]

Disputed Narratives about Electoral Violence in Ethiopia

What matters for future electoral cycles is how actors—the state, political parties, and average citizens—come to characterize any electoral violence that occurs. In Ethiopia's election-related violence, a few noteworthy features stand out. At the public level, the demonstrations appeared to have been mostly peaceful and only semiorganized and highly diffuse in intent and strategy. The regime has argued that the protesters were not peaceful and that they aimed at overthrowing the government despite the EPRDF's claim that it had won the majority of seats and, thereby, the right to form the government. There is an interesting contradiction in the regime's narrative about the violence. On the one hand, the prime minister was adamant in dispelling any possibility of a so-called Orange Revolution—an allusion to the method of peaceful protest to bring about a change of government in Ukraine in 2004–05, which spawned several similar protests. This would reinforce the opposition's claim that the protests were peaceful in intent and form though aimed at overthrowing the government. At the same time, both the federal police commissioner's testimony and the official statements about the protests frequently cited limited use of violence by the protesters as evidence of the violent nature of the protests, thereby justifying the extent of the crackdown by state security forces. For instance, the regime made a great deal of the deaths of six police officers and the evidence of property damage, nearly all of which occurred in Addis Ababa. The EPRDF's argument has been that this violence was a threat to public safety and to the elected government of the country and that, therefore, the use of force was justified and occurred at the appropriate level. It was portrayed as a series of isolated political disturbances requiring the state to intervene to restore public order.

The narrative framed by key members of the main opposition political parties and their supporters differs. Most claim that the protests were peaceful and spontaneous. Some who disputed the official election results would agree that the aim of the protests was to overthrow the govern-

---

10. By the fall of 2008, there were at least four factions of what was formerly the CUD coalition, including parties led by Hailu Shawel, Lidetu Ayalew, Birtukan Mideksa (Andenet, or the Unity for Democracy and Justice Party), and Berhanu Nega (Ginbot 7: Movement for Justice, Freedom and Democracy), and other new parties such as the Tigray for Unity and Democracy Party. Birtukan Mideksa was returned to prison in early 2009, accused of violating the conditions of her pardon. She was released again in October 2010 after again seeking a presidential pardon and has gone into exile.

ment peacefully (the "Orange Revolution" strategy), but would argue that this was a valid aim since the election was stolen. Other groups within the opposition similarly assert a peaceful intent to the protests but accept the general legitimacy of the government that formed in the postelection period. There is a distinction to be made between an assertion that the opposition won the actual vote in 2005 and the charge that the results were mostly legitimate (with some few exceptions) even though acquired through coercion and intimidation. The former view is generally held by those opposition members who did not take their parliamentary seats, and the latter by those who did. Of course, as in all disputed elections, particularly those that occur over multiple cycles of violence, it is impossible to know. The overall national-level electoral results were accepted by the European Union and Carter Center observation missions. What is fascinating is that, in a sense, both the ruling party and at least one of the segments of the political opposition agree on one point: that the aim of the protests was to remove the government from power.[11]

While the establishment of the Parliamentary Commission of Inquiry represented an exciting opportunity for Ethiopia to explore the nature and consequences of the violence, the application of political interference from the highest levels undermined the commission's legitimacy. Few citizens have accepted the ruling party's narrative of the scale or causes of the violence. The popular understanding of the 2005 protests is that they were peaceful and semiorganized, though the views on the protesters' intended aims mirror the two perspectives noted above. That is to say, some Ethiopian citizens agree that the election results were flawed and that the state used excessive force in responding to the protests, but would have preferred the parliamentarians-elect to have taken their seats and worked within the Parliament for change. Others argue that the elections were stolen completely and that the CUD should not legitimate the results by assuming its seats in the House of People's Representatives.

Notwithstanding these differences of opinion over the appropriate response to the postelection dispensation, a far share of Ethiopians consider the 2005 elections to have represented a "massacre," while the regime has generally referred to the protests over the elections as a series of political "disturbances." The regular use of the term "massacre" and, sometimes, "bloodbath," when referring to the 2005 elections does not conform to social science or international donor definitions of what constitutes a mas-

---

11. The subsequent founding by Berhanu Nega, one leader in the diaspora, of a political party that does *not* renounce the option to remove the government by force (the Ginbot 7 Party) reflects one response to the failure of peaceful opposition.

sacre. It is certainly meant to signal the belief that the country has returned to the brutality of the Derg.

Types of Electoral Violence

An important factor, not only in the regime's response to the 2005 protests but also in the narrative it has developed about the causes and extent of the violence and in its subsequent electoral strategy of political repression, is the ruling party's electoral platform, before and after the 2005 elections. The EPRDF ran in 2005 on the strength of two policy platforms: one related to ethnic self-determination and the other to economic growth. It regularly cited, and continues to highlight, economic growth numbers of 7–11 percent annually. Party leadership, mainly Prime Minister Meles Zenawi, pointed to infrastructure development, dramatic gains in education and health care delivery, and rural development as evidence of its successful leadership of the Ethiopian state. It generally has used a rhetoric of a "developmental state."

Rural Ethiopians have arguably benefited more in real terms from the EPRDF's policy and developmental interventions than have urban citizens, and this is in part because the government has focused more of its interventions on the more than 80 percent of the population living in rural areas. This is where a single all-weather road, a school building, or a clinic can be perceived as a significant accomplishment. In towns and cities, where literacy, education levels, access to media outlets, access to health care facilities, visits of diaspora returnees, and so on are all much greater, it is not surprising that voters' demands are considerably higher. Notwithstanding these indicators, however, some large subsection of citizens, particularly urban citizens, who perceive themselves as definitely not having benefited to the same extent as rural Ethiopians, are unmoved by the economic figures that the EPRDF repeatedly cites. They focus instead on high urban unemployment, inflation, and the costs of basic urban goods, as well as demands for even more attention to secondary and higher education. These dissatisfied citizens voted against the EPRDF in 2005, and at least some of them protested against the election results. The regime has not changed its policy platform or its claim to success based on economic indicators, nor has it become any more persuasive about why urban citizens, for instance, should share in and celebrate rural successes. Therefore, it had to find other ways to control the outcome of the subsequent 2010 elections.

What is also significant in the Ethiopian cases is what did *not* happen. The protests in June and November 2005 were mainly peaceful and were not intercommunal, interethnic, or interreligious in nature or form. Most of the violence that resulted in personal injury or loss of life was at the hands of the security forces, not the civilians. Even when protesters were not entirely peaceful, violent action was directed at members of the Ethiopian security forces, not at particular ethnic communities seen as supporting either the ruling party or one of the opposition coalition parties.[12] This is especially significant since the policy differences between the regime and the CUD were largely based on differences in how to incorporate and accommodate these diverse ethnic communities within the unified Ethiopian polity. The ruling party continued to defend the principles of ethnic group rights and collective ownership of land, which are enshrined in the 1995 Constitution. For example, the largest opposition party, the CUD, sought major constitutional changes that would "enhance individual rights . . . and allow for the privatization of rural and urban lands" (Arriola 2008, 121).

The relationship between the political issues that are the focus of electoral competition, and the grievances of members of ethnic communities is complex and intertwined. We might have expected more interethnic violence in Ethiopia than in neighboring Kenya, for instance, because of Ethiopia's history of civil war and ethnically based conflict (Smith 2009). Voting results in Ethiopia's 2005 elections revealed ethnic patterns to voting preferences, and the history of land alienation and economic and political disparities structurally related to ethnic and religious identity groups could have served as the basis for interethnic resentment and led to violence. Arriola (2008) discusses voting patterns in the 2005 Ethiopian elections, including ethnic patterns, as well as the influence of religious identities (Muslim populations in particular) and economic variables such as food aid dependence, degree of urbanization, prevalence of poverty, and the type of cash crop grown (see also Donham and James 1986; Keller 1988; Smith 2007). For instance, on the question of land reform, Ethiopian ethnic communities have widely divergent land grievances, even if most share a concern to improve land access, tenure, and productivity. Certain groups favor a privatization of land, because they are convinced that security of tenure will improve farmer productivity. Others, who lost ancestral land to highlander ethnic groups in the expansion of the modern Ethiopian state, are mostly opposed to the privatization of land, even as they favor some sort of legal reforms.

---

12. This conclusion is based on a review of media reports, interviews, the findings of various reports, including those by the official observation missions, and the unofficial report of the Parliamentary Commission of Inquiry. The Parliamentary Commission of Inquiry ended with a deeply politicized final report, resulting in the flight of both the commission's chairman and its vice chairman from the country, and the rejection of the report's findings by most opposition members of Parliament. As mentioned earlier, neither of these reports was made public.

In Ethiopia, the contestation over constitutionally protected rights for ethnic groups and the rhetoric of individual rights and Ethiopian nationalism are intertwined with what we might call contemporary and historic "identity politics." The perception of some voters, for instance, is that ethnic federalism benefits numerically smaller groups or could benefit groups that are a plurality, but do not serve the interests of communities who have generally dominated modern Ethiopian political life. The objective reality belies this view, at least for ordinary citizens who face similar challenges of poverty and underdevelopment. But the powerful perception persists and could have been expected to trigger communal violence after the elections, yet it did not.[13]

Similarly, these "identity" questions are intimately linked with very real economic and development concerns relating especially to land, port access (symbolic and practical), and privatization/marketization. Political elites used the election campaign to signal support for, or opposition to, existing policies, based on a complicated mix of policy (e.g., pro-market) and identity questions (e.g., "new" groups, such as members of particular ethnic groups, getting benefits under the current system). New religious and linguistic rights of the post-1995 Constitution became a focus of some debate during the election campaign, again pointing to identity-group concerns and interests. Arriola (2008) highlights the interconnection of economic interests with ethnicity in voting patterns, while Pausewang (n.d.) offers a nuanced and detailed narrative accounting of the various interests at play in Ethiopia, arguing that the "view from below" involves a number of disparate groups, including "peasants," ethnic communities, women, and so on.

In many ways, the opportunity has come and gone for extended national dialogue on contentious issues in Ethiopia, particularly those related to specific controversial provisions of the constitution. Preelection debates highlighted fundamental disagreements over the post-1991 governance structures, putting them on the national agenda for the first time in a very long while. But the 2005 election results and the subsequent crackdown by EPRDF security forces stifled that dialogue. Since 2005, the ruling party has become increasingly authoritarian, reversing previous gains in media and personal freedoms, suppressing dissent, and punishing urban voters with new taxes and restrictions on civil and political rights. (See Human Rights Watch 2005, 2006, 2010a, 2010b; U.S. State Dept. 2007, 2008; Aalen and Tronvoll 2008.) The Ethiopian Parliament passed a new press law in 2008,

---

13. Both main political parties' leadership made allusions to the ethnic underpinnings of these policies in the preelection period, with the ruling party disparaging the CUD as an "Amhara chauvinist party" akin to the Rwandan *interhamwe*, and the opposition referring to the EPRDF as "Woyane thugs" or "Tigrayans" (see Carter Center 2009).

and a new law with harsh restrictions on civil society organizations in 2009, both of which significantly limit the functioning of press and civil society (Arriola 2011). Almost none of the political elites of either the ruling party or the main opposition parties have suggested areas of potential agreement or compromise. Unresolved political tensions among various communities across the country, articulated by political elites, have been left to simmer without an outlet for dialogue and compromise. What started as an elite conflict that was not localized or intercommunal could certainly become so.

Subsequent Elections in Ethiopia

Ethiopia's recent episodes of electoral violence reveal important patterns in both the state's and citizens' responses to periods of sustained or episodic electoral violence. Unsurprisingly, the long-delayed 2008 local elections were an across-the-board sweep for the EPRDF and a successful test run for the strategies deployed in the 2010 elections. A combined strategy of patronage and intimidation ensured a dramatic win for the regime. The EPRDF increased its party membership nationwide from 760,000 in 2005 to 4,000,000 by 2008. This was accomplished through threats of withholding valuable resources, as well as promises of resources, but also by massively expanding the actual size of local government councils, essentially turning substantial numbers of citizens into employees of the state and the ruling party. The *kebele* (village-level) councils were increased from 15 to 300 members, for instance. One analysis concludes that "up to one third of the inhabitants are [now] members of the local government councils, and a similar number of members of the party, resulting in overwhelming control of the local community" (Aalen and Tronvoll 2008, 116).

This was the context for the 2010 national and regional elections. Analysts both inside and outside Ethiopia did not see any reason to be optimistic that the election would produce genuine political competition (Aalen and Tronvoll 2008; Human Rights Watch 2005, 2006, 2010a, 2010b). Violence was not expected, in large part because of the chastening impact of the 2005 violence and subsequent political changes. The EPRDF and its affiliate parties won all but two seats in the House of People's Representatives. The major opposition parties that had reformed in the wake of the 2005 elections included the coalition referred to as Ethiopia Federal Democratic Unity Forum, or Medrek, which is composed of eight parties, including the United Ethiopian Democratic Forces, the Oromo People's Congress, the Oromo Federalist Democratic Movement, the All Ethiopian Unity Party, and the Arena Tigray Party. The reformed CUD of 2005, called the Unity for Democracy and Justice Party, also participated in the

Medrek coalition. Only one Medrek candidate won a national seat, one independent candidate won a seat, and the opposition gained only one seat in all the nine regional state councils—a 99 percent win in both national and regional elections for the EPRDF and its affiliate parties.

Election day was peaceful and generally well organized. Voter turnout was a staggeringly high 93 percent, following what all analysts describe as years of ruling party coercion, intimidation, and harassment. Citizens were told that to keep access to resources—including food aid and fertilizer in rural communities, and jobs and university placements in towns—they were to register with the ruling party and vote on election day.[14] Some were told to bring five people to the polling station on election day if they wanted to keep their jobs. While this may not have been an official statement of the ruling party leadership, the fact that it did not occur in the 2005 elections— though it surely is similar to political strategies employed in earlier elections in Ethiopia—clearly confirms that directives "from above" led to pressure on ordinary party operatives to ensure an EPRDF win.[15]

Significantly, there were no reported protests or demonstrations of any kind in the months since the election. So, while the targeted killings in the months before the election would lead Straus and Taylor to classify the 2010 elections as level 2 (as noted above), the striking difference in popular perception about violence over multiple electoral cycles is significant. Ethiopians seem to have taken the lesson from 2005 that at least for now, protests and violence are not worth the consequences, and they have acquiesced to very old and familiar patterns of political conformity, though perhaps not agreement. This demonstrates what Höglund points out as a consequence of electoral violence: that "the fear created by such tactics can substantially influence not only if people vote, but also who they will vote for" (Höglund 2009, 417).

The message of the 2010 elections was intended for the Ethiopian people: the EPRDF is firmly in charge.[16] And the "lessons learned" from the 2005 elections were not only for citizens (vote, and vote for the ruling

---

14. These strategies were openly discussed by Ethiopians throughout 2009 and 2010 and are documented meticulously by the Human Rights Watch Report of 2010.

15. Directives emanating "from above" or "from the top" is a commonly used expression, encountered regularly in Ethiopian citizens' discussions of almost all policy, particularly during fieldwork on language policy in 2003. Ethiopians rarely indicate a notion of participation in policy formation, whether directly or indirectly through elected or appointed representatives, and are much more likely to describe most policies as coming "down through a chain" (see also Lefort 2007; Vaughn and Tronvoll 2003.)

16. The idea that the EPRDF was "embarrassed" by the results is inaccurate. The message was for Ethiopian citizens (and maybe the influential Ethiopian diaspora, so influential in the 2005 elections)—in any event, not the international community—and therefore, this outcome was the one that EPRDF preferred.

party) but for the state as well (make sure you leave no doubt in citizens' minds that the ruling party is in control). In light of long-documented patterns of hierarchy and authority in Ethiopia, this result should not be particularly surprising. Ethnographic studies of Ethiopian sociopolitical life clearly demonstrate that the tradition of rigid social hierarchy and the legacy of political authoritarianism collude to create a political culture that is extremely cautious, risk-averse, and calculating (Lefort 2007; Vaughn and Tronvoll 2003; Pausewang n.d.). While the analysts who suggest the impenetrable nature of the ruling party's leadership and decision-making structure are correct, there is also a certain conformity with more general patterns of Ethiopian political life. Political parties, as embedded in the surrounding political milieu, are likely to resort to familiar patterns of political action—in this case, a return to high levels of coercion, intimidation, and surveillance to ensure political control.[17] The 2010 elections demonstrate that the political space that was opened in the years before 2005 has decisively closed, at least for now.

Civil Society Involvement in Ethiopia's Elections

The 2005 elections represented a significant upsurge in citizen and voter participation and enthusiasm—something of a "return to politics"—and the subsequent targeted political violence and repression was surely a disciplining tool of the state. That violence and intimidation has generally returned the citizenry to a fear and apathy all too familiar in Ethiopian history. Nonetheless, the elections of 2005 did involve unprecedented collective action. In this vein, attempts by civil society to intervene in preventing the violence and the subsequent state crackdown on civil society merit analytic consideration.

If civil society across Africa is still mostly nascent, the involvement of nonstate organizations and associations in electoral politics is even more uncommon. This is because the state continues to view elections as threatening to regime security. Although outside organizational representatives have been (reluctantly) allowed to observe national and local elections in Africa, these observer teams are often short in duration, quite weak in local expertise, and mostly symbolic in their coverage of the totality of the electoral process. There can be little doubt that local observation teams, if well-trained and well-resourced, can provide critical local knowledge to

---

17. Abbink concludes that "hierarchy, obedience and forceful authority, inherited from the old imperial system and reinforced by the Marxist-military regime until 1991, are still dominant" (Abbink 2009, 24).

inform and support democratic procedural outcomes (Nevitte and Canton 1997, 47–61). In particular, where local observation teams have been most effective in preelection and election day activities, they have also been able to serve as a force for conflict prevention and mitigation throughout the entire electoral process. This was not the case in Ethiopia, however, and it suggests that a more robust role for Ethiopian civil society in election-related activities might support peaceful conditions around elections.

The civil society sector in Ethiopia is much smaller and weaker than in many other parts of Africa, but it was growing rapidly in recent years under the EPRDF. The number of civil society organizations and non-governmental organizations (NGOs) registered by the Ministry of Justice rose from only 24 in 1994 to a staggering 1,742 in 2007. Most of these are engaged in poverty alleviation and development work, but some advocacy and democracy and governance civil society organizations (CSOs) have also started up (Rahmato, Bantirgu, and Endeshaw 2008). In general, "civil society" can be used to refer to those "networks of intermediary associations [that] act as a counterweight to vested interests, promote institutional accountability among states and markets, channel information to decision-makers on what is happening at the 'sharp end,' and negotiate the social contracts between government and citizens" (Edwards 2009, 13).

It is worth considering what, exactly, a domestic observation mission composed of trained local citizens can contribute to electoral processes. In one study on the topic, Nevitte and Canton conclude that "the sheer numbers of observers provided by the domestic monitoring groups far exceeds the capability of international observations, allowing the former to provide much more comprehensive coverage" (Nevitte and Canton 1997, 60). The authors note that in addition to their strength in numbers, the extensive citizen education activities that these groups often engage in, both before and between elections, as well as the channels they provide for citizen participation in a general sense, are particularly important in building trust in political parties and processes in societies emerging from authoritarian regimes or in transition.

It is interesting that Nevitte and Canton do not note the possible increased legitimacy of the entire electoral process that monitoring by domestic groups might provide, but refer only to the potential benefits of "compatible conclusions about an election" that might arise from a coordinated announcement by international and domestic observation missions (Nevitte and Canton 1997, 60). While it is true that domestic observation missions face a hurdle that international missions generally do not—which lies in convincing the various parties (both average citizens and the main political parties) that the observers are not motivated by what the authors call "oppositional" instincts—there seem to be few examples where the kinds of organizations that participate in these observation teams are political parties in the making, as is sometimes the charge. In fact, as the comparative cases discussed below illustrate, these coalitions are generally composed of civic associations (youth, women, trade unions) and faith-based groups that have little interest in acting as political parties in future electoral contests.

Ghana's recent election (considered in depth in chapter 8 of this volume) provides an instructive example of this. As the final report of the Coalition of Domestic Election Observers (CODEO) in Ghana's 2008 elections suggests, domestic observation teams can help promote free and fair elections in part by "instill[ing] confidence in the electoral process and in the Ghanaian public at large in the building of democratic structures . . . prevent[ing] and/or manag[ing] conflicts . . . [and] encourag[ing] citizens' participation in the election" (CODEO 2009). Illustrative of the manpower mobilized by domestic observation initiatives, Ghana's coalition deployed 60 trained preelection observers for the nine-month period preceding the December 2008 elections, and 4,000 election-day observers for the December 7 election and the December 28 presidential runoff elections. It also fielded a twenty-five-person team to monitor electoral violence specifically and created a consortium of security, media, and other civil society representatives to respond to emerging issues in all three phases: preelection, election day, and postelection (CDD-Ghana 2009). Finally, the coalition engaged in proactive peace and civic education activities. CODEO even undertook the effective method of parallel vote tabulation of the presidential election—a process that provides "specially trained and accredited nonpartisan observers to . . . collect data on the voting process and the official vote count for each polling station within their catchment area" (CODEO 2009). All these structured and coordinated activities built confidence in the final announced election results.

Much as was done in Ghana, the Kenya Elections Domestic Observation Forum deployed 17,000 election-day observers during the 2007 elections, to cover as many polling centers in the country as possible, building on a tradition of using domestic monitors in Kenya's multiparty elections. The monitors were able to conclude that "the 2007 General Elections were credible in as far as the voting and counting process is concerned. The electoral process lost credibility towards the end with regard to the tallying and announcement of the presidential results" (Kenya Elections Domestic Observation Forum 2007). Such reports, though not able to prevent the types of violence that engulfed Kenyan society in the weeks after the elections, did provide the framework for promoting cooperation and compromise among the two main contenders, arguably contributing to the conditions for a power-sharing agreement, which did facilitate the conditions to end the violence. Civil society has continued to play a dynamic role in monitoring the postelection peace agreement, including the recent constitutional referendum in 2010.

Unlike Ghana and Kenya, Ethiopia has almost no tradition of meaningful domestic observation activities during previous election cycles, making the initiative of civil society to contribute to the electoral process in early 2005 yet another indicator to donors and Ethiopian citizens alike that this election was genuinely different in form from those that had come before (Polhemus 2002; Organization for Social Justice in Ethiopia 2004). In preparation for the 2005 elections, a coalition of civil society organizations called the Ethiopian Civil Society Network for Elections formed in December 2004. The Network, as it was known, was a consortium of over thirty local NGOs organized to participate actively in various aspects of election monitoring, including voter education, media monitoring, and direct observation of all phases of the electoral process. The Network planned to train and deploy over 3,000 observers on polling day. In addition, they organized to participate in preelection monitoring activities related to voter and party registration, campaigning, and media in particular (Organization for Social Justice in Ethiopia 2004). The leadership of these organizations saw civil society's role as that of an intermediary with no stake in a particular political outcome and, therefore, a natural and effective leader in violence prevention and in creating the conditions for a legitimate election.

But at all stages, they faced a surprising lack of support from international donors and various legal barriers from the NEBE. The NEBE refused to share basic data such as the number of registered candidates within each constituency (necessary for planning deployment activities) and eventually issued a late directive restricting accreditation to organizations with "election observation" in their statutes of incorporation. This measure effectively made all members of the network ineligible for accreditation. A legal battle ensued, and the Federal High Court and the Federal Supreme Court eventually ruled in favor of the observer group—but in a decision that came only three days before the polling day. As analysis from those involved in the leadership of the Network's secretariat demonstrates, "this obstruction effectively sabotaged the planned large scale domestic observation. ESCE-Net was forced to cut its observers from 3,000 to just over 250 and to restrict them from nationwide coverage to only the capital city and its surroundings" (Demissie 2009).

In its concept paper on election monitoring, the Network envisioned that the impact of its educational and monitoring activities around the

2005 elections would "contribute to strengthen public confidence in Ethiopia's elections, thus enforcing our democracy" (Organization for Social Justice in Ethiopia 2004). However, its efforts were repeatedly stymied by staff at the NEBE before the May elections, and by members of the ruling party after the elections. Even though the Network members were legally registered and acting within the parameters of the relevant electoral laws, and even after winning the High Court case, they continued to face substantial barriers to meaningful participation in observation activities on election day. As both scholars and observer missions noted at the time, had there been domestic observer reports in the country, the confusion and uncertainty in the days and weeks immediately after the election could have been minimized, potentially limiting the violent incidents that did occur (Abbink 2005, 105, 187–90, 419; Carter Center 2005, 2009).

Also, in the wake of the initial round of violence in Ethiopia in June 2005, the Network sought to introduce a postelection code of conduct to calm the various parties and provide the context for dialogue in the aftermath of the earliest episodes of violence in Addis Ababa. But their efforts were quickly rebuffed and they were not able to assume this role in any meaningful way. By the second outbreak of violence, in October and November 2005, the regime had moved to implicate the Network leadership in serious crimes. Several leaders were detained, and some charged and found guilty of major offenses against the constitutional order (Smith 2007; Human Rights Watch 2006).

The role of civil society is certainly disputed by many state actors, but scholars generally agree that the history of democratization points to a robust role for nonstate actors. Some, such as Michael Bratton, would argue that "the alternation of political initiative between state and civil society is necessary for the legitimation of state power" (Bratton 1994, 59). In this argument, because "the right of any elite to exercise state power is ultimately dependent upon popular acceptance," which is created and organized by civil society, then "civil society is sovereign" (Bratton 1994, 59). This expands on Nevitte and Canton's earlier discussion of the legitimacy argument created by the involvement of domestic observation missions and suggests that domestic observation groups have substantial potential to legitimate state power in electoral exercises. Where elections are close— and this is happening more and more across Africa—a neutral third-party group such as a domestic electoral observation team can enhance the legitimacy of the exercise and have a positive influence in supporting the conditions for peace before, during, and especially after elections.

While it is, of course, impossible to know for sure, the periods of tense but hopeful peace after the June 2005 demonstrations, throughout the highly polarized months of September and October, and again after November show that the Ethiopian citizenry at large was interested in a peaceful resolution. There was no resort to widespread violence or any targeted violence or intercommunal violence of any kind. Rather, it seems that the Ethiopian public, as well as the voting constituencies of all the major parties, was anxious for a resolution to the disputes over results and for some kind of elite pact to resolve the deadlock. In such a context, civil society involvement can facilitate not only peace talks but public education, reassurance, and, eventually, public support. Kenya's experience also suggests this. Although the power-sharing deal that broke the postelection deadlock was brokered by international personalities—notably former UN secretary-general Kofi Annan—Kenyan civil society organizations closely monitored and publicly reported on these processes as well as on the post-violence inquiry commission's activities and final reports. There can be little doubt that the CSOs filled a vital role as a neutral and trusted source of information for Kenyan citizens anxious to interpret activities and outcomes.

Ethiopian civil society's experience in elections was quite unlike the examples of Ghana and Kenya, where civil society had a role in either preventing violence or at least mitigating its impacts and even promoting a postelection justice framework. The failure of civil society to manage and prevent violence in Ethiopia can be seen as symptomatic of the sector's overall weakness compared to civil society elsewhere in sub-Saharan Africa, but this must be better understood. The Carter Center, an organization of international experts on elections and peace promotion, concludes its assessment of the 2005 elections by noting that not only political party agents but also "civil society observers provide the most effective assurance of accountability and fair conduct of elections. . . . Domestic observers should be allowed access to all aspects of the electoral process" (Carter Center 2009, 41).

Not only have the Ethiopian state and opposition political parties seen the nascent civil society as irrelevant to peace-promotion and conflict-prevention activities, but legislation in the post-2005 election period has significantly narrowed the space in which nonstate and nonpolitical actors can operate inside the country. The Charities and Societies law (Proclamation No. 621/2009) sharply limits the work of civil society but is focused particularly on limiting activities of those groups doing human rights, conflict prevention, and civic and voter education and advocacy work, and on creating a monitoring agency and establishing stiff penalties for violations. In particular, the law makes it illegal for Ethiopian organizations engaged in these types of activities to receive more than 10 percent of their funding from international sources—a prohibitive figure in a poor country with little opportunity for, or history of, private philanthropy. The "CSO law" has had ripple effects in the country, with the flight of the leadership of several prominent human rights and advocacy organizations, and the closure or significant scaling-back of many others.[18]

Not surprisingly, in the wake of the challenges the Network faced in 2005, the arrest and charging of two prominent civil society activists, and the restrictive CSO law, the 2010 national and regional elections saw very little civil society involvement. Voter education, a crucial activity in a country with limited literacy and media reach and a history of politicized elections, was left entirely to the NEBE, an organization with almost no domestic credibility. An umbrella of domestic civil society organizations, called the Coalition of Ethiopian Civil Societies for Election Observation (CECSEO), gathered together eleven organizations, including, prominently, the reorganized Ethiopian Teachers' Association, widely regarded as an instrument of the ruling party. The CECSEO was accredited by the NEBE. It fielded observers in most polling stations, but those observers cannot be considered organic or autonomous representatives of civil society, as the 2005 Network observers were.[19] More significantly, as the persistent nature of electoral violence in Ethiopia suggests, to be effective, civil society must be more than simply deployed on election day, but embedded in the accountability and legitimacy processes of state-society relations over many cycles. This has not happened in Ethiopia, nor is it likely to under the current dispensation.

Conclusion

A number of conclusions emerge from analyzing Ethiopia's experience with election-related violence. Clearly, it is important to view the totality of an electoral event rather than focus on voting day exclusively or even primarily. Incidences of violence are to be expected on other days. In Ethiopia's case, this involved some coercion and violence in the preelection period, and the possibility for substantial violence in the postelection period, extending well beyond a three-month horizon. It is imperative that violence be analyzed along a trajectory of multiple electoral cycles. Violence that followed the 2005 election clearly led to the preelection violence and coercion in the run-up to the 2008 local elections and the 2010 national and regional elections. The lessons of electoral violence extended

---

18. Among those who fled were the executive director of the Ethiopian Women Lawyers Association and the head of the Ethiopian Human Rights Commission, two of the oldest and most influential civil society groups in the country. See also McLure 2010.

19. EU Election Observation Mission—Ethiopia 2010.

far beyond the election of 2005 and even 2010, for voters and the ruling party alike.

This reality also necessitates more than an empirical consideration of numbers relating to scale (e.g., loss of life, numbers wounded, property damage) or labeling of perpetrators of violence (e.g., incumbents or challengers, civilian protesters or police/security forces). As the Ethiopian case suggests so poignantly, the narratives of electoral violence can diverge in ways that do not easily lend themselves to classification schemes or standards of identification. Both the regime and popular understandings of the causes and consequences of the violence will play a role not only in the structure of future electoral contests but also in the nature of sociopolitical life in the intervening years. Where one sees a disturbance to be put down in order to restore public order, another sees a massacre and will judge the perpetrator accordingly, regardless of "objective" policies such as economic growth or education and health care spending.

The other significant feature of Ethiopia's election-related violence concerns the targets of the violence. The fact that Ethiopia saw almost no interethnic or intercommunal violence while countries such as Kenya did highlights the factors that underlie the violence. In Ethiopia, it is often said that even if the violence of the Derg was harsher in some sense, it made no pretension to democracy, while the EPRDF has talked of democracy throughout its tenure.[20] Therefore, Ethiopians, particularly urban, engaged, and better-informed citizens, have held the EPRDF to a higher standard of political openness. This was then reflected in the popular rage when the regime clamped down so sharply in the weeks and months after the 2005 elections. Public acquiescence since 2005 similarly reflects an understanding by citizens that the transition has been stymied and a certain resignation to returning to the usual cautious and quiescent approach to political engagement. With most private press and civil life dismantled, with so many activists abroad, and with such intense pressure to join the ruling party, citizens now have adapted to the return to the "norm" of democratic performance, though not democratic substance (Pausewang, Tronvoll, and Aalen 2002). Still, it is important to note that while a promise of a job or educational placement (or the threat of losing either) may coerce a young voter to vote once or even multiple times, at some point, if the promise is not delivered on, voters may weary of acquiescing. The EPRDF's ability to make good on threats and promises of the 2010 election cycle will influence voters' choice sets in future elections. The wide-ranging political opening of the late 1990s and early 2000s, before the dramatic reversals of

---

20. But its "revolutionary democracy" was never meant to be liberal democracy. See Abbink 2010.

2005 and beyond, are still in living memory and inform popular expectations of what the possibilities of full citizenship include.

Finally, despite the notable and historic efforts of Ethiopian civil society organizations to participate in the 2005 elections in unprecedented ways, they faced legal and political obstacles through every step of the process. Significantly, these groups could not play a role in mitigating the violence in the postelection period, as their counterparts in Ghana and even Kenya could, which reflects not only the general weakness of Ethiopian civil society but also a distinctly narrower view of nonstate actors' role within larger Ethiopian political discourse. It is striking that the ruling party and state actors, as well as opposition party leaders and even international donors, failed to appreciate the critical role of a vibrant civil society in facilitating the peaceful and legitimate conduct of the 2005 elections. The postelection environment has proved even harsher for Ethiopian civil society, and we can expect to see a more restricted conception of political life outside direct political contestation as a result. This is unfortunate, since it is impossible to envision a democratic future for Ethiopia that does not include civil society's diverse and active representation of citizens' interests. Although this condition is not likely to persist indefinitely, it should nonetheless be a matter of concern to donors and policymakers in Ethiopia and beyond.

References

Aalen, Lovise, and Kjetil Tronvoll. 2008. "Briefing: The 2008 Ethiopian Local Elections: The Return of Electoral Authoritarianism." *African Affairs* 108 (430): 111–20.

Abbink, Jon. 2005. "Discomfiture of Democracy? The 2005 Election Crisis in Ethiopia and Its Aftermath." *African Affairs* 105 (419): 187–90.

———. 2009. "The Ethiopian Second Republic and the Fragile 'Social Contract.'" *Africa Spectrum* 44 (2): 3–28.

———. 2010. "Political Culture in Ethiopia: A Balance Sheet of Post-1991 Ethnically Based Federalism." African Studies Centre Info Sheet 8/10.

Amnesty International. 2006. "Ethiopia: Prisoners of Conscience on Trial for Treason: Opposition Party Leaders, Human Rights Defenders and Journalists." Amnesty International AFR 25/013/2006. www.amnesty.org/en/library/info/AFR25/013/2006.

Arriola, Leonardo R. 2008. "Ethnicity, Economic conditions and Opposition Support: Evidence from Ethiopia's 2005 Elections." *Northeast African Studies* 10 (1): 115–44.

———. 2011. "Countries at a Crossroads: Ethiopia" Freedom House report. www.freedomhouse.org/sites/default/files/inline_images/ETHIOPIAFINAL.pdf.

Bratton, Michael. 1994. "Civil Society and Political Transitions in Africa." In *Civil Society and the State in Africa*, ed. John W. Harbeson, Donald Rothchild, and Naomi Chazan. Boulder, CO: Lynne Rienner.

Carter Center. 2005. "Final Statement on the Carter Center Observation of the Ethiopia 2005 National Elections, Sept. 2005." www.cartercenter.org/documents/2199.pdf.

————. 2009. "Observing the 2005 Ethiopia National Elections: Final Report." Dec. www.cartercenter.org/resources/pdfs/news/peace_publications/election_reports/Ethiopia-2005-Finalrpt.pdf.

CDD-Ghana. 2009. *Preventing and Managing Conflict in Election 2008*. Legon, Ghana: CDD-Ghana.

Coalition of Domestic Election Observers (CODEO). 2009. *Final Report on Ghana's 2008 Presidential and Parliamentary Elections*. Accra: CODEO Secretariat. www.cddghana.org/documents/CODEO%20Report%20for%202008%20(PDF).pdf.

Demissie, Netsanet. 2009. "Domestic Election Observation in Ethiopia: Retrospect and Prospect." Master's thesis, Queen Mary, Univ. of London.

Donham, Donald, and Wendy James, eds. 1986. *The Southern Marches of Imperial Ethiopia: Essays in History and Social Anthropology*. New York: Cambridge Univ. Press.

Edwards, Michael. 2009. *Civil Society*, 2nd ed. Malden, MA: Polity.

European Commission. 2005a. "Election Observation Mission—Ethiopia 2005. Preliminary Statement on the Election Appeals' Process, the Re-run of Elections and the Somali Region Elections." Aug. 25. www.eueom.eu/ethiopia2005.

————. 2005b. "Ethiopia Legislative Elections 2005, EU Election Observation Mission Final Report." Sept. http://eeas.europa.eu/eueom/pdf/missions/final-report-ethiopia-2005.pdf.

EU Election Observation Mission—Ethiopia 2010. 2010. "Preliminary Statement." May 25. www.eueom.eu/files/pressreleases/english/eu-eom-ethiopia-preliminary-statement-25052010_en.pdf.

Gebeyehu, Workineh. 2005. "Report of the Federal Police Commissioner to Parliament." Nov. 14. Addis Ababa.

Harbeson, John. 2005. "Ethiopia's Extended Transition." *Journal of Democracy* 16 (4): 144–58.

Höglund, Kristine. 2009. "Electoral Violence in Conflict-Ridden Societies: Concepts, Causes and Consequences." *Terrorism and Political Violence* 21 (3): 412–27.

Human Rights Watch. 2005. "Suppressing Dissent: Human Rights Abuses and Political Repression in Ethiopia's Oromia Region." May. www.hrw.org/sites/default/files/reports/ethiopia0505.pdf.

————. 2006. "Ethiopia: Hidden Crackdown in Rural Areas." Jan. 13. www.hrw.org/news/2006/01/11/ethiopia-hidden-crackdown-rural-areas.

———. 2010a. "'One Hundred Ways of Putting Pressure': Violations of Freedom of Expression and Association in Ethiopia." Mar. www.hrw.org/sites/default/files/reports/ethiopia0310webwcover.pdf.

———. 2010b. "Ethiopia: Donor Aid Supports Repression." Oct. www.hrw.org/news/2010/10/18/ethiopia-donor-aid-supports-repression.

Keller, Edmond J. 1988. *Revolutionary Ethiopia: From Empire to People's Republic.* Bloomington, IN: Indiana Univ. Press.

Kenya Elections Domestic Observation Forum. 2007. "Preliminary Press Statement and Verdict of the 2007 Kenya's General Elections." http://kenyastockholm.files.wordpress.com/2008/01/kedof-statement-31-12-07.pdf.

Lefort, René. 2007. "Powers—*mengist*—and Peasants in Rural Ethiopia: The May 2005 Elections." *Journal of Modern African Studies* 45 (2): 253–73.

Lyons, Terrence. 2006. "Ethiopia in 2005: The Beginning of a Transition?" *CSIS Africa Notes,* 25. http://csis.org/files/media/csis/pubs/anotes_0601.pdf.

McLure, Jason. 2010. "Ethiopian Rights Groups Forced to Reduce Work before Elections." *BusinessWeek,* May 14.

Nevitte, Neil, and Santiago A. Canton. 1997. "The Role of Domestic Observers." *Journal of Democracy* 8 (3): 47–61.

Organization for Social Justice in Ethiopia. 2004. "A Concept Paper on Election Monitoring by a Network of CSOs in Ethiopia." Unpublished, author's personal copy.

Pausewang, Siegfried. n.d. "Ethiopia: A Political View from Below." Unpublished draft.

Pausewang, Siegfried, Kjetil Tronvoll, and Lovise Aalen, eds. 2002. *Ethiopia since the Derg: A Decade of Democratic Pretension and Performance.* New York: Palgrave.

Polhemus, James. 2002. "An Action Plan for Useful Donor Involvement in Ethiopia's 2005 National Elections." Unpublished working paper.

Rahmato, Dessalegn, Akalewold Bantirgu, and Yoseph Endeshaw. 2008. "CSOs/NGOs in Ethiopia: Partners in Development and Good Governance. A Report Prepared for the Ad Hoc CSO/NGO Task Force." NGO report, Addis Ababa. www.crdaethiopia.org/Documents/CSOs-NGOs%20in%20Ethiopia%20-%20Partners%20in%20Development.pdf.

Rahmato, Dessalegn, and Meheret Ayenew. 2004. *Democratic Assistance to Post-Conflict Ethiopia: Impact and Limitations.* Addis Ababa: Forum for Social Studies, FSS Monograph Series 3. http://books.google.com/books/about/Democratic_assistance_to_post_conflict_E.html?id=JACNAAAAMAAJ.

Samuel, Frehiywot. 2006. "Testimony before the US House of Representatives: Congressional Briefing on November 16, 2006."

Smith, Lahra. 2007. "Political Violence and Democratic Uncertainty in Ethiopia." USIP Special Report 192, Aug.

———. 2009. "Explaining Violence after Recent Elections in Ethiopia and Kenya." *Democratization* 16 (5): 867–97.

Tronvoll, Kjetil. 2000. "Ethiopia: A New Start?" Minority Rights Group International NGO report. www.minorityrights.org/?lid=1052.

U.S. State Dept. 2005. "Country Reports on Human Rights Practices: Ethiopia." www.state.gov/j/drl/rls/hrrpt/2005/61569.htm.

———. 2006. "Country Reports on Human Rights Practices: Ethiopia." www.state.gov/j/drl/rls/hrrpt/2006/78734.htm.

———. 2007. "Country Reports on Human Rights Practices: Ethiopia." www.state.gov/j/drl/rls/hrrpt/2007/100481.htm.

———. 2008. "Country Reports on Human Rights Practices: Ethiopia." www.state.gov/j/drl/rls/hrrpt/2008/119001.htm.

Vaughn, Sarah, and Kjetil Tronvoll. 2003. "Structures and Relations of Power: Ethiopia." NGO report, SIDA Background Documents to the Country Strategy. www.sida.se/Documents/Import/pdf/No10-The-Culture-of-Power-in-Contemporary-Ethiopian-Political-Life2.pdf.

8

Preventing Electoral Violence

Lessons from Ghana

Franklin Oduro

T his chapter discusses the lessons to be learned from Ghana's experience in preventing electoral violence. In the 2008 general elections, a combination of policies and programs by independent state and nonstate actors aiming to build trust and confidence in the electoral system, deepen interparty dialogue, and expose undercurrents of violence through early warnings forestalled postelection violence in Ghana. Complementing these efforts were several layers of election dispute resolution mechanisms. Also, eminent Ghanaians were strategically deployed to mediate on the electoral and political disputes that occasionally flared up during the election process.

The relatively peaceful conduct and outcomes of December 2008 elections in Ghana distinguished it from several other African countries and showcased it as an exemplar. Coming as it did after a disheartening string of postelection clashes—in Ethiopia (2005), Togo (2005), Kenya (2007), and Zimbabwe (2008)—the Ghanaian experience constitutes a welcome success. At the outset of the 2008 election season, Ghana seemed predisposed to experiencing postelection violence. Despite the stakeholders' violence prevention efforts, however, 2008 revealed grave flaws in election processes and administration, and critical institutional weaknesses.

In particular, lack of clarity and transparency in the rules and conventions affecting political party agents' representation at polling stations, those agents' endorsement of declared results sheets, and the transmission of results from the constituency level to the headquarters of the electoral commission (EC) exposed potential sources of violence. The limitations of the decentralized security arrangements, such as the regional and district security councils, in combating election violence became apparent. Since successful violence prevention in one election cycle does not guarantee the same in the future, election stakeholders need to learn how to fill these gaps.

Following this introduction is a brief account of what we know about election violence in Ghana. Then follows an overview of Ghana's 2008 elections, the threat of violence, and the nature of the tensions and the violence that surrounded the elections. The next section presents an analysis of triggers, patterns of violence, and perpetrators' motivations for election violence. We examine the preventive mechanisms throughout the three phases of an election: preelection, polling, and postelection. The discussion concerns three types of intervention: by state or public institutions such as the judiciary and the EC, by quasi-state bodies such as the National Peace Council (NPC), and by civil society organizations (CSOs). The discussion focuses on the complementary approach adopted among CSOs, between CSOs and public institutions, and between CSOs and external groups. The next section of the chapter examines the deficits in the election administration and in the institutional arrangements for violence prevention. The final section draws lessons from the relative success of the Ghanaian case in preventing and managing electoral violence.

The discussion and analysis in this chapter rely on research sources and data on election-related activities from the Coalition of Domestic Election Observers (CODEO) gathered during the 2008 election cycle. CODEO is the single largest domestic election observer group in Ghana. Formed in 2000 by the Ghana Center for Democratic Development (CDD-Ghana), it is an umbrella body of professional, secular, and religious groups.[1] In 2008, CODEO drew from thirty-four organizations to mobilize its domestic observation project. The analysis in this chapter draws from a three-month systematic study of patterns of election violence, conducted by CDD-Ghana and CODEO in selected constituencies across the country. It also draws from the activities of other Ghanaian CSOs during the period.[2] Although the December 2008 election serves as the context, a broader historical approach also involves delving into instances from previous elections.

---

1. The author was a founding coordinator of CODEO and has been involved in its activities since its formation. In 2008, the author spent about six months in Ghana and worked with CDD-Ghana and CODEO to mobilize civil society toward conflict-free elections.

2. The author's own independent research during this period also informs the analysis and discussion.

Election Violence in Ghana: What We Know

While the history of Ghana has no recorded widespread postelection violence, past elections have not been violence free. The interparty violence that occurred during the preindependence 1954 and 1956 elections are particularly insightful (see Austin 1966). The incidence of postindependence election violence in Ghana has also been recorded elsewhere (Chazan 1987; Boahen 2004). In the period of the fourth republic, which began in 1993, violent attacks by supporters of political parties against one another have been frequent during election years. Despite a history of isolated cases of election violence, until the 2008 elections there was no countrywide attempt to systematically study and analyze patterns, triggers, and perpetrators of election violence.[3] Nonetheless, anecdotal evidence suggests that Ghana may not be very different from other African countries, particularly when it comes to machinations and engineering of violence by politicians.

The Northern, Ashanti, and Greater Accra regions have been cited as the three areas with the most recurrent election violence since the 1992 elections. The period before polling day, particularly between eight weeks and four weeks before election day, has generally seen increased violence. However, there has been almost no electoral violence following the polling day and subsequent declaration of results. In other words, postelection violence that threatens national stability has been rare. Whereas a broad range of factors, including the disregard of electoral rules, defacement of political party posters, and hate speeches by leading politicians, have triggered election violence, what has become obvious during recent elections is politicians' manipulation and politicization of existing chieftaincy disputes in some areas of the country.

In particular, in certain parts of the Northern and the Upper East regions of Ghana, the recurrence of election violence is largely traced to ongoing chieftaincy feuds. In the Dagbon traditional area of the Northern region, the dispute between the Andani and Abudu families over the rightful successor to the kingdom has led to repeated clashes, during elections, between members of the two families, who are perceived to be supporters of the two leading parties, the National Democratic Congress (NDC) and the New Patriotic Party (NPP), respectively. Similarly, in the Bawku traditional area of the Upper East region, the chieftaincy dispute between the Mamprusi and the Kusasi ethnic groups has been politicized, generating

---

3. The only exception is a pilot project carried out by CDD-Ghana and the Tamale-based Institute of Policy Alternatives (IPA) in monitoring election violence in the three northern regions during the 2004 election.

electoral violence between the supporters of the NDC (Kusasi sympathizers) and the NPP (Mamprusi sympathizers).

Despite the existence of several undercurrents that provide a groundswell for widespread and intense electoral violence, Ghana has been spared the ordeal of dealing with postelection violence. The design and administration of the electoral system has greatly reduced the incentives for widespread electoral violence. Managing election conflicts and threats of violence in past elections has involved the deployment of both formal and informal strategies to address disputes and to moderate tensions (Gyimah-Boadi 1998; Agyeman-Duah 2008). The strengthening of the EC's independence and technical competence, coupled with the vibrancy and watchfulness of the media and CSOs in campaigning for election peace, have also contributed.

Background to the December 2008 Elections

The 2008 general elections presented three main challenges to Ghana's democratic development. The first challenge was to match its record of fairly peaceful, transparent, and generally conflict-free election outcomes or, better yet, improve on this record in the fifth successive multiparty elections since the 1992 democratic transition. The second challenge was, in the event of an opposition victory, to repeat the 2000 experience, in which an incumbent party was defeated and a smooth and peaceful turnover of political power ensued (see Ayee 2001; Gadzekpo 2001; Smith 2002a, 2002b; Van Walraven 2002; and Agyeman-Duah 2008).[4] In other words, would an opposition victory result in a peaceful change in government, and, conversely, would the opposition accept a victory by the incumbent? The third challenge was to break the cycle of sour and stalemated election outcomes that had engulfed the continent in recent years, and to continue to lead Africa in democratic development. These challenges presented a test for the country's growing democratic institutions. As Gyimah-Boadi has ably noted, "The [2008] polls in Ghana tested the prospects of sustaining multiparty democracy at precisely the moment when its success on the continent appeared most tenuous" (2009, 138–39).

A number of events in the run-up to the elections seemed to portend a hotly contested campaign that held the potential for violence. Three events in particular are worth mentioning. One was the heated and acrimonious exchanges between the incumbent NPP and the main opposition, the NDC, regarding the enactment of an amendment to the Representation of

---

4. For the NDC, winning the 2008 elections was a task deemed vital if the party was to remain relevant in Ghanaian politics and not fall apart.

the Peoples' Amendment Law (ROPAL) in 2006. That law allowed Ghanaians living abroad to register and vote in general elections. The NDC, which had strongly opposed the amendment and resisted the legislative process, vowed to resist its implementation, arguing that the EC did not have the capacity to implement such a law. Further, the party argued that implementing ROPAL would have serious financial implications for the state and would not be a prudent economic management decision. Significantly, the NDC feared that potential manipulation by the ruling NPP would affect the outcome of the 2008 elections (Oduro 2009). The party threatened to boycott the 2008 election and reject the results if ROPAL was implemented. The EC decided early in 2008 to defer implementation of ROPAL.

A second significant threat to the peace surrounding the 2008 elections was the persistent but unsubstantiated allegation by the NDC that the NPP had rigged the 2004 elections. This became part of NDC's election-year propaganda, insinuating that the NPP could not otherwise win in 2008. The NDC viewed the surfacing of a flawed voter register with ostensibly inflated voter rolls for some constituencies in the Ashanti region—the stronghold of the NPP—as one of the NPP's rigging methods. A bipartisan investigative committee formed by the EC ruled that the error was not the work of any political party but a genuine computer glitch that did not affect the original register of voters who were available at the constituency and regional levels. NDC allegations of NPP fraud continued, however.

Unfortunately, the subsequent bloating of the voters' register, by about 16 percent over the 2006 register, undermined its credibility. The bloat was a result of poor management by the EC, with the political parties' connivance, during the registration process (CDD-Ghana 2009). Meanwhile, the NDC continued its allegations of NPP attempts to rig the polls, circulating among the foreign missions in Ghana what the NDC referred to as an NPP "top secret" strategy document that purported to reveal the rigging scheme (Gyimah-Boadi 2009).

A third compounding preelection event was the discovery of large deposits of oil in western Ghana in 2007. The expected large infusion of petrodollars that will accrue from this discovery colored the 2008 election process in a phenomenon described elsewhere as petropolitics (WANEP 2008). The two main parties' desire to manage and control the proceeds from the oil raised the stakes. The prospect of state capture and control—which, obviously, is a question of who wins the presidency—suddenly infused the electoral contest with an oppressive and violent atmosphere as management of the oil resources filled the dreams of the presidential aspirants (WANEP 2008, 2).

These events and others, in particular the cyclical electoral violence in northern Ghana, increased the potential for widespread election violence. Mistrust increased between the parties, between the parties and the EC, and also between the NDC and the security forces.

2008: Threat and Nature of Electoral Violence

The atmosphere of the preelection environment appeared to threaten Ghana's political stability. Some violence did occur during the preelection period, exacerbating tensions in the political environment. In a nine-month preelection observation covering fifty-six selected constituencies throughout Ghana, CODEO noted that political intolerance among supporters of the two main parties had risen and had led to violent clashes in several parts of the country, notably the Volta, Central, Ashanti, Greater Accra, Brong-Ahafo, Upper East, and Northern regions.[5] Most were instigated by events associated with voter registration and campaigns by political parties (CODEO 2009).

CODEO preelection observers noted several forms of violence perpetrated by political party supporters, including shootings and arson, vandalism of opponents' campaign posters, exchanges of insults, obstruction of political opponents from campaigning in another party's home communities, and clashes between youth groups belonging to different political parties during campaign rallies. These violent behaviors were committed with blatant disregard for the parties' own code of conduct and for the public order law in scheduling campaign events. The simultaneous scheduling of campaign events by opposing political parties in the same locality often triggered violent behavior by supporters.

In the three constituencies located in the city of Tamale and its environs in the Northern region, for example, this particular flouting of the laws on campaigning was a common feature leading to repeated clashes between the NPP and the NDC, resulting in injuries and arson. These threats and actual occurrences of violence observed by CODEO were generally noted by the European Union Election Observation Mission (EU Election Observation Mission 2009). For example, the report cites tension between supporters of the NDC and the NPP throughout the campaign in the Brong-Ahafo region.

Apart from the CODEO preelection observation, close monitoring of election violence in twenty-five selected constituencies, for three months up to the December 7 polls, confirmed some of the general findings in the

---

5. Although the observers were deployed in these specific constituencies, they were responsible for covering adjoining constituencies as well. CODEO received reports from about 183 constituencies during this period.

Table 8.1 Twenty-five Constituencies Selected for Monitoring Electoral Violence in Ghana's 2008 Elections

No.	Constituency	Region	Selection Indicator
1	Bunkpurugu/ Yunyoo	Northern	High security risk
2	Tolon	Northern	
3	Tamale Central	Northern	
4	Mion	Northern	
5	Kumbungu	Northern	
6	Zibilla	Upper East	
7	Bongo	Upper East	
8	Bawku Central	Upper East	
9	Wa Central	Upper West	High electoral
10	Nkwanta North	Volta	competitiveness
11	Ho East	Volta	
12	Sunyani West	Brong Ahafo	
13	Asokwa East	Ashanti	
14	Asante Akim South	Ashanti	
15	Oforikrom	Ashanti	
16	Odododiodio	Greater Accra	
17	Okaikwei North	Greater Accra	
18	Ablekuma North	Greater Accra	
19	Ledzokuku	Greater Accra	
20	Ayawaso Central	Greater Accra	
21	Cape Coast	Central	
22	Effutu Awutu	Central	
23	Asawasi	Ashanti	High volatility
24	Jomoro	Western	
25	Ellembelle	Western	

Source: Lartey and Aning 2008.

CODEO report. In the absence of any systematic study or meaningful analysis of election violence in Ghana, the selection of the twenty-five constituencies for close monitoring of election violence followed a method of newspaper content analysis and other anecdotal evidence that indicated variously a history of communal violence, prevailing security threats, a history of local violence triggered by elections, and a trend of electoral competitiveness.

These constituencies, chosen according to three indicators—high security risk, high degree of electoral competitiveness, and high level of volatility—cut across all ten regions of Ghana. Table 8.1 shows the identified constituencies. Nine of these constituencies were located in the three regions of northern Ghana: the Northern, Upper East, and Upper West. The patterns of electoral violence in the three northern regions confirmed earlier findings of a similar project conducted only in these regions during the 2004 elections.[6]

---

6. The 2004 project, the Election Violence Education and Resolution Project, was supported by the International Foundation for Electoral Systems (IFES) and implemented jointly by CDD-Ghana and IPA.

In the current study, the Northern and Greater Accra regions had the highest number of monitored constituencies (five each). In this focused study, ninety election-related violent incidents were recorded in the selected constituencies. Of this number, the largest percentage (about 48 percent) involved defacement of party posters, followed by physical harm to individuals (about 15 percent) and group clashes (about 10 percent). The remaining incidents of violence were noted as verbal harassment, intimidation, disruption of campaign rallies, property damage, and other violent acts. Perpetrators of these acts of violence were mainly supporters of the NPP and the NDC. The study also revealed that many of the acts of violence occurred during the day of campaign events, where there were large gatherings of party supporters. The findings from the study showed that these selected constituencies were indeed prone to electoral violence, with the Northern and Greater Accra regions especially vulnerable.

Foreshadowed by preelection strife, violence recorded on both polling days—December 7 and 28 (the presidential runoff)—was rife, and more of the same to come seemed inescapable. On the polling days, incidents were recorded in the Ashanti, Central, Greater Accra, Eastern, Brong-Ahafo, Upper East, and Volta regions. According to CODEO, incidents on December 28, during the presidential runoff, almost doubled those on December 7. The acts occurring at polling stations involved clashes between supporters of the NDC and the NPP and were mainly triggered by voting procedure violations that prevented eligible voters (accused of being "underage") from casting their ballots and by the snatching of ballot boxes by thugs, as witnessed in the Akwatia constituency in the Eastern region.

Significantly, in the twenty-five constituencies selected for election violence scrutiny, the atmosphere at the polling stations was generally calm during December 7, perhaps due to the high level of security. But the same could not be said for the presidential runoff on December 28. The observers witnessed isolated cases of violence in observed constituencies in the Northern, Greater Accra, and Central regions, and violence also occurred in constituencies in the Ashanti and Volta regions, considered the strongholds of the NPP and the NDC respectively (Smith 2002a; Jockers, Kohnert, and Nugent 2010).

The postelection phase also saw some isolated violent acts between the supporters of victorious and vanquished parties. The atmosphere in the interim between December 7 and the presidential runoff and in the days immediately following the runoff was so charged that the NPP government nearly declared a state of emergency.[7] The EC only exacerbated the

---

7. This became imminent when supporters of both parties besieged the EC premises, holding members hostage and threatening mayhem if the results of the presidential runoff were not declared in their favor.

tension when it took two extra days to declare a stalemate in the runoff, necessitating a rerun in the Tain constituency in the Brong-Ahafo region, on January 2, 2009, before a winner could be declared.[8] The atmosphere worsened between December 30, 2008, and January 3, 2009, with the Tain constituency becoming the focus of a probable violent outbreak. The NPP's last-minute boycott of the polls may have averted what was likely to be a violent end to the 2008 election.[9]

In the twenty-five selected constituencies, there was no significant post-election violence except in some constituencies in the Northern, Greater Accra, and Upper East regions. In these constituencies, the observers witnessed and recorded intermittent postelection violence on days following the December 28 presidential runoff. For instance, in the Okaikwei North and Ablekuma North constituencies in the Greater Accra regions, angry NDC supporters damaged campaign billboards belonging to the NPP on December 29. Similarly, in the Bawku Central constituency in the Upper East region, NDC supporters allegedly attacked NPP supporters residing in NDC strongholds for voting out the incumbent NDC member of parliament for the area.

Fortunately for Ghana, the incidents during the three phases of the elections were not severe enough or widespread enough to seriously undermine the integrity of the elections. Thus, Ghana did not experience postelection violence on the scale seen in Kenya and Zimbabwe. Through pragmatic and direct measures, Ghana managed to prevent postelection turmoil. It survived arguably the most competitive elections since 1992, with the eventual presidential winner determined, as in 2000, by two rounds of polling—and this time by less than 1 percent of the vote. On January 7, 2009, an opposition party took the mantle of governance from incumbents in a peaceful and smooth transition. This political transformation enabled Ghana to meet Samuel Huntington's two-turnover test (Huntington 1991). This achievement also scaled back, at least in the interim, the widespread pessimism over Africa's democratic development.

Electoral Violence in Ghana: Triggers, Patterns, and Actors

Gyimah-Boadi points out that since Ghana's independence in 1957, localized conflicts and electoral violence have afflicted every election. Significantly, this recorded experience has persisted since the fourth attempt at

---

8. The Tain constituency was unable to hold the election on December 28, due to logistical challenges.

9. In addition to the threat of violence in Tain, back in Accra the NPP brought a lawsuit at the High Court, setting in motion its attempts to halt the Tain runoff and to stall the EC's declaration of the presidential runoff results. For a discussion of this event, see Gyimah-Boadi 2009.

democratic governance, which began with the transitional election in 1992 (Gyimah-Boadi 1998). These violent acts occur in all three phases of the process. They manifest in particular areas of the country and appear to be triggered by factors associated more with contentious electoral competition or vote contestation, exacerbated by institutional and structural deficiencies, than with ethnic tension, economic factors, or resource control and allocation. Resource control and allocation plays a role of stimulating electoral competition rather than appropriating electoral support, as the oil discovery during the 2008 elections exemplified. The elections that year revealed the significance of five triggers of election violence in Ghana.

Trigger: A Contentious Competition

The more competitive that Ghanaian elections become and the more effort that parties make to protect electoral ballots and prevent fraud, the more likely election violence becomes. At the local or constituency level, where the competition between leading contenders was keen, violence was more likely. The election violence monitoring study confirmed this tendency in the fourteen constituencies identified in the second cluster—high electoral competitiveness. (See table 8.1). Especially in constituencies such as Odododiodio, Okaikwei North, and Ayawaso Central in the Greater Accra region, Cape Coast constituency in the Central region, and Nkwanta North in the Volta region, where the contests had been closely fought in previous elections (and electoral violence occurred), the 2008 polls recorded a series of preelection and polling-day outbreaks.

In the Akwatia constituency in the Eastern region, for example, where competition was close during the 2008 elections, repeated violence was recorded during the preelection phase.[10] Because of this, the election for the parliamentary seat was suspended in six polling stations during the December 7 polls, following clashes between NDC and NPP supporters (CODEO 2009). When the EC held the rerun of the vote in that constituency in August 2009, supporters of the two parties exchanged gunfire again (CDD-Ghana 2010a).[11]

At the national level, the increasing parity in electoral strength between the two main parties intensified the struggle for votes. Significantly, the 2000 election was the first to confirm that the NDC and the NPP had become the dominant parties in Ghana. The elections that year were determined by two rounds of polling. Although the NPP won the first round for

---

10. Akwatia was not included in the sample of twenty-five constituencies selected for close monitoring.

11. One of the contestants took the matter to the courts after the EC decided to conduct a rerun in only the polling stations where voting had been suspended. The court's ruling sided with the EC, resulting in the rerun.

the presidency in the 2004 elections, its victory was not a landslide. (The margin of difference was less than 10 percentage points.) In any case, the NDC disputed the NPP victory. Similarly, the two parties have shared the parliament almost equally.[12] This rivalry between the two parties has made the electoral competition aggressive, resulting in an energetic struggle for votes, with violence as a consequence.

It is interesting to glean from CODEO's report that recorded cases of violence at polling stations on December 28 almost doubled those of December 7. Recorded violent incidents increased from fifteen on December 7 to twenty-eight on December 28 (when the competition was just between the two presidential candidates of the NPP and the NDC). The spirited contestation of the 2008 polls by both parties reflected their belief that victory was a matter of being more forceful, manipulating the electoral process, and securing ballots by preventing fraud in the other party's stronghold. In this context, both the Ashanti and Volta regions, the strongholds of the NPP and the NDC respectively, were the most affected areas, with prominent electoral violence.

CODEO, for example, reported that on election day (both December 7 and December 28), violence was rampant in these regions. It noted scuffles between supporters of the two leading parties at some polling stations in the Ashanti region, and in the Volta region it recorded the presence of militant vigilante groups, supposedly sympathetic to the NDC, mounting roadblocks and threatening mob action against suspected NPP supporters (CODEO 2009). The Northern region, which, to some extent, has become another stronghold for the NDC, was also the scene of violent acts between NPP and NDC supporters. This uncompromising determination on the part of both parties led to two significant electoral malpractices during the preelection and polling day phases of the 2008 elections.

First, as noted before, both parties had strategies that they tried in their own strongholds. Several forms of intimidation, including defacement of posters, physical harm to individuals, verbal harassment, disruption of rallies, and damage to property, were common. The strongholds were declared no-go areas for opponents (CDD-Ghana 2009; Gyimah-Boadi 2009). Second, the effect of this no-go-area politics was further misconduct, where each party excluded agents of the opposing party in order to manipulate the casting and counting of votes. The ability of opposing-party agents to be present at polling stations is one of the trust-building norms that the parties themselves agreed on, and thwarting it sowed sus-

---

12. In the aftermath of the 2000 elections, NPP secured 100 seats against 92 by the NDC, with the remaining seats going to the other parties in a 200-member house; after the 2004 elections, NPP had 128 and NDC 94 seats in a 230-member house; and in the latest 2008 elections, NPP secured 107 and NDC 116 (in a 230-member house).

picion—and the actual perpetration—of fraud. Attempts by both parties to resist such intimidation and manipulation led to violent clashes in both the Ashanti and Volta regions during the presidential runoff.

Interestingly, these acts were inflicted on party opponents who were ethnically connected. In the Volta region, for example, where agents of the NPP were attacked, some of the perpetrators actually hailed from the region; thus, both victims and perpetrators were from the same ethnic group. Similarly, in parts of the Northern region (in Dagbon land), the scene of much of the violence during the 2008 cycle, perpetrators and victims were ethnic kin. One would expect ethnic groups to gang up against others, but this was not typically the case in Ghana in 2008.

This is not to suggest that ethnic undertones dividing Akans from non-Akans, and, at the microlevel, Ashantis from Fantis, Gas, or Ewes, did not feature significantly in the campaign rhetoric on both sides (CDD-Ghana 2009; Gyimah-Boadi 2009). And certainly, there are significant relationships between ethnic mobilization and electoral violence. However, the principal trigger of election violence in this case was not mobilization of one ethnic group against another, but electoral competition and attempted vote rigging. If true, it confirms an earlier observation that in some African countries, including Ghana, the mobilization of ethnicity is not a direct consequence of the electoral process, nor is it employed as divisive force (Hayward 1987). That view is also consistent with the results of a recent study of Ghanaians' opinions on democracy and intercommunal violence (Sharif 2010). In it, 51.4 percent of Ghanaians perceived voting irregularities as more likely to incite electoral violence, whereas 42.3 percent of Ghanaians saw the manipulation or exploitation of ethnic-tribal sentiments by power-driven politicians as a more likely trigger.

Apart from the Ashanti and Volta regions, acts of violence were evident in areas that were not strongholds but, rather, swing regions, and also in particular constituencies within regions. For example, the Greater Accra and Central regions, which are increasingly swing regions in determining the presidency, became key battlegrounds for both parties. Of the five constituencies selected for election violence monitoring in the Greater Accra region and the two in the Central region, repeated clashes between supporters of competing parties, intimidation, and other identified forms of electoral violence were recorded. Not surprisingly, the recorded incidence of violence in these regions during the preelection phase and on both election days was prominent (CODEO 2009).

Both the parties and their candidates (more so in the case of parliamentary candidates) were involved in mobilizing and transporting supporters across constituencies and regions during voter registration. The same tactics were employed in similar constituencies in other regions. The intention was to facilitate registration of mobilized voters. In some instances, the strategy—which contributed to the bloating of the voters' register—was to orchestrate double voting. As already observed, the limited voter registration exercise was engulfed by violent clashes between supporters of the two parties as each attempted to resist the registration of persons who appeared underage or whom they suspected of living outside the area. CODEO also noted that Central and Greater Accra regions figured in some of the few reported incidents of violence recorded by its observers at polling stations, confirming these regions as prone to electoral violence.

Trigger: Institutional and Structural Weaknesses

Institutional and structural deficiencies in the work of the EC proved significant factors in electoral violence. The EC's occasional lapses in election management and process enabled political parties to carry out violent acts in an atmosphere of heightened electoral competition. To be fair, Ghana's EC has grown in technical competence. Several features of the election management body have contributed to its independence and expertise. In particular, security of tenure in its executive membership has liberated it from influence and promoted continuity in the commission's administration. This has also made it possible for the EC to learn from past elections. But the EC has also, whether out of complacency or for reasons beyond its control, acted in ways that exacerbated election contestation and exposed the process to bloody turmoil. Perennial structural and management weaknesses have involved the preparation of a credible voters' register, the production of ballot papers and transportation of ballots cast, the vote tabulation process, and the transmission of results.

Since 1992, a credible electoral or voters' roll has been something of a holy grail for the EC. In 2008, it became an issue again, when an unreliable register put the two main parties on a path to confrontation. The EC appeared to have been operating a densely packed election calendar with little or no flexibility to manage lapses and disputes as they arose. As Gyimah-Boadi notes, "The Commission presented the nation with a crowded and somewhat compressed electoral timetable, leaving too little time to resolve irregularities, such as the voters' register that was most likely bloated" (2009, 142). Such an administrative bottleneck obviously primed the parties, particularly the NDC, to express a lack of confidence in the EC and the election process. The slowness with which disputes over the process were resolved led to violent acts by party supporters in some places. The fears surrounding the unreliable voters' roll, including the bloated register, were rooted in the possibility of electoral fraud that the situation invited.

Trigger: Social Conflicts

Unresolved and politicized social conflicts, especially chieftaincy disputes, have also become critical flashpoints for election violence. While some of these disputes predate 1992 and result from conflicts over the traditional and customary rights to succession, they have become political. In northern Ghana, particularly parts of the Northern and Upper East regions, these conflicts have divided the geographical areas along the two main political traditions. Since 1992 in the Northern region, for instance, the general view is that members of the Abudu family of the Dagbon traditional kingdom are allied to the NPP, with their "brothers," members of the Andani family, linked to the NDC. Although these two families belong to the same ethnic fraternity, they are divided by a dispute over the right of succession to the headship of the Dagbon kingdom. Likewise, in the Bawku traditional area of the Upper East region, two different ethnic groups, the Mamprusis and the Kusasis, who have disputed each other's claim over the right of succession to the traditional leadership of Bawku, are divided between the NPP and the NDC respectively.

These conflicts, which in the past have produced violent confrontations with deadly outcomes following political interference, have become electoral conflicts as well. Politicians from both parties have sought electoral support from potential allies by giving tacit promises to support or restore their claim to succession once elected. In some instances, campaigning parties have openly promised justice for a group, as in the 2008 elections, when the NDC promised the Andani family that it would find and prosecute the perpetrators of the gruesome murder of the Dagbon chief and his household in 2002.[13]

Politicizing these social conflicts has perpetuated electoral violence in these areas for years. As noted, constituencies in these two traditional areas were the scenes of much of the recorded 2008 brutality. For example, the clashes, during the latter months of the preelection phase, in the towns of Yendi, Gushiegu, and Tamale and their environs in the Northern region, involving supporters of the NDC and the NPP, had more to do with the stalemated Dagbon chieftaincy conflict than with the actual election. The bloody strife in the Bawku area during the elections was similarly fueled by a chieftaincy succession dispute.

Successive Ghanaian governments lacked the necessary commitment to resolve these conflicts, thereby allowing them to gather momentum dur-

---

13. The murdered chief belonged to the Andani family, and the crime is alleged to have been committed by members of the Abudu family. The failure or unwillingness of the then NPP government to fully pursue the case and secure justice for the Andanis lends credence to the allegations.

ing elections. Politicians took advantage of the tension to inflame passions in an effort to bolster their electoral support bases in these constituencies. Compounding this challenge is the bureaucratic and logistical inability of security agencies, particularly the police, to arrest, investigate, and prosecute the perpetrators in these chieftaincy conflicts. Nevertheless, in April 2010, under the NDC government, the police arrested several members of the Abudu family in connection with the murdered Dagbon chief and his household. The government has initiated court proceedings against some of those arrested.

This effort by the ruling NDC Party has been given a political slant, interpreted by members of the Abudu family (and, to some extent, the NPP) as a predictable attempt to placate members of the Andani family. Although these arrests may be based on genuine investigative work by the police, the manner of the arrests and pronouncements by the NDC government have deepened the politicization of the conflict. This culture of politicians' using chieftaincy disputes to further their political interests is the bane of peaceful elections.

Since the 2008 elections, the deepening of political interference and the manipulation of these existing conflicts for political gain in these two regions make them a potential source of violence during the next round of elections. In the Bawku area, for example, a state of emergency instituted after the 2008 violence remains in effect to this day, with sporadic clashes between the two groups. Unfortunately, there seems to be no breakthrough in resolving any of these conflicts. Going into the 2012 general elections without any real resolution of these conflicts, and without politicians' willingness to stop using the divisions in these areas as electoral campaign issues, constituencies in these areas will remain at risk of violence.

Trigger: Weak State Security Sector

The inability of the state security agencies to impose appropriate sanctions against perpetrators of election violence seems to have become another source of violence (WANEP 2008; Aning 2009). The institutional weakness of the police regarding swift arrest and prosecution of known party thugs responsible for violent attacks in certain constituencies exacerbated election violence during the preelection phase in 2008. This impunity for perpetrators was prominent in northern Ghana (CDD-Ghana 2009). Perpetrators feared neither prosecution nor arrest because they were protected by their political benefactors, who are leading personalities in the party hierarchies. Police ineffectiveness encouraged the victims to retaliate further.

The political and administrative arrangement of various decentralized security bodies prevented the police from effectively dealing with clashes as they happened at the local level. Equally important, while deficits in infrastructural resources, investigations, and forensic skills affected police ability to prevent and contain election violence, so did political interference. During the 2008 elections, this political manipulation appeared common (WANEP 2008; CDD-Ghana 2009). In one instance, the political head (the district chief executive) of Gushiegu, an area prone to violence, was implicated in a preelection-related incident that claimed six lives (*Daily Graphic* 2010; WANEP 2008). Yet the police could not arrest him. In this case, the political head continued to chair the Security Council even when investigations into his culpability were instituted.[14]

Trigger: Migrant Communities and Social Groups

Finally, some migrant communities in southern Ghana, particularly in the Greater Accra region, experienced repeated incidents. These migrants are mostly from the north, where unsolved communal conflicts fester. Several incidents in the Greater Accra region occurred among these communities, indicating the export of the communal and chieftaincy conflicts from their home regions. For example, the violent exchanges between NPP and NDC supporters in the Old Fadama suburb and in the Agbobloshie market in Greater Accra during the pre- and postelection phases were provoked by the Dagbon chieftaincy dispute.

Social network groups that sprang up during the election period were also identified as arenas for violence. "Keep fit clubs" became affiliated to political parties and, thus, politically charged and mutually antagonistic.[15] In the Cape Coast constituency in the Central region, where these party-affiliated clubs are popular, violence between supporters of rival politically colored clubs was common. These clubs behaved as watchful agents for their preferred parties and candidates and, in their exuberance, clashed violently (Gyimah-Boadi 2009, 143).

* * *

The 2008 elections also confirmed that perpetrators of election violence are mostly supporters of the two leading parties. Systematic acts, though, were traced to the parties' youth groups. As observed elsewhere, some party leaders deliberately recruit idle youths and thugs, famously known as "macho men," to commit brutality for their party (WANEP 2008).[16] In the

---

14. A member of parliament for the then-opposition NDC called for the sitting political head to proceed on leave while the investigations were ongoing. See Daabu 2011.

15. "Keep fit clubs" are popular Ghanaian apolitical social groups. Their members engage in weekly fitness and sporting activities and also compete across clubs.

16. These are bodybuilders whose muscular physiques enable them to intimidate people, causing havoc at polling stations and even snatching ballot boxes.

Northern region, the regional party youth wings of both the NDC and the NPP, named after their leaders (Azorka boys for the NDC, and Addoo boys for the NPP), were cited for many of the threats and violent acts.[17] These grassroots youth wings, known in Ghanaian political discourse as party "foot soldiers," are sometimes incited to violence by their leaders.

In addition to the youth, former paramilitary groups, known as the "cadres" and associated with the NDC, were also identified as potential perpetrators. The cadres were official militias connected to the old military junta, the Provisional National Defence Council (PNDC), led by Flight Lieutenant Jerry John Rawlings, who is also the founder of the NDC. The lead-up to the 2008 election saw reports that the NDC was mobilizing some of these cadres and ex-army chiefs who had served under Rawlings to prepare to defend the interests of the party by extrajudicial force if necessary (CDD-Ghana 2009; Gyimah-Boadi 2009). Interestingly, these identified actors (former army officers and militia members) of election violence in the Ghanaian context are among the list of potential perpetrators of election violence in Africa, as observed by Laakso (2007).

What motivates these actors is the lack of speedy and effective sanctions by the security agencies, furthered by the absence of any meaningful reprimand from party leadership. The leaders of both parties sometimes publicly condone the deeds of these thugs, in addition to offering them protection against police. The absence of public denunciation means continuing the cycle of repetition and revenge. Perpetrators are also motivated by the leadership's or candidate's promises of monetary reward or political appointments and control of public assets should the party win.

The NDC foot soldiers' widespread and violent manifestations since the party took office in 2009, demanding access and control of public assets and institutions at the district levels, attest to this quid pro quo arrangement. Immediately after the swearing in of President Mills in early 2009, NDC foot soldiers (mostly youth) went on a rampage in parts of the country, forcibly taking control of toll collection booths, public toilets, public car parks, and roads, as well as attacking staff offices of the National Health Insurance Scheme and the National Youth Employment Program and locking up the people apparently seeking work.[18] As observed in *Democracy Watch*, "The NDC foot-soldiers demanded that their contribution to the success of the NDC in the 2008 elections be acknowledged in bread-and-butter terms" (CDD-Ghana 2010b, 6).

---

17. These personalities, Azorka and Addoo, are high-ranking party officers in the Northern region and noted to be "fathering" these groups of young men. In addition to the "Azorka and Addoo boys," other youth groups identified in the region were the NPP Kandahar boys and NDC Aluta boys.

18. This unruly behavior has continued to date, with the NDC party leadership unable or unwilling to stop it. Ghanaian newspapers have reported extensively on these acts.

Managing and Preventing Electoral Violence

Managing the upheavals during the 2008 election cycle and preventing their later recurrence demanded a combination of state-led and quasi-state-led interventions as well as nonstate civic initiatives. Taking into account the repeated patterns but also the sometimes sporadic nature of electoral violence, the programs aimed to build confidence and trust in the election process and to heed early warnings and promote interparty dialogue. This section documents these activities.

Interventions by State Actors

The measures adopted by state-led actors included assuring the speedy adjudication of disputes; facilitating dialogue among the political parties and between the parties and the EC to resolve differences; enhancing mediation efforts; and making a robust and comprehensive national security arrangement to secure polling areas.

The judiciary and judicial speed. The record of timely adjudication of election disputes through the courts has been lackluster for years. The most famous case regarding the courts and election result contestation is one that occurred during the fourth republic, when it took nearly four years for the courts to dispense justice in favor of the complainant, who was the true winner of a parliamentary seat in one of the constituencies in the Greater Accra region. By the time the court gave its ruling, the defendant had already completed her four-year term as a member of parliament, thereby forever denying the complainant his rightful place in the legislature.

To remedy this slowness and as part of the measures to build trust, the judiciary assigned automated high courts, popularly known as the "fast track" courts, across the country to handle election-related disputes exclusively during the 2008 contest. Two judges were assigned to deal specifically with election cases in each of the regional capitals. Three fast-track high courts were set up in Accra. To make the courts accessible to political parties and the public, the judiciary published a manual of election adjudication. These initiatives marked a significant departure from the previous election seasons. They also seem to have contributed to building confidence in the electoral system (EU Election Observation Mission 2009).

Although the mechanism put in place by the judiciary left out timelines and deadlines for petitions to be cleared, evidence from the 2008 election cycle suggested that the judiciary's work had been timely and professional. At the end of 2009, of the twenty-three election disputes that came before the courts, only one was outstanding.[19] Among the cases was the last-minute attempt by the NPP to place an injunction on the EC to prevent it from declaring the winner of the presidential runoff. Within forty-eight hours (and on a weekend, no less), the high court sat. After the initial dismissal by the court, the NPP did not follow the case through to its conclusion, thereby allowing the EC to go ahead and declare the NDC candidate the winner and paving the way for the transition (Gyimah-Boadi 2009; EU Election Observation Mission 2009).

The EC and interparty dialogue. During the 2008 elections, the EC continued to use its interparty advisory council (IPAC) platform to promote dialogue and build consensus and trust in the electoral process. The IPAC is one of the significant innovations in Ghana's electoral system. It was initiated in 1993 as one of the electoral management reforms following the disputed outcomes of the 1992 transitional elections (Gyimah-Boadi 1999; Agyeman-Duah 2005, 2008). It sought to manage political parties' distrust of the EC and of each other.[20] It has since lived up to expectations, becoming the stage on which the parties resolve differences, develop electoral norms, and promote dialogue toward electoral integrity. In 2008, IPAC helped deal with several lapses of the election administration and with rumors and disagreements among parties. Among the notable cases were the viability of ROPAL for the 2008 elections, an allegedly inflated voter registration disk for selected constituencies in the Ashanti region, and the bloated voters register and its use for the 2008 polls.

During the 2008 election cycle, IPAC expanded its frontiers. For the first time, it was decentralized to the regional and district levels. In the past, its decisions at the national level were expected to be communicated to the party representatives at the regional, district, or constituency levels. In many cases, though, they were not properly communicated. The decentralization of IPAC was to promote this interparty dialogue at the grassroots, where many of the threats and actual occurrences of violence were common. The effect of this effort was to deepen conversation among political parties and the EC representatives at the regional and district levels on matters concerning the election. It aimed to provide a forum where political parties could address issues and concerns that were of local rather

---

19. Information on election petitions comes from an interview with a senior official at the EC. Most of the cases related to parliamentary seat petitions. The remaining case, concerning the Bawku Central constituency in the Upper East region, is a dispute about the elected candidate's eligibility to contest the elections and not the declared results.

20. IPAC brings the EC and representatives of all registered political parties together in regular meetings to discuss preparations for each election cycle.

than national interest, and also to resolve differences among the parties that might otherwise degenerate into conflict and violence.

The National Peace Council and peace mediations. The National Peace Council (NPC) became a significant factor in preventing election violence in 2008. The NPC is a quasi-national institution established by the Government of Ghana in 2005 with support and funding from the United Nations Development Programme (UNDP). It is a national infrastructure for peacebuilding and seeks to promote nonviolent means to peacebuilding and national reconciliation. It is composed of respected and eminent Ghanaians representing civil society, religious leaders, traditional leaders, community elders, and local government authorities. The NPC was established initially to promote dialogue and peace in northern Ghana, which is known for ongoing communal conflict. It has since spread its peace mediation programs to all issues of national importance, including election conflicts.

In 2008, the NPC's main agenda was to promote election peace (Bawumia 2007). Adopting the mediation mechanism, the NPC implemented a series of peace education programs with the political parties at the national, regional, and district levels through its decentralized Regional Peace Advisory Councils and District Peace Advisory Councils. It also employed the mediation approach in peacefully resolving election disputes and relieving tensions between political actors and among the parties. The space provided by the NPC and its decentralized organs promoted dialogue among the political parties and helped inculcate peaceful management of conflicts, thereby calming tensions during the elections (Ojielo 2009).

The NPC collaborated with governance structures and security agencies at both the national and decentralized levels. The nature of its membership, which includes respected religious and traditional leaders, enabled the NPC to motivate political actors in the advancement of peace. Its chair, Cardinal Peter Turkson, a respected Catholic cleric, was instrumental in moderating a deadlock in the aftermath of the presidential runoff, calming the waters when supporters of the two main parties appeared ready for confrontation (EU 2009).[21] It has been suggested that Cardinal Turkson conducted many behind-the-scenes meetings and discussions, persuading political leaders to embrace peace and dialogue rather than conflict and violence in resolving electoral disputes.

The National Election Security Task Force. The National Election Security Task Force was a comprehensive arrangement to ensure a safe and secure

---

21. The role of Cardinal Turkson, and the influence of the entire NPC leadership in prevailing on both parties' leaders to rein in their supporters, helped make possible the peaceful election and subsequent transition.

environment for peaceful electioneering in the days before, during, and after the election, to ensure postelection peace. It has been a part of Ghana's electoral security infrastructure since 2004. For the 2008 polls, the task force was made up of 36,000 security operatives from the various regions as well as from all the security agencies in Ghana.[22] Each of the ten regions of Ghana had its own security task force, spearheaded by the police service but also with representatives of the EC and other public institutions, including the Information Service Department, the National Commission for Civic Education (NCCE), and the regional coordinating councils.

The force's main tasks were to ensure incident-free elections by strategically deploying on polling day and to coordinate the administrative and operational aspects of general security at all 230 constituencies and 22,000 polling stations nationwide. Part of the program was to deploy unarmed security operatives (both uniformed and plainclothes) at all the polling stations and to escort and protect election officers and materials and monitor situation reports.[23]

Despite some lapses by the Ghanaian security agencies in stemming repeated violence in the preelection phase, the National Election Security Task Force was very helpful in promoting peace and stability on polling days and achieving peaceful outcomes (CDD-Ghana 2009). The task force's continuous monitoring of the postelection phase, dubbed Operation Calm Life, helped in quickly halting the isolated violent clashes between supporters of the two main parties following victory and protest rallies in parts of Greater Accra and the Upper East regions (Salia 2009).

* * *

These interventions by independent Ghanaian state and quasi-state institutions, working with the EC, affirmed the growing view within the Ghanaian political system that the peaceful conduct and outcomes of elections are not the sole responsibility of the EC. Indeed, public institutions that are not directly mandated to conduct elections have played significant roles in the election process. For example, in the 2008 elections, the Commission for Human Rights and Administrative Justice mounted an election observation project for the first time. The active participation of some of these public institutions helped instill trust and, more important, assured Ghanaians that significant measures were in place to promote peaceful and credible elections, notwithstanding identified challenges in the election administration process during the preelection phase.

---

22. Security personnel were drawn from the army, police, prison administration, fire service department, customs service, immigration service, defense intelligence, and the Bureau of National Investigations.

23. Armed security operatives, particularly from the army, were posted not at polling stations but at strategic points miles away, to be called in to restore calm only if the stationed security personnel could not handle the situation.

Interventions by Nonstate Actors

Nonstate actors focused on election monitoring and observation to make public the sources of violence, promote civic and peace education programs, mandate protection for all peaceful voters, election workers, and campaign workers, and promote conversations and consensus building among political parties. Some of these activities were in collaboration with other nonstate actors and with some state institutions.

Early warning. Through preelection observation of areas known or suspected to be prone to election violence, several CSOs undertook a systematic observation of events in the political environment. The primary objective was to draw attention to practices and breaches likely to undermine the freedom, fairness, and peacefulness of the elections. CODEO, for example, deployed sixty long-term preelection observers in selected constituencies for a nine-month monitoring project. It was the longest preelection observation exercise since 1992. Also, as already noted, the CDD-Ghana, in collaboration with CODEO, mounted election violence monitoring exercises during the last quarter of the year in selected constituencies.

It is worth noting that the CSOs involved in this activity took steps to share information about their findings and also exchanged ideas to those ends. Findings from these exercises were publicly shared through monthly press releases. Confidential briefings were also presented to key stakeholders and public institutions, including the security agencies, the EC, the NCCE, and the NPC.[24] Information was also shared with some international election observation teams and with representatives of donors and diplomatic missions in Ghana. CSOs adopted a strategy of engaging Ghanaian development partners to enlist public institutions in addressing deficits in the electoral process. Since these partners have unrestricted access to government officials and public agencies, including the EC, and can therefore give these actors critical information on potential electoral violence, it was felt that the information would reach the appropriate actors in time and would be treated more seriously than if merely put in the public domain by the CSOs.

These preelection observation activities by CSOs, including religious and professional bodies as well as the media, helped expose suspected wrongdoers and publicly identified constituencies that were trouble spots, thereby drawing national attention and resources. In one of these confidential briefings, held in November 2008, CODEO shared with participants information on violence-prone areas in the northern region, and

---

24. The purpose of these private meetings was to give these key stakeholders sensitive findings about names of suspected perpetrators of violence, which would not be publicly released.

names of suspected perpetrators of attacks, as reported by its observers. It is no surprise that the security presence in northern Ghana was beefed up during the polling days. These efforts did much to keep the 2008 elections generally peaceful (Gyimah-Boadi 2009).

Civic and peace education. The early-warning activity was complemented by civic and peace education programs. These programs have become hallmarks of Ghanaian election cycles (Gyimah-Boadi 1998; Agyeman-Duah 2005, 2008). Statutorily, the NCCE and the EC are required to conduct civic and voter education respectively. Since 1996, however, the CSOs, religious bodies, traditional authorities, and even musical groups have consistently been involved in these endeavors, either on their own or in partnership with these statutory bodies (WANEP 2008; Agyeman-Duah 2008). The rationale behind this collective effort toward peace promotion is the recognition that Ghana, like its neighbors, is not immune to election violence and conflict in general. The 2008 election cycle was no different. Organizations such as the Institute of Economic Affairs (IEA), the Institute of Democratic Governance (IDEG), CDD-Ghana, and CODEO implemented several components of civic and peace education programs in selected regions and locations. Many of the peace activities were concentrated in areas where preelection monitoring reports suggested a high risk of election violence.

The CDD-Ghana/CODEO, for example, mounted various peace and civic education programs in the three northern regions and the migrant communities, popularly called "Zongos," in the Greater Accra region. Using the findings from election violence monitoring, the program aimed at engaging youth against election violence. This peace education activity by CDD-Ghana and CODEO showed how early-warning programs can result in advance conflict-prevention actions. In this instance, community-based peace education teams drawn from resident members were established in these areas. In some areas, the CDD-Ghana/CODEO peace education and community-based teams drew from officials of the EC, the NCCE, and the security agencies to assist in civic, voter, and peace education.

Although it is typically difficult to quantify the extent to which civic and voter education or the work of peace missions affects election violence, it is reasonable to suggest that the more intensive the interventions, the greater the restraining power they exert. In Ghana, these activities have been a significant factor in preventing or mitigating the escalation of electoral competitionrelated discontent that can set off violence.

Securing and protecting the vote. Nonstate actors implemented two main activities to complement the effort by the EC and the political parties to

not been arrested. The Northern region Police crime officer conveyed the impotence of the police, saying that soon after someone was arrested for an offense, calls came from various politicians requesting the suspect's release (*Ghana Web* 2011). This is how effectively the politicization of the decentralized security councils hamstrung the police's efforts to do their job.

These defects in the electoral management and governance arrangements, as evidenced in the 2008 elections, deserve serious attention from all stakeholders. They require urgent institutional responses if those arrangements are to serve the purposes for which they were created. If any future election is to be violence free, much will depend on how these challenges are addressed.

The violent acts, by both NDC and NPP supporters, that engulfed the two post-2008 by-elections in the Akwatia and Chereponi constituencies in the Eastern and Northern regions are a clear reminder that Ghana needs to prepare adequately if it is to avoid repetition (CDD-Ghana 2010a). If these challenges are not made an urgent priority, the success of the competitive and closely contested 2008 elections my be a one-off occurrence.

Lessons Learned

Notwithstanding these challenges, the Ghanaian account presents five useful lessons. Although contextual differences may prevent these lessons from being amenable to generalization, they are helpful as guideposts for new initiatives.

Early-Warning Programs

To start with, mounting long-term early-warning programs to highlight conflict-prone areas, triggers, and perpetrators of electoral violence is critical. Activities such as preelection observation and monitoring, stakeholder briefings, regular public dissemination, and media advocacy are some of the activities that yielded beneficial results in the Ghanaian case. The publicized format of these preelection observation findings had the unintended benefit of shaming the constituencies that were noted for habitual election strife. It thus galvanized opinion leaders and members of the community to mobilize for election peace.

If such activities and advocacy are to have legitimacy, it is crucial that they be led by credible, independent, and nonpartisan individuals and organizations. Also, if these early-warning programs are to be implemented by nonstate actors, it is essential that these groups build constructive working relationships with state actors, in particular the security services, so that they can easily share findings with them.

Complementary Approach

To maximize the typically limited resources available for indirect election activities, election stakeholders should take a complementary and coordinated approach to their electoral violence prevention programs. In Ghana, this harmonizing approach among CSOs and between CSOs and state actors has become a recurring practice during elections. Agyeman-Duah notes a growing sense of collective duty on the part of state institutions, CSOs, traditional chiefs, and artists in developing programs to support the EC in organizing credible and peaceful elections (Agyeman-Duah 2005). In 2008, this complementary and coordinated approach to preventing election violence was intensified and expanded. CSOs worked with state institutions such as the EC, the NPC, and the Election Security Task Force in sharing critical information and implementing coordinated peace education programs. This working relationship was fundamental to the generally peaceful outcome of the elections.

Interparty Dialogues

Decentralized interparty dialogues, initiated by both state and nonstate actors, were critical to the 2008 elections' success. They offered the parties opportunities to make public their concerns and grievances and underscored the necessity for the parties to resolve election conflicts themselves. These forums helped build trust and opened communication channels between political opponents. The importance of these decentralized interparty dialogues and peace forums lies in their framing the peace process and election violence prevention mechanisms as a bottom-up, rather than a top-down, process. Such an approach gives local communities a greater awareness of the consequences of not preserving the peace. The challenge, though, is how to avoid politicizing the process.

Making Use of External Actors

Local CSOs' tactical engagement of development partners and other external partners to create some leverage in interactions with the government appears to have been very helpful. Whether for good or for ill, these developmental partners do have some leverage with domestic governments. In situations where agents of the incumbent party are the obvious main perpetrators of violence, or where the incumbents are unwilling to provide the necessary support to prevent these acts, it may be helpful for CSOs to engage these partners creatively as intermediaries. Since inputs from CSOs are seen largely as advisory and since governments and public institutions are not bound by them, such a dynamic can be helpful.

Where CSOs' access to state agencies such as the EC or the police is limited, this approach may facilitate the sharing of critical information about defects in the electoral system and about signs of potential electoral violence—the developmental partners can bring these concerns forward in their regular meetings with government agencies. CODEO, for example, found this strategy useful in the confidential briefings held on election violence monitoring. CODEO ensured that these external stakeholders were always invited to the briefings and also that reports from field observations were transmitted to them. Even though CODEO could not be privy to discussions and negotiations between these external partners and public officials, the continuing presence of these agents at CODEO briefings, and the requests by some of them for reports, suggested that the external stakeholders found these interactions useful.

Making Use of Eminent Citizens

Finally, the strategic deployment of eminent and respected Ghanaians as election peace mediators was extremely helpful. Ghana has been fortunate to have such personalities whose opinions and interventions are respected by both sides of the political divide. These persons have offered themselves as peace brokers, and society expects them to serve in that function in times of conflict. The NPC, for instance, is led by just such distinguished people. Religious leaders from both Christian and Muslim faiths, as well as traditional leaders, have also been among the strategic stakeholders promoting election peace. Emphasizing and deploying influential domestic actors to mediate political and electoral disputes promises better and more sustainable conflict resolution. Unlike externally led mediators, the local actors live with the parties in dispute and, as representatives of the people, can share their concerns as well as monitor their behavior over time.

Conclusion

Elections in Ghana since 1992 have witnessed repeated patterns of violence. These acts occur in all three phases of the electoral process. While the violence may not have engulfed the nation as it has elsewhere in Africa, it tends to undermine the internal peace and stability of the country's political foundations. In the past, the politicization of chieftaincy disputes resulted in cyclical violence. But in 2008, new issues, such as diaspora voting and persistent allegations of vote rigging, created additional security fears.

Ghana succeeded in preventing large-scale electoral violence after the 2008 election primarily because of the acknowledgment beforehand that the violence could happen. In response, civil society, in partnerships with state and international actors, intervened in an attempt to forestall electoral violence. Also, civil society was inspired to demand an effective and efficient approach from public institutions (such as the EC and the police) in preventing postelection violence. These efforts were translated into trust-building processes, mediation efforts, secured polling environments, and swift and fair adjudication of disputes. In addition to advocating for peace in the 2008 elections, state and nonstate actors intervened proactively to prevent electoral violence and advocated for a peaceful electoral transition.

The combined precautionary measures appear to have helped avert postelection violence during the 2008 polls. These targeted prevention and mediation measures that occurred during the three phases of the election—before, during, and after the polling—were generally successful in deterring large-scale electoral violence. These measures worked in Ghana because, as noted before, at the onset of the election year there was a general unease among Ghanaians that the country could experience postelection violence similar to Kenya's. A combination of election-related events and political and resource-control interests that characterized the election-eering campaign, raising the stakes for the election outcomes, portended violence. The awareness, among both state and nonstate actors, of the potential for election violence provided the needed context for marshaling policy and programmatic efforts to forestall it.

In a nutshell, what does the Ghana story teach us about preventing electoral violence? Does this suggest that similar combined approaches could work in future elections in Ghana? And do the lessons from the Ghana case hold any relevance in other political environments?

As mentioned in this chapter's introduction, successful violence prevention in one election cycle does not necessarily mean peaceful future elections. Each election cycle has its own dynamics, and the political context at any particular time matters significantly. Nonetheless, in the case of Ghana, if similar or even more contentious and acrimonious conditions exist during the run-up to future elections, combined approaches and interventions, especially in the decentralized units of the political and administrative structures, will be essential in the effort to prevent postelection violence. And focusing on the structural and institutional weaknesses in election administration that manifested during the 2008 elections will be critically important.

Regarding the possible application of lessons derived from the Ghanaian case to other political jurisdictions, much will depend on the nature of the political environment and the electoral context, and the levels of civil society engagement with the electoral process. These variables, among others, that allow state and nonstate actors to develop complementary approaches to such an exercise will be fundamental to its success. Indeed, such a joint effort will require a shared recognition of the potential for electoral violence. Positing further, if similar conditions to those that existed in Ghana during the 2008 elections arise elsewhere, some of the programs used in Ghana may well help turn the tide. In particular, developing early-warning systems, creating avenues and opportunities for interparty dialogues, and harnessing the potential of respected and eminent citizens as conflict prevention mediators and peace ambassadors may be adaptable to other countries.

In the end, preventing electoral violence is a continuous process, an ongoing act of consciously engaging with all three phases of the election, and it requires identifying the specific threats to electoral peace and legitimacy during any electoral cycle. The mechanics of this exercise, however, will vary from one political context to another.

References

Agyeman-Duah, Baffour. 2005. "Elections and Electoral Politics in Ghana's Fourth Republic." Critical Perspective Monograph no. 18. CDD-Ghana.

———. 2008. "Elections Management and Electoral Politics." In *Ghana: Governance in the Fourth Republic*, ed. Baffour Agyeman-Duah, 155–94. Tema, Ghana: Digibooks Ghana.

Aning, Kwesi. 2009. "Actors in Election Violence: Motivations, Causes, and Manifestations." Paper presented at roundtable conference, "Preventing Election Violence through Legal Enforcement and Political Tolerance." Ghana Center for Democratic Development (CDD-Ghana) and Coalition of Domestic Election Observers (CODEO), Accra, Nov. 3.

Austin, Dennis. 1966. *Politics in Ghana, 1946–1960.* Oxford: Oxford Univ. Press.

Ayee, Joseph R. A., ed. 2001. *Deepening Democracy in Ghana: Politics of the 2000 Elections.* Vol. 1. Accra: Freedom Publications.

Bawumia, Abdulai M. 2007. "Building Peace in Ghana: Capacity Building for Conflict Prevention." *CPR Newsletter* 3 (1). UNDP.

Boahen, Albert Adu. 2004. "Ghana: Conflict Reoriented." In *Africa in the Twentieth Century: The Adu Boahen Reader,* ed. Toyin Falola. Trenton, NJ: Africa World Press.

Chazan, Naomi. 1987. "The Anomalies of Continuity: Perspectives on Ghanaian Elections since Independence." In *Elections in Independent Africa*, ed. Fred M. Hayward. London: Westview.

Coalition of Domestic Election Observers (CODEO). 2009. *Final Report on Ghana's 2008 Presidential and Parliamentary Elections.* Accra: CODEO Secretariat.

www.cddghana.org/documents/CODEO%20Report%20for%202008%20 (PDF).pdf.

Daabu, Malik Abass. 2011. "Haruna Iddrisu Calls for Gushiegu DCE's Head." Joy Online. http://edition.myjoyonline.com/pages/news/200809/20198.php.

Daily Graphic. 2008. "Gushiegu DCE Denies Complicity in Violence." http://edition.myjoyonline.com/pages/news/200809/20184.php.

EU. 2009. "Ghanaians Have Elected Their New President and Parliament." Newsletter of the Delegation of the European Union (EU) in Ghana, Accra.

EU Election Observation Mission. 2009. *Ghana: Final Report, Presidential and Parliamentary Elections 2008.* Accra: EU Election Observation Mission. www.eeas.europa.eu/eueom/pdf/missions/eu_eom_final_report_ghana.pdf.

Gadzekpo, Audrey. 2001. "Reflections on Ghana's Recent Elections." *Review of African Political Economy* 28 (88): 267–73.

CDD-Ghana. 2009. "Special Issue on Election 2008." *Democracy Watch* 8 (2). www.cddghana.org/documents/D-Watch%2027.pdf.

———. 2010a. "The Akwatia and Chereponi Elections: The Unlearned Lessons." *Democracy Watch* 8 (4). www.cddghana.org/documents/D-%20Watch%2029%20&%2030.pdf.

———. 2010b. "The 'Foot-Soldier' Phenomenon Revisited: Rewarding the Party versus Rewarding Ghanaians." *Democracy Watch* 8 (4). www.cddghana.org/documents/D-%20Watch%2029%20&%2030.pdf.

Ghana Web. 2011. "Policeman in Northern Region Complains about Political Interference." Mar. 11. www.ghanaweb.com/GhanaHomePage/NewsArchive/artikel.php?ID=178285.

Gyebi, Edmond. 2010. "Fallout from the 2008 Election Violence: Police Arrest 23 Suspects." *Ghanaian Chronicle.* Apr. 15. www.modernghana.com/news2/271577/1/fallout-from-the-2008-election-violence-police-arr.html.

Gyimah-Boadi, Emmanuel. 1998. "Managing Electoral Conflicts: Lessons from Ghana." In *Elections and Conflict Management in Africa,* ed. Timothy D. Sisk and Andrew Reynolds. Washington, DC: United States Institute of Peace Press.

———. 1999. "Institutionalizing Credible Elections in Ghana." In *The Self-Restraining State: Power and Accountability in New Democracies,* ed. Andreas Schedler, Larry Diamond, and Marc F. Plattner. Boulder, CO: Lynne Rienner.

———. 2009. "Another Step Forward for Ghana." *Journal of Democracy* 20 (2): 138–52.

Hayward, Fred M. 1987. "Conclusion." In *Elections in Independent Africa,* ed. Fred M. Hayward. London: Westview.

Huntington, Samuel P. 1991. *The Third Wave: Democratization in the Late Twentieth Century.* Norman, OK: Univ. of Oklahoma Press.

Jockers, Heinz., Dirk Kohnert, and Paul Nugent. 2010. "The Successful Ghana Election of 2008: A Convenient Myth?" *Journal of Modern African Studies* 48 (1): 98–115.

Laakso, Liisa. 2007. "Insights into Electoral Violence in Africa." In *Votes, Money and Violence: Political Parties and Elections in Sub-Saharan Africa,* ed. Matthias Basedau, Gero Erdmann, and Andreas Mehler. Scottsville, South Africa: Univ. of KwaZulu-Natal Press.

Lartey, Ernest Ansah, and Kwesi Aning. 2008. "Mitigating Electoral Violence in Ghana: Challenges and Prospects for Peaceful Elections." Unpublished report commissioned by CDD-Ghana.

Oduro, Franklin. 2009. "The Quest for Inclusion and Citizenship in Ghana: Challenges and Prospects." *Citizenship Studies* 13 (6): 621–39.

Ojielo, Ozonnia. 2009. "Prevention of Electoral Violence: Experiences in Ghana, Kenya and Sierra Leone." *CPR Newsletter* 5 (1). UNDP.

Salia, Albert. 2009. "Election Task Force Shifts to 'Operation Calm Life.'" *Daily Graphic.* Jan. 7. www.modernghana.com/news/197645/1/election-task-force-shifts-to-operation-calm-life.html.

Sharif, Idris. 2010. "Ghanaian Opinions on Democracy, Inter-communal Violence, and Conflict in Sub-Saharan Africa." *African Journal of Political Science and International Relations* 44 (4): 150–63.

Smith, Daniel. 2002a. "Ghana's 2000 Elections: Consolidating Multi-Party Democracy." *Electoral Studies* 21: 519–26.

———. 2002b. "Consolidating Democracy? The Structural Underpinnings of Ghana's 2000 Election." *Journal of Modern African Studies* 40 (4): 621–50.

Van Walraven, Klaas. 2002. "The End of an Era: The Ghanaian Elections of December 2000." *Journal of Contemporary African Studies* 20 (2): 183–202.

West African Network for Peacebuilding (WANEP). 2008. "December 2008 Elections in Ghana: Stakes, Challenges and Perspectives." Accra: WANEP Warn Policy Brief. www.wanep.org/wanep/attachments/article/86/pb_ghana_nov08.pdf.

9

Conclusion

Implications for Research and Policy

Dorina A. Bekoe

This book is an attempt to analyze the scope and nature of electoral violence in Africa by developing a dataset and using the conclusions drawn from a set of important cases to understand the conditions enabling or mitigating electoral violence. Much of the current literature treats electoral violence as *part* of a case, rather than a focus in its own right. Little has been done to produce a body of work that looks at the issue in a more targeted manner, addressing electoral violence as a separate phenomenon. The cases and data in this book make clear that electoral violence merits its own field of study. While it certainly falls under the rubric of political violence, electoral violence is time-bound and issue-specific. Even though, as Straus and Taylor show, the episodic incidence of electoral violence does not constitute a significant portion of a nation's overall level of violence, it nonetheless carries long-term latent costs: diminished support for democracy, reduced legitimacy of leaders, and, possibly, the seeds of civil war. Indeed, Sisk writes, "It doesn't take much overt violence to deeply and widely influence the electoral process . . . élites have learned that election violence has both direct and indirect effects."

This book is a step in defining electoral violence and developing theoretical frameworks for understanding and preventing it in Africa. In this, it stands alone in its field. This book deepens understanding of several aspects:

- incidents, patterns, and scope of electoral violence in sub-Saharan Africa since the dawn of democracy's third wave

- the context of electoral violence, by accounting for how democratization, conflict drivers, institutional capacity, and political patronage norms affect its probability of occurrence
- the use of land as a source of patronage in electoral politics, highlighting its role in ensuring politicians' survival
- the impact of postelection political agreements on curbing electoral violence
- the danger of focusing on institutional reform while ignoring the incentives actually driving political decisions
- the consequences of electoral violence
- possible strategies for preventing and mitigating electoral violence

In recent years, the international and regional communities have intervened more decisively in cases of electoral violence. The book provides a number of conclusions that have direct impact for policymakers and for international and regional institutions that may respond to reduce or prevent its occurrence. The empirical evidence demonstrates that electoral violence is not inevitable and indeed may be preventable and that the political context in which an election takes place is critical to predicting and resolving electoral violence. Both these broad conclusions offer policy recommendations for international and regional intervention.

Electoral Violence Is Not Inevitable and May Be Preventable

Most African states have experienced some degree of violence surrounding elections. But the intense violence that the world witnessed in Zimbabwe, Côte d'Ivoire, and Kenya is not common, occurring only about 10 percent of the time. Instead, as Straus and Taylor document, the bulk of the violence consists of harassment, intimidation, and other clashes that do not result in a high number of deaths. While it is not difficult to see how intense electoral violence can weaken voters' support for democracy and their willingness to participate in it, we know from surveys conducted by Afrobarometer that even the low-level violence of harassment and intimidation can have lasting harmful effects. Thus, violence of any kind can diminish citizens' appetite for participating in future voting, discourage candidates from running for office, weaken civil society's scrutiny of elections and democratization generally, and hurt a government's legitimacy.

Many of the chapter authors allude to several indicators that policymakers and experts can use to predict electoral violence and then take steps to prevent it or reduce its impact. Specifically, the case studies, coupled with Straus and Taylor's African Electoral Violence Database (AEVD), point to four areas that place a country at high risk of electoral violence: a history of electoral violence, close elections, declining state resources, and weak institutions.

History of Electoral Violence

The AEVD shows that about half of all African countries have persistent electoral violence. Thus, knowing that a country is prone to electoral violence is a fairly strong alert to prepare for more of the same. In the case studies, similar patterns of recurrent violence during elections were seen in Kenya, Côte d'Ivoire, Zimbabwe, Nigeria, and Ghana.

Close Elections

In Ghana, Kenya, Ethiopia, and Zimbabwe, close elections resulted in violent clashes between political supporters. In many African countries, predicting the closeness of a poll may be logistically and organizationally difficult. Still, when it appears that a vote may be close, it is important to regard this as a sign of high risk of electoral violence and to begin taking steps to counter it.

Declining State Resources

Sisk's chapter illustrates the significance of understanding the political economy of state capture in different countries. In other words, what are the expected benefits in gaining state office? What are the consequences of losing office? In either case, the groups most affected are the core supporters of a political party or politician, and the candidate must devise ways and means for keeping the support of the base. When the resources for keeping that support are under threat, violence can be expected to play the role of driving away opponents. The cases of Côte d'Ivoire, Zimbabwe, and Kenya demonstrate that declining state resources for supporting patronage networks can lead to violence in the quest to shore up supporters. In each of these cases, violence was used, in lieu of land or other resources, to intimidate or remove opponents in a bid to secure a political win.

Weak Institutions

Sisk, along with Mueller in her chapter on Kenya, dramatically shows the effects of weak institutions on managing conflict. Sisk focuses on the electoral commission, but as Kenya shows, the decline of other institutions related to electoral politics can also increase the chance of violence. In Kenya's case, it is particularly disturbing to see the impotence of relatively strong institutions to guard against the 2007 violence. But as Mueller demonstrates, the strength of the institutions was deceptive because it did not change the underlying incentives driving politicians to use violence.

Indeed, the failure of institutional reform in Togo and Zanzibar to change politicians' incentives for using violence ultimately unraveled the political agreements meant to end the cycle of electoral violence. It is therefore important to understand not only the formal and informal rules of governance but also the incentives they generate to use violence to obtain political victories.

The Political Context of an Election Is Important

In his chapter on the roots of electoral violence, Sisk demonstrates that political and historical context matters. He lays out a framework that takes into account a country's democratic path and trajectory, the political economy of state capture, the structural and institutional drivers of conflict, and the capacity of national institutions to manage the elections. Using the case of Nigeria, Sisk shows that when a leader in a semiauthoritarian state is facing a formidable challenger and dwindling patronage resources and has the advantages of centralized political and economic resources, the ready availability of ethnic mobilization, and the easy manipulation of election administration, violence is more likely. These themes, including the use of dwindling land supplies as a patronage resource, also resonate in Boone and Kriger's chapter on Zimbabwe and Côte d'Ivoire.

On the other hand, with Sudan, Sisk shows that the violence did not take on a national dimension, because the focus of the parties, guided by the CPA-mandated referendum on secession, was more regional. As the dominant political parties of the north (the National Congress Party, or NCP) and south (the Sudan People's Liberation Movement, or SPLM) faced the inevitability of southern Sudan's secession, they focused on shoring up their political power, and consequently, violence was largely within their respective political bases rather than between the NCP and the SPLM, as was widely anticipated. And Smith's analysis of Ethiopia's 2005 postelection violence, documenting the seemingly paradoxical outcome that the violence revolved not around existing ethnic and resource-based grievances in the country but around the opposition parties' expectations, also demonstrates the importance of the context in which an election takes place.

For the international and regional communities, these conclusions reinforce the need for in-depth country knowledge. One program does not fit all situations. Where a country sits on the democratic trajectory, its capacity to manage elections, the role of ethnicity in its politics, and the sources of patronage are key to understanding the elites' behavior and their responses to threats. Without question, this is a long-term problem, which may not be solved by the next election. But it speaks to the need for a more coordinated investment in governance reforms, development, and social and economic mobility.

Policy Recommendations for International and Regional Intervention

The findings from the AEVD and the case studies provide guidance and opportunities for policymakers, international and regional institutions, and locally based stakeholders to draw useful conclusions about the outcome of upcoming elections, identify points of tension, and devise strategies for defusing the tension or violence. International and regional stakeholders can help reduce the prospects of violence, using such tools as foreign aid policies, diplomatic and economic sanctions, and the provision of mediators to devise political agreements between opponents.

Certainly, tensions exist around calling for international involvement when the domestically based reasons for electoral violence include a lack of political will to stop the use of violence. The chapter discussing Kenya, for example, documents that despite the international community's satisfaction with Kenya's progress on institutional reform, the persistence of informal norms and incentives that encouraged politicians' use of violence eventually led to the bloodshed in 2007. Boone and Kriger's chapter on Côte d'Ivoire and Zimbabwe shows how the need for internal resources to shore up patronage led to the use of violence to secure political ends.

And yet, even in the face of strong local causal factors in fueling electoral violence, there is a role for outside entities, particularly in shoring up local capacity and reducing some of the incentives for using violence. Indeed, donors have routinely used foreign aid, diplomacy, and institutional sanctions to change the internal incentives driving political decisions. Responding to electoral violence is no different. What international and domestic entities must guard against is distorting incentives to the point that decisions about the use of violence are counterproductive. The international and regional communities, through a combination of development assistance, diplomacy, and various sanctions, can provide support to internal conflict prevention networks, contribute to ending the impunity enjoyed by many politicians who use violence to achieve their goals, and monitor postelection power-sharing agreements more closely.

Supporting Internal Conflict Prevention Networks

The international community, through development agencies, can support internal networks to combat and understand electoral violence. In this regard, Ghana's approach to combating electoral violence is notable. Ghana's experiment in creating advisory groups to review information from specially trained election violence observers and in developing programs to intervene at the source of tension deserves further study and perhaps replication on a larger scale with donor assistance.

Ending Impunity in the Use of Violence

The international community can also remove the impunity enjoyed by many politicians who use violence to win seats—thus changing the incentives that influence politicians' choices. This is most evident in the International Criminal Court's (ICC's) indictment of the four Kenyans judged most responsible for the postelection violence and in the referral of Ivorian former president Laurent Gbagbo to the ICC.

Stronger Monitoring of Postelection Power-Sharing Arrangements

The power-sharing agreements in Togo and Zanzibar involved some of the most intensive international involvement ever in elaborate cease-fire agreements meant to create space for peace talks and reforms. To varying degrees, they met their primary goal—to stop the killing—yet many of the reforms that were meant to resolve the underlying causes of conflict remained mostly unaddressed. Importantly, power sharing can also have significant costs, such as the weakening of democratic principles, the rewarding of violence, and a reduced role for political opposition. The attractiveness and expediency of postelection power-sharing agreements must be balanced with important measures that mitigate the detrimental effects on democratization processes. Also, agreements should focus on bolstering the credibility of reforms taken; otherwise, any peace and cooperation obtained through a PPA will be short-lived.

Conclusions and Implications for Future Research

The new data, analyses of electoral violence's triggers and political contexts, and the tracing of particular grievances to electoral violence answer many questions, but they also reveal the need for continued research. We have only begun to scratch the surface of understanding electoral violence in general, and in Africa specifically. Only by knowing more about why electoral violence happens, why it can vary over time and within a country, and what incentives underlie politicians' choices to forgo the use of formal institutions in favor of protests and even deadly clashes can reliable strategies for its prevention and management be developed.

Three broad areas await future research: patterns of electoral violence, strategies for preventing it, and costs and benefits of power-sharing agreements. Research in these areas will not only illuminate the processes and triggers of electoral violence in Africa but will perhaps serve as the basis for studying it in other regions as well.

Patterns of Electoral Violence

Straus and Taylor's AEVD should serve as the basis for further inquiry into the patterns of electoral violence in Africa and for additional refinement of its causes. In particular, more research is needed to understand why high levels of electoral violence are a regular occurrence in some cases (ten countries) but not in others. Equally important, what accounts for the twenty-two countries that have never had high levels of electoral violence, and the ninety-two elections that have been free of violence altogether? Lahra Smith reminds us that a violence-free election is not necessarily a positive outcome. Ethiopia's "peaceful" 2010 parliamentary election had its roots in the very violent 2005 election and the harassment, intimidation, and repression that characterized the next five years. Thus, the peaceful 2010 election was the result of violence. How many other "peaceful" elections are rooted in the fear of violence? Should this type of intimidation be counted even though no one was physically injured? What implications do such "peaceful" elections have for the intervention of regional or international entities focused on advancing democracy? The AEVD can serve as the launching pad for examining these nuanced characteristics on a large scale.

Just as important, what makes some regions within a country more prone to violence than others? As Straus and Taylor write, electoral violence in Africa varies over space and time. It is important to understand how some regions remain free of violence. Again, Smith provides an answer, in pointing out that the violence in Ethiopia during the 2005 elections was restricted to the urban areas (despite deeply held grievances elsewhere) because of the nature of the opposition's protest. The Coalition for Unity and Democracy was protesting that the Ethiopian People's Revolutionary Democratic Front had ignored basic democratic tenets—a sentiment felt more in the cities than in the countryside. Oduro's chapter on Ghana describes regular electoral violence in northern Ghana arising from political manipulation of chieftaincy disputes. Thus, not just the existence of grievances in a country is important, but also the source of the protest, and its propensity for manipulation by politicians or other community leaders. To understand when and where to expect violence, we may ask similar questions about Kenya (why is the violence worst in the Rift Valley?) or Zimbabwe (why is Matabeleland since 2000 less violent than other parts of the country?). Boone and Kriger's chapter on land-related conflicts offers possible answers to these questions and to others involving geographic patterns of rural violence in Côte d'Ivoire. With this information, it will be easier to devise strategies to prevent the escalation of electoral tension into violent acts.

Also, researchers should look more closely at the electoral environment—specifically, at whether the election will produce close results and whether the type of electoral system matters. Among the cases in this book, the elections in Ghana, Ethiopia, Kenya, Nigeria, and Zimbabwe all seem to have some source of violence based on the closeness of the election. Certainly this speaks to the capacity of institutions and the will of political leaders to manage conflict, but it is conceivable that other relevant stakeholders could help absorb such shocks. Do Africa's heavily centralized governments make close elections more threatening? Can a more decentralized system reduce the threat of a close election? Have other countries been able to manage close elections more peacefully? Similarly, do certain electoral systems generate more violence than others? Many criticize the first-past-the-post system as inappropriate for deeply divided societies. Should new democracies adopt a different electoral system to avoid electoral violence? These questions remain unanswered beyond anecdotal cases and would benefit from further research.

Finally, a central conundrum presented by Straus and Taylor's work is why the level of electoral violence has not fluctuated significantly since 1990. Particularly troubling is the continuing electoral violence in at least ten countries, even in the face of increasing adoption of democratic tenets and institutions by some of them. The case study on Kenya provides a rich illustration of how increasing the capacity of institutions, such as the judicial sector, did not prevent Kenya from repeatedly descending into violence. And yet, international and regional institutions continue to emphasize the development of institutional capacities in Africa. While institutionalization is important, the Kenya case suggests that it does not necessarily help in providing the political development and maturity to resist electoral violence. It is important, therefore, to understand the limitations of institutional reform in affecting governance and democratic development.

Strategies for Preventing Electoral Violence

Oduro's case study on Ghana's 2008 general elections is notable for the description of several measures adopted to prevent electoral violence. Especially noteworthy is the coordination between the civil society observation team, local organizations, national institutions, the security services, and the media. Can this model work elsewhere in Africa? It is important to understand how other countries have addressed electoral violence, reduced its intensity, or prevented it altogether. The United Nations Development Programme (UNDP) and the U.S. Agency for International

Development (USAID) have recently released guidebooks that may be used for addressing electoral violence, and the International Foundation for Electoral Systems (IFES) proposes the adoption of a conflict cycle perspective to address electoral violence (UNDP 2009; USAID 2010; Bardall 2010). But without a more concrete understanding of how some strategies have worked (or not worked) in practice, it is difficult to propose particular practices with any confidence.

To complement local strategies for forestalling electoral violence, regional and international institutions must develop more robust sanctions to discourage the use of violence during elections. Article four of the African Union's (AU) Constitutive Act highlights a number of important principles that can be brought to bear in addressing electoral violence: it calls for intervening in member states to combat crimes against humanity, genocide, and war crimes; upholding the tenets of democracy; and denouncing unconstitutional changes in government (African Union 2000, art. 4). But violation of these principles has not resulted in more than a temporary suspension of membership in the AU (as it did in the aftermath of coups d'état in Mauritania [2005 and 2008], Guinea [2008], Niger [2010], Madagascar [2009], and Mali [2012]). The Economic Community of West African States (ECOWAS) also has a practice of suspending member states that stage coups d'état. In contrast, the reaction to electoral violence by Africa's institutions has been more interventionist than punitive—such as sending in diplomatic delegations to quell tensions and seek a way out of the political crisis. This was the case, for example, in Togo (2005), Kenya (2007), and Zimbabwe (2008). In fact, among countries that experienced electoral violence, only Côte d'Ivoire was suspended (by both the AU and ECOWAS). Even then, its suspension was tied to Laurent Gbagbo's refusal to recognize Alassane Ouattara as president following the 2010 polls. Currently, there are no mechanisms (beyond appeals for peace) or sanctions in place in regional or continental institutions to intervene early to reduce the prospect of electoral violence—seriously hampering efforts by local institutions to ensure peaceful polls.

Costs and Benefits of Power-Sharing Agreements

Third, although postelection political agreements have produced mixed results, it seems likely that they will remain a tool for the international community in designing a cease-fire and creating the space to negotiate an end to conflict. With the costs to democratization in mind, more research needs to take place on the optimal lengths and tasks assigned during a PPA. The international and regional communities' insistence that a power-sharing agreement as proposed by Gbagbo would not resolve the Ivorian electoral stalemate seemed to suggest uneasiness with the previous high-profile agreements in Kenya and Zimbabwe. These are important policy responses that will also begin to solidify the rules by which the AU and regional institutions operate.

* * *

Disputing the validity of elections ahead of the polls, during elections, and after the announcement of the results is a regular phenomenon in Africa. In 2011, for example, with the exception of Cape Verde, all the remaining sixteen elections in Africa were disputed or characterized as fraudulent, noncredible, or rigged. But not all the disputes turned violent. Indeed, of the seventeen elections in 2011, roughly half had some degree of violence (Nigeria, the Democratic Republic of Congo, Liberia, Cameroon, Djibouti, Gambia, Uganda, and Zambia). Why did violence take place in some countries and not in others? What conflict drivers lay behind the violence that did happen? Could it have been prevented? The empirical work in this book reveals that by understanding a country's history of electoral violence and grievances, the context in which an election takes place, the structure of the patronage system, and the country's institutional capacity, we can find ample opportunities for predicting electoral violence. Most important, because the date of a poll is usually known well beforehand, the international, regional, and domestic stakeholders are in opportune positions to put in place programs far in advance, when they can be most useful, to forestall or reduce the threat of violence during elections.

References

African Union. 2000. "Constitutive Act of the African Union." July. www.au.int/en/sites/default/files/ConstitutiveAct_EN.pdf.

Bardall, Gabrielle. 2010. "A Conflict Cycle Perspective on Electoral Violence." *Monday Developments* 28 (3): 15–16, 29. www.ifes.org/~/media/Files/Publications/Article/2010/1682/MD_March_10_small_2.pdf.

United Nations Development Programme (UNDP). 2009. *Elections and Conflict Prevention: A Guide to Analysis, Planning and Programming.* Aug. web.undp.org/publications/Elections_and_Conflict_Prevention.pdf.

U.S. Agency for International Development (USAID). 2010. *Electoral Security Framework: Technical Guidance Handbook for Democracy and Governance Officers.* July. www.usaid.gov/our_work/democracy_and_governance/publications/pdfs/1-Electoral-Security-Framework.pdf.

About the Contributors

Dorina A. Bekoe is a research staff member of the Africa program at the Institute for Defense Analyses. Before that, she was a senior program officer in the Center for Conflict Management at the United States Institute of Peace. She specializes in Africa's conflicts, political development, institutional reform, including the New Partnership for Africa's Development and the related African Peer Review Mechanism, peace agreements, and electoral violence. She is the author of *Implementing Peace Agreements: Lessons from Mozambique, Angola, and Liberia* (Palgrave Macmillan, 2008).

Catherine Boone is professor of government at the University of Texas at Austin. She is the author of *Merchant Capital and the Roots of State Power in Senegal, 1930–1985* (Cambridge Univ. Press, 1992), *Political Topographies of the African State: Rural Authority and Institutional Choice* (Cambridge Univ. Press, 2003), and numerous journal articles and book chapters. In 2011, she completed the book manuscript "Property and Political Order: Land Rights and the Structure of Politics in Africa."

Norma Kriger is an independent consultant. She is currently a research associate in the Department of Anthropology and Development Studies, University of Johannesburg, and a research consultant at the Federal Research Division, Library of Congress, Washington, D.C. She is the author of *Zimbabwe's Guerrilla War: Peasant Voices* (Cambridge Univ. Press, 1992), *Guerrilla Veterans in Post-War Zimbabwe: Symbolic and Violent Politics, 1980–1987* (Cambridge Univ. Press, 2003), and numerous articles on politics in Zimbabwe.

Susanne D. Mueller lived in Kenya for twenty years through the mid-1990s, doing doctoral and postdoctoral research, teaching at the University of Nairobi and at Princeton University, and working as a consultant in most of the countries of East and southern Africa. Her article "The Political Economy of Kenya's Crisis" won the 2009 Best Article of the Year Award from the African Politics Conference Group (APCG), an affiliate of the American Political Science Association. She has a PhD from Princeton University.

Franklin Oduro is head of research and programs at the Accra-based Ghana Center for Democratic Development (CDD-Ghana), a research- and policy-oriented think tank. Since 2000, he has played several roles in Ghana's Coalition of Domestic Election Observers, including managing the parallel vote tabulation process in 2008. He has published in *International Journal of Human Rights, Journal of African Elections, Citizenship Studies*, and other journals. He has a PhD in political science from Carleton University, Ottawa, Canada.

Timothy D. Sisk is professor and associate dean for research at the Josef Korbel School of International Studies, University of Denver, and director of Korbel's Center for Sustainable Development and International Peace. He specializes in civil wars and political violence, and in conflict prevention, management, and peacebuilding in fragile and postwar contexts. He is the author most recently of *International Mediation in Civil Wars: Bargaining with Bullets* (Routledge, 2009) and the editor of *Between Terror and Tolerance: Religion, Conflict, and Peacebuilding* (Georgetown Univ. Press, 2012).

Lahra Smith is a political scientist and assistant professor at Georgetown University, with a particular interest in African politics. Her recent research focuses on the study of citizenship and citizen education in post-transition reforms, the role of political institutions in addressing conflict based largely on ethnic and language identities in Ethiopia, and women and gender politics.

Scott Straus is professor of political science and international studies at the University of Wisconsin, Madison. He is most recently coeditor, with Lars Waldorf, of *Remaking Rwanda: State Building and Human Rights after Mass Violence* (University of Wisconsin Press, 2011). In addition to electoral violence, his current research focuses on why some armed conflicts escalate to genocide and similar forms of mass violence while others do not. He is working with Andy Kydd on developing a game-theoretic model on third-party intervention to stop mass atrocities.

Charlie Taylor is a PhD candidate in the Department of Political Science at the University of Wisconsin Madison, studying transitions to democracy in Africa. His dissertation examines presidential campaign strategies across African elections since 1990. He has worked or conducted research in Sierra Leone and Ghana.

Index

Page numbers followed by *t*, *f*, and *n* denote tables, figures, and footnotes, respectively.

Abiola, Moshood, 36
Abubakar, Atiku, 49, 51, 57
Acemoglu, D., 164
Addoo boys (Ghana), 225
African Electoral Violence Dataset
  (AEVD)
  overview of, 8, 17–18
  construction of, 22–23
  data collection, 18–23
  data sources, 22
  findings, 32–33, 36–37
  patterns of violence, 23–33
    level of violence, 23–26, 25*t*–27*t*,
      30*t*, 31*t*, 33
    perpetrators, 29–31, 30*t*, 32–33
    pre- versus post-election, 28–31,
      30*t*, 33, 182–83
    trends over time, 27–28, 28*f*
  policy implications, 247–48
  research implications, 248–52
  risk factors identified by, 244–45
  scenarios, 9, 33–36, 107
  scope and concepts, 18–23
African Union, 40*n*2, 66, 185, 188, 251
Africa Report, 22
Africa Watch, 154
Afrobarometer, 5, 53, 244
Agar, Malik, 62
Agyeman-Duah, Baffour, 237
Akindès, Francis, 94
Akiwumi Commission (Kenya), 153–54,
  162

al-Bashir, Omar, 60, 62, 66
Albin-Lackey, Chris, 54
allochtones (Côte d'Ivoire), 99
al-Sir, Hatim, 62
Amah, Gnassingbé, 126
Amnesty International, 22
Amum, Pagan, 66
Anderson, David M., 151
Anglo-Leasing scandal (Kenya), 164–65
Angola, 6
Arman, Yasir, 62
Armenian brothers scandal (Kenya), 165
Arriola, Leonardo, 17, 17*n*4, 193, 194
Asingo, P. O., 164
autochtones (Côte d'Ivoire), 90, 100–101
Ayalew, Lidetu, 190*n*10
Azorka boys (Ghana), 225

Babo, Alfred, 99
Bakassi Boys (Nigeria), 52
Balint-Kurti, Daniel, 105
Bates, Robert, 16, 19, 45, 158
Bédié, Henri Konan, 95–102
Bednik, Anna, 98
Bekele, Daniel, 189*n*9
Bekoe, Dorina A., 1, 10, 17, 117, 243
Besigye, Kizza, 1
Biwott, Nicholas, 150, 163, 168, 169
Blair, Tony, 86
Bolivia, 46
Boone, Catherine, 9–10, 44, 75, 154, 249
Botswana, 5

257

Bratton, Michael, 53, 201
Buhari, Muhammadu, 49, 59

Canton, Santiago A., 198, 201
Carter Center
    Ethiopia, 185, 187, 191, 202
    Sudan, 67–68
challengers, 20–21
    as perpetrators, 29–31, 30*t*, 33
Chauveau, J. P., 77, 91, 100, 101
Cingranelli, David, 22
citizenship disputes
    Côte d'Ivoire, 91, 94–106
    Zimbabwe, 78–79, 86, 88, 106
civic education, 231
civil society organizations (CSOs). *See also*
        specific organization
    democratization and, 201–03
    Ethiopia, 183, 197–203, 205
    Ghana, 183, 202, 205, 210, 230–33,
        237–39
    Kenya, 202, 205
    Togo, 128
    violence prevention by, 237–38
civil war
    Côte d'Ivoire, 1, 5, 7, 105
    electoral violence linked to, 1, 5, 7, 39,
        41, 154–55, 243
    Sudan, 59–62, 65
co-ethnics, 169
Collier, Paul, 16
    on democratization, 5, 16
    on electoral tactics, 47
    on greed, 157
    on origins of violence, 21
    on perpetrators, 31
    violence definition, 19
Commonwealth Observer Group (COG),
        56, 56*n*12
Compaoré, Blaise, 125–27
complementary approach to violence
        prevention, 237
Congo, Democratic Republic of, 6, 75, 83,
        87, 120
Congo, Republic of, 6, 7, 29*n*13
corruption, 44–45
Côte d'Ivoire
    civil war in, threat of, 1, 5, 7, 105

constitutional referendum (2000),
        101–02
    electoral violence in
        1990 elections, 95
        1995 elections, 97
        2010 elections, 105
        citizenship disputes, 91, 94–106
        coup d'état (1999), 101
        land patronage and, 77–78, 90–106
        post-conflict environment, 5
        scenario, 9–10, 35–36, 107
    Land Code *(Code Foncier)*, 98–101
    Marcoussis Accords, 104
    Ouagadougou Accords (2007), 104
    political parties
        Front Populaire Ivoirien (FPI),
            94–100, 102–05
        Parti Démocratique de Côte
            d'Ivoire (PDCI), 93–96,
            98–100, 105
        Rassemblement des Républicains
            (RDR), 95–98, 105
    postelection political agreement, 118
    Pretoria Agreement (2005), 104
    structural adjustment programs (SAPs),
        100
Cowen, M., 167
crime, in Kenya, 146, 155–58, 171–73
Curless, Gareth, 64*n*20
Curley, James, 152–53
cutoff points, 23

Daddieh, Cyril, 100
Dahl, Robert, 15–16
Daramola, Ayodeji, 55, 56*n*12
Darfur (Sudan), 59–62
dataset. *See* African Electoral Violence
        Dataset
Demissie, Netsanet, 189*n*9
Democratic Republic of Congo, 6, 75, 83,
        87, 120
democratization
    causes of conflict and, 40–43
    civil society organizations and, 201–03
    effect of violence on, 4–5
    institutional factors, 10, 45–46, 120,
        159–66, 174
    patterns of violence and, 15–38

demographic factors, 46
demonstrations. *See* protests
Deng, Francis, 61
developmental assistance, 122, 124, 126,
    128–29, 131
de Waal, Alex, 62–63
displaced people. *See* internally displaced
    people
Droz, Yvan, 99

early-warning programs, 230–31, 236
Economic Community of West African
    States (ECOWAS), 40*n*2, 124,
    251
economic factors, 40, 42
election(s)
    dispute adjudication, 226–27
    security related to, 47, 229, 231–33,
        235–36
    types of, 22–23, 31, 31*t*, 33
election management, 46–47
    Ghana, 213, 231–35
    Kenya, 46–47
    Nigeria, 50–51, 56–59
    Sudan, 67–68
election monitoring
    Ethiopia, 197–203
    Ghana, 199, 210, 214–17, 215*t*,
        229–36
    Kenya, 199–200
    Sudan, 66–68
electoral administration, 42, 47
electoral environment, variables affecting,
    121, 121*f*
electoral fraud, 47, 69
    Ghana, 213, 220–21, 238
    Sudan, 67
    Togo, 125
electoral system, 42, 47
    Ethiopia, 184–86
    Kenya, 151–55
    Nigeria, 53
    Sudan, 47, 64
electoral violence
    case studies, 8–9. *See also specific country*
    concept of, 20–21
    consequences of, 4–5

dataset. *See* African Electoral Violence
    Dataset
    defined, 2, 19–20
    democratization and (*See*
        democratization)
    evaluation of, 39–74
        approach and methods, 40–42
        case studies. *See* Nigeria; Sudan
        causal drivers, 42–47
        conclusions, 68–70
        framework, 48
    extent of, 3, 15–16, 32, 36–37, 40, 117,
        182, 243–44
    future research on, 248–52
    general patterns of, 23–33
    level of, 2–4, 21–26, 25*t*–27*t*, 33
        by timing and perpetrators, 29–31,
            30*t*
        by type of election, 31, 31*t*, 33
    origins of, 20
    perpetrators, 3–4, 29–31, 30*t*
    versus political violence, 19, 32–33, 69
    prevention of, 11, 236–38, 244–51
        case study. *See* Ghana
        postelection agreements. *See*
            postelection political
            agreements
    reasons to study, 4–7
    risk factors, 5–7
    scenarios of, 8–9, 33–36, 107
    time frame, 2–3, 20–21, 28–31, 30*t*, 33,
        69, 182–83
    victims, 3–4
environmental scarcity, 46
Equatorial Guinea, 34
Ethiopia, 121, 181–208
    Charities and Societies (CSO) law,
        202–03
    civil society organizations in, 183,
        197–203, 205
    Coalition of Ethiopian Civil Societies
        for Election Observation
        (CECSEO), 203
    election monitoring in, 197–203
    electoral system, 184–86
    electoral violence in
        1995, 2000, and 2001 elections, 185
        2005 elections, 185–90, 197, 203

2008 elections, 195, 203
2010 elections, 195–97, 203
  consequences of, 196
  data sources, 183–84
  land patronage and, 193
  level of, 182, 196
  narratives about, 190–92, 204
  perpetrators, 193, 204
  postelection, 182, 203, 205
  preelection, 185, 187, 203
  scenario, 9–11
  types of, 192–95
Ethiopian Civil Society Network for
  Elections, 200–201
Ethiopian Teachers' Association, 203
ethnic diversity in, 193–95, 204
National Electoral Board of Ethiopia
  (NEBE), 186–87, 200–201
Parliamentary Commission of Inquiry,
  191, 193n12
political parties
  All Ethiopian Unity Party, 187, 195
  Arena Tigray Party, 195
  Coalition for Unity and Democracy
    (CUD), 185–88, 190n10,
    193, 195
  Ethiopia Federal Democratic Unity
    Forum (Medrek), 195
  Ethiopian People's Revolutionary
    Democratic Front
    (EPRDF), 184–86, 190,
    192, 195, 196, 204
  Oromo Federalist Democratic
    Movement, 185, 195
  Oromo Liberation Front (OLF),
    184
  Oromo National Congress (ONC),
    187
  Oromo People's Congress, 195
  Southern Nations, Nationalities and
    People region (SNNPR),
    187
  Tigray People's Liberation Front,
    184, 190n10
  United Ethiopian Democratic
    Forces, 185, 195
  Unity for Democracy and Justice
    Party, 195
political system, 197, 197n17

ethnic diversity, 6–7, 40, 45–46
  Ethiopia, 193–95, 204
  Ghana, 220
  Kenya, 166–71, 193
  Nigeria, 50, 56
  Sudan, 61, 65–66
European Union (EU), 191
  developmental assistance, 122, 124,
    128–29
  election monitoring, 185, 191, 214
Eyadéma, Gnassingbé, 123–24

farm workers
  Côte d'Ivoire, 101, 103–04, 106
  land patronage and, 76
  Zimbabwe, 76–77, 79, 83–89
"fast track" courts (Ghana), 226–27
Fearon, J. D., 170
Fischer, Jeff, 3
fraud. *See* electoral fraud
Freedom House, 16, 28

gangs
  Ghana, 224–25
  Kenya, 150, 153, 155–58, 171–73
  Nigeria, 52, 55–56
  youth. *See* youth militia
Gbagbo, Laurent
  citizenship dispute, 94–95, 101–05
  ECOWAS suspension, 251
  ICC referral, 248
  power-sharing arrangement, 118, 139
Gecaga, M., 157
generalized violence, 22–23, 25t–26t
gerrymandering, 153
Ghana, 209–42
  Center for Democratic Development
    (CDD-Ghana), 210, 230–31,
    233
  Civic Forum Initiative, 232
  civil society organizations in, 183, 202,
    205, 210, 230–33, 237–39
  Coalition of Domestic Election
    Observers (CODEO), 199,
    210, 214–21, 230–31, 233, 238
  data sources, 210
  election management in, 213, 231–35
  election monitoring in, 199, 210,
    214–17, 215t, 229–36

electoral commission (EC), 210, 212,
    213, 216–17, 221, 227–28, 231,
    233–35
electoral violence in, 211–12
    1954 and 1956 elections, 211
    1992 elections, 211, 227
    2004 elections, 213
    2008 elections, 209, 212–17, 223,
        227, 238
    consequences of, 5
    gangs, 224–25
    institutional and structural factors,
        221, 223–24
    lessons learned, 236–38
    patronage resources and, 213, 218
    perpetrators, 216, 218–21, 224–25
    postelection, 216–17
    preelection, 214–15, 220–21
    prevention of, 11, 226–40, 250
    scenario, 9, 36
    social factors, 222–23
    triggers and patterns, 217–25
ethnic diversity in, 220
Ghana Conference for Religions for
    Peace, 232
Ghana Political Parties Program, 233
Institute for Economic Affairs (IEA),
    231–33
Institute of Democratic Governance
    (IDEG), 231–32
interparty advisory council (IPAC) plat-
    form, 227–28, 233, 234, 237
National Election Security Task Force,
    228–29
National Peace Council (NPC), 210,
    228, 238
political parties
    National Democratic Congress
        (NDC), 211–13, 216,
        218–25, 234
    New Patriotic Party (NPP), 211–13,
        216, 218–25, 234
political violence in, 223
Representation of the Peoples'
    Amendment Law (ROPAL),
    212–13, 227
Gimonde, E. A., 162
Giorgis, Girma Wolde, 189
Githongo, John, 165

Glaeser, E. L., 153
Gnassingbé, Faure, 124
"godfather" syndrome, 52–53, 68
Goldenberg scandal (Kenya), 164–65
government of national unity (GNU)
    Togo, 125–26, 138
    Zanzibar, 138
greed, 40, 42, 69–70, 155, 157
Guéi, Robert, 101–02
Gyimah-Boadi, Emmanuel, 100, 212, 217,
    221, 233

Hailemariam, Mengistu, 184
Hamad, Seif Sharif, 134
harassment. See violent harassment
Hartzell, Caroline A., 120
Hemmer, Jort, 63
historical factors, 245–46
Höglund, Kristine, 3, 6, 10, 196
horizontal inequalities, 40, 44–45
Houphouët-Boigny, Félix, 90–93, 95, 100
Human Rights Watch, 22
    Côte d'Ivoire, 104, 104n27
    Nigeria, 52, 54
    Sudan, 61, 66
    Zanzibar, 132n3
Huntington, Samuel, 217

identity politics, 194
immigrants. See also citizenship disputes
    Côte d'Ivoire, 93
    Ghana, 224
incumbents, 20–21
    as perpetrators, 29–31, 30t, 32–33
Indonesia, 46
Institute for Democracy in Southern
    Africa, 58
institutional factors, 10, 45–46, 245–46
    Ghana, 221, 223–24
    Kenya, 159–66, 174
    power-sharing and, 120
    violence prevention, 234–36
internally displaced people (IDP)
    Côte d'Ivoire, 103–04
    Kenya, 173
    Sudan, 66
    Zimbabwe, 87–88
international community
    peace mediation by, 228

postelection political agreements and, 120–22, 139
Togo, 124, 126, 128–29, 131, 139
Zanzibar, 136–37, 139
role of, 10, 247–48
International Criminal Court (ICC), 105, 248
International Crisis Group (ICG), 57, 59, 99n19, 104
International Foundation for Electoral Systems (IFES), 251
interparty dialogues, 237

Jesuit Refugee Service of East Africa, 154
joint governance, 118, 140
Jonathan, Goodluck, 49, 59
Joseph, Richard, 40n1
judiciary speed, 226–27
Justice and Equality Movement, 66
justice for victims, 118

Kamungi, P. M., 178
Kanyinga, K., 167
Katumanga, M., 150, 157
Keefer, Phil, 175
Kenya, 145–80
    civil society organisations in, 202, 205
    constitutional referendum (2010), 46
    economic development in, 145–46
    election management in, 46–47
    election monitoring in, 199–200
    Electoral Commission of Kenya (ECK), 160, 165–66, 172
    electoral violence in
        2007 election, 159, 160, 169, 171
        consequences of, 4
        deliberately weak institutions and, 159–66, 174
        diffused, 148–50, 171, 173
        land patronage and, 75, 77, 154
        postelection escalation, 170–74
        precipitating factors, 146–47
        prevention of, 11
        scenario, 9–10, 18, 35–36
        trickle-down, 158–59
    ethnic diversity in, 166–71, 193
    executive presidency in, 161–63
    financial scandals in, 146, 164–65
    High Court, 165–66

Kenya National Commission of Human Rights (KNCHR), 171
Kenya Posts and Telecommunications Company (KPTC), 162
Kenya Power and Lighting (KPL), 162
political mobilization in, 43
political parties, 167–70
    clientist, 166–67, 170
    Gikuyu Embu and Meru Association (GEMA), 169–70
    KAMATUSA, 151
    Kenya African Democratic Union (KADU), 151, 170
    Kenya African National Union (KANU), 149, 151, 153, 161, 167–68
    Kenya People's Union (KPU), 149, 161
    Liberal Democratic Party (LDP), 167
    National Rainbow Coalition (NARC), 164–65, 167–68
political system, 151–55
postelection political agreement, 118–19, 119t
privatized violence in, 32, 146, 150–55, 171–73
Kenyatta, Uhuru, 149, 157, 161, 167–69
Kibaki, Mwai, 157
    institutional weakness under, 160, 164, 165
    political allegiances, 167–69
    privatized violence and, 148, 172
    reform efforts, 145, 157
    vote rigging dispute, 36
Kiir, Salva, 60
Kikwete, Jakaya, 134
Kolelas, Bernard, 29n13
Koné, Mariatou, 102, 105
Kriger, Norma, 9–10, 44, 75, 249

Ladhu, Ismail Jusa, 134
Laitin, D. D., 170
land patronage, 75–78, 105–07
    Côte d'Ivoire, 77–78, 90–106
    Ethiopia, 193
    Kenya, 75, 77, 154

Sudan, 63
Zimbabwe, 76–89, 106
Lebanon, 120
legislative elections, 22–23, 31, 31*t*, 33
Lesotho, postelection political agreement, 118, 119*t*
Lewis, Barbara, 94, 99, 100
Liberia, 120
Lindberg, Staffan, 17*n*4, 22, 39, 50
Lissouba, Pascal, 7, 29*n*13
local elections, 22–23
localized violence, 9, 18, 35–36, 45, 183

macroeconomic factors, 96, 100
Madagascar, postelection political agreement, 118, 119*t*
majimboism (Kenya), 151
Matiba, Kenneth, 157
Mbadinuju, Chinwoke, 52
Meagher, Kate, 52
measurement error, 23
mediation approach, 228, 238
Michuki, John, 157
Mideksa, Birtukan, 190*n*10
Mkapa, Benjamin, 134, 135, 137
mobile text messaging, 232
Moi, Daniel arap
    as executive president, 161–63
    institutional weakness under, 164
    patronage, 10
    political allegiances, 167–69
    privatized violence under, 148, 151–55
    repression under, 4, 145
Movement for Democratic Change (Zimbabwe), 9
Mueller, Susanne D., 10, 145, 245
Mugabe, Robert, 78, 80–86, 89
Mungiki (Kenya), 155–58, 172–73

Namibia, 5
National Democratic Institute (NDI), 58
Nega, Berhanu, 190*n*10, 191*n*11
neopatrimonialism, 44, 69, 168–69
Nevitte, Neil, 198, 201
Nigeria, 48–59
    democratization context, 43, 49–51
    election management in, 50–51, 56–59
    Electoral Act (2006), 51*n*8, 53*n*10, 54
    electoral system in, 53

electoral violence in, 41–42
    2007 elections, 48–49, 54–59
    2011 elections, 59
    consequences of, 4–5, 58–59
    gangs, 52, 55–56
    scenario, 9, 20*n*9, 36
    state capture and, 46, 51–53
    violence-management efforts, 58
ethnic and religious diversity in, 45, 50, 56
Independent National Electoral Commission (INEC), 48–49, 51, 57
political parties
    Action Congress (AC), 49
    People's Democratic Party (PDP), 48–49, 51, 55, 57, 59
Njonjo, Appollo, 175
Nkomo, Joshua, 78, 81
nongovernmental organizations (NGOs), 58, 198. *See also* civil society organizations; *specific organization*
North, Douglas, 159, 175
Norwegian Refugee Council (NRC), 103
Ntimama, William, 150, 152, 153

Obasanjo, Olusegun, 49, 51, 55
observation. *See* election monitoring
Odhiambo-Mbai, C., 161, 162
Odinga, Raila, 121, 167–70, 172
Oduro, Franklin, 11, 209, 250
oil resources
    Ghana, 213, 218
    Nigeria, 50–53
    Sudan, 63
Operation Murambatsvina (Zimbabwe), 9
opposition, elimination of, 9, 18, 34, 107, 152–53
Orange Revolution (Ethiopia), 190–91
Orengo, James, 173
Osaghae, Eghosa E., 52
Ouattara, Alassane
    citizenship dispute, 96–97, 102, 104–05
    ECOWAS suspension, 251
    power-sharing arrangement, 118, 140
Ouattara, Fambaré Natchaba, 124

parallel vote tabulation (PVT), 232
parliamentary elections, 22–23, 31, 31*t*, 33

path dependence, 175
patronage resources, 245
    as causal driver, 40, 44–46, 68–70
    Ghana, 213, 218
    land. *See* land patronage
    Nigeria, 50–53, 58
    scenario, 9–10, 18, 107
    Sudan, 61–63
Pausewang, Siegfried, 194
peace education, 228, 231, 238
peace mediation, 228, 238
perpetrators, 3–4, 29–31, 30*t*, 32–33
petrostates
    Ghana, 213, 218
    Nigeria, 50–53
    Sudan, 63
Philippines, 46
pockets of violence, 9, 18, 35–36, 45, 183
policy implications, 247–48
political context, importance of, 246–47
political economy
    Kenya. *See* Kenya
    of state capture, 40, 42, 44–45, 68–70.
        See also patronage resources
    Nigeria, 51–53, 58
    Sudan, 62–63
Political Instability Task Force (PITF),
        Worldwide Atrocities Event
        database, 32
political mobilization, 42–43
    land patronage linked to, 83, 104–07
political violence, 19, 32–33, 69
polling day violence, 2–3, 20–21
    patterns of, 28–30, 33
Posner, D. N., 170
postelection political agreements (PPAs),
        10, 117–44
    case studies. *See* Togo; Zanzibar
    characteristics of, 119–21
    conclusions, 138–40
    cost-benefit analysis of, 251–52
    monitoring of, 248
    power-sharing arrangements in, 118,
        120, 122–23, 140, 248, 251–52
    variation in, 118–19, 119*t*
postelection violence, 2–3, 20–21, 182–83
    patterns of, 28–31, 30*t*, 33
poverty, 53, 63

Praia Declaration on Elections and
        Stability in West Africa, 40*n*2
prebendalism, 40, 40*n*1, 69, 168–69
preelection violence, 2–3, 20–21
    electoral fraud and, 69
    monitoring of, 230–31, 236
    patterns of, 28–31, 30*t*, 33
    presidential elections, 22–23, 31, 31*t*, 33
    prosecutions, lack of
        Ghana, 223–25
        Nigeria, 58
    protests, 9, 36
        Ethiopia, 182–83, 186, 187, 192, 196
        Kenya, 121
        Togo, 131

Rawlence, Ben, 54
redistribution of resources, 9, 18, 35. *See
        also* patronage resources
redistricting scenario, 9, 18, 34–35
religious diversity, 40, 45
    Nigeria, 45, 50
    Sudan, 45, 61, 65–66
Reno, William, 69
rent-seeking. *See* patronage resources
Republic of Congo (ROC), 6, 7, 29*n*13
research implications, 248–52
resources, redistribution of, 9, 18, 35. *See
        also* patronage resources
Richards, David, 22
Robinson, J. A., 164

Sassou-Nguesso, Denis, 7, 29*n*13
Schleifer, A., 153
security, election-related, 47, 229, 231–33,
        235–36
security forces, violence perpetrated by, 193
Selassie, Haile, 184
Shamuyarira, Minister, 81
Shawel, Hailu, 190*n*10
Shigolla, Brigadier, 156
Short Message Service (SMS), 232
Sisk, Timothy D., 9, 10, 39, 243, 245, 246
Smith, Ian, 80, 81
Smith, Lahra, 10–11, 181, 249
Snyder, Jack, 16, 19
social factors, 42, 45–46
    Ghana, 222–24

South Africa, 29*n*13
Soyinka, Wole, 49
state capture. *See also* patronage resources
  political economy of, 40, 42, 44–45, 68–70
    Nigeria, 51–53, 58
    Sudan, 62–63
state formation, 43
Straus, Scott, 2, 15
  dataset. *See* African Electoral Violence Dataset
street brawls scenario, 33–34
structural factors, 45–46. *See also* institutional factors
  Ghana, 221, 223–24
  violence prevention, 234–36
Suberu, Rotimi T., 52
Sudan, 59–68
  civil war-to-democracy transition, 60–62, 65
  Comprehensive Peace Agreement (CPA), 42, 59–61, 63
  election management in, 67–68
  election monitoring in, 66–68
  election observers in, 66–68
  electoral system in, 47, 64
  electoral violence in, 42
    2010 elections, 65–67
    consequences of, 4
    resource control and, 61–63
    scenario, 9
  ethnic and religious diversity in, 45, 61, 65–66
  National Elections Act, 64
  National Elections Commission, 67
  political parties
    Democratic Unionist Party, 63
    Government of South Sudan (GOSS), 60*n*17, 61–64
    National Congress Party (NCP), 59*n*16, 60–62, 64, 66
    Sudanese People's Liberation Army (SPLA), 60*n*17
    Sudan People's Liberation Movement (SPLM), 60–66
    UMMA Party, 63
  Sudan Armed Forces (SAF), 60*n*17

Tanzania, 36. *See also* Zanzibar
Taylor, Charlie, 2, 15
  dataset. *See* African Electoral Violence Dataset
Togo, 123–31
  civil society organizations, 128
  Comité de Suivi (CS), 123–31
  Commission Electorale Nationale Indépendant (CENI), 125–31, 127*t*, 139
  Comprehensive Political Accord (APG), 122–23, 125–28
    scope of, 118–19, 119*t*
  electoral violence in
    2005 elections, 124–25
    2007 elections, 129–31
    2010 elections, 130–31
    background to, 123–24
    scenario, 9–10, 34
  government of national unity (GNU), 125–26, 138
  international community's role in, 124, 126, 128–29, 131, 139
  political parties
    Cadre Permanent du Dialogue (CPD), 125, 139
    Cadre Permanent du Dialogue et de Concertation (CPDC), 130–31
    Comite d'Action pour le Renouveau (CAR), 129–31
    Convergence Patriotique Panafricaine (CPP), 128
    Front Républicain pour l'Alternance et le Changement (FRAC), 130–31
    Ligue Togolaise des Droits d l'Homme (LTDH), 124
    Parti pour la Démocracie et le Renouveau (PDR), 128
    Rassemblement du Peuple Togolais (RPT), 124, 126, 127, 129, 139
    Union des Forces de Changement (UFC), 124, 126, 127, 129–31, 139
Treisman, D., 174
Tsvangirai, Morgan, 4, 79, 86, 89

Turkson, Peter, 228

United Nations
    Development Programme (UNDP),
        126, 228, 250
    Office for the Coordination of
        Humanitarian Affairs
        (OCHA), 104
    Praia Declaration on Elections and
        Stability in West Africa, 40n2
urbanization, 46
U.S. Agency for International
        Development (USAID), 250–51
U.S. State Department, 183
    Human Rights reports, 22, 187

Vicente, Pedro C., 21, 31
victims, 3–4
vigilante gangs. See gangs
violence-management efforts, 42
    Ghana, 226–34
    Nigeria, 58
    postelection. See postelection political
        agreements
violent harassment
    defined, 17
    patterns of, 21–23, 25t–26t, 37
    scenario, 33–34
violent repression
    patterns of, 21–22, 25t–26t
    scenario, 34
voters
    bribery of, 47, 53
    civic education of, 231
    intimidation of, 47
    registration of, 135–36, 213, 220–21
vote tallying process, 232, 234–35

Wambui, Mary, 165
Wamwere, Koigi wa, 163, 170
Weber, Max, 148
World Bank, Governance Indicators,
        145–46

Yar'Adua, Umaru, 4, 48
Yevou, Marc, 104
youth demographics, 46

youth militia
    Côte d'Ivoire, 103
    Ghana, 224–25
    Kenya, 150, 151, 153, 173
    Nigeria, 56
    Zanzibar, 137

Zanzibar, 132–38
    electoral violence in
        2005 and 2010 elections, 136–38
        background to, 132
        scenario, 9–10, 36
    government of national unity (GNU),
        138
    international community's role in,
        136–37, 139
    Joint Presidential Supervisory
        Committee (JPSC), 123,
        133–35
    Muafaka Accord, 122–23, 132–36, 139
        scope of, 118–19, 119t
    permanent voters registry (PVR),
        135–36
    political parties
        Chama Cha Mapinduzi (CCM),
            132–33, 136–37, 139
        Civic United Front (CUF), 132–33,
            136–37, 139
    shehas (community leaders), 135–36
    Zanzibar Electoral Commission
        (ZEC), 133–36
Zenawi, Meles, 192
Zimbabwe
    constitutional referendum (2000), 83
    electoral violence in
        1990 elections, 81
        2000 and 2002 elections, 84–87
        citizenship dispute, 78–79, 86, 88,
            106
        consequences of, 4–5
        land patronage, 76–89, 106
        scenario, 9, 34–35, 107
    General Agricultural and Plantation
        Workers Union of Zimbabwe
        (GAPWUZ), 83
    Global Political Agreement (GPA), 89
    Land Acquisition Act, 81–82, 85

political parties
  Movement for Democratic Change
    (MDC), 79, 84–86
  Zimbabwe African National Union
    (ZANU PF), 77–89
  Zimbabwe African People's Union
    (ZAPU), 78, 81
Zimbabwe Unity Movement
  (ZUM), 81
political violence in, 32
postelection political agreement,
  118–19, 119*t*

United States Institute of Peace Press

Since its inception, the United States Institute of Peace Press has published over 150 books on the prevention, management, and peaceful resolution of international conflicts—among them such venerable titles as Raymond Cohen's *Negotiating Across Cultures*; John Paul Lederach's *Building Peace*; *Leashing the Dogs of War* by Chester A. Crocker, Fen Osler Hampson, and Pamela Aall; and *American Negotiating Behavior* by Richard H. Solomon and Nigel Quinney. All our books arise from research and fieldwork sponsored by the Institute's many programs. In keeping with the best traditions of scholarly publishing, each volume undergoes both thorough internal review and blind peer review by external subject experts to ensure that the research, scholarship, and conclusions are balanced, relevant, and sound. With the Institute's move to its new headquarters on the National Mall in Washington, D.C., the Press is committed to extending the reach of the Institute's work by continuing to publish significant and sustainable works for practitioners, scholars, diplomats, and students.

Valerie Norville
Director

About the
United States Institute of Peace

The United States Institute of Peace is an independent, nonpartisan institution established and funded by Congress. The Institute provides analysis, training, and tools to help prevent, manage, and end violent international conflicts, promote stability, and professionalize the field of peacebuilding.

Chairman of the Board: J. Robinson West
Vice Chairman: George E. Moose
President: Jim Marshall